Speechmaking

An Introduction to Rhetorical Competence

FREE
COPY

Speechmaking

An Introduction to Rhetorical Competence

J. Michael Sproule
San Jose State University

Wm. C. Brown Publishers

Book Team

Editor *Stan Stoga*
Developmental Editor *Jane F. Lambert*
Production Editor *Anne E. Gardiner*
Art Editor *Jess Schaal*
Photo Editor *Carol M. Smith*
Permissions Editor *Vicki Krug*
Visuals Processor *Amy L. Saffran*

WCB **Wm. C. Brown Publishers**

President *G. Franklin Lewis*
Vice President, Publisher *George Wm. Bergquist*
Vice President, Publisher *Thomas E. Doran*
Vice President, Operations and Production *Beverly Kolz*
National Sales Manager *Virginia S. Moffat*
Advertising Manager *Ann M. Knepper*
Marketing Manager *Kathleen Nietzke*
Managing Editor, Production *Colleen A. Yonda*
Production Editorial Manager *Julie A. Kennedy*
Publishing Services Manager *Karen J. Slaght*
Manager of Visuals and Design *Faye M. Schilling*

Cover design by John R. Rokusek

Cover image © Steve Hunt/The Image Bank

The credits section for this book begins on page 474, and is considered an extension of the copyright page.

Library of Congress Catalog Card Number: 89-082701

ISBN 0-697-07639-3

Printed in the United States of America by Wm. C. Brown Publishers, 2460 Kerper Boulevard, Dubuque, IA 52001

10 9 8 7 6 5 4 3 2 1

▶To Betty, John, and Kevin

Contents

Sample Speeches

Preface

For many college students, a course in public speaking is a required part of basic education. If you are like most of your classmates, you are wondering what to expect. What kind of assignments are to come? How is public speaking similar to other courses in the arts and sciences? How is the course different?

The *skills orientation* of public speaking is probably the major difference between this course and your other requirements in the humanities and social sciences. You probably share the common expectation of students that public speaking will encompass fundamental tactics for communicating. This assumption is true of the university as a whole. Ability in public speaking is a mark of the educated person. In days gone by, public speaking—then called "rhetoric"—was one of the seven liberal arts. Today, public speaking is part of what colleges call their "basics." Contemporary universities frequently require a class in public speaking because the course shapes skills of coherent thought and articulate expression.

The direct focus on skills distinguishes public speaking from many other required college courses, but do not expect to shed at the doorway of your public speaking class the intellectual curiosity and study methods you exercise elsewhere. Like other components of the college core, speechmaking draws from and exhibits the heritage of classical and modern thought. No one looking for practical skills will ever be disappointed with a class in basic speaking, but much lies below these skills. In particular, three resources will provide the solid foundation you need to master and retain skills of speech. Like other courses in the arts and sciences, public speaking draws from classical studies, history, and social science research. The classical heritage of speechmaking comes from the theory and practice of the Greeks and Romans. A second resource is the example of how American speakers, historical figures as well as students, have successfully managed their materials. Third, today's speakers can tap the wealth of experimental and survey findings that clarify how to win over audiences.

Americans of the 1990s are hardly the first people to find themselves giving talks at civic organizations and business meetings. Speech is basic to any society that makes decisions by open deliberation and debate. Ancient Athens, the world's first great democracy, also spawned the first important writers on speechmaking or rhetoric. Writings on rhetoric by such

Greeks as Aristotle and such Romans as Cicero supply a reservoir of ideas that we modern speakers ignore at our peril. Aristotle's advice on how to organize ideas and how to argue remains fundamental. Cicero's tips on how to speak without bulky notes remain fresh and challenging.

Just as classical rhetoric supplies the intellectual framework of modern speechmaking, American history helps exhibit the purpose and scope of public speaking. The history of our nation is one of great speakers confronting great issues. The story of America's speakers, their successes and failures, gives us useful examples. Choices made by Abraham Lincoln, Franklin Roosevelt, Harry Truman, Barbara Jordan, Jesse Jackson, and Ronald Reagan show public speaking in action, fulfilling its purpose to give practical advice and persuasion. However, examples of speaking need not be great to be useful. Speeches by ordinary individuals, including students in basic speech courses, give significant illustrations of rhetorical practice. Taken together, speeches of the great and the ordinary, speeches of today and yesteryear, all serve as guideposts along the pathway toward rhetorical success.

Complementing the tradition of classical rhetoric and the example of American speakers is a third important resource—social science research. Your speech class presents much advice on what to do. Techniques of speaking, however, function like any tool. You may use the skills with a clumsy hesitation or with an educated confidence. No book or class can detail every possible application of a speech skill. If we turn to social science research, however, we have access to hundreds of specific experiments on the application of skills to problems of informative and persuasive speaking. During the last sixty years, and particularly between 1950 and 1980, hundreds of researchers have tested variations in speech organization, proof, language, and delivery. When incorporated into your speech course, this research supplies a reservoir of specific tactics for meeting varying needs of communication.

Public speaking differs from other arts and sciences courses because of its skills orientation. Yet, the course is similar to other components of the curriculum because it draws from a common intellectual and historical legacy. Balancing the dual goals of practical skill and academic substance is not easy, even though the two are mutually supporting. In fact, some teachers complain that the skills component of public speaking is so wide-ranging that they have no time for treating the classical heritage, or historical examples of speaking, or even social science research. Must the skills orientation blot out the many links between public speaking and the rest of the arts and sciences? I think not.

To the contrary, today's academic climate calls for a merging of speech skills and substance. Contemporary educators face simultaneous demands to get "back to the basics" (skills) and to improve quality (substance). In this atmosphere, a public speaking course that ignored its rich cultural heritage would be one at risk. Offered only the bare bones of skills, students would risk receiving a poorer education. Faculty would risk giving the impression that their course was nothing more than an excessively prolonged training workshop.

The mission of *Speechmaking* is to have you benefit from an optimal merging of speech skills and substance. Your textbook reconciles the skill and substance components of speechmaking through the concept of *rhetorical competence.* When aiming for rhetorical competence, you build your speaking skills on a firm foundation of *knowledge* and *attitudes* springing from classical principles, social science research, and historical examples. For the rhetorically competent speaker, substance acts not as a diversion from skills but, rather, as a steering mechanism for them. The rhetorically competent speaker is able to apply skills effectively to differing speech situations chiefly because those skills are propelled by a knowledge of and appreciation for good speaking. The substance of speechmaking helps you understand and appreciate the practical power and social significance of speech in a democratic society. Building on this foundation, you know when, where, and how to apply your skills of analysis, organization, delivery, language, and adaptation to a situation.

Your textbook divides the task of acquiring rhetorical competence into five component parts. Preparing you for the first classroom speeches is Part I (chapters 1–3). Your educational goal of rhetorical competence is set in chapter 1. The essential knowledge, attitudes, and skills needed for the first speech are summarized in chapter 2. Your introduction to speechmaking from the point of view of a critical listener is rounded out in chapter 3. To help bridge the gap between your present skills and future goals, the models of speaking in Part I are drawn chiefly from student speeches. Drawing more from social science research and from examples of important American speakers are Parts II through V.

The building blocks of speechmaking are set in Part II (chapters 4–7). Why speech preparation must begin with a clear notion of purpose is shown in chapter 4. Why and how you plan the speech with the audience in mind is explained in chapter 5. In chapter 6, you learn methods for developing, analyzing, and researching your main idea (thesis). Your options for supporting your thesis—arguments, evidence, and visual materials—are presented in chapter 7.

How to transform the building blocks of speech into well-organized speeches is shown in Part III (chapters 8–9) . Methods for outlining, with focus on transitions between points in the speech, are summarized in chapter 8. Your options for beginning and ending the speech are reviewed in chapter 9.

Rounding out your education in the steps of speechmaking is Part IV (chapters 10–12). Its focus is on how to transform a speech you have planned and prepared into a speech actually delivered. In chapter 10, you review options for using language to make the speech clear and interesting. The hows and whys of good voice, movement, and gesture are treated in chapter 11. How you adjust your planned speech to actual circumstances of time, place, and people is explained in chapter 12.

Focusing your rhetorical education on important kinds and types of speeches is Part V (chapters 13–15). The essentials of putting together an informative speech are set in chapter 13. Key characteristics of persuasive speaking are reviewed in chapter 14. Examples of and tips for presenting such special occasion speeches as introductions, nominations, and accepting gifts—situations you are sure to face at some time in your life—are given in chapter 15. Throughout the text, key points and speeches are emphasized in a variety of ways to give you the clearest possible understanding of rhetorical competence.

Finally, suggestions for speaking in group situations are given in two appendixes. Tips for group meetings are given in Appendix A, and some basics of parliamentary speaking are set out in Appendix B.

What, then, can you expect from your basic public speaking course? Expect to exit the class with greater powers of analysis, research, organization, language, and delivery. Expect that your coordinated knowledge, attitudes, and skills will serve as a foundation for a lifetime of better speech.

A speech education rooted in rhetorical competence will not merely propel your speaking skills; it will give two additional benefits. First, your dual introduction to the classical heritage of rhetoric and to social science research will acquaint you with some of what is essential in the study of human communication. The result is a better view of speech communication as a field of inquiry than if your course focused solely on skills. Introductory courses such as public speaking offer a look at different options open to you for further college study. You may find yourself wanting to talk to your teacher about additional courses in speech communication.

The rhetorical competence approach offers a second supplementary benefit. Some educators and national leaders today complain that modern Americans know too little of their democratic history. The 1990s may be just the time to reemphasize the traditional link between public speaking and democratic life. Nothing reveals democracy at work more than the historical panorama of significant speakers putting great issues before the public. By stressing the historical link between the good speaker and the good society, the public speaking course promotes what some call "cultural literacy." And the history of public speaking shows that ours is a culture built by the rhetorical efforts of men and women, racial majorities and minorities, young and old, expert and student, liberal and conservative.

Welcome to the basic speech course. Best wishes on beginning your quest for rhetorical competence.

Acknowledgments

I would like to thank my colleagues who gave me their counsel as I wrote this text: John Bee, University of Akron; David S. Birdsell, City University New York–Baruch; Randall Bytwerk, Calvin College; Ann Darling, University of Illinois; Charles C. DeLancey, Furman University; Ray Ewing, Southeast Missouri State University; James J. Floyd, Central Missouri State University; Thurmon Garner, University of Georgia; Robert Jackson, Ball State University; Robert Pruett, Wright State University; Arlan Ropp, Brevard Community College; Michael Schliessmann, South Dakota State University; Larry Schnoor, Mankato State University; Lee Snyder, Kearney State College; James S. Taylor, Houston Baptist University; Susan Thomas, University of Illinois; Sally Widenmann, University of California–Davis.

Recognition is also due to my students and colleagues at Indiana University Southeast and San Jose State University who nudged me in many helpful directions.

Part

I

Getting Started

Chapter

1

Theory and Research into Practice

Outline

Public Speaking Today

Rhetorical Competence
- Knowledge about Speechmaking
- Attitudes toward Speechmaking
- Skills of Speechmaking

The Roots of Rhetorical Competence
- The Rhetorical Tradition
- The Classical Approach
- The Social Science Contribution

Concepts for Review

Things to Try

If you want to improve your public speaking skills, you are in good company. Thousands of today's men and women are vitally interested in becoming better able to organize and present ideas. People all over America, at work and in community life, want to speak competently and confidently to groups, both small and large.

Like most students, you probably bring expectations and hopes of personal improvement to your speech course—even though a graduation requirement also may have prompted you to sign up. Asked what they wanted from the course, two of my public speaking students recently replied:

- "I need to work on becoming more at ease in front of people and to learn how to speak eloquently and effectively."
- "I have had to lead meetings at work and I would like to feel more comfortable."

America's great speakers all express a similar desire to attain good speech—and they pursue this desire with determination. Consider the case of Cesar Chavez, founder of the United Farm Workers. Having no formal education beyond the seventh grade, Chavez nevertheless worked on his own to develop effectiveness in speaking. He sought opportunities to talk before groups, often replaying tapes of these meetings to discover what brought responses from the audience. Chavez developed a skill in public speaking that helped him do what many labor leaders thought impossible—to organize California's disadvantaged migrant farm workers.[1]

To what extent are your expectations of personal improvement reasonable? To get a greater idea of what you may expect from a basic speech course in the 1990s, let's take a close look at speechmaking today. Is speechmaking important in modern life? What does it mean to have *competence* in speaking? What can we learn about speechmaking from significant speakers, researchers, and teachers?

Public Speaking Today

Worried about giving your first speech? Would you believe that thousands of men and women, who are actively pursuing their careers, envy your chance to take a college course in public speaking? It's true. People in the "real world" need and want competence in public speaking.

As you and other students of today seek careers in business, service, and government, it is important to know that college graduates draw every day upon their competence in public speaking. One survey showed that 98 percent of executives in the nation's largest corporations regularly use skills of public speaking. Ninety percent of these executives recommended that

Speechmaking skills made Cesar Chavez a leader in the labor movement.

the college course in business communication should include a "strong emphasis" on oral presentations.[2] Competence in public speaking is also valued by industrial scientists and engineers. Even members of these behind-the-scenes professions need to convey successfully their ideas to work groups.[3]

Box 1.1

Today's Corporate Speechwriting

A corporate speechwriter may help formulate op-ed columns in newspapers and prepared remarks for annual meetings or television appearances. He may even draft the allegedly "unprepared remarks" so often delivered to industry groups. . . .

"I write a lot of speeches in honor of new building openings," said Katie Nutter, speechwriter for Hewlett-Packard CEO John Young. "But when speechwriting is at its best, it's taking something that's not totally crystallized and forcing people to clarify their thoughts."

Evidently most large corporations keep full-time speechwriters on their staffs, but a few find this too costly and choose instead to hire freelancers—at as much as $5,000 per speech. Top speechwriters on or off the staff make as much as $150,000 a year, but most earn between $50,000 and $80,000, according to Judy Cushman, president of a Seattle recruiting firm.

Source: Jamie Beckett, *San Francisco Chronicle* (8 November 1988), C1.

Competence in public speaking is so important that speech education often does not stop with college. One barometer of the vitality of public speaking is the large number of brochures business people receive that promote commercial speech workshops and materials:

> "Announcing an easy, effective way for you to unleash your hidden 'Speech Power.' " (for a cassette package by American Express Company)
> "Speak Out With Clout!" (for the *Decker Communications Report*)

To meet the needs of today's professionals, dozens of speech coaching firms have emerged to offer speech education to managers and executives. Some of these programs charge participants a thousand dollars or more for two days of instruction. In addition, a large percentage of American businesses have always offered in-house public speaking training to employees.[4]

Many working people wish they had used their college days to gain greater knowledge and skill in public speaking. A survey of alumni of the College of Charleston found that the graduates rated public speaking the top choice as most "helpful in your life since graduation" compared to other language arts courses. Public speaking was not a required course for these graduates. However, "alumni felt so strongly about the importance of oral communication that some of them voluntarily recommended a requirement in public speaking."[5]

Public speaking will prove its value not only in your work but also in your civic and social life. "Real people" use speechmaking skills in everyday situations. In Albany, New York, researchers found that 46.5 percent of residents had spoken to a group of ten or more persons "at least once in the last two years"; 31.7 percent spoke on more than four occasions. These speaking experiences occurred at church, banquets, and union meetings, and in community organizations. These results came from an area of the city containing a high proportion of non-college-educated blue collar workers. We would expect college-educated persons to report even more speechmaking activity.[6]

If you want to improve your public speaking skills, you *are* in good company. Thousands of men and women—in and out of college—share your interest. But you still may be wondering exactly what you are going to gain from a college course in speechmaking. What does it mean when we identify someone as a well-educated, *rhetorically competent,* speaker?

Rhetorical Competence

People just like you are spending money and are taking time to learn about public speaking. This fact conveys an important message. You are now in the perfect position to set a foundation for a life-long ability in speechmaking. What will serve you best is what we may call *rhetorical competence.*

Rhetorical competence is the key term of this textbook. What does it mean? "Rhetorical" comes from the root word, *rhetoric*, meaning persuasive speech. The Greeks and Romans of ancient times did more than give us this original word for speechmaking. They also began the systematic study of speech concepts. Since classical times, good speaking has been seen as a product of *knowledge, attitudes,* and *skills.* We hear the term *skill* used frequently, today, but knowledge and attitudes are equally important in your education as a speaker. Your knowledge and attitudes enable you to use your skills appropriately and well. Taken together, your knowledge of, your attitudes about, and your practical skills in speechmaking will combine to make you a *rhetorically competent* individual. We should examine these three aspects of rhetorical competence carefully, both individually and in combination.

The first measure of achieving rhetorical competence is *knowledge* gained about several basic mechanics of public speaking. You need to know the ways of analyzing a topic as well as the options for putting together and delivering messages. Beyond this, rhetorical competence means to understand how long-term success flows from good ethics and logic as well as from high quality techniques of delivery.

Second, as a competent speaker, you will possess *attitudes* that enhance effective communication. The attitudes that distinguish the able speaker from the novice are confidence in oneself, a positive interest in the topic, enthusiasm for sharing ideas with people (instead of giving a one-way monologue), and a strong desire to present the best possible speech. The third component of rhetorical competence is your demonstrated *skill* in constructing and delivering messages. To use a phrase popular today, skills are the "bottom line" of speaking. However, you will realize that outward skillfulness—what the audience sees and hears—is the product of your prior knowledge and attitudes about speechmaking.

If we look at one specific skill—that of organization, for example—we will see how rhetorical competence requires a close marriage of knowledge, attitudes, and skills. Organization in public speaking is your ability to put ideas into the most advantageous sequence. To organize a message for an actual occasion, you will need to know the many alternatives for arranging ideas and arguments, as well as the implications of each alternative. Theory and research in speechmaking tell us that messages may be organized according to one of two general options. First, you may organize your speech around the topical information that needs to be given. Second, you may arrange information according to how you predict the audience will respond to the ideas.

Beyond knowledge, you need to hold positive *attitudes* about speaking in order to skillfully project your ideas to listeners. If you also hold two positive *attitudes* about speaking, you will be more likely to put your knowledge successfully into practice. These two attitudes are, first, your desire to know everything about your subject, and second, your appreciation for the opinions of other people. What does interest in your topic and audience have to do with successfully organizing your material? Attitudes toward topic and audience enhance your skill of organization because these attitudes inevitably guide you in applying your knowledge. Your interest in the topic motivates you to look at a wide range of ideas, to find out what points *are* available to be presented first, second, or third. At the same time, your interest in the audience helps you decide what are the stronger ideas *for this audience.* Your attitude prompts you to find out the likely knowledge and opinions of listeners on the subject. Only with favorable attitudes toward your topic and audience will you be motivated to review fully the many possible ways for putting together the speech.

In sum, your ability to organize your speech skillfully rests upon knowledge of how speeches generally may be organized. Skillful organization also flows directly from attitudes that help you apply general knowledge to a particular topic and audience.

Rhetorical competence grows naturally with age. As people mature during grade school and high school, they become increasingly able to deal with complex concepts. Twelfth graders are more successful than younger students in recalling information from a speech. Also, the older students demonstrate an increased capacity to see possibilities other than those mentioned in a speech, and thus are better able to resist attempts at persuasion.[7] Throughout adolescence, a person's rhetorical capacities increase, including "the ability to think about one's own thinking and the ability to recognize possibilities in addition to the actualities of everyday experience."[8]

The entire rhetorical process—from selection of a topic to presenting the speech—requires that you exercise your advanced powers of analysis. Although your power to prepare and analyze messages effectively has grown with maturity, you also may expect to benefit from formal speech education. Your public speaking course offers an ideal time and place for honing your rhetorical competence. Let's look at what you can expect to gain from your public speaking course in the way of knowledge, attitudes, and skills.

Knowledge about Speechmaking

Your speech education is focused on the crucial things you need to know about giving speeches. We speakers of today benefit from 2500 years of accumulated observations and advice on public speaking. Your rhetorical education will give you new ways to think logically and systematically about communication. You will understand that speaking is a process that helps you make beginning hunches, helps you surmount hurdles of analysis and research, and finally, guides you in practicing delivery.

In one sense, the nature of speechmaking as a process makes gaining knowledge of public speaking easy. After all, everything you learn fits in immediately with what you already know about communicating with people. At the same time, however, the nature of speechmaking as a cumulative learning process can be difficult for beginners. Every classroom speech, from the first to the last, is an exercise that spans the whole process. Because public speaking is part of an integrated complex of steps, the first three chapters of this book are designed to give you a good mental picture of the whole process. They get you ready for delivering and evaluating the first classroom speech. The remaining chapters then turn you loose to focus in depth on different facets of public speaking.

Part II of this book brings you to the first building blocks of speech preparation. An in-depth view of how to develop your purpose as a speaker is given in chapter 4. Implementing your speech purpose requires that you fully research your audience and topic. Why and how to learn about your listeners are two important facets of chapter 5. Your goal is to discover what the audience believes about your topic and what impression they have about your competence and preparation to speak on that topic. In fact, a very important attitude of the competent speaker is one of audience-centeredness. Communication researchers sometimes use the term *perspective taking* to describe how you can sense an audience's slant on a subject and how you can thereby adjust your speech.[9]

The second part of research, covered in chapter 6, calls for you to take apart the topic of the speech to discover the major points and their relationships. Chapter 6 will sharpen and focus your abilities to analyze the content of messages. The chapter shows the importance of developing a thesis, and it introduces a system for assembling what you know about the topic. Furthermore, competence in analysis includes being able to gather the outside evidence and arguments that tighten, elaborate, or back up your points. The kinds of speech materials that the rhetorically competent speaker usually finds valuable are introduced in chapter 7.

Once you grasp analysis and research, Part III takes you to the point of fashioning speech materials into a coherent whole. In speechmaking, analysis of the subject and audience leads to ideas for organization. You work to find different ways that individual points may best be arranged to respond to a particular topic and audience. Given that listeners can remember only three to five key ideas in a speech, placing your ideas carefully is crucial. For this reason, the two chapters devoted to organization, chapters 8 and 9, will be crucial to your speech education. They will give you tips for successfully highlighting just those major points you want to convey.

The connection between highlighting major points and achieving your goals as a speaker cannot be too greatly emphasized. Part IV explains how you may transform a planned speech into one successfully presented. How wording the speech can help win attention and interest, keeping the minds of listeners open to information and open to persuasion, is shown in chapter 10. Your voice and movement during the speech also highlight the ideas you present, so specific advice on such good habits of delivery as straight posture, direct eye contact, and variety in vocal expression is given in chapter 11. Since vocal and body action are personal, however, your delivery will not markedly improve without your individual commitment to practice and improve these facets of speechmaking. Your options for preparing speech notes and for responding to unforeseen events are explained in chapter 12.

Finally, helping you put together your rhetorical knowledge as you prepare informative, persuasive, and special occasion speeches is Part V (chapters 13–15).

Attitudes toward Speechmaking

Rhetorical competence begins, but does not end, with knowledge about the process of speechmaking. Turning your knowledge into skill requires something further—an appreciation for good speaking. Attitudes of rhetorical competence will make you want to model your own communication on examples given in your course. We need to review four specific attitudes that will help you take on competence in the rhetorical arts.

Enthusiasm for speaking to people

Does the prospect of speaking to a group make you feel nervous? Of course it does! Speakers, regardless of age or experience, all report having "butterflies" before the speech. The term we will use in chapter 2 is *speech anxiety.* Such feelings are only natural. Increased heart rate and other symptoms of nervousness are part of the body's way of responding to a demanding situation. As we will observe in chapter 2, the symptoms of nervousness are greatest at the beginning of the speech, and they routinely decline as we get deeper into our presentation.

Since *all* speakers experience the knee-knocking sensations that accompany a speech, why are some people eager to talk and others reluctant? The difference is a matter of attitude. Experienced speakers view the tension as excitement, not fearfulness. They expect the bodily tension, even welcome it, since they know the sensations mark a heightened state of readiness to perform. To reinforce their attitude that speaking creates an enjoyable excitement, seasoned speakers look out at members of the audience as they speak. They view listeners as individual people, not a faceless crowd.

Box 1.2

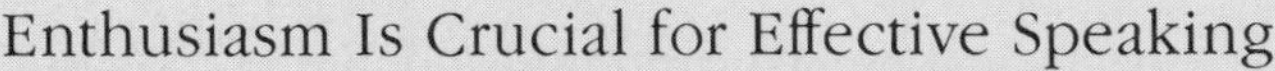

Enthusiasm Is Crucial for Effective Speaking

Is it necessary to catch a speaker off guard and off platform in order to get his best speech? I thought of Jack London who, directly after making a dull speech on socialism at Bowdoin College, sat by our fireside and thrilled us half the night with his adventures in Alaska. I thought too of Henry van Dyke who, after an undistinguished sermon in the College Chapel, sat by the same fireside, smoked a pipe, and fascinated us.

Source: William T. Foster, "Random Notes on Public Speaking," *Quarterly Journal of Speech*, 33 (1947), 139.

Begin to cultivate the positive attitude toward speechmaking. This will mark an important early lesson in your speech education. Chapter 2 contains many specific suggestions concerning how to make the act of speaking an enjoyable, less fearful, experience.

Balanced interest in content and delivery

Have you ever heard the remark that successful speakers choose sizzle over substance? Sometimes we associate public speaking exclusively with the techniques of posture, gesture, eye contact, and voice. A survey of students at Pennsylvania State University revealed that "a majority of beginning speech students expected their instructors to emphasize aspects of speech delivery while they ignored speech content."[10] Experienced speakers would *not* agree. They know that you cannot be a competent speaker if you lack an understanding of your topic.

The view of public speaking as only training in delivery is often reinforced by short workshops that take a few techniques out of the supporting context of theory and research. A study of in-house business public speaking courses showed that "the major concern of these training programs was delivery." One participant in a Communispond executive speech workshop recalled that the training focused so completely on techniques that participants "learned nothing about improving the content of our future speeches." Indeed, the narrow view that public speaking equals delivery exists occasionally even in higher education. For instance, two psychologists studying speech argued that "the 'gift' of public speaking involves a number of specific target behaviors that can be acquired with a minimum amount of instruction." The psychologists listed these simple behaviors as eye contact, gestures, smiling, "pausing momentarily before beginning to speak," and using anecdotes.[11]

Speech communication faculty do not deny the importance of good delivery habits. Far from it, they view delivery as important, and they will give you ideas for improving your delivery. But experience has taught instructors of speech that people cannot speak well on a topic unless they have a thorough knowledge of the subject matter. Audiences are surprisingly able to see through a technique when it is not supported by full knowledge of the topic. Further, it is difficult for speakers to bring confidence and poise to the speech situation unless they are in command of the content.

Dating from ancient Greek times, the most significant writers on public speaking have always counseled speakers to embrace both content and delivery. One of the most important of these writers was the Roman philosopher and statesman, Marcus Tullius Cicero, who wrote on rhetoric from his own observations and experiences in the Roman Senate. Cicero recognized that the best speakers were those who used a complete rhetorical approach, sensitive to content and delivery. Cicero's ideal speaker was one who discovered good arguments, carefully organized them, worked for a good style of words, and practiced methods of good oral delivery.[12] Expect your speech education to include an integrated study of content and delivery.

Desire to perfect knowledge

Another sign that you share the attitudes of rhetorical competence will be when you find yourself wanting to perfect your knowledge about a subject. The rhetorically competent speaker understands that knowledge is something always subject to improvement. This point is well put by Eugene Garver, a teacher of critical thinking. Garver observes that a rhetorical argument is "not an invulnerable argument but the best argument possible in a given situation."[13] Arguments *never are final,* since people, groups, even nations change their minds. If we accept that our claims are neither invulnerable nor final, we respect our opponent's arguments and we readily admit that our own arguments need improvement. These views are crucial in helping us to adopt the attitude of wanting to perfect our knowledge. They are crucial for a lifetime of rhetorical competence.

To understand the implications of perfecting our knowledge, let's compare the rhetorically competent to the rhetorically *in*competent attitudes about speech content. Suppose, for example, that a speaker decided to talk on the subject of the 55 mile-per-hour speed limit. This speaker would begin with a particular knowledge of and view toward the subject. A rhetorically *in*competent attitude would be one of satisfaction with this state of knowledge. The speaker might halfheartedly look up some information about traffic fatalities in an almanac or copy some data from a recent magazine article. The basic approach would be to give the speech with essentially the same level of knowledge as when the speaker first began work. This unprepared individual would be likely *not* to look confident in dealing with opposing points of view. The speaker's own limited knowledge and insight would make confronting the opposing view risky and threatening.

In contrast, consider the thought processes of the rhetorically competent speaker. This speaker would also begin with knowledge and opinions on the 55 MPH limit. But the competent speaker would realize two things about his or her existing knowledge. First, the speaker would appreciate the benefits of learning more about the history, operation, and effect of the national speed limit law. Second, the rhetorically able speaker would be careful not to fall into the trap of searching only for information that supports initial opinions.[14] Conducted on the basis of these two assumptions, the speech preparation of the rhetorically competent speaker would be sure to produce good results. Either this competent speaker would have an unchanged opinion that was better supported, or the speaker would possess a modified opinion that better accounted for all available information on the topic. In either case, because the competent speaker had already considered many of the opposing ideas, he or she would be less afraid to fully and authoritatively confront them.

Set as your goal becoming a speaker who "thinks rhetorically." Constantly evaluate the information you encounter while working on your topic.[15] Moreover, keep striving to judge whether your opinions are reasonable, ethical, and true. If you do this, you will be less likely to be surprised by an opponent who mentions contrary information. The idea of constantly evaluating our sources of information is an ancient one. This practice is embodied in Aristotle's contention that one of the basic functions of public speaking is to make truth prevail.[16]

Desire to advise the audience

Karl Wallace, the revered American scholar of rhetoric, described public speaking as an exercise in *advising*. When we view ourselves as advisers, we perceive our speeches as supplying "specific information and advice" concerning "what should or ought to be done." Our listeners, in turn, reflect on our information and advice as they make reasoned choices. Part and parcel of rhetorical competence is treating your listeners as valued people worthy of your best counsel. One sign that you are coming to rhetorical competence is looking for ways to help listeners make an informed choice. Although your aim is to educate or influence listeners, your speech methods neither selfishly manipulate them nor give in totally to their whims.

As Wallace points out, the advice-giving notion of communication holds speaker and listener jointly responsible for good speechmaking. The responsibility of the speaker is to keep well informed about the subject to give good advice. The speaker also keeps "sensitive to the climate in which advice is appropriate" and is careful to recommend only a course of action "that he believes is in the best interest of the audience." The listener, in turn, remains aware of his or her responsibility to weigh the advice and make a decision. Considered as an advice-giving activity, rhetorical communication is a *balanced process* in which the speaker is informed, the message is relevant, and the listeners are aware that they must make their own decisions.[17]

Wayne Booth, an expert on composition and rhetoric, identifies three all-too-common approaches to speechmaking that lack the balance of the advisory method. Each one of these three errors of rhetorical perspective finds the speaker giving too much stress to one dimension of communication—either speaker, message, or audience. The communicator who emphasizes his or her personal role as speaker becomes an *entertainer.* Such a speaker typically is willing to "sacrifice substance to personality and charm." On the other hand, emphasis on the message makes one a *pedant,* someone who presents a message whether or not anyone cares to hear it. Finally, Booth terms the *advertising* approach as one preoccupied with the audience. The advertiser tends to aim for pure effect and therefore is tempted to use any way—fair or foul—to promote a point of view.[18]

The concept of rhetorical sensitivity provides us with a closely related way to understand and correct a possible imbalance in our attitude toward the act of communication. If we are *rhetorically sensitive* persons, we communicate in a manner appropriate to the subject, audience, and situation. This balanced attention to communication may be compared to two unbalanced approaches to speaking. One kind of rhetorical imbalance is exhibited by the self-centered egoist, who gives thought to nothing but his or her own opinion. Another form of imbalance is shown by the overly devious speaker who advances a cause by saying whatever the listeners want to hear.[19]

The attitude of the rhetorically competent speaker is embodied in the ancient ideal of the *golden mean.* As a rhetorically competent speaker, you chart a middle course between a variety of extremes. With the onset of rhetorical competence, you begin to feel a zest for speaking that is produced by your controlled apprehension and excitement. Further, you seek to understand your material as well as to look impressive. Third, you begin to view your ideas as good, but imperfect. Finally, rhetorical competence helps you strike a balance between promoting ideas and helping the audience. Together these four attitudes will put you on the route to a life-long program of competence in speechmaking.

Skills of Speechmaking

Though knowledge and attitudes are essential for good speech, so are competent practices. Exactly what practices, however? Has anyone developed a short list of public speaking skills? The problem of listing skills is a real one. Not only is public speaking a continuous process, but your textbook spreads advice among fifteen chapters. Are we therefore prevented from making a thumbnail sketch of the skills required for mastery of speaking? Does it somehow distort the process of speechmaking to mark out certain crucial skills?

The Romans pondered these very questions, and they developed a shorthand roster of speaking skills. The classical catalogue of speech methods is termed the *canons of rhetoric.* The canons divide speechmaking into five parts: invention, organization, style, delivery, and memory. These traditional divisions mark for us five crucial categories of rhetorical skill.

Invention

Invention is the process that we use to gather the "stuff" of the speech—the arguments and evidence that make our case, pro or con. One mark of a skillful speaker is the ability to use analysis and research to get strong arguments and evidence for the speech.

When you attain a full measure of competence in invention, you will seek and obtain materials that meet the two traditional tests of validity and ethics. First, valid materials are those ideas and arguments that remain sound when everything about them is public knowledge. Valid supporting materials provide substantial facts, statistics, and examples. At the same time, the fruits of your speech invention may be considered valid when they neither overstate a point nor omit relevant information about it. When you test speech materials for their ethical implications, you enter a contract that binds you, the ethical speaker, to your audience. You pledge that your advice is thoughtful, truthful, and in the best interests of the listeners.

In our pragmatic, what's-in-it-for-me culture there is a tendency to dismiss questions of validity and ethics. However, to the rhetorically competent speaker, such a view of effective speechmaking is shallow, short-term, and ultimately self-defeating. To the competent speaker, effective speaking means a *career* of rhetorical success as you build a reputation in front of many audiences.

Organization

Organization is the arranging of the parts of the speech. You may approach the skill of organization from one or both of two directions. On the one hand, your presentation may be structured to reflect what you think should be said about the topic. For instance, you may decide that a complicated concept of psychology must be explained before you can clearly convey a technique of counseling therapy. On the other hand, speeches may be organized according to the expectations or background of the listeners. Such a case would be when you first build up favorable points to prepare the audience for a disagreeable idea to be presented later.

Organization also includes the practice of presenting the speech in a way that gives listeners a verbal road map of your thoughts. You put this kind of map before your listeners when you repeat key ideas, use brief capsule statements to highlight major points, and use transitions to connect ideas.

Style

Style is a matter of wording ideas effectively. Good style means phrasing your arguments to make them clear, interesting, and appropriate to the occasion. When you attain rhetorical competence in the area of style, you understand how word choices influence the responses of listeners. If an idea may be likened to a rough, uncut diamond, then style supplies the general shape and polished facets of the idea. Cut and polished through words, ideas can either gain speedy acceptance or be snagged by their rough edges.

How do you develop and implement a fine sense for style? The only sure way is to become a student of words. Develop an ear for the sound of words. Watch how people react to words and phrases. Practice different wordings for key ideas in your speeches.

Delivery

When your speech "goes public," your delivery is at the forefront of attention. The ideas, words, and structure of a speech all lie hidden until delivered in public. Therefore, you would do well to *practice* skills of bodily and vocal communication. True, when a speaker lacks either a command of content or a sensitivity to audience, he or she will profit little from merely knowing how to control voice and gesture. On the other hand, when you see skills of delivery in their proper relation to content and audience, you will realize the profit possible from drilling yourself on delivery. Neither you, nor any other speaker, has anything to fear from working on skills of voice and movement—as long as you also attend to matters of content and audience analysis.

Experienced speakers use few, if any, notes.

Memory

Memory is that facet of speechmaking that allows you to put content and delivery together at the moment of speaking. Memory in public speaking begins when you first organize your ideas and practice the speech. But this skill is most closely associated with the use of technical aids to help you recall the speech while you deliver it. For most speakers, the familiar techniques of memory are those that involve preparing and using written speech notes. Closer to the classical conception of memory are those techniques of aided memory (treated in chapter 12) that allow you to recall the organization and arguments of the speech with few or no notes.

The five parts of rhetoric are doors through which anyone desiring rhetorical competence must pass. Skilled public speaking works through five categories of thought and talk to bring together your intention and the expectations of your audience.

The Roots of Rhetorical Competence

In chapter 2, we will get down to the specifics of how to prepare for your first classroom speech. Before embarking on the road of advice, however, we should consider the source of all these suggestions. Exactly *who* vouches for the many recommendations about public speaking given in the fifteen chapters of this textbook? Obviously, your instructor and the author of your textbook are the immediate "whos" in your speech education. Yet, this advice on speech practice comes from a long tradition of theory and research in speechmaking. Both your public speaking textbook and class have one mission, that of helping you put theory and research into practice.

Today's knowledge of speech comes from two major sources. The first of these is the 2500-year long classical tradition of rhetoric, exemplified by such writers as the Roman senator, Cicero, and the Greek educator, Aristotle. The second important source of information about public speaking is twentieth century social science research in communication. Since World War II, and especially between 1950 and 1980, social scientists worked to test the traditional advice on speaking given by the classical writers. A clearer notion of these two roots of speechmaking will help you get the most out of this text and from your course in public speaking.

The Rhetorical Tradition

The theory of public speaking already was well developed in the Greek society of 300 B.C. By this time, speechmaking had served as a recognized social force for 150 years, and a theory of public address was emerging in the works of several teachers and writers, notably the Athenian scholar, Aristotle.

Box 1.3

Good Public Speaking Helps Truth Prevail

Rhetoric is useful because things that are true and things that are just have a natural tendency to prevail over their opposites, so that if the decisions of judges are not what they ought to be, the defeat must be due to the speakers themselves, and they must be blamed accordingly.

Source: Aristotle, *Rhetoric,* I. 1. 1355a.

In the decades before and after the Christian era, Roman writers continued and systematized the rhetorical theory of the Greeks. The Roman work is best exemplified by Cicero, Quintilian, and the unknown author of the *Rhetorica ad Herennium* (a work on rhetoric dedicated to Gaius Herennius). By 430 A.D., St. Augustine, an early father of the Christian church, had written a treatise, *On Christian Doctrine,* applying classical rhetoric to the needs of early Christian preachers. During the Middle Ages, much of the classical learning was lost. Certain practices and some theory of rhetoric remained, since speech helped the church fathers both to interpret scripture and to preach, but it was not until the rediscovery of the ancient writers on rhetoric, after A.D. 1400, that the classical tradition reestablished itself.

In the European Renaissance, rhetoric gained strength as one of the traditional seven liberal arts, mastery of which was the mark of an educated person. However, opportunities for open political and legal expression were limited in those days. Thus rhetoric was more often used as an art of literary technique than a method of persuasive speaking. Nevertheless, major writings on rhetoric as persuasive speech have been published since the beginning of the modern period right up to the present.

In contemporary society, however, the classical teachings of rhetoric sometimes have less prestige and importance than they commanded in the classical Greek and Roman world. The tendency of today's Americans to forget the tradition of rhetoric began after the Civil War. That was a time in which university studies were being reorganized to include more education in science and technology. Such restructuring grew from the idea that science provided all the knowledge needed for modern people. Many educators argued that rhetoric was now useless. Such a viewpoint helped to produce today's popular conception of rhetoric as the opposite of science, that rhetoric was overblown, artificial, and deceitful speech. In contrast, for the ancient world, mastery of speechmaking was viewed as *the* essential goal of education. The classical view held that knowledge was complicated and often contradictory when applied to matters of public policy. Accordingly, the ancients saw rhetorical studies as the only sure route to analyzing and presenting ideas effectively in a democratic climate.

The philosophy of the ancients may be compared to the contemporary illusion that ours is a world of objective facts that speak for themselves. How often do today's leaders suggest that their "facts" need no human analysis and interpretation? How often do the powerful want to make us feel embarrassed to ask tough and probing questions? Too often we sit back, watch television, and let the experts make our decisions for us. People today often feel excluded from such vital matters as nuclear policy, AIDS, economics, and environmental safety. The widespread modern myth of a purely technical world makes the study of rhetoric more socially important today than at any other time. If citizens are to understand and control their society, then they must be skilled in the arts of reasoned speech.

The Classical Approach

But exactly what does the legacy of classical rhetoric have to offer the modern student of public speaking? Does the classical tradition supply only a few high-minded, but impractical thoughts? To answer such questions, we must begin with the early works of rhetoric, books that contain purely practical advice mixed with deep philosophical insights. Since Greek and Roman times, public speaking—the art of rhetoric—has been understood to provide specific benefits both for the individual speaker and for the society at large. The benefits to be gained from study of our rhetorical tradition arise from four key themes that are found in these writings. Traditional teachers of speechmaking focus on four important outcomes for their students: (1) personal discovery, (2) practical wisdom, (3) personal prestige, and (4) improvement of society.

Personal discovery

Speechmaking is the art and science of communication. In studying how best to communicate, people make discoveries about themselves and about others who may be different. Faced with the need to prepare messages for listeners, speakers take a close look at their own beliefs, attitudes, and values. To prepare a persuasive speech, you must run through a host of personal opinions and values to select the topic and content that best suit you. So, speechmaking provides you with an opportunity to understand yourself better. In addition, you must go beyond yourself and observe, read about, and question other human beings. You begin to improve your ideas at the same time that you become wiser about people.

Practical wisdom

Most of the great books of traditional rhetorical study are a fascinating mixture of the practical and the philosophical. Aristotle's *Rhetoric* is a good example. A keen observer of speakers and of speech preparation, Aristotle wrote about all the nitty-gritty things that concern a speaker, including making a good impression on listeners, getting striking content for the speech, and making the speech interesting.

Aristotle's method of invention is practical. It helps us discover intelligent, interesting, and impressive things to say about a subject. In addition, Aristotle's theory of invention helps us gain *practical wisdom.* Not only does Aristotle's method supply immediately useful speech content, but it also promotes habits of thought and inquiry that can be applied anytime we must "deliberate well" and take action "with regard to things that are good or bad."[20]

Personal prestige

Commercial public speaking workshops illustrate well one practical aim of speech education—the ability to speak with confidence and power. One such program, the Communispond workshop for executives, encourages speakers to use a few hand-drawn pictures, called *pictographs,* instead of preparing an elaborate outline or a complete manuscript. The pictograph method allows speakers to exhibit an obvious command of their subject, speaking virtually without aid.

Pictures and drawings may substitute for written notes.

Although the pictograph method may represent the cutting edge of today's high-priced workshops, the method is not new. In fact, this technique is found in the classical Roman textbooks of rhetoric, notably Cicero's *De Oratore* and Quintilian's *Institutio Oratoria.* By using pictographic symbols, classically-trained speakers were ready to speak in the extemporaneous mode, with a minimum of notes.

But we should note that the classical view held that impressive speaking resulted from exhibiting integrity and ability as much as from executing various techniques of presentation. For instance, Aristotle viewed the character, or *ethos,* of the speaker as particularly crucial in persuasion. He noticed that at the same time audiences listened to words, they also looked for what the address revealed about the speaker's general character, understanding of the subject, and apparent intentions. Aristotle observed that listeners asked questions of a kind expressed in the modern phrase: "Would I buy a used car from this individual?"

This view of personal credibility as a persuasive force shows the genius of speech education in the classical tradition. To the Greek and Roman teachers, the only way to be *perceived* as credible was *actually to possess* the traits of character, competence, and sincerity. Quintilian put the point in this way:

> Bad men, in their contempt for public opinion and their ignorance of what is right, sometimes drop their mask, unawares, and are impudent in the statement of their case and shameless in their assertions . . . however we strive to conceal it, insincerity will always betray itself.[21]

For the ancients, then, education in public speaking was also training in the development of good character. The natural outgrowth of this rhetorical study was a speaker who was en route to deserving, and therefore possessing, great prestige. Quintilian's often-repeated description of the effective speaker of his day was "a good man, skilled in speaking."[22]

Improvement of society

Marcus Tullius Cicero certainly was the greatest combiner of rhetorical practice and theory in the ancient world. While other leading Romans of the time used military force (Julius Caesar) or wealth (Crassus) as springboards to political power, Cicero's abilities as a speaker won him a commanding influence in the Roman Senate. A careful observer and thinker, Cicero also wrote seven significant works on the philosophy, theory, and history of public speaking.

Box 1.4

Free Speech Is Protected as Vital for Society

A principal who was dismissed after accusing school committee members of interfering too much in his high school's operations was ordered reinstated Monday by a Middlesex Superior Court judge.

The principal, Michael G. Waring, was dismissed from Lexington High School in June 1987. He filed a lawsuit contending that he was dismissed in retaliation for a speech he made at a faculty meeting on June 16, 1987.

In the speech, Mr. Waring accused the Lexington School Committee of "excessive interference" with routine operations of the high school. . . .

The principal was reinstated by Justice Hiller Zobel, who ruled that the speech was protected under the Constitution and could not be used as a basis for dismissal, said Mr. Waring's lawyer, Roderick MacLeish, Jr.

From the Associated Press, as appeared in *The New York Times,* August 31, 1988, p. B8.

To Cicero, the very survival of a nation depended on the ability of wise citizens to communicate effectively on matters that concerned the public. He was convinced that open deliberation and debate were vital for society, and he cautioned that "mute and voiceless wisdom" could not advance humanity. Cicero saw a second danger when a society did not provide its public with a balanced education in rhetoric. He pointed to abuses that occurred when persons "of eloquence unaccompanied by any consideration of moral duty" temporarily fooled and misled the public. To avoid these extremes of rhetorical failure, Cicero recommended that a society should actively cultivate the eloquent habits of good speech. In this view, those who attained mature eloquence would "obtain glory, honor and high esteem." At the same time, society would benefit by fluent speech whenever, "it is accompanied by wisdom."[23]

The above four themes of the rhetorical tradition have continued to the present day. Modern writers on composition, such as Wayne Booth, remind us that the good speaker gives us good reasons for believing and acting. Contemporary writers on ethical communication, such as Richard Johannesen, remind us that listeners adjust their belief in what we say to their confidence in our character and motives.[24] Today, we can draw from the longstanding philosophy of rhetorical competence, a view that integrates the knowledge, attitudes, and skills of speechmaking.

The Social Science Contribution

Although the rhetorical tradition of speechmaking is many centuries old, only in the last generation has social science research made a major mark on public speaking. The term *social science research* can be defined narrowly, to include only the most recent and sophisticated study methods and interests, or broadly, to account for all work done under the heading of social science. In speechmaking, social science research has taken chiefly the form of controlled experiments in which researchers study the reaction of listeners to carefully crafted messages. Less frequently used methods include field studies and survey research. Most often, statistical analysis is used to interpret and report findings. Much of the specific advice now given to students of speech flows from findings gained during the last thirty years from hundreds of communication experiments and other research. To understand the modern theory and practice of speechmaking, we must know something about each of three important facets of social science research in public communication.

Experiments

To the experimental researcher, the key concepts of public speaking are termed variables. Experimental controls make possible a microscopic analysis of how two or more variables of speaking work in an artificial, but nevertheless revealing, situation. Experimental analysis of public speaking gives a limited, but quite specific, insight into what is otherwise a very complicated process of human interaction.

John Baird, Jr.'s study of the effect of summaries in a speech is a useful illustration of experimental research in public speaking. Baird began with Aristotle's advice on the desirability of restating major points in the conclusion of a speech. From this background, he stated four predictions, hypotheses, about what he expected to happen when audiences listened to speeches having various degrees of organization. One of these hypotheses

Among Aristotle's pupils in philosophy and rhetoric was Alexander the Great.

was that "inclusion of either a preview, a review, or internal summaries will produce significantly greater comprehension than will inclusion of no summaries."[25]

To test his hypothesis about the effect of previews, internal reviews, and concluding summaries, Baird created four versions of a speech. One version was a speech prepared without any of the various organizing statements being studied; another speech possessed an introduction that previewed the major points to be covered; a third version of the speech contained three short internal summaries placed after each of the major points of the speech; and a final version contained a summary of points at its conclusion. Baird chose to compare these speeches, experimentally, by observing how much student audiences remembered after hearing tape recorded speeches—that is, how great was their comprehension. Comprehension was measured by multiple-choice questions. Baird found that previews and reviews increased comprehension to a statistically significant degree, but learned that "inclusion of internal summaries produced no appreciable effect."[26]

Experimental research has provided a wealth of information about many facets of speechmaking, including speech anxiety, the credibility of speakers, the impact of evidence, verbal style, and the effects of eye contact, vocal articulation, and gestures. Although we may profit from this information, we should be aware of one weakness of the experimental study—its artificiality. In the Baird study, for example, the listeners heard only a taped voice; they knew they were going to be tested on the content of the speech; and they were a captive audience. Moreover, the subject of the speech—how to listen—was rather academic in nature. Whether or not the same results would appear with a live, "real world" audience that listened to a speech having rousing emotional content is open to question. Because of the issue of artificiality, as well as other considerations, the specific advice given to speakers always occurs in a *context of possibility and probability.* Experimental studies of speaking always bring up points of possible help. When the real world situation approximates the assumptions of the laboratory, this help is highly likely to yield good effects.

Field studies

While relatively few field studies of speechmaking have been conducted, a representative study is that reported by Lynda Kaid and Robert Hirsch. These researchers attended a campus rally for Edmund Muskie, Democratic presidential candidate, held at Southern Illinois University on January 25, 1972. Kaid and Hirsch wanted to collect information relating to three questions: (1) "Are those who come to hear a political candidate speak favorably predisposed toward him?" (2) "Does a single appearance by a political candidate produce a favorable shift in his image?" and (3) "If there is a favorable shift in his image, will it persist over time?" To answer these questions, the researchers distributed questionnaires to about 600 persons as the listeners entered the auditorium. Some members of the audience received questionnaires asking for their initial impressions of Muskie; others were asked to give after-the-speech impressions. In a second part of the study, follow-up questionnaires, also asking for impressions of Muskie, were sent to a number of attendees two or three weeks after the rally.[27]

The results showed that attendees had an initially slightly favorable opinion of Muskie and that Muskie's speech significantly improved his image. The authors further reported that the listeners judged Muskie according to two major standards: first, his trustworthiness, and second, his demeanor. Finally, Kaid and Hirsch reported that elements of the favorable shift toward Muskie persisted after three weeks. These results supplied concrete support for the standard principle that speeches do make a difference in such real social situations as political campaigning.

Survey research

Surveys in the form of questionnaires, interviews, or telephone calls also shed light on a number of facets of speechmaking. A classic survey study presented sound recordings of different dialects to listeners in all parts of the United States. Among the eight conclusions reported by the authors was that "speech preferences of college students in all sections of the United States are similar, and show a tendency to accept General American speech as the preferred dialect."[28] A second example of survey research in speechmaking is a useful study of what college students believe and feel about stage fright. Various findings from this study are helpful in controlling speech anxiety. For instance, the researchers discovered that students who are especially nervous about speaking hold the false belief that other people have no stage fright while speaking.[29]

Social science research offers important ideas about specific ways you can attain rhetorical competence. For this reason, research findings are built into the advice given in every chapter of this textbook. However, because differences discovered through scientific procedures may be small ones, do not expect that by following any particular item of advice you can double your effectiveness as a speaker. Recommendations based on social science research are likely to produce subtle rather than massive improvements in your public speaking.

In addition to giving tips on speech preparation, social science research makes a further contribution by giving us specific objectives for a course in public speaking. Modern research on speech communication provides a list of documented outcomes of the college class in public speaking. Research shows ten ways that students improve their abilities. Compared to students who have not yet completed their speech instruction, public speaking students have:

1. Greater confidence in their speech abilities.[30]
2. More favorable attitudes toward speech—attitudes that enhance competence in communication.[31]
3. Significantly less nervousness about speaking—that is, less stage fright or speech anxiety.[32]
4. Better writing skills; public speaking courses have been found to enhance essay writing skills as much as classes in English composition.[33]

5. Better skill in presenting information and giving directions, based on tests of the information recalled by listeners.[34]
6. Better ability to organize and deliver speeches in later speech situations, outside of class.[35]
7. Greater comprehension in listening.[36]
8. Greater fluency of speech.[37]
9. Better movement, gestures, and eye contact.[38]
10. More awareness of how messages should be constructed to respond to the particular audience.[39]

The research results are consistent. Students of public speaking improve their rhetorical attitudes and skills as a result of the instruction and directed practice they receive. If you put the necessary effort into the course, you *will* make important improvements in a number of areas. The knowledge, attitudes, and skills you gain are directly applicable to *any* situation in which you have to prepare and organize material for presentation to a group of listeners.

Remember, however, that speech instruction is not strictly a consumer product given to you in ready-to-use form, such as a garden hoe. What you gain from your instruction in speech is more akin to a package of seeds that, once purchased, will grow only if properly planted and tended by the owner. Your rhetorical instruction truly gives you something usable, but your competence will increase only in proportion to how much personal study, practice, and effort you give to it.

This textbook and your class sessions in public speaking are your guide to putting theory and research into practice. If you signed up hoping to learn things that will benefit both your career and general human relationships, your hopes probably will be realized. Research shows that public speaking students improve not only in ability to prepare public messages, but also as writers and listeners, and as individuals having greater confidence and better attitudes toward human interaction. Further, surveys attest to how public speaking is valued by college graduates, both those well established in a wide variety of careers and those rising in their professions.

You have been set on the route to rhetorical competence. Your class in public speaking represents a program that gives you relevant knowledge, helpful attitudes, and useful skills of communication. The education you receive is based on a 2500-year classical tradition that demonstrates the historical benefits of rhetorical competence both to speakers and to their society. Further, because you are part of America's current crop of speech students, you can gain from a generation of social science research on speech. These scientific studies have refined the traditional advice on rhetoric into even more specific and useful helps and hints.

Concepts for Review

Can you summarize the meaning of these terms or expressions? How does each relate to speechmaking?

"real people" speaking
rhetorical competence
knowledge
attitudes
skills
perspective taking
speech anxiety
content vs. delivery
perfecting knowledge
advisory approach
rhetorical sensitivity
canons of rhetoric
invention
organization
style
delivery
memory
classical tradition
Aristotle
Cicero
Quintilian
pictographs
ethos
social science
experiments
field studies
survey research

Things to Try

1. Real people give speeches. You are a real person, so identify two times during the last year that you have given a speech. Were you more successful in the general areas of content or delivery? Why?
2. You have probably heard or read of advice on how to make an effective speech. Identify three items of advice you remember. Do these points pertain to content or to delivery? What does this textbook say about this advice? Use the table of contents and index to find out.
3. Consider the four attitudes associated with rhetorical competence. Are these attitudes you already possess? Do these attitudes correspond to what you believe is good public speaking? Do you have difficulty understanding the importance of any of these attitudes? Why?
4. Consider the five areas of public speaking skills as summarized in the five canons of rhetoric: invention, organization, style, delivery, and memory. In which of the five areas are you *now* best prepared as a speaker? Which of the five is *now* your weakest point?

Endnotes

1. John C. Hammerback and Richard J. Jensen, "Cesar Estrada Chavez," *American Orators of the Twentieth Century,* ed. B. K. Duffy and H. R. Ryan (New York: Greenwood Press, 1987), 55–61.
2. James C. Bennett and Robert J. Olney, "Executive Priorities for Effective Communication in an Information Society," *Journal of Business Communication 23* (1986): 16, 19.
3. Suzanne P. Fitch, "Communication Education for the Research Scientist," *Communication Education 29* (1980): 60–64, and Sidney W. Wilcox, "Engineering Communication: An Analytical Method of Teaching Engineers to Communicate," *Journal of Communication 20* (1970): 387–394.
4. James E. Wasylik, Lyle Sussman, and Robert P. Leri, "Communication Training as Perceived by Training Personnel," *Communication Quarterly 24,* No. 1 (1976): 32–38.
5. M. Sue Hetherington, "The Importance of Oral Communication," *College English 44* (1982): 572.
6. Kathleen E. Kendall, "Do Real People Ever Give Speeches?" *Central States Speech Journal 25* (1974): 233–235.
7. Don M. Boileau, "An Investigation of the Effects of a Persuasive Speech: An Application of Piaget's Developmental Theory," *Speech Teacher 24* (1975): 1–14.
8. Ellen M. Ritter, "The Socio-Cognitive Development of Adolescents: Implications for the Teaching of Speech," *Communication Education 30* (1981): 1–10.
9. Ruth A. Clark and Jesse G. Delia, "*Topoi* and Rhetorical Competence," *Quarterly Journal of Speech 65* (1979): 187–206.
10. Kathryn B. De Boer, "Protecting the Voice," *Communication Education 29* (1980): 256.
11. Mark L. Knapp, "Public Speaking Training Programs in American Business and Industrial Organizations," *Speech Teacher 18* (1969): 131; Herbert E. Meyer, "A $900 Lesson in Podium Power," *Fortune* (August 1977): 204; Edward L. Black and Garry L. Martin, "A Component Analysis of Public-Speaking Behaviors Across Individuals and Behavioral Categories," *Communication Education 29* (1980): 280.
12. Cicero, *De Oratore,* I. 3–6.
13. Eugene Garver, "Rhetoric and Essentially Contested Arguments," *Philosophy and Rhetoric 11* (1978): 159.
14. Thomas M. Conley, " 'Logical Hylomorphism' and Aristotle's Koinoi Topoi," *Central States Speech Journal 29* (1978): 92–97.
15. Vernon E. Cronen, "Teaching Students to Evaluate Arguments," *Speech Teacher 22* (1973): 107–113.
16. Aristotle, *Rhetoric,* I. 1. 1355a.

17. Karl R. Wallace, "Rhetoric and Advising," *Southern Speech Journal 29* (1964): 279–287.
18. Wayne C. Booth, "The Rhetorical Stance," in *Contemporary Rhetoric: A Reader's Coursebook,* ed. Douglas Ehninger (Glenview, IL: Scott, Foresman, 1972), 218–225.
19. Roderick P. Hart and Don M. Burks, "Rhetorical Sensitivity and Social Interaction," *Speech Monographs 39* (1972): 75–91, and Roderick P. Hart, Robert Carlson, and William F. Eadie, "Attitudes Toward Communication and the Assessment of Rhetorical Sensitivity," *Communication Monographs 47* (1980): 1–22.
20. Aristotle, *Nichomachean Ethics,* VI. 5. 1140a-1140b.
21. Quintilian, *Institutio Oratoria,* XII. i. 12 and 29, respectively.
22. Quintilian, *Institutio Oratoria,* XII. i. 1.
23. Cicero, *De Inventione,* I. ii. 3, and I. iv. 5, respectively.
24. See Wayne Booth, *Modern Dogma and the Rhetoric of Assent* (Notre Dame: University of Notre Dame Press, 1974), and Richard L. Johannesen, *Ethics in Human Communication.* 2nd ed. (Prospect Heights, IL: Waveland Press, 1983).
25. John E. Baird, Jr., "The Effects of Speech Summaries Upon Audience Comprehension of Expository Speeches of Varying Quality and Complexity," *Central States Speech Journal 25* (1974): 119–127.
26. *Ibid.*
27. Lynda L. Kaid and Robert O. Hirsch, "Selective Exposure and Candidate Image: A Field Study Over Time," *Central States Speech Journal 24* (1973): 48–51. Kaid and Keith R. Sanders reported a similar study, "Political Rallies: Their Uses and Effects," *Central States Speech Journal 32* (1981): 1–11.
28. Walter H. Wilke and Joseph F. Snyder, "American Speech Preferences," *Speech Monographs 9* (1942): 91–110.
29. Gerald M. Phillips and Nancy J. Metzger, "The Reticent Syndrome: Some Theoretical Considerations about Etiology and Treatment," *Speech Monographs 40* (1973): 220–230.
30. Robert S. Cathcart, "A Study of the Effect of Course Length on Student Improvement in the Basic Speech Course," *Southern Speech Journal 25* (1959): 34–42; James C. McCroskey, "The Effect of the Basic Speech Course on Students' Attitudes," *Speech Teacher 16* (1967): 115–117; William D. Brooks and Sarah M. Platz, "The Effects of Speech Training Upon Self-Concept as a Communicator," *Speech Teacher 17* (1968): 44–49; Bedford H. Furr, "Influences of a Course in Speech-Communication on Certain Aspects of the Self-Concept of College Freshmen," *Speech Teacher 19* (1970): 26–31; Larry Judd, "Research in Improving Self-Concept in the Basic Course: Review and Recommendations," *Today's Speech 21,* No. 3 (1973): 49–52; Larry Judd and Carolyn B. Smith, "A Study of Variables Influencing Self-Concept and Ideal Self-Concept among Students in the Basic Speech Course," *Speech Teacher 23* (1974): 215–221.
31. Franklin H. Knower, "The College Student Image of Speech, Communication, and Speech Instruction," *Speech Teacher 15* (1966): 108–112.

32. Howard Gilkinson, "Social Fears as Reported By Students in College Speech Classes," *Speech Monographs 9* (1942): 141–160; Stanley F. Paulson, "Changes in Confidence During a Period of Speech Training," *Speech Monographs 18* (1951): 260–265; Theodore Clevenger, Jr., "The Effect of a Physical Change in the Speech Situation upon Experienced Stage Fright," *Journal of Communication 9* (1959): 131–135; Eldon E. Baker, "An Experimental Study of Speech Disturbance for the Measurement of Stage Fright in the Basic Speech Course," *Southern Speech Journal 29* (1964): 232–243; Anthony Mulac and A. Robert Sherman, "Behavioral Assessment of Speech Anxiety," *Quarterly Journal of Speech 60* (1974): 134–143; Anthony Mulac and A. Robert Sherman, "Relationships Among Four Parameters of Speaker Evaluation: Speech Skill, Source Credibility, Subjective Speech Anxiety, and Behavioral Speech Anxiety," *Speech Monographs 42* (1975): 302–310.

33. Galen L. Wenger and Arlo L. Schilling, "Speech as Preparation for High School Writing: An Experiment," *Speech Teacher 14* (1965): 136–137, and William H. Edwards, "The Relationship Between Performance in a Basic Speech Course and Performance on a Test of Writing Skills," *Indiana Speech Journal 15* (1980): 24–27.

34. Paul D. Holtzman, Robert E. Dunham, and Richard E. Spencer, "Direct Assessment of Effectiveness of Student Speakers," *Journal of Communication 16* (1966): 126–132.

35. William D. Semlak and Donald C. Shields, "The Effect of Debate Training on Students Participating in the Bicentennial Youth Debates," *Journal of the American Forensic Association 13* (1977): 192–196.

36. Charles R. Petrie, Jr., "Listening and Organization," *Central States Speech Journal 15* (1964): 6–12.

37. Baker, "Speech Disturbance."

38. William D. Brooks and Judith Strong, "An Investigation of Improvement in Bodily Action as a Result of the Basic Course in Speech," *Southern Speech Journal 35* (1969): 9–15.

39. Glen E. Hiemstra and Ann Q. Staton-Spicer, "Communication Concerns of College Undergraduates in Basic Speech Communication Courses," *Communication Education 32* (1983): 29–37.

Chapter

2

The First Speech

Outline

Soon you will give your first speech. You are likely to begin with an assignment to introduce yourself, to relate an experience, or to present an opinion. Whatever the specifics of your first speech, you can be sure of two things. First, that you will be nervous about it—everyone is. Second, that you won't have time to read this entire book before giving that initial speech. It is important for you to get started speaking even before your book-learning is completed. Even before you hone each element of rhetorical competence, you need to get the feel of preparing ideas and delivering them to your fellow students. Would any of us take a trip, begin college, or do anything else, if we waited until we knew everything beforehand?

Box 2.1

The First Speeches of American Women

Every first speech presents a challenge. Since your classmates are a sympathetic audience, your first speech will be relatively easy.

But consider the situation of the first women public speakers in America. During the 1830s, women began to speak to large audiences in support of abolition, temperance, and peace. However, these pioneer women speakers faced a tradition against women addressing public meetings. The first women speakers found that their "meetings were frequently broken up, they experienced riots and mobbings, and they dodged the flying missiles, the favorites among which seem to have been rotten and fresh eggs, dried apples, beans, rocks, smoked herring and tobacco quids. . . . But the early women speakers seemed to have enough determination to overcome all obstacles, and their very courage in the face of opposition won for them many friends."

Source: Doris G. Yoakam, "Pioneer Women Orators of America," *Quarterly Journal of Speech, 23* (1937), 257.

Chapter 2 is designed to get you on your feet speaking—*right now.* Each of the three sections of the chapter is designed to give you a head start on your long march to rhetorical competence. After reading the section "Key Elements of Speechmaking," you will have the rudiments of rhetorical knowledge. The next section, a survey of speech anxiety, should help you acquire the single most important attitude about speaking—confidence. Finally, the six steps of speech preparation give you a list of bases to touch before you step up for that first speech.

The Key Elements of Speechmaking

We have all listened to speeches and we have delivered them. A public speech obviously brings together speaker, message, and audience. Though these ingredients of speechmaking may be familiar enough, the exact features and relationships among the ingredients are less obvious. Grounding yourself in the rhetorical process is a foundation for your first speech.

Public speaking may be described as a process involving five key elements: (1) the speaker as a person, (2) the speaker's intention, (3) the audience's need for communication, (4) the situation or occasion of the speech, and (5) the structure of the message.

The Speaker

The individual characteristics of the speaker have much to do with the outcome of a speech. In making this point, it is useful to contrast the different responses of the public to the two presidential and the two vice-presidential candidates during their debates in 1988. During their presidential debates, Vice President George Bush and Governor Michael Dukakis each benefitted from distinctly different ways of speaking. Dukakis, who once moderated a television program, gave a more polished presentation. He was careful to look straight into the camera, and he spoke in a steady, even manner. Bush appeared less at ease, as shown by much miscellaneous movement of head and body. On the other hand, Bush's more animated manner helped the Vice President seem friendlier.

Personal characteristics of speaking were even more important during the single debate between the two candidates for vice president, Lloyd Bentsen and Dan Quayle. Reports about Senator Quayle's college records and his special admission into law school had called into question Quayle's competence for the office of vice president. The nationally-televised debate was crucial for Quayle, since it offered him a chance to demonstrate credibility through speech, thereby counteracting past reputation. The results were mixed. On the one hand, Senator Quayle did not say anything embarrassing, nor did he contradict himself. On the other hand, Quayle seemed ill at ease, and he alternated between hesitation and launching into apparently memorized answers. In contrast, Senator Bentsen seemed less surprised and more confident in responding to tough questions. An instant poll by ABC News indicated that viewers rated Senator Bentsen as the more impressive speaker by a margin of 51 percent to 27 percent (with 22 percent not expressing a preference).[1] Personal characteristics of speechmaking kept Senator Quayle from being much help to George Bush in winning the presidency. Chapter 11 gives more detail on impressions given by our voice and movement.

Credibility is not simply a matter of the appearance we give while speaking. Early experimental studies showed the relevance of reputation to how a communicator's message is received. Social scientists found that "the very same presentation tends to be judged more favorably" when attributed to a speaker having higher levels of prestige—for instance, a college professor compared to a student.[2] The complex mixture of past reputation and present performance is well-illustrated by the case of Senator John Glenn in his campaign for president in 1984. Nationally known as a former astronaut, Glenn enjoyed high initial credibility with his campaign audiences. Unfortunately, Glenn usually received his biggest ovations at the beginning of the rallies, *before* he spoke. Glenn's speeches were typically lengthy and sprinkled with unexplained technical terms. His addresses seemed to weaken rather than improve his standing.[3]

Although reputation may influence how your remarks are received, the chief barometer of your credibility frequently will be the impression you make *on the spot,* as you speak. Even when the audience already knows you, it is wise not to rest on reputation. Aristotle advised speakers not to assume that their credibility was completely fixed. He reminded them, and reminds us now, that every speech marks an opportunity to give an impression by what we say.[4] In chapter 5, we will further explore how audiences judge the credibility of speakers.

Prepare your speeches on the basis of the known connection between credibility and success in communication. Jack Dodds, a student preparing a classroom speech, gave this analysis of how credibility would probably figure in his speaking. (The text of his persuasive speech is found at the end of this chapter.)

> My being a Vietnam era veteran, having served six years on active duty myself, will help to establish a great deal of credibility. Also, the many hours of research are evident in the content of the speech and this will reinforce argument. The sources are good and work well in reinforcing the credibility I need to project on a topic not well known.

As you embark on this course in public speaking, take stock of your strengths as a speaker. Your interest in or familiarity with the subject of your speech may be what is working for you. You may possess other qualities of thought or expression that can translate into effective speaking; these include wide interests in reading, a clear voice, natural gestures, or a liking for people.

A final key personal factor that bears on the outcome of your speeches is alertness to the situation. To what extent are you ready to respond to audiences and events? Successful speakers are able to adjust plans to make their speech more effective. Both Franklin D. Roosevelt and John F. Kennedy kept news reporters on their toes by constantly changing the advance speech texts released to the media. A successful speaker, such as suffragette

Susan B. Anthony, is often known for being able to give an impromptu retort. Horace Greeley, the newspaper editor, once confronted Anthony with the argument that women's demand for the vote presumed the obligation to fight in time of war. Anthony replied that women would be happy to fight for their country just the way Greeley himself had fought during the Civil War—by wielding a sharp pen.[5] The more you are alive to what is going on, the more likely you will prosper as a speaker. Responding to feedback is a major theme of chapter 12.

The Speaker's Intention

Speech tends naturally toward a purpose. Imagining a speaker who had no intention of influencing listeners in some way is difficult. On one level, we enter a speech situation with basic human needs. On a more sophisticated level, a prepared speaker develops specific aims regarding (1) the subject and (2) the audience of the speech.

A young child quickly learns that speech allows for control of events. It is no accident that "mine" and "more" are two of the first words that children pick up. Speech is one of the basic ways we establish our own personal identity—the very reason that a two year old delights in saying, "No!" Further, whether we are speaking to a few friends, or to a larger group, speech gives us an ego boost. Our self-esteem increases as we become the center of attention. Control, self-identity, and self-esteem are basic human needs, and all relate directly to speaking.

When we move into the realm of carefully planned speech, we enter another level of speech purpose. During the preparation phase of a speech, your general needs to control, to establish identity, and to gain self-esteem evolve into two specific rhetorical intentions. One of your intentions points in the direction of speech subject; the other points toward the audience.

Jack Dodds, student speaker, began with a strongly-developed attitude toward the subject of his message, the defoliant, Agent Orange. He studied testimony by Vietnam veterans about how Agent Orange had afflicted them, and he amassed scientific evidence about the toxic nature of this chemical. Jack decided that these two elements of the subject cried out for emphasis. In contrast, Jack wanted to minimize the arguments that the effects of Agent Orange were unknown during the Vietnam War and still are a subject of controversy.

Jack's developing intention toward the subject was paralleled by an emerging orientation toward his listeners. Jack worked to predict how the audience would react to his ideas. First he considered what the audience might already know about the dispute. Jack decided that listeners probably knew little in specific about the controversy over Agent Orange. Second, Jack considered where the sympathies of listeners might lie. He expected that the audience would be more responsive to the plight of the veterans than to efforts of the government and chemical companies to avoid paying compensation. In short, *Jack planned what to say about his subject in view of the audience's probable knowledge of and attitude toward the subject.* Jack organized his speech to convey factual information about Agent Orange, relying on the assumption that the audience would favor the side of the veterans. How you can prepare by developing a clear statement of your specific speech purpose is discussed in chapter 4.

The Audience's Needs

It is not just speakers who bring needs to the speech situation. Audiences, too, have specific expectations and wants concerning what you should say on the topic. For example, I have heard many speeches on child abuse, all focusing on how to detect child abuse and report it. Not a single speaker has treated the subject of child abuse from the parents' perspective. Why do student speakers show disinterest in examining the behavior of abusive parents? I believe that popular attitudes toward the subject of child abuse prevent public speaking students from considering the situation of abusive parents. Student speakers sense the strong feelings against child abusers held by the general public. Speakers know that an audience might view a speech focusing on the parents as an attempt to excuse a socially unacceptable behavior. Such an impression by listeners might fatally undermine the speaker's credibility and persuasiveness.

This example suggests that speakers intuitively pay attention to the audience's views. This principle can help you prepare speeches when you accept that *every* audience you address enters the speech situation with *existing preferences and ideas.* The audience's needs and expectations about your speech come from the cultural, sociological, and psychological backgrounds of listeners. Members of a *cultural group* share perspectives on what constitutes appropriate forms of speaking. Senator Robert Dole aptly noted that Americans generally expect short speeches when he chastised speakers at the 1980 Republican National Convention. Dole complained that "the introducers spoke longer than the speakers, and the speakers spoke too long."[6] Gone are the days of Daniel Webster and the two-hour oration! Today's audiences also hold beliefs about the proper content of political speaking. For instance, Americans expect some meaningful content in speeches. In 1960, Senator Frank Church delivered a keynote address to the Democratic National Convention that was long on high-sounding phrases but short on substance. As a result, Church was criticized for sounding like a schoolboy orator.[7]

General cultural expectations often are contradicted by beliefs particular to a specific *social group.* For instance, Americans generally have a great faith in progress and technology. If you were preparing a speech in favor of nuclear power, you could capitalize on these national assumptions to contend that nuclear power inevitably will become safer. However, not all Americans embrace technology; in fact, many are suspicious of it. In other words, general cultural beliefs do *not* hold true for all segments of society. In the case of nuclear power, members of environmental protection groups worry about what science and technology are doing to Planet Earth. Environmental groups have much support among the college age population. You might expect a college audience to be more receptive to arguments based on environmental principles than to points founded on the cultural ideal of progress.

Though cultural and sociological factors influence audiences, the reactions of individual listeners to a speech are not identical. Particular *psychological factors* may cause individuals to deviate from general cultural and group trends. A student once told me of attending a Sunday service in which listeners vehemently applauded the preacher's attacks on other churches. Not holding these beliefs, the student kept silent and looked forward to leaving.

How should you respond to the inevitable cultural, sociological, and psychological needs of listeners? To prepare your speech with the audience in mind, learn about the needs and expectations of listeners. Then try to construct a message that *reconciles the needs of the audience with your own intention.* How? Here is how one student speaker dealt with constraints that she predicted would apply to her speech on the subject of birth defects.

> Because most people like to think that there is no chance that they will be a parent of a child with birth defects, I will emphasize the effects that smoking, drinking and drugs have on an unborn child. In response to this, people will think, "well I knew someone who both drank and smoked during pregnancy and her child was born normal." I will bring up that the baby probably was a low birth weight baby and will tend to be a slow learner when he or she starts to school. I will also question why anyone would want to take a chance with her unborn child.

This student effectively anticipated the response of her listeners. Knowing the importance of audience attitudes, she was able to use her predictions about listeners to prepare her speech. More about audience analysis will follow in chapter 5.

The Speech Situation

Both speakers and audiences bring needs and intentions to the speech; thus, speechmaking is an interactive process. The mutual influences between speaker and listener are best seen from the perspective of what we may call a *speech situation* (see fig. 2.1). A speech situation is a specific

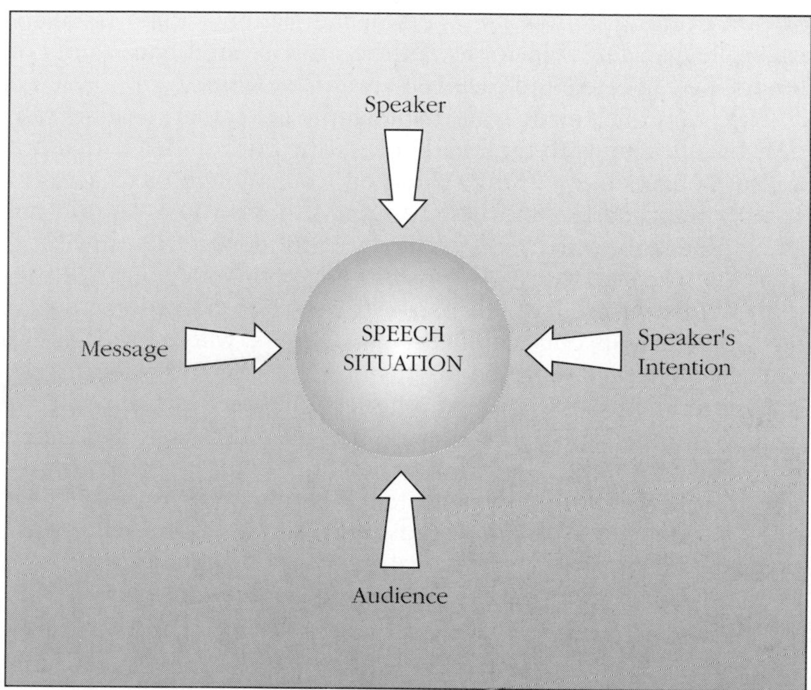

Figure 2.1
The speech situation.

occasion (a time and place) in which your intention and the audience's needs are reconciled—or not—by a message.

In one sense, you, the speaker, always remain in complete charge of the situation. After all, you hold the floor. You enjoy a freedom to make whatever points you believe are necessary. Yet, listeners are moving, breathing, active human beings. The speech situation represents mutual influence of speaker and listener. The success of your speech in a given speech situation depends on the interaction of your purpose with the needs of the audience.

An episode during the 1980 campaign season illustrates how the needs of two different speakers interacted with the preferences of two audiences. On February 18, 1980, a group of 1000 members of Gun Owners of New Hampshire (the immediate audience) assembled to hear the major candidates for the presidential nomination. The speeches also were broadcast to a wider audience of voters. Two of the speakers were John Anderson, United States Representative from Illinois, and Ronald Reagan, then a former California governor, both seeking the Republican presidential nomination. In his speech, Anderson took the position that "gun owners should be licensed, just as car drivers are." Anderson's stance contradicted the desires of the immediate audience of Gun Owners, and the result was a chorus of boos. In contrast, candidate Reagan began his speech with the greeting,

"Good evening, fellow members of the National Rifle Association." Because Reagan felt able to accept the topic-related constraints of the listeners, he expected and received a warm welcome.[8]

The point to be made with this example is *not* that speakers can succeed only by agreeing with their audiences. The crucial idea is that predictable consequences follow from a decision to challenge or to accept the constraints imposed by listeners. Though Anderson lost support among the assembled gun owners, his choice was not necessarily unwise, given his objectives. For one thing, if we assume that both Anderson and Reagan chose their words on the basis of personal convictions, Anderson was not in a position to satisfy completely the gun owners, whereas Reagan was. True, Anderson might have stated his position less explicitly to give less offense. Anderson knew, however, that other candidates would embrace the views of the gun owners. Since Anderson was trailing Ronald Reagan and other Republican contenders, Anderson had little to lose by challenging the gun owners. Furthermore, he had potentially much to gain in the way of support from people listening on radio and television. By challenging the immediate audience, Anderson actually may have sought to embrace the needs of an important group in the remote media audience.

Box 2.2

Speech Content Must Fit the Situation

The speaker of the West German parliament resigned yesterday, saying he was "shocked and depressed" by the political storm he set off with a speech in which he tried to show how Germans were taken in by Hitler fifty years ago.

"My speech was not understood in the way I meant it by many of those who heard it," Speaker Philipp Jenninger, a senior member of the governing Christian Democratic Party, wrote in his letter of resignation. . . .

Jenninger's address was the keynote speech of a special session of the Bundestag on the fiftieth anniversary of Kristallnacht, the nationwide pogrom that first signaled the full fury of Nazi Germany's war on the Jews. . . .

"He had no sense of occasion," said Sebastian Haffner, a prominent publicist who has written extensively about German history. "He said true things at the wrong moment."

"The 10th of November is not the right moment to think of fascination with Hitler, which certainly existed. If a man has been murdered, one doesn't speak at his funeral about the interesting personality of the murderer."

Source: Serge Schmemann (NEW YORK TIMES), *San Francisco Chronical,* 12 November 1988, A1, A14.

Crucial to speech success is how we respond to the constraints of a particular speech situation. How our own attitudes interact with those of listeners will be developed in greater detail in chapters 3 and 12.

The Structure of the Message

Your speech is what reconciles your intention to the audience's expectations. How you put together your remarks—how you structure them—determines whether you will succeed in merging your needs with those of the listeners. Three elements of your speech—the ideas, the language, and the arrangement of points—have a bearing on its ability to produce a meeting of minds. Jack Dodds's speech on Agent Orange will help clarify the role of structure in speechmaking.

Jack held strong personal beliefs that the government should help Vietnam veterans who were exposed to Agent Orange. However, he was realistic, recognizing that Agent Orange was a matter "overlooked by those not involved." Further, Jack saw a danger in using only statistics to educate the audience, because such an approach might make the listeners knowledgeable at the cost of losing their interest. He therefore selected *ideas* that would reconcile his view of the importance of Agent Orange with the audience's lack of knowledge and possible disinterest. Jack began the speech with facts. He defined Agent Orange as a toxic dioxin chemical used to defoliate five million acres in Vietnam. He explained that 50,000 Vietnam veterans were exposed to Agent Orange. By the fourth paragraph of the speech, however, Jack was focusing on an individual case. "Very little concern was given to these claims until 1977 when veteran Paul Reutersham discovered he had abdominal cancer. This is very rare for young men." By quickly relating statistics to a real example, Jack was able to capitalize on the tendency of people to respond to individual stories.

Regarding Jack's *language,* we may notice how the wording of ideas contributed to reconciling Jack's intention with the interests of listeners. Jack began with a play on the word "orange." Holding up a citrus orange, Jack compared this wonder of nature to the man-made "deadly type of orange," Agent Orange. This comparison developed interest, and it also had the effect of setting up the contrast between safe and deadly, an idea that was the heart of Jack's position. Throughout the speech, Jack used terms such as "victims" and "chemical time bombs" to make real the human crisis he saw. Jack's emotion-laden presentation of the veterans contrasted with the words he used to portray the bureaucratic Veterans Adminstration. Jack quoted a VA staff physician who cynically said, "Just hope you don't have an Agent Orange problem." This quotation helped communicate the stark difference between the human tragedy of Agent Orange and the impersonal response of the Veterans Administration. Such a contrast supported Jack's request that his listeners write letters to support legislation that helped veterans.

Finally, speech structure had an important bearing on the success of Jack's speech. Jack arranged his points both to promote his views and to capitalize on where he believed the sympathies of the audience would lie.

Jack began by focusing the attention on a problem. He stated an argument about the toxic nature of Agent Orange and the inevitable consequence of the disease for veterans exposed to it. By getting listeners to believe that a problem existed, Jack made the VA and Dow Chemical appear merely self-serving in their effort to deny that Agent Orange created a health problem. Also, Jack began his speech from the perspective of veterans, instead of beginning with the official positions of the VA and Dow. This arrangement of ideas helped lead the audience to side with the veterans.

Use the key elements of speechmaking as a starting point in your preparation for the first speech. Reflect about what you bring to the lectern as an individual speaker. Next, look at your speech topic. What are your options for bridging the gap between your intention and the needs and interests of listeners? Select and arrange ideas in ways that better reconcile your intention with the expectations of listeners.

The Problem of Speech Anxiety

Now that we have some essential knowledge about speechmaking, it is appropriate to turn to the matter of attitudes. As we saw in chapter 1, attitudes are important in rhetorical competence because they determine whether you possess the will to excel. Probably the *single most important attitude toward speechmaking* is the feeling of confidence that experienced speakers cultivate. Confidence about speaking always represents a cultivated attitude because stage fright is an ever-present feeling, even for veteran speakers. Experienced communicators, however, have learned to let their anxiety feelings work *for* them, not against them. To best understand how experienced speakers manage stage fright, we must look at the nature and source of the anxiety reaction.

The Nature of Speech Anxiety

If you are a typical public speaking student, you will feel anxious as the time for your speech approaches. This feeling is to be expected. After all, a public speech *is* a performance. You naturally worry whether you will "do OK." You look at the audience and wonder how you are coming across. And you are not alone. *Everyone* who is placed in the situation of giving a speech feels some anxiety. Both men and women experience the anxiety. Research shows that neither age nor birth order among brothers and sisters affects whether or not a person experiences speech anxiety. Furthermore, people experience speech anxiety regardless of their performance on intelligence tests or their academic rank in school.[9]

Box 2.3

Jack Kennedy Grew Out of His Speech Anxiety

During his early years in public life he [Jack Kennedy] hated shaking hands, which was highly unusual in a city where some politicians had been known to shake hands with fire hydrants and wave to telephone poles. They say that a good Irish pol can carry on six conversations at once, but Jack was a different breed, a new breed. He hated crowds. When we went into a hall together, he'd immediately look for the back door. . . .

He was very bashful in the early days, but that soon changed. In all my life, I never saw anybody grow the way Jack did: he turned into a great personality and beautiful talker. But until he was in the Senate you just couldn't imagine that he was really going anywhere.

Source: Tip O'Neill and William Novak, *Man of the House: The Life and Political Memoirs of Speaker Tip O'Neill* (New York: Random House, 1987), 85–86.

Researchers working on human fears like to distinguish between anxiety as a trait and as a state. *Trait anxiety* refers to the different levels of anxiety possessed by each individual. On the other hand, *state anxiety* results when people are placed in a specific performance situation—such as giving a speech. In the case of public speaking, anxiety appears primarily as a factor of the speaking situation and only secondarily a factor of individual personality. In other words, speech anxiety is *not* a generalized fear. We know why we are nervous—we are performing in front of an audience! The nature of stage fright as a situational fear is shown in studies of the physical responses of public speakers. Both heart rate and self-reported anxiety increase when the speech is begun and then decline when the speech is completed.[10] In other words, we are nervous in response to the uncertainty of facing the audience. As we present the speech successfully, our worries decrease.

Social science research gives us additional ideas on how to handle speech anxiety as something arising from the situation of speaking. Findings document that anxiety decreases when we know personally the people we are addressing. Further, studies of speech anxiety show that stage fright increases when we lack confidence in our communication skills. Anxiety correspondingly decreases when we possess high expectations of success and predict that the audience will view us as credible. Even the physical environment of the speech can affect anxiety. A researcher found evidence that using a lectern lessened the stage fright of public speaking students.[11]

The above findings suggest that speech anxiety chiefly is a problem of *self-perception*. When we expect to do well and view the audience as supportive, our fear is lessened. A study by Michael Motley further suggests that, to borrow a famous line from Franklin D. Roosevelt, "the only thing we have to fear is fear itself."[12] Motley was interested in whether a person's actual stage fright (measured by heart rate arousal) would be affected by the speaker's being *told* he or she had high or low speech anxiety. Motley arranged for student speakers to be shown, during their speeches, data from a monitor that supposedly revealed their stage fright to be high or low. Although the speakers thought they were being shown their own heart rates, actually they saw only randomly chosen high or low readings. The results of the experiment suggested that "a correlation did indeed exist between the stage fright level that a speaker believed himself/herself to be experiencing and the stage fright level truly being experienced." In other words, actual speech anxiety was increased or decreased by perceived anxiety. When the speaker was shown data indicating that his or her anxiety was low, actual anxiety decreased. Correspondingly, when the person believed that his or her level of anxiety was high, actual anxiety increased.[13]

The findings about speech anxiety contain some good news. First, if everyone experiences anxiety, then we need not be embarrassed to admit that we are nervous. Second, if actual speech anxiety is modified by perceived anxiety, then we can reduce our stage fright by developing a positive attitude toward public speaking. Finally, if speech anxiety is a known fear that is the result primarily of the speaking situation itself, then the anxiety can be removed by greater skill in handling occasions of speechmaking. The point is that once we admit we have speech anxiety, we can manage and control it through techniques of attitude and behavior. Let's look now at some of the ways to channel speech anxiety into better performance.

Building a Positive Speech Attitude

If a certain amount of anxiety is a normal part of speechmaking, our attitude toward the anxiety is the key to developing the confidence that supports rhetorical competence. Why not set out consciously to acquire the positive attitude that experienced speakers possess?

As you take up the challenge of developing a confident outlook about speaking, remember two things. First, *everyone experiences anxiety before a speech.* This simple reminder is important. Interviews with hundreds of college students show that those who label themselves as high in speech anxiety tend to believe that "other people have no apprehensions or concerns" about speaking before an audience.[14]

Second, *do not underestimate yourself.* Interviews show that students who perceive themselves as prone to stage fright tend to think that their speaking skills are low compared to the skills of others. This lack of confidence in our skills can lead to a vicious circle. Experimental evidence suggests that as that speech anxiety increases, expectations of success in speaking decline. It is important to *think realistically about your skills.* Be sure to give yourself credit for the many experiences you have had as a speaker—in clubs, at church, on the job. Include your experiences in conversation and your participation in groups. Also, be sure that you are not setting up unrealistically high expectations. Let's face it, even the greatest orators usually fail to impress and persuade everyone in the audience.

Clearheadedness about your abilities and expectations has an important bearing on speech anxiety. Research shows that *rational thinking* is a successful therapy for anxiety. In other words, as you think more realistically about your speech, your anxiety decreases. Furthermore, research shows that *motivation* to achieve (which you have as a student) is connected to confidence as a speaker. Take advantage of the fact that you have placed yourself in an academic setting in which your desire to do well can boost your confidence about speaking.[15]

After you realize that your anxiety is normal and that certain factors are working in your favor, what comes next? At this point, you are ready to take four specific steps to change your thinking about public speaking. First, relabel your anxiety feelings so that they work for you. Second, notice that anxiety declines naturally as you give a speech. Third, realize that increasing your skills in public speaking—a key component of your college course—is a recognized way of handling speech anxiety. Fourth, visualize yourself speaking successfully. Let us consider each, in turn.

Research suggests that there are two facets of speech anxiety. The first is your observation that you are experiencing tension in the form of changes of breath, heart rate, and so on. The second facet of speech anxiety is your labeling of the arousal: "Oh no, I'm nervous!"[16] This two-part theory indicates that one way to reduce speech anxiety is to *relabel it.* Instead of looking at the physical tension as a negative experience, why not look at your feelings as the kind of excitement that accompanies something you enjoy? Have you ever felt the excitement of opening a long-awaited package or letter? Did you describe yourself as suffering from speech anxiety? Probably not, but the physiological symptoms were similar. Experienced speakers know they will experience "butterflies" as the time for the speech approaches. What separates them from beginners is that experienced speakers welcome feelings of anxiety as an additional boost of energy to enhance performance. The evangelist Harry Emerson Fosdick went so far as to say that "any man who isn't tense before he speaks can't speak."[17]

Another way to help cultivate a positive frame of mind toward speechmaking is to observe how your anxiety declines as you get busy speaking. Research findings are consistent that a decline in anxiety typically takes place as you get farther along into your remarks. Speech anxiety seems to follow a four-stage pattern of development. The first stage is before-the-speech *anticipation,* characterized by a rise in anxiety compared to your anxiousness at rest. The second stage may be called *confrontation,* moments of increased anxiety as you first look out and speak to the audience.

Speakers cope with anxiety by concentrating on giving the speech.

Third, you begin a period of *adaptation* as anxiety declines continuously during the speech. Finally, you experience *release* when, after the speech, anxiety declines to a level equal to or below that of the stage of anticipation.[18] (See fig. 2.2.) What this progression suggests is that most speakers naturally cope with speech anxiety by concentrating on giving the speech. Practice taking advantage of the natural tendency of anxiety to disappear. Instead of focusing on the fact that you are "up there" giving a speech, concentrate on the speech you have prepared. Abraham Lincoln reported he always felt uncomfortable at the beginning of a speech. However, as Lincoln warmed up to the situation, observers noted that his eyes began to sparkle and his body moved as one with his words.[19]

A third basic step in developing a positive attitude toward speechmaking is to concentrate on gaining skills in speaking. Your public speaking course is organized to provide you with a large number of specific skills in content and delivery. Research shows that acquiring skills in speechmaking reduces unproductive anxiety. Many psychological therapies have been applied to problems of speech anxiety. Although all of these therapies seem to work, research shows that *training in speech skills is equally effective in reducing speech anxiety.* Whether or not you do anything else about your stage fright, the skills training you receive in your public speaking class will help you manage speech anxiety. One researcher, Gerald Phillips, is particularly keen on the idea that students should concentrate on honing their skills rather than looking for specific therapies to reduce anxiety. He contends that "when a person wants to improve speaking skill, removing

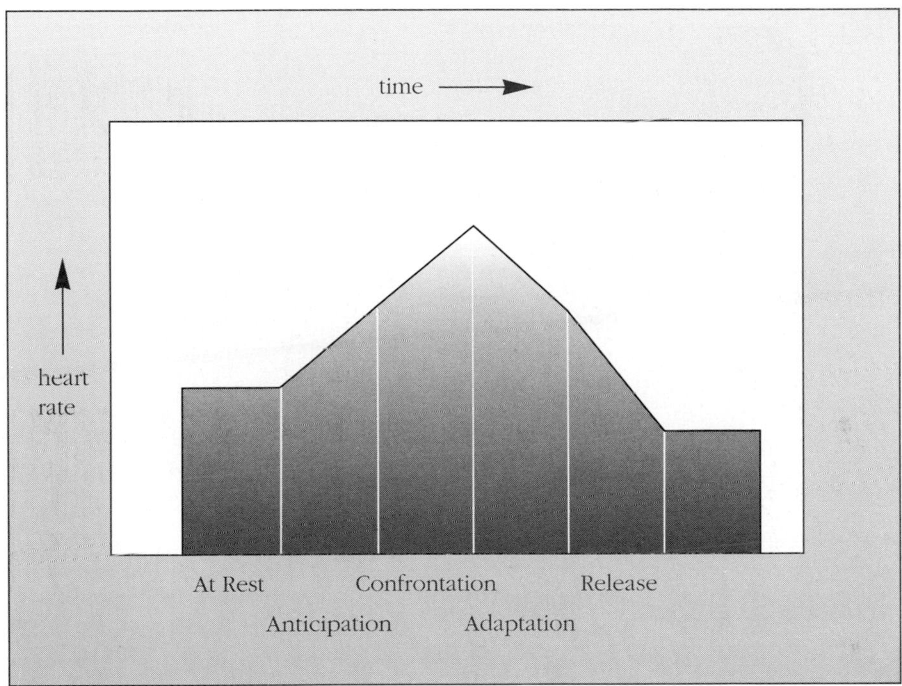

Figure 2.2
The pattern of speech anxiety.

anxiety does nothing more than reduce the incentive to attain skill. A little healthy tension is important."[20]

Fourth, after you have planned and practiced your speech, visualize yourself successfully giving your speech. Mentally picture yourself walking to the lectern, beginning to speak, making your most important points. Get in your mind a specific image of the audience responding favorably. Research findings suggest that visualization techniques significantly reduce speech anxiety for persons having initially moderate or high levels of stage fright.[21]

Management of Speech Anxiety

Developing a positive attitude is the long-range response to speech anxiety. Over the weeks of your public speaking course, this advice should help you make physical tension work for you. But during the short term—say, tomorrow's speech—there are some specific actions you can take to make the experience more comfortable.

In the days before your speech, do everything you can to make yourself look forward positively to the opportunity. Pick a topic that is of special interest to you. Your excitement about your material and your desire to share it with others will make you more eager to talk. Once you have picked

Practicing the speech outloud several times is one way to manage anxiety.

your topic, dig into the subject and study it thoroughly. Surveys show that speakers worry whether the listeners will perceive them as knowledgeable. You may banish this worry by becoming a kind of expert through good preparation.[22]

Practicing the speech several times aloud is another vital way to reduce your anxiety. Speech anxiety interferes with good communication only when you are preoccupied with the fact that you are standing in front of people. The more you practice the speech, the more you will become accustomed to focusing on the message you are giving. Practice helps you *know* you can present the speech.

We considered earlier the finding that speakers are more nervous the less they know their audience personally. Make a point of talking to people in your public speaking class. Get to know some of your classmates, certainly the ones who sit close by. As you begin to look out and see familiar faces while speaking, you will tend to look at listeners less as a faceless crowd. Your worries about speaking will lessen.

On the day of the speech, take steps to avoid unnecessary additional mental and physical stress. Avoid accepting extra obligations for the day. Don't dwell on your nervousness by making it the focus of your conversations. Control your food to minimize unnecessary stress. Avoid greasy foods for the day. Eat protein a couple of hours before the speech. Don't consume more than your average of caffeine. Avoid alcohol or nonprescription drugs. In addition, your level of physical stress will be lessened if you walk to class at a normal rate and arrive on time.

As class begins, if you perceive an uncomfortable level of anxiety, you may choose to concentrate on listening to the other speakers. The class period is a kind of great conversation, after all. Get into your role as a listener instead of dwelling on your role as speaker. Sometimes, however, speakers find paying attention to the other speeches difficult. If this proves to be the case, try using methods of body relaxation. Jean Bertram-Cox developed this regimen for students as they walk to class or sit waiting for their turns to speak: (1) breathe deeply, taking in air up to a count of twenty, then fully exhale; (2) loosen the tongue and jaw, let them drop into relaxed positions; (3) maintain good posture; (4) relax hands and wrists; (5) settle the shoulders in proper position, straighten the back and pull in the stomach; and (6) relax the head and neck, turn slowly from side to side and up and down.[23]

The above techniques should help you manage anxiety up to the time of the speech. However, the period of peak anxiety is the first few moments of the speech itself—the period of confrontation. Therefore, mind a few pointers on dealing with this crucial phase of speech tension. Assume the attitude of confidence from the time of your turn to speak. Walk briskly to the front of the room—do not drag your way up. When you have reached the front, pause to look at the audience. Smile. Recent research shows that facial expressions can trigger alterations in your mood. Ninety percent of persons actually begin feeling the emotion they are asked to express facially.[24] Establish real eye contact with some of the students and/or with your instructor before you begin speaking. This routine will help you keep in mind that your speech has some of the attributes of a conversation. Remember, you are communicating to real people.

As you launch into the speech, you will find keeping good eye contact helpful. Actually look at individual people around the room. Concentrate on some of the ones who seem most attentive and friendly. At the same time, mentally focus on the ideas you are presenting. Remember, the whole idea of managing speech anxiety is to focus on elements of the speech *other* than the fact that you are standing alone in front of listeners.

Occasionally, a speaker will become so tense that he or she finds it difficult to continue speaking. If this possibility worries you, take some steps to combat it. First, take solace in the research finding that audiences typically observe *less* speech anxiety in you than you perceive yourself.[25] If you find your mind going blank, then pause for a moment. Consider where you left off; review your notes; get the main purpose or whole plan of your speech back in mind. *The pause will seem longer to you than to the listeners.* Smile as you reorient yourself. Your listeners are sympathetic—they have to give speeches, too. If reorienting yourself seems to be taking you a bit long, do not be afraid to acknowledge the problem. You might say something such as, "I'm so nervous I lost my train of thought; just give me a second." The public speaking classroom is a laboratory for learning, so acknowledging your temporary problem to other listeners is only natural.

Your listeners will be concerned for you, since all of them have experienced something of what you are feeling. In fact, audiences outside the classroom situation tend to be supportive when the speaker acknowledges a problem with nervousness.

Speech Anxiety and Your Public Speaking Course

Your public speaking course is designed to help you manage the anxiety feelings that accompany speaking. Of course, you do not want to *eliminate* the anxiety. Such feelings mark a state of physical-mental readiness that can enhance your performance. However, you might find reassuring the knowledge that the average amount of anxiety experienced by students declines during a course in public speaking. Consistently, students report feeling less anxiety about speaking at the end, as compared to the beginning, of their public speaking class.[26] When independent observers rate the apparent nervousness of student speakers, the finding is the same: nervousness declines by the time of later speeches.[27] What you need to do is build on the gains you have made. Seek other opportunities for public speaking, and keep practicing your skills in building confidence. People who have the most public speaking experience tend to have the least anxiety.[28]

In sum, you can expect your public speaking course to help reduce your speech anxiety. Nevertheless, some students perceive themselves as having a severe level of anxiety that precludes success in the class. Based on the experiences of teachers at Pennsylvania State University, we may assume that between one and two percent of students would desire special attention from their instructors.[29] If you are among this number, contact your teacher individually. He or she will listen to you describe your feelings about public speaking and will work with you to set specific goals for building confidence. Penn State researchers contend that public speech anxiety can be reduced by setting such general goals of communication as asking questions in class and participating in a group discussion.[30]

Overall, then, speech anxiety is normal. The anxiety can be managed, and stage fright actually can be a helpful stimulus for rhetorical competence. If you acquire a positive attitude and good speech skills, you will make public speaking an enjoyable experience—exactly what it should be.

Basic Steps of Speech Preparation

Giving your first speech requires having a general sense of the speech-making process as well as ideas for managing speech anxiety. In addition, you need *specific skills* for putting your ideas into the form of a speech. To transform knowledge and attitude into a skillful performance, let us proceed by example and by principle. Read the following sample of a first classroom speech given in a basic public speaking course. Next, consider the six preparation steps below that provide an overview of how to put together your speech.

Sample Speech

How I Survived "The All-New Dating Game"

By Monica L. Haller[31]

"Wanted, irresistible singles to win exciting trips to places like Jamaica, the Bahamas, Switzerland." Interested? Who wouldn't be? There was just one catch, though. You had to be a contestant on "The All-New Dating Game." I know, I was hesitant too at first when I was recruited last June at a Universal Studio tour. But the thought of sipping tropical drinks on an exotic isle with a hunk in tight shorts was too *irresistible* to pass up. So I signed up.

Actually, I thought, how hard could it be to get on a game show. Huh. But take it from a veteran—the real game begins behind the camera. There are three characteristics a contestant hopeful must possess in order to get on a game show. I call them the Three A's: appearance, attitude, and ability.

In the category of appearance, the Dating Game interviewers in particular were looking for individuals who are sexy, innocent, and sweet; sort of a Gidget with silicon implants. This category took a little more effort. So, two beauty parlor appointments, a bottle of fake tanning lotion, and fasting for four days later, and I was Hollywood bound.

I walked into the studio starring not only a new appearance, but also a new attitude as well. I was energetic, enthusiastic—instantly larger than life. Sort of like a Disneyland tour guide with pom-poms. I walked in to greet the producers and yelled, "Hi, I'm Monica Haller from sunny Mission Viejo, California." I smiled so much it hurt.

The final clincher was the category of ability. Now in the Dating Game it's not the ability to spew out trivial facts or spell multisyllabic words, but rather the ability to lie—and lie with conviction. This category I excelled in. I lied about my weight, my height, even my natural hair color.

Now that I've mastered the game show technique, I plan to make it a life long series. What next? The Love Connection, The Newlywed Game, and Divorce Court. Let the games begin!

Steps of Speech Preparation

Now that you have read Monica Haller's first speech, consider how you should prepare your own. Your first speech may require you to introduce yourself, to relate an experience, or to state an opinion. In any case, what you need is a road map of steps leading to a finished speech. The process of speech preparation may be organized into six steps: (1) develop the purpose, (2) analyze the audience, (3) develop the thesis, (4) investigate the subject, (5) structure the message, and (6) ready the message for oral presentation. To help you get more information where necessary, each step includes appropriate references to later chapters.

Develop the purpose

When you speak, you aim at one of four broad purposes: (1) to *inform,* or impart understanding about the topic; (2) to *persuade,* or to modify the beliefs and attitudes of listeners; (3) to *inspire,* or to deepen the audience's appreciation of a person, event, or object; and (4) to *entertain,* or to interest and amuse the listeners by treating the light side of a subject. What would you say was Monica's chief purpose? To entertain? To inform?

To be sure, the four aims of speechmaking overlap. But experienced speakers find themselves emphasizing one of the purposes; they realize that a single speech will fail when attempting everything at once. Because her speech focuses on the light side of game shows, Monica's purpose would be classified as chiefly one of entertaining. Her secondary purpose seems informative, presenting the basic steps to becoming a contestant on a game show.

When you have settled upon one of the four general purposes for your speech, you are ready to develop your *specific purpose.* A statement of specific purpose links your general purpose to the subject of the speech and to the specific audience. In the case of Monica's speech, an appropriate specific purpose statement would be "to entertain [general purpose] the public speaking class [specific audience] with the story of how I became a contestant on "The All-New Dating Game" [the subject]. Chapter 4 conveys more on how a specific purpose statement helps in your speech preparation.

Analyze the audience

As you become more competent in the rhetorical arts, you will recognize that your audience is vital to your speech plans. You will become more sensitive to the characteristics and expectations of listeners, and you will take this information into account in preparing a message. Begin by surveying the objective features of the audience, including such characteristics as sex, age, and ethnic origins. Look for ways that these characteristics might help you predict the audience's reaction to your message. For instance, if most students are over twenty-five years of age, you will have to work harder to impress them with the importance of a legal drinking age of 18. Beyond noting observable characteristics of your listeners, remember things that classmembers say about themselves. Information about hobbies, academic majors, and the like will not only sensitize you to your listeners, but also may give some useful clues about how to make your points.

After you have found characteristics of your listeners, try to generalize on the audience's knowledgeability and opinions on your subject. Put yourself in the audience's place. Just how much information does the typical person in your class possess about the topic you have chosen? Monica rightly assumed that few members of her audience had auditioned for a game show, but that most had watched the programs.

Try to get some specific information on how people in general (culturally) and specific members of your audience view your subject. You might question your family and friends to get ideas. Why not ask three or four classmates to comment on points you will be making? Suppose you are planning to give a talk on car seats for children. Possibly you will learn that people consider a baby to be safer in an automobile when held by an adult than when sitting in a car seat. If so, then you will want to emphasize that the arm-held baby actually is in greater danger. Further, you may be able to construct a mini-poll to find out specifics of what the whole class thinks about your topic. Write out a couple of yes-no questions on slips of paper and distribute your poll before class. If you planned to talk about smoking, you might ask whether people smoked and also whether they approved of prohibiting smoking in public areas.

The final step in audience analysis is *using your knowledge of the audience to structure the speech.* Your scrutiny of the audience gives insight into whether listeners are familiar with or favorable to your material. This information should help you select, word, and arrange your ideas in the speech. Even very general predictions could help you decide how much background explanation is necessary and which of your arguments is strongest. For instance, if you wanted to argue that smoking should be limited to designated public areas, you might capitalize on the tendency of most adults to worry more about their children's safety than their own. You might argue that smoking creates a special danger for the very young. Also, if you used a mini-poll to gather ideas for an anti-smoking message, you might uncover the troubling information that half of your listeners were smokers. This finding might prompt you to begin the speech with points generally agreeable to smokers. For instance, you could start with the argument that people in society get along better when clear rules exist to control their conflicting interests. More about using audience data is found in chapter 5.

Develop the thesis statement

A thesis statement is a one-sentence summary of the content of your speech. You build a thesis statement by taking your key points about the topic and merging them into a single statement. When you prepare your speech around a clear thesis, both your needs and those of the audience are served. The thesis helps you decide what material should be included or excluded. At the same time, organizing your speech around a clear thesis helps listeners remember what you have to say.

To develop your thesis, first list the two to five points you want to make. Next, write a sentence that states and relates these points. Here is a thesis statement for Monica Haller's speech that meets the criteria described above:

> When I decided to audition for "The All-New Dating Game," I began an adventure in making an impression through appearance, attitude, and ability.

This thesis statement indicates the general topic of Monica's speech and identifies her three major points. Look in chapter 6 for more instruction on the thesis statement.

Most people work on speech topics they already know something about or in which they have a real interest. Whenever you have pre-existing knowledge or interest, you probably also have an overall conclusion (thesis) in mind as you start preparing the speech. However, you should expect to modify and reword your thesis as a result of your further analysis and inquiry.

Investigate the subject

Chances are good that you chose your speech topic partly because you already knew something about it. Possibly you already are more knowledgeable about the subject than most of your listeners. It is unlikely, however, that you are aware of even a fraction of everything that could be said on the topic. Adlai Stevenson, Democratic candidate for president in 1952 and 1956, was one of America's most experienced politicians. Nevertheless, after he prepared the first draft of a speech, Stevenson always asked his aides to check on facts.[32]

There are two basic ways to investigate the subject: first, identify what you know and need to know; and second, consult outside sources to fill in the cracks that lie between your current knowledge and what the speech requires. The classical teachers of speech recommend that students begin research by using a category-based system for gathering and organizing details. This category format for research is traditionally known as the *topoi* (TOW-pee) system, and is fully explained in chapter 6. The *topoi* method begins when you write headings to designate important divisions or ideas included relating to a subject. These categories include such general headings as the familiar *topoi* of journalists: who, what, when, where, and how. Or the headings might mark key points of a given subject. For instance, a public speaking student used these categories on the subject of abuse of tranquilizers: (1) reasons that people use and abuse tranquilizers, (2) types of tranquilizers, (3) side effects, and (4) history of tranquilizers. Each heading, each category, was useful in speech preparation because it brought up ideas for possible inclusion in the speech.

Let's assume that you have chosen several categories and have written out several ideas suggested by each heading. Now it is time to follow up with outside ways of getting information. Outside research includes library work, interviews, questionnaires, and actual participation in events. Finally, summarize on paper the key points made by your sources of information. Chapter 6 shows how your research data are most effectively summarized on note cards.

Structure the message

The three essential elements of speech structure are ideas, the wording of ideas, and the arrangement of ideas. Preparing a sentence outline is the best way to massage your material into its most useful shape. The best thing about an outline is that it allows you to experiment. If you do not like the way points are shaping up, all you have to do is shift a few sentences to create an entirely new format for your speech.

A sure sign that you are straying from the road of rhetorical competence is an unwillingness to outline. Motivation and attitude are the keys to using the skill of outlining. Unless you are using chisel and granite to sketch out your ideas for the speech, you should not regard your first words as unchangeable. Maybe some of your ideas and phrases are truly inspired, but problems can result when you regard your first notations as finished masterpieces rather than rough blueprints. Your presentations will improve to the extent that you prepare and revise your outlines.

A relatively simple outline will probably suffice for your first speech. Consider this outline of Monica Haller's speech. This outline shows two useful features. First, it makes separate entries for introduction, body, and conclusion. Second, it is built upon more than just words and phrases. Sentences are useful in outlines because the sentence expresses a complete unit of thought.

I. Introduction: At Universal Studios
II. Thesis: How hard can it be?
III. Body: The Three A's
    A. Appearance: They want sexy, innocent, sweet
    B. Attitude:
        1. They want energetic, enthusiastic
        2. I walked in: "Hi, I'm . . . "
    C. Ability:
        1. Lie with conviction
        2. Lied about weight, height, hair color
IV. Conclusion: Now that you've mastered the game show technique.

A more complete introduction to techniques of outlining, including basic rules for outlining and more sample outlines is given in chapter 8.

Prepare for oral presentation

Remember that a course in public speaking aims to make you an effective *extemporaneous* speaker. To extemporize is to speak spontaneously, using brief notes. Two qualifications exist, however; first, "spontaneous" here means the presentation of the results of practice. Whereas an impromptu speaker creates the speech spontaneously, the extemporaneous speaker *re*-creates a practiced talk. Second, notes for the speech are not exactly the same as the outline you prepared. An outline is most effective when it consists of whole sentences, because the sentence is the basic unit of reasoned thought. In contrast, notes for the speech are most effective if they condense the original outline. As you deliver the speech from your outline, you find yourself able to boil down the sentences of the outline into key phrases or words. Ideally, each run-through of the speech will lead to a modification of the notes, usually in the direction of fewer words. More information on extemporaneous speaking is given in chapter 12.

Notes for the speech should be written clearly so as not to interfere with direct communication between you and your listeners. Write the notes onto something that you can use easily during the speech—a 5 x 8 card or a sheet placed in a plastic folder. Be careful about notes that flop, sag, rustle, or shuffle. Also, avoid using thin pieces of loose paper or a stack of twenty-five note cards.

Can you take the outline of Monica Haller's speech and transform it into useful notes? Something like this, perhaps?

I. Introduction: Scene at Universal
II. Thesis: How hard?
III. Three A's
    A. Appearance
    B. Attitude
    C. Ability
IV. Master the Games Technique

It is difficult to practice a speech too much and so easy to practice too little. You should run through the speech several times before you deliver it—improvement will come with each session. When you begin to find that the speech is coming along naturally, you are ready to pay attention to your voice and movement. Are you speaking loudly and clearly enough? Try to make your voice just a bit louder and your words a bit more distinct than in ordinary conversation; this way you easily can be heard by a class of twenty or thirty people. Try for some gestures. Do not force the gestures; let them come naturally at points where you feel that emphasis is required. Details on voice and body action during the speech are found in chapter 11.

Six useful steps of speech preparation include (1) developing the purpose, (2) analyzing the audience, (3) developing the thesis, (4) investigating the subject, (5) structuring the message, and (6) preparing for oral presentation. These steps take you from rough ideas about your topic to a practiced, relatively polished talk. The steps represent a progression through which you gradually become master of your material. Rhetorical success is directly linked to how much you personally work with your ideas and research. This principle holds true even for important speakers who have a staff of speech writers. Recent history shows that those United States presidents who actively participated in the preparation of their speeches were best able to use speechmaking as a tool of leadership.[33]

Box 2.4

Preparation Steps Lead to Speech Success

After studying speech manuscripts at the Roosevelt, Truman, Eisenhower, Johnson, and Ford libraries, I have come to the conclusion that those most intimately involved with their addresses are also those whose additions, modifications, and deletions have contributed in a positive way to the success of the speech as delivered. There seems to be a direct link, both in specific speeches and across an entire administration, among involvement, attitude, editorial ability, and the success or failure of rhetorical efforts. Even presidents such as Gerald Ford whose general involvement was slight, whose attitude was somewhat lackadaisical, and whose editorial abilities were limited, even such a one as this could improve his rhetorical success, as evidenced in his 1976 nomination address, through greater involvement. . . .

Source: Martin J. Medhurst, "Ghostwritten Speeches: Ethics Isn't the Only Lesson," *Communication Education, 36* (1987), 243–244.

Chapter 2 is your one-chapter overview of rhetorical competence. The key elements of speechmaking show the importance of reconciling your needs to the demands of your audience. What you are seeking is a message that takes good ideas and makes them appealing through effective wording and arrangement. Attitude is important in this unfolding rhetorical process. One particularly important attitude for beginning speakers is the feeling of animated confidence that makes speaking simultaneously exciting and enjoyable. Finally, to construct your first speeches, follow the six-step roster of speech preparation skills.

This panorama of rhetorical knowledge, attitude, and skill sets the agenda for your education in speechmaking. As you grow in experience, your habits of speech (skills) will be supported by firmer knowledge of and appreciation for the rhetorical process.

Sample Speech

Don't Blame Mother Nature

By Jack C. Dodds*

Good afternoon. The other day, when I asked my family what they thought about when I said the word, "orange," they said, like many of you probably would, "a citrus orange." The orange, I think, is one of nature's perfections. Not only does it look beautiful, it smells pretty good, and I think it tastes even better. So I can say nature has truly created something that we can all enjoy—something that many people believe has vitamin C and it's really good for you. But today, I want to tell you about a different type of orange—a man-made type of orange. It's a deadly type of orange. I'm going to speak to you today about Agent Orange.

What is Agent Orange? Agent Orange was a herbicide used during the Vietnam War to defoliate over 5 million acres of land to destroy enemy cover. Agent Orange is a dioxin, which is a contaminant created during its manufacturing, and is also linked to cancer-causing diseases. Agent Orange is the most toxic of 75 dioxin chemicals known to man. And according to biochemist Matthew Meselson of Harvard, he says the safe level has yet to be determined, and if you feed a guinea pig one billionth of its weight in dioxin, it will kill the guinea pig.

* Transcript of a speech delivered in S121, Public Speaking, Indiana University Southeast, Spring 1981.

And the February 23, 1980, *Congressional Quarterly* stated 10.7 million gallons of undiluted dioxin were sprayed during the 1965–1970 period.

That's the cause. What are the effects of this spraying? Well, for 50,000 Vietnam veterans who served in the areas of spraying (of which I am not one, but I am a Vietnam-era veteran, I served six years in the Navy), they claim that Agent Orange exposures cause cancer, liver damage, psychological and neurological disfunctions, malfunction of the body's immune system, stillbirths, miscarriages, and numerous birth defects in their children. A *New York Times* article reported some veterans say that the outstanding questions about Agent Orange have left them reluctant to even have families.

Very little concern was given to these claims until 1977 when veteran Paul Reutersham discovered he had abdominal cancer (this is very rare for young men), and in a chance meeting with a Chicago TV producer, told his story to the producer and this led to numerous radio and TV appearances. He also founded Agent Orange International. Paul died the following year at the age of 28. The furor really didn't exist until January 1978, when 300 Long Island, New York, Vietnam veterans, along with their wives and children, gathered in Bay Shore, New York, and exchanged horror stories that have been a part of their lives since Vietnam. By July 1979, the Veterans Administration, also known as the VA, had received over 500 claims for disability benefits due to their exposure to Agent Orange. At this time, the Carter Administration ordered the widening of research on the long-term effects of Agent Orange to persons exposed to Agent Orange.

For the first time in December 1979, almost ten years after the halt of spraying, the VA reported, through lab tests, that it revealed that dioxin was found in Vietnam veterans who had been exposed to Agent Orange. In January 1980, Dow Chemical, one of the manufacturers of Agent Orange for the government during the Vietnam War, reported that the government acted negligently and recklessly in failing to adequately test the herbicide, using it in ways that they did not anticipate. Yet, on July 22, 1980, before a House sub-committee, Dr. Samuel S. Epstein, professor of occupational and environmental medicine at the University of Illinois School of Public Health, stated Dow Chemical company knew as early as 1964 that Agent Orange contained a strongly toxic substance called dioxin, but failed to notify appropriate federal agencies of this fact.

This has led Agent Orange International to file suit on behalf of over 5,000 veterans against the manufacturers. The suit asks for a provision authorizing either a special compensation fund for victims—as done in the past for black lung exposure, radioactive exposure, or PCB contamination—or procedural changes to ease the burden of proof for individuals suing for damages. A VA official said that veterans are being alerted to the fact that a chemical time bomb may be ticking away inside them. Yet, the VA says that they need more scientific facts before they will admit that Agent Orange is the cause of the conditions of the Vietnam veterans. One VA staff physician told a vet: "Just hope you don't have an Agent Orange problem. We really can't help you because there is no cure."

"We really can't help you" and "there is no cure" are echoing in the minds of thousands of innocent victims. But you and I can help. We can help establish a compensation fund and lessen the burden of proof. We can do this by writing our congressmen, our senators, or even the president himself to let them know that we care and that we support legislation such as S1872, S1480, HR6050, and HR5291, which will create a superfund, financed largely by industry, and would pay benefits to their families. They have failed in the past due to the lack of support of the public or apathy.

The war for many vets did not end when they left Vietnam, but it continues to be fought here in the United States against the government that sent them there—a war to survive both psychologically and physically. The question being asked by them today is "I was there when my country needed me, where is my country now that *I* need help." The next time you think about one of nature's best, the orange, won't you think about one of man's worst, Agent Orange? Thank you.

References

"Agent Orange: 10-Year Controversy Over Effects on Humans," *Congressional Quarterly,* 23 Feb. 1980, 550.

DeWitt, Karen. "House Hearing is Told Dow Knew in 1964 That Defoliant Was Toxic," *New York Times,* 23 July 1980.

Henig, Robin M. "Congress Calls for 2, 4, 5-T Ban After Dramatic Herbicide Hearings," *Bioscience,* August 1979, 454.

Severo, Richard. "Veterans, Fearful of Bias, Challenge Defoliant Study," *New York Times,* 8 May 1980.

Concepts for Review

Can you summarize the meaning of these terms or expressions? How does each relate to speechmaking?

speaker
reputation vs. performance
speaker's intention
audience's needs
speech situation
structure of message
speech anxiety
trait anxiety
state anxiety
rational thinking therapy
anticipation phase
confrontation phase
adaptation phase
release phase
skills training therapy
body relaxation therapy
the four general purposes
specific purpose
audience analysis
thesis
sources of research
extemporaneous speaking
topoi
the outline

Things to Try

1. Identify a time that you have experienced a misunderstanding. Try to discover where in the rhetorical process the problem lay. Which one (or more) of these elements do you believe accounted for the misunderstanding: speaker, speaker's intention, audience's needs (cultural, sociological, psychological), speech situation, structure of message (ideas, words, arrangement)?
2. Try the visualization technique in preparation for your first speech. Imagine that you are in the classroom and your turn to speak has arrived. Can you picture yourself walking up to the front? Can you mentally take yourself through your speech, point by point? Try to see your audience of classmates. Picture yourself working through your points smoothly and finishing your speech.
3. Stumped for topics for the first speeches? Try the interview approach. Choose a partner from the class, and interview this person about his or her interests, goals, ideas, plans, experiences. Then switch roles.
4. Here's a challenge. See if you can boil down your speech notes to fewer than twenty words. Start with a complete outline. Practice the speech several times, each time using a dark marker to black out some words and phrases. How about trying for just a dozen words?

Endnotes

1. *San Francisco Chronicle,* 6 October 1988, A11.
2. Carl I. Hovland, Irving L. Janis, and Harold H. Kelley, *Communication and Persuasion* (New Haven, CT: Yale University Press, 1953), 35.
3. "This Time Out, He Had the Wrong Stuff," *Newsweek,* November-December 1984 special issue, 44.
4. Aristotle, *Rhetoric,* I. 2. 1356a.
5. Doris Y. Twichell, "Susan B. Anthony," *A History and Criticism of American Public Address,* ed. M. K. Hochmuth [Nichols], 3 vols. (New York: Russell & Russell, 1955), 3:126.
6. Dole quoted in James J. Kilpatrick, "Oratory's Decline," *Courier-Journal* (Louisville), 2 August 1980, A5.
7. Reactions to Church recalled in *Courier-Journal* (Louisville), 8 April 1984, A4.
8. See Ellen R. Gold and Judith S. Trent, "Campaigning for President in New Hampshire: 1980," *Exetasis* 6, No. 2 (1980): 3–21.
9. See Keith Jensen, "Self-Reported Speech Anxiety and Selected Demographic Variables," *Central States Speech Journal 27* (1976): 102–108, and Howard Gilkinson, "Social Fears as Reported by Students in College Speech Classes," *Speech Monographs 9* (1942): 141–160. Although both men and women experience speech anxiety, women tend to exhibit fewer outward signs of the anxiety, see Theodore Clevenger, Jr., "A Synthesis of Experimental Research in Stage Fright," *Quarterly Journal of Speech 45* (1959): 134–145. On the other hand, the heart rate arousal of women speakers tends to be higher, see D. Thomas Porter, "Self-Report Scales of Communication Apprehension and Autonomic Arousal (Heart Rate): A Test of Construct Validity," *Speech Monographs 41* (1974): 267–276.
10. See Porter, "Apprehension and Autonomic Arousal"; Ralph R. Behnke, Larry W. Carlile, and Douglas H. Lamb, "A Psychophysiological Study of State and Trait Anxiety in Public Speaking," *Central States Speech Journal 25* (1974): 249–253; Steven Booth-Butterfield, "Action Assembly Theory and Communication Apprehension: A Psychophysiological Study," *Human Communication Research 13* (1987): 386–398.
11. See Malcolm R. Parks, "A Test of the Cross-Situational Consistency of Communication Apprehension," *Communication Mongraphs 47* (1980): 220–232; Joe Ayres, "Perceptions of Speaking Ability: An Explanation for Stage Fright," *Communication Education 35* (1986): 275–287; Dominic A. Infante and Jeanne Y. Fisher, "Anticipated Credibility and Message Strategy Intentions as Predictors of Trait and State Speech Anxiety," *Central States Speech Journal 29* (1978): 1–10; Theodore Clevenger, Jr., "The Effect of a Physical Change in the Speech Situation Upon Experienced Stage Fright," *Journal of Communication 9* (1959): 131–135.
12. Franklin D. Roosevelt, *Inaugural Addresses of the Presidents of the United States* (Washington, D.C.: House Document No. 540, 1952), 225.

13. Michael T. Motley, "Stage Fright Manipulation by (False) Heart Rate Feedback," *Central States Speech Journal 27* (1976): 186–191.

14. Gerald M. Phillips and Nancy J. Metzger, "The Reticent Syndrome: Some Theoretical Considerations about Etiology and Treatment," *Speech Monographs 40* (1973): 220–230.

15. See Phillips and Metzger, "Reticent Syndrome"; Michael D. Miller, "The Relationship of Communication Reticence and Negative Expectations," *Communication Education 36* (1987): 228–235; David P. Himle, Bruce A. Thyer, and James Papsdorf, "Relationships Between Rational Beliefs and Anxiety," *Cognitive Therapy and Research 6* (1982): 219–223; Arden K. Watson and Carley H. Dodd, "Alleviating Communication Apprehension Through Rational Emotive Therapy: A Comparative Evaluation," *Communication Education 33* (1984): 257–266; Kim Giffin and Shirley M. Gilham, "Relationships Between Speech Anxiety and Motivation," *Speech Monographs 38* (1971): 70–73; Michael J. Beatty, Edmund C. Forst, and Robert A. Stewart, "Communication Apprehension and Motivation as Predictors of Public Speaking Duration," *Communication Education 35* (1986): 143–146.

16. Ralph R. Behnke and Michael J. Beatty, "A Cognitive-Physiological Model of Speech Anxiety," *Communication Monographs 48* (1981): 158–163.

17. See Roy C. McCall, "Harry Emerson Fosdick: Paragon and Paradox," *Quarterly Journal of Speech 39* (1953): 289.

18. See Larry W. Carlile, Ralph R. Behnke, and James T. Kitchens, "A Physiological Pattern of Anxiety in Public Speaking," *Communication Quarterly 25,* No. 4 (1977): 44–46.

19. See Mildred F. Berry, "Abraham Lincoln: His Development in the Skills of the Platform," *A History and Criticism of American Public Address,* ed. William N. Brigance, 3 vols. (New York: Russell & Russell, 1943), 2:847.

20. See Michael Weissberg and Douglas Lamb," Comparative Effects of Cognitive Modification, Systematic Desensitization, and Speech Preparation in the Reduction of Speech and General Anxiety," *Communication Monographs 44* (1977): 27–36; Susan R. Glaser, "Oral Communication Apprehension and Avoidance: The Current Status of Treatment Research," *Communication Education 30* (1981): 321–341; Watson and Dodd, "Rational Emotive Therapy"; Joe Ayers and Theodore S. Hopf, "Visualization, Systematic Desensitization, and Rational Emotive Therapy: A Comparative Evaluation," *Communication Education 36* (1987): 236–240. See Gerald M. Phillips, "On Apples and Onions: A Reply to Page," *Communication Education 29* (1980): 107.

21. Joe Ayres and Theodore S. Hopf, "Visualization: A Means of Reducing Speech Anxiety," *Communication Education 34* (1985): 318–323, and Ayres and Hopf, "Comparative Evaluation."

22. See Infante and Fisher, "Anticipated Credibility."

23. See William T. Page, "Helping the Nervous Presenter: Research and Prescriptions," *Journal of Business Communication 22,* No. 2 (Spring 1985): 16–17, and Jean D. Bertram-Cox, "Relaxation: An Approach to Platform Poise," *Speech Teacher 14* (1965): 235–236. John Stoudenmire,

"Effects of Muscle Relaxation Training on State and Trait Anxiety in Introverts and Extraverts," *Journal of Personality and Social Psychology 24* (1972): 273–275, found that muscle relaxation reduced performance state anxiety, with the reduction reaching statistically significant levels for introverts.

24. See "Changes in Facial Expression Can Alter a Person's Moods," *Chronicle of Higher Education,* 5 June 1985, 9.

25. See Ralph R. Behnke, Chris R. Sawyer, and Paul E. King, "The Communication of Public Speaking Anxiety," *Communication Education 36* (1987): 138–141, and Judee K. Burgoon, et al., "Nonverbal Communication Performance and Perceptions Associated with Reticence: Replications and Classroom Implications," *Communication Education 36* (1987): 119–130.

26. See Gilkinson, "Social Fears"; Stanley F. Paulson, "Changes in Confidence During a Period of Speech Training," *Speech Monographs 18* (1951): 260–265; Theodore Clevenger, "The Effect of a Physical Change"; Robert S. Littlefield and Timothy L. Sellnow, "The Use of Self-Disclosure as a Means for Reducing Stage Fright in Beginning Speakers," *Communication Education 36* (1987): 62–64.

27. See Eldon E. Baker, "An Experimental Study of Speech Disturbance for the Measurement of Stage Fright in the Basic Speech Course," *Southern Speech Journal 29* (1964): 232–243; Anthony Mulac and A. Robert Sherman, "Behavioral Assessment of Speech Anxiety," *Quarterly Journal of Speech 60* (1974): 134–143; Mulac and Sherman, "Relationships Among Four Parameters of Speech Evaluation," *Speech Monographs 42* (1975): 302–310.

28. Howard Gilkinson, "A Questionnaire Study of the Causes of Social Fears Among College Speech Students," *Speech Monographs 10* (1943): 74–83; Gordon M. Low and Boyd V. Sheets, "The Relation of Psychometric Factors to Stage Fright," *Speech Monographs 19* (1951): 266–271; W. Clifton Adams, et al., "Effects of Radio Announcing Experience on Self-Perceived Anxiety," *Western Speech Communication 39* (1975): 120–122; Jensen, "Speech Anxiety and Demographic Variables."

29. Phillips, "Reply to Page."

30. Phillips and Metzger, "Reticent Syndrome."

31. The following text is a transcription of a first speech, given extemporaneously from notes, presented as an assignment in the introductory public speaking course, San Jose State University, September 1988.

32. Russel Windes, Jr. and James A. Robinson, "Public Address in the Career of Adlai E. Stevenson," *Quarterly Journal of Speech 42* (1956): 225–233.

33. Martin J. Medhurst, "Ghostwritten Speeches: Ethics Isn't the Only Lesson," *Communication Education 36* (1987): 241–249.

Chapter

3

Listening to Evaluate

Outline

Listening and Rhetorical Competence

Content Listening

- Abstracting
- Outlining

Critical Listening

- Principles of Critical Analysis
- Five Standards of Speech Criticism

Critiquing Classroom Speeches

- Focusing on Specifics
- Focusing on Criteria
- Focusing on a Constructive Attitude

Listening is sometimes called the "forgotten skill" of public speaking. Speech researchers write far more articles on problems of presentation than of reception. Similarly, if you are like most public speaking students, you are chiefly concerned with personal ability to execute skills. Public speaking students express far more worries about how they *themselves* will perform than how *others* might react to the speech.[1]

Seen from the vantage point of "giving a speech," it is only natural to subordinate skills of listening. Putting together the message itself is work enough, even without thinking about the audience. Yet, speaking always presupposes that someone will be listening. In fact, the best speakers are those persons who are able to see public speaking from the perspective of the listener. Booker T. Washington, the early civil rights leader, made a point to pick out the listener who seemed particularly skeptical or cold. "When I have found him," Washington stated, "I usually go straight at him, and it is a great satisfaction to watch the process of his thawing out."[2]

Box 3.1

Fewer Listeners When the President Speaks

Over Mr. Reagan's term thus far, an average of 61 percent of American households have watched his prime-time speeches and news conferences—compared to 77 percent for President Carter and 79 percent for Presidents Ford and Nixon. In this year alone, only about half the households have been watching Mr. Reagan [according to Joe S. Foote, chairman of the department of radio and television at Southern Illinois University].

. . . Television, Mr. Foote said, no longer guarantees a president "that block-buster power" to take his message directly to the people.

Source: *The Chronicle of Higher Education,* 1 June 1988, A4.

Cultivate an interest in listening to the first classroom speeches. Your early practice in evaluative listening will lay the foundations for later work in audience analysis (chapter 5). More generally, your evaluative listening in class will make an important contribution to your speech education. Every time you listen to a speech, you have a chance to observe principles of rhetorical competence. This chapter on listening is designed to help you extract real paydirt from the many speeches you will be hearing. Your speech education becomes complete when you look at communication from the perspective of listener as well as speaker.

How exactly should we listen to speeches? To answer this question, chapter 3 begins with a treatment of basic features of evaluative listening. The next two sections give suggestions for effectively applying methods of content and critical listening. The chapter concludes with suggestions on how to critique and discuss classroom speeches so as to maximize the impact of speaking assignments.

Listening and Rhetorical Competence

What precisely is listening? Most definitions tell us that to listen is to hear and interpret sounds. In addition, watching the speaker can increase the accuracy of our interpretations, provided that delivery cues do not distract us from ideas. Facial expressions and body action could help us be sure whether a mumbled comment was intended as "no way" or "OK." For our purposes, listening amounts to hearing and watching speakers to best understand and evaluate their presentations.

Listening is a particular kind of role we play as receivers of communication. How well we listen depends upon (1) our general personality, (2) the environment in which the message is presented, and (3) our immediate intentions and needs. We may begin with the idea that listening is partly a function of personality. Have you noticed that some people feel comfortable listening, whereas others show impatience while waiting for a turn to speak? Our American culture predisposes us to be assertive—to talk. Yet, we should not forget the remark attributed to President Calvin Coolidge that "I don't have to explain anything I don't say." Silent Cal's observation reminds us that listening complements speaking.

In addition to personality, the environment exerts an influence on listeners. Obviously, background noises can create blocks to listening. Our own thoughts can set up similar distractions. If we are wondering whether our parking meter time has expired, we will be apt to miss some of a speaker's points. Others in the audience also can influence our reactions to a speaker. Research shows that heckling of the speaker by members of the audience makes other listeners less likely to find the speaker credible and the message persuasive.[3]

Our personal needs and intentions are a third influence on effective listening. For instance, when we seek to enjoy communication, we are listening *appreciatively*. Musical performances and other situations of entertainment bring out our appreciative responses. On the other hand, our listening intention may shift quickly in response to a new need or challenges. Imagine yourself at an orientation lunch for new employees, listening in a relaxed way to an interesting story. Suddenly you notice that the speaker is now presenting specific facts that you must remember about the afternoon's schedule. Your interest in appreciative listening quickly shifts to a need to *gather information*. You may find yourself quickly shifting

Television magnifies the need for excellence in speech content and delivery.

posture or fumbling for a pen—signs that you are taking on a new role. Clearly, something important is in the air as day-dreamy appreciation quickly shifts to an attitude of frantic straining for content.

Research shows that our listening is powerfully influenced by the specific interests that we bring to the speech situation. In chapter 5, we will consider findings that people tend to recall information that supports their preexisting viewpoints. A good illustration of this point comes from the classic first Kennedy-Nixon debate of 1960. Political professionals generally agreed that Richard Nixon appeared strained and nervous during his first confrontation with Kennedy. Further, the hot television lights highlighted Nixon's facial stubble and recent loss of weight. Nevertheless, television viewers who supported the Republican ticket were able to focus on Nixon's ideas despite his comparatively unpolished performance. Nixon supporters remembered more ideas they liked from Nixon's speeches and more ideas they disliked from Kennedy's.[4]

When we listen to speeches, we find ourselves not only interested in content, but also frequently wanting to test the information we receive. *Critical listening* is a role we might take on when hearing a sales presentation. Sure, we want to retain information, but that is not our most pressing need. We realize that the salesperson is trying to win a commitment from us, so our need is to evaluate whether a product deserves our dollars. To fulfill the role of critical listener we not only retain information, but also actively work with the data. We look for clues about whether the salesperson truly is knowledgeable and trustworthy. We compare what the salesperson says to what we already know about competing products. In short, we make decisions to discount or accept the information.

The listening you will do in your public speaking class will require you to play appreciative, information-gathering, and critical listening roles. An important part of your speech education is to measure what you hear and see against the criteria of good thinking and speaking. When you first apply elements of rhetorical competence to speeches, you will work with one or two performance criteria at a time. With practice, you will be able to apply to a single speech many, if not most, of the evaluation factors listed on the checklist given in table 3.2 (p. 83).

Content Listening

Listening to get speech content is a familiar role. We take on this perspective whenever we take notes in class, remember directions, or report to a friend on the day's doings. The goal in content listening is to achieve *exact correspondence* between the message, as presented, and our recollection of it. Note that the emphasis here is on recollection of ideas, not on words. Unless you can boast total recall, or know shorthand, your recollections will not be verbatim.

Content listening encompasses two basic skills. The first is called *abstracting,* the ability to identify the main ideas of the message. The second is *outlining,* the ability to identify and organize those major points that elaborate, support, clarify, or prove the main idea.

Abstracting

When we abstract a speech, we boil down the whole content into a brief summary. Abstracting is a two-stage process. The listener first identifies the key terms of the message and then recombines them in a summary statement. Evaluative listening requires that we construct what is called a *main idea abstract* of the speech. Such an abstract summarizes the key terms of the speech into a couple of sentences. The abstract allows you to get hold of and work with the speech in a convenient capsule form.

To get some practice in abstracting a speech, let's take a further look at the persuasive speech "Don't Blame Mother Nature," prepared by Jack Dodds for his public speaking class. (This speech is reprinted at the end of chapter 2, pp. 58–60.) Read the speech aloud in a fast but not hurried pace, occasionally jotting down a word or phrase. Now, put away the speech. Try to abstract the remarks by reviewing your brief notes. Use these notes to find the essential idea of the speech. Combine the phrases into a brief summary. Make sure that your synopsis makes sense and that it adequately reflects the content of the speech.

At this point, I myself took a few minutes to apply the principles of abstracting to Jack Dodds' speech. Without trying to create an actual outline of the talk, I read the speech aloud, periodically writing down a key term or phrase. The result was the following list:

- deadly Agent Orange
- herbicide
- toxic dioxin
- defoliant used in Vietnam
- 50,000 veterans exposed
- Reutersham's cancer
- veterans claim harms
- Dow blames government
- Agent Orange International sues manufacturers
- legislation to help veterans
- veterans need help

These notes I jotted down are somewhat sketchy; but these words and phrases are not random. The extracts from the speech reduce a long message into a small set of key ideas and terms. Putting together these notes of Jack Dodds' speech results in the following main idea abstract:

> Agent Orange is a toxic herbicide used as a defoliant in Vietnam. The 50,000 veterans exposed to Agent Orange have filed suit claiming that they have suffered health harms. We should support legislation to assist and compensate these veterans.

This main idea abstract compresses the ideas of the speech. In some cases, you may find it useful to make an abstract that not only compresses but reorganizes major points. This kind of compressing and reorganizing is necessary to produce a short summary that captures the essence of a long train of argument. The speech abstract is a listener's effort to extract the main idea of the speech—what in chapter 6 we will call the *thesis.* (However, in preparing a thesis, a speaker goes one step further and summarizes speech content in a single sentence.)

Outlining

Outlining and abstracting are complementary activities. Abstracting gives us the overall theme or point of a message, providing the focus for listening. Outlining produces a step-by-step development in which we gather details that explain, elaborate, or justify the theme. When we outline a speech, we identify and show the relationship of important ideas in the message. For the listener, the outline makes a long message into something that can be analyzed at a glance. For the speaker, the outline allows quick and relatively easy experimentation with the whole material of the speech. (In chapter 8, we will look more closely at outlining as a tool for speakers.)

The way to outline is to catch each idea as it comes. Fit each point into a developing framework that consists of *major ideas* (or contentions) and *subpoints.* To take an everyday example, suppose you volunteer to fetch snack items for a group studying in the student union. When taking note of the requests of your friends, you might quickly classify the specific choices under the main headings of "drinks" and "food." The individual items—hot dog, cheeseburger, coke, juice—would amount to the subpoints.

In a similar fashion, your outline of a speech would identify major and supporting points. We customarily divide an outline of a speech into three parts. The first part of a speech outline is the *introduction,* containing ideas that arouse interest and give brief orientation to the content. Second comes the outline of the *body* of the speech. Here we note those major ideas that the speaker states and supports. Finally comes the *conclusion* portion of the outline, which usually summarizes points or emphasizes the main idea. About 80 percent of the outline is made from the body of the speech. The outline of the body gives the two to five major points the speaker is presenting and lists the relevant supporting details under each.

Here is an outline of Jack Dodds' speech prepared according to the format we have been considering:

Introduction

The citrus orange versus Agent Orange.

Body

I. During the Vietnam War, Agent Orange was used as a defoliant.
   A. Agent Orange contains toxic dioxin.
   B. 10.7 million gallons were sprayed in Vietnam.
II. Veterans report bad health effects from Agent Orange exposure.
   A. Veterans filed claims with the Veterans Administration (VA).
   B. VA tests show dioxin in veterans.
   C. Agent Orange International filed suit against manufacturers.
   D. The VA calls for more tests.
III. We can help by supporting legislation.
   A. Write members of Congress.
   B. Legislation requires public support.

Conclusion

Veterans answered the call of their country; now they are calling for our help.

Listening for content means remembering accurately what was said. The abstract and the outline capture the essential content of a speech. Content listening serves as the foundation for intelligent evaluations of a speech. Once you have a good idea of content, you are ready to apply skills of critical analysis.

Critical Listening

The content listener functions as a note-taker. On the other hand, the critical listener acts not only as recorder but also as judge. Having first identified the key concepts of the message, the critic evaluates their worth against standards of reasoning and expression.

Principles of Critical Analysis

To evaluate a message sensibly, we must be aware of two basic dimensions of criticism. First, we have to know the difference between *fact* and *opinion*. Second, we have to know that statements should not always be taken at face value—that sometimes important *assumptions* lie beneath any statement.

Facts may be distinguished from opinions. A fact is a statement that can be verified directly by one or more of the five human senses. A speech gains logical credibility by offering us facts that invite testing. Jack Dodds' speech gained strength from factual information and evidence. Jack gave significance to the Agent Orange issue by showing that 10.7 million gallons of Agent Orange were used in the Vietnam War to defoliate 5 million acres. We could verify this statement as factual by reading the source Jack cited. Similarly, Jack invited us to check his factual data that guinea pigs died from ingesting one-billionth of their body weight in dioxin. Factual arguments of this kind supply us with precise information that can be checked and compared to other sources.

Unlike factual statements, opinions cannot be directly verified by things seen, heard, and read. Opinions are *interpretations of fact.* Opinions are statements that make facts meaningful by putting them into categories. Jack argues by interpretation when he deals with the cancer death of Paul Reutersham, a young Vietnam veteran. Jack explains that abdominal cancer is "very rare for young men." Since abdominal cancer rarely occurs in the young, Jack is suggesting an interpretation that the cancer was caused by Agent Orange. Here Jack interpreted the fact of one veteran's cancer by suggesting the cancer belonged in the category of "caused by Agent Orange" rather than that of "other causes." In this argument, and in others, the function of interpretations is to extract the implications of facts—to make facts meaningful.

For the critical listener, the relationship between facts and opinions is important for two reasons. First, facts normally serve as support for interpretations. The alert listener is always interested in whether an opinion has factual support. Are the facts really something that can be tested, or are they vague, second-hand, pseudo facts? Second, contrary to the popular saying, facts do not really speak for themselves. Any fact suggests many possible interpretations, so the critical listener is concerned with whether the speaker has presented the best interpretation of facts.

Box 3.2

Vague, Second-Hand, Pseudo-Facts?

Ann Landers wrote a column telling a reader that "there was some pretty convincing evidence that Elvis Presley died on Aug. 17, 1977." Since that time, Ann notes, she has been "swamped with letters from readers who say I am mistaken." Among the various "Elvis Lives" interpretations are:

- "Elvis was not in that casket. It was a wax dummy."
- "The man they buried was an Elvis look-alike."
- "I have seen Elvis in the supermarket" [in Bay City, Michigan].
- "Elvis' coffin was ordered several weeks in advance, which proves that his 'death' was planned long before the public was told that he died."
- "The original [death] certificate stated that the body weighed 170 pounds. The paramedics who picked him up said he weighed at least 250 pounds. Looks like there were two corpses, doesn't it."

Source: *Times Tribune* (Palo Alto), 23 October 1988, 24.

In addition to noting the relationship between the facts and opinions of a message, the critical listener stays on the lookout for hidden *assumptions.* Assumptions are ideas taken for granted by a statement. For instance, a major point of the speech by Jack Dodds is that the Veterans Administration has received 500 claims from veterans claiming health problems resulting from Agent Orange. On the one hand, this factual argument ties in well with Jack's other evidence about the health risks of Agent Orange exposure. However, Jack's argument about the 500 veterans *assumes* that a claimed harm is the same as an actual harm. Further, the argument takes for granted that any actual harm would very likely result from Agent Orange exposure—not from some other cause. Given Jack's point that the Veterans Administration wants to continue testing Agent Orange, we have reason, for now, to withhold our full agreement from Jack's argument about harmful health effects.

Beyond testing the major and supporting ideas of a message, the critical listener often gives attention to whether the speaker is credible. It is natural for listeners to question whether a speaker is believable, since human experience tells us that a speaker may be ignorant, may harbor base motives, or may lie. Therefore, considering the words themselves is not enough; we must give at least some thought to the person speaking. Credibility springs from two general sources—first, the reputation of the speaker, and second, the performance of the speaker during the speech. Speakers are strongest when they excel in both reputation and performance.

How did Jack Dodds, a student speaker, establish his reputation and performance credibilities? Jack mentions that he is a Vietnam-era veteran. This statement about his background helps give Jack a credible reputation. He has a personal connection to the topic without being obviously self-serving or biased. At the same time, Jack establishes credibility through performance when he uses strong evidence and factual support. His speech gives a commanding level of details about Agent Orange—its chemical composition, its use, its likely effects, and legislation pending in Congress about it. Further, Jack's speaking performance conveys the impression of someone who has a sincere interest in the welfare of others. Jack is factual rather than sentimental; but he is persistent in his real concern for veterans exposed to Agent Orange.

Box 3.3

Theodore Roosevelt's Performance Credibility

Early in his career, Theodore Roosevelt tried to link himself closely to listeners. For instance, Roosevelt would often read about the history of a locality in which he was to speak. However, in the estimation of speech critic, Richard Murphy, "after the Progressive campaign of 1912, Roosevelt began to lose rapport with his audiences." Roosevelt had always been a demanding speaker, even instructing one group to "applaud!" when they overlooked what he believed was an important remark. But in his later years, Roosevelt lost the ability to keep contact with the sentiments of listeners. Roosevelt tried to use his great energy as a speaker to cure the apathy of his later audiences. However, Roosevelt's public image began to suffer because of "the shouting and the ranting of the later years when he no longer was attuned to his audiences."

Source: Richard Murphy, "Theodore Roosevelt," in *A History and Criticism of American Public Address*, ed. M. K. Hochmuth [Nichols] (New York: Russell & Russell, 1955), 338–339, 341–342, 360.

Facts versus opinions, statements versus assumptions, reputation versus performance credibility—all these considerations are preliminary to critical judgments about a speech.

Five Standards of Speech Criticism

Listening contributes to rhetorical competence when you draw conclusions from observing classroom speeches. As you gain experience as a critical listener, you will be able to evaluate speeches according to five standards: validity, ethics, quality, truth, and effectiveness. (See table 3.1, p. 80.)

Validity

A speech may be considered valid when the conclusions of the message make good sense given the supporting information provided by the speaker.

The gist of testing ideas for validity is to question whether the points presented (1) are *sufficient* to establish a claim and (2) have *omitted* nothing crucial. (These two principles are refined into an extensive roster of particular tests in chapter 7.) For an example of testing validity, we may turn to a speech by Henry Kissinger, former Secretary of State, on the fall of the Shah of Iran. Kissinger's main contention was that the collapse of Shah Mohamed Reza Pahlevi's pro-American government in Iran presented the U.S. with one of its worst foreign policy setbacks in recent history. Kissinger's overall point would seem valid given the subsequent Iranian hostage crisis of 1979–1980.

However, less immune to criticism was Kissinger's supporting argument that the collapse of the Shah's government "has raised doubts all over the Middle East as to our ability to protect our friends."[5] The relationship between the main idea and this supporting argument seems vulnerable to tests of both sufficiency and of omission. First, on the point of sufficiency, we should note that the Shah's government was not toppled by a foreign invasion. The United States had no official commitment to the Shah to maintain his regime against internal opposition. Second, analyzed from the point of omission, Kissinger's argument was also vulnerable. Kissinger does not mention the relevant point that the Shah himself was responsible for having alienated the religious leaders who overthrew his regime. Tests of sufficiency and omission suggest that Kissinger may have overstated both the U.S. commitment to the Shah and the United States ability to "protect" the Shah from his own people.

Ethics

The term *ethics* refers to the principles of right action. Ethical principles apply to speechmaking because speaking is a public act; visible actions are open to analysis for their rightness or wrongness.

Perhaps the most important principle of public speaking ethics is that the speaker should keep to worthy motives. An ethical public speaker respects the best interests of audience members and of the society as a whole.

An *un*ethical speaker treats the interests of the listeners as but temporary obstacles to attaining desired aims. Applied to the society as a whole, ethics are embodied in legal limits set on freedom of speech. Legal protections of free speech do not apply when a speaker incites a crowd to illegal mob actions. To incite people directly to riot is to place a democratic social structure in jeopardy.

Matters of speech ethics are inherent to a democratic society in which competing groups and individuals struggle to have their voices heard. A persistent ethical dilemma of a liberal democracy occurs in courtrooms. Here defense attorneys struggle with dual responsibilities. They must give their client the best possible defense while, at the same time, they serve the public interest. Attorney Seymour Wishman reflected over the ethical paradox of courtroom speaking. Whereas he entered law school "to defend the innocent," his actual criminal practice found him constantly asking, "Why have I fought so hard for the interests of the guilty?"[6]

The 1984 presidential campaign saw many complaints about the ethics of hecklers who sought to prevent candidates from having their messages heard. There is no easy solution to balancing the rights of vocal activists with the right of campaign speakers to address their supporters. An informal ethical standard holds that major political parties should not incite heckling of the opposing candidates. Yet there are legal limits to the power of police forcibly to silence protesters.

Box 3.4

Listening is Essential for Free Speech

Lawyers and philosophers have been wrestling with the question of how to define free speech for at least 200 years. Now Harvard Law School has weighed in.

After nearly a year of study, a committee of students, faculty members, and administrators has produced guidelines on free speech for student groups that want to bring speakers to the campus.

[One of the guidelines states:] "Responding vocally to the speaker, spontaneously and temporarily, is generally acceptable, especially if reaction against the speaker is similar in kind and degree to reaction in his or her favor. Chanting or making other sustained or repeated noise in a manner which substantially interferes with the speaker's communication is not permitted, whether inside or outside the meeting."

Source: *New York Times* (National Edition), 12 October 1988, B9.

Quality

Since 500 B.C., teachers have prescribed rules of good speechmaking. Standards of quality in speech come from each of the various canons of rhetoric mentioned in chapter 1. Speeches show good quality when they are based on strong arguments and when they show good organization, good style of language, and good delivery. A useful way of evaluating a speech is to question whether it conforms to the traditionally-accepted practices of good speaking.

Political commentators frequently applied standards of quality to the speaking of Ronald Reagan. Analysts generally agreed that Reagan exhibited a good quality of delivery. It was not long after Reagan assumed the presidency that columnists dubbed him "The Great Communicator" in view of his ability to deliver speeches effectively. Columnists did not limit themselves to assessing the quality of Reagan's delivery, however. From time to time, they also offered opinions about the quality of the content in Reagan's messages. For instance, after President Reagan spoke to the National Association of Evangelicals in Orlando, Florida, three important national news commentators critically examined the quality of ideas conveyed by the president. Ernest Conine, of the *Los Angeles Times,* faulted Reagan for using "confrontational rhetoric" to condemn the Soviet Union. William Safire, former speech writer for Richard Nixon, believed that Reagan unwisely attempted to give moral guidance to religious leaders. Anthony Lewis of the *New York Times* chided Reagan for using religion as a basis for arguing against the nuclear freeze movement.[7] These three commentators seemed to agree that Reagan's speech used ill-advised and inappropriate ideas. That is, they judged the quality of ideas in the speech to be poor.

Truth

Most often when we listen to a speaker, we take for granted that he or she is speaking the truth. Speechmaking would lose much of its force if we doubted that speakers usually told the truth. If we were suspicious of all the speakers we heard, then our world would be a more difficult and a less civilized place. We would be forced to narrow our participation in life as we verified everything personally.

Though distorted communication remains the exception in life, most of us stand ready to test speeches against the criterion of truth. Let's look at an example of why listeners should be alert to the truthfulness of speechmaking. Consider the case of psychic Tamara Rand's alleged advance prediction of the March 1981 assassination attempt on President Reagan. The United States communication media gave wide circulation to Rand's claim that she had correctly predicted, a month beforehand, many details of the attempted assassination. Both NBC's *Today* show and ABC's *Good Morning*

America presented a videotape of Rand making her predictions—a recording that was described as having been taped on January 6, 1981. The tape, in fact, showed that Rand gave approximations of the date, type of wound, and name of the would-be assassin. But the story was untrue. The film of Rand's prediction, alleged to have been recorded on January 6, actually was produced on March 31—one day *after* the president was shot. The tape had been faked. Rand's claim failed the test of truth, even though her tale had been broadcast on television as fact.[8]

Wayne Minnick argues that the truth standard is vital for the public speaking classroom. He describes the introductory public speaking course as one "dedicated to the purpose of training young people to speak the truth honestly and to speak it well."[9] Judged according to the benchmark of truth, speeches must present ideas without conscious distortion or purposeful slanting. Outright faked evidence is not the only sign that a speech is vulnerable to the truth standard. Reliance on exaggerations may also create problems as in the case of the Lincoln-Douglas debates of 1858. History rightly credits Abraham Lincoln and his opponent, Senator Stephen Douglas, for giving generally strong and well-supported speeches. However, these two debaters did offer some arguments based on nebulous conspiracy theories. Lincoln accused Douglas of being part of a conspiracy to spread slavery to the entire nation. Douglas accused Lincoln of advocating mob rule.[10] These particular assertions were more fanciful exaggerations than realistic, truthful interpretations.

Effectiveness

The general purposes of public speaking are to inform, to persuade, to inspire, and to entertain. One way of judging a speech is for listeners to decide whether the speech attained one or more of these purposes as sought by the speaker.

A study by William D. Brooks illustrates the careful analysis of speech effectiveness. Brooks conducted a field study of campaign speeches given in 1964 by Lyndon Johnson and Barry Goldwater. Brooks randomly selected thirty rows of seats in the Pittsburgh Arena and distributed questionnaires to individuals seated there. The questionnaires measured the attitudes of the listeners before and after the candidates spoke. Results showed that in some cases the campaign speeches had changed the attitude of listeners. For instance, the questionnaires indicated that Johnson's speech made him appear more intelligent and emotionally stable to Republican listeners. Results showed that Goldwater improved his credibility among his Republican supporters but not among Democrats in the audience. Brooks's survey is useful because it provides specific statistical support for judgments about speech effectiveness.[11]

Table 3.1 Standards for speech criticism

Standard	How applied to a speech
Validity	Adequate proof; nothing important is omitted
Ethics	Fairness to listeners and to opponents
Quality	Recognized principles of good content and delivery
Truth	Honest facts, accurate interpretations
Effectiveness	Measurement of how listeners actually responded

No ordinary speech critic is able to distribute surveys to a random sample of listeners. Critics of speech effectiveness, however, can use the same general approach as Brooks. We can always observe listeners throughout the speech. We can listen for their responses—are they laughing or clapping? We can look at faces in the crowd. Are listeners appreciative; are they puzzled, staring blankly? We can watch for movement. Are listeners attentive, restless? With just a little practice, we are able to pick up on various verbal and nonverbal cues that indicate attention or inattention, support or opposition.

Critiquing Classroom Speeches

Students of public speaking inevitably learn a great deal of information from the talks they hear in class. This holds true for teachers as well. When talking casually on matters of current interest, I occasionally comment that my information came from "one of my public speaking students." Gaining useful information about topics of the day is a nice bonus for classroom audiences. Better still, you can use listening as a means to refine your own speaking skills. Principles of content and critical listening can be applied in the classroom as a way of advancing and refining rhetorical competence. Achieving such gains requires that you listen to speeches in the same way your instructor does. You need to pay attention to some particular guidelines shortly to be described.

Student critics also contribute to the education of the speakers they evaluate. Of course, student speakers expect to receive criticism from their instructor, and almost all speakers report that such criticism helps them attain rhetorical competence.[12] However, student critics can also contribute positively to the discussion of speeches. Overall ratings of speeches by peers are generally consistent with the ratings given by faculty members.[13] Furthermore, speech researchers have found that student critics make specific comments of a kind similar to that given by teachers.[14] Student critics can enhance the climate of learning in the speech classroom.

Good critical skills are not something you should take for granted, though. Effective speech criticism demands thought and practice in addition to basic knowledge of content and critical listening. Below are certain technical considerations that will better enable you to offer useful feedback to your peers.

Focusing on Specifics

To act as an effective student critic, you must gather plenty of specific data about the speech. It is not enough to comment that "I liked it," or "it was good." Remarks of this kind are not criticism; they tell us nothing about how the speech stood up against the standards of good public speaking.

Remember, speakers want to know their strengths and weaknesses. Comments about particular moments in the speech are preferable to general observations. Research shows that student speakers prefer criticism that gives precise observations about individual elements of speechmaking.[15] For example, a speaker gains specific knowledge from hearing that "your transitions between major points were clear." On the other hand, when a critic says, "I approved of your organization," the speaker is left to puzzle over the many possible meanings of this comment.

As a rule, student critics should follow a three-fold format in giving feedback. First, you should present an observation. Identify something you actually heard or saw. For instance, tell the speaker that "I understood the preview in your introduction in which you listed three points you would be making." Second, you should give an evaluation of your observation. State how you assess the speaker's action. For instance, you might comment that "I thought your speech was helped by having a preview of major points." Third, give reasoning to explain your evaluation. For instance, you might say: "The preview helped me follow your major points, and the book says that previews are usually a good idea in informative speeches."

Taking a few notes will help you to make good, specific remarks. But be sure not to write volumes, because notes can interfere with listening. Make occasional notation of something the speaker says or does. Specific marks of this kind will help you stick to the format of observing, evaluating, and explaining.

Focusing on Criteria

To function as a good student critic, you should focus on a limited number of the criteria of good speechmaking. Furthermore, try to emphasize what is unique to each speech exercise. For example, if the assignment is to give a speech using visual aids, pay special attention to visual evidence and to delivery. If the speech is persuasive in nature, concentrate on evidence and proof.

A general evaluation form for analysis of in-class speeches is presented in table 3.2. This critique sheet includes twenty-eight separate items divided into eight categories: (1) introduction, (2) organization of body, (3) content of body, (4) style, (5) voice, (6) other nonverbal factors, (7) conclusion, and (8) purpose. The criteria pertain both to content and to delivery, with a somewhat greater attention to content.

How should you use the critique sheet? When first using a general checklist such as this, it is often helpful to focus on just one or two criteria instead of everything. Be sure to make written comments about how the speaker stacks up against whatever standards you are using.

In the early speeches, you will not yet have a full background of knowledge about all the speech criteria, so let's take a look at some of the key ideas that lie behind the criteria given on the critique sheet. In your evaluation of the *introduction* to the speech, take note of anything the speaker does to spark *interest and attention* in listeners. Also, identify what, if anything, the introduction does to give *orientation* to the topic of the speech. For instance, the speaker may state his or her main idea. Finally, look for whether the speaker includes some kind of *transition* between the introduction and body of the speech. The speaker may give a preview of points or state the overall purpose of the speech.

To help you evaluate the *body* of the speech, the critique sheet lists separate criteria for organization and content. Regarding *organization of the body,* check to see whether the speaker *clearly presents between two and five major points.* Each major point should be not only stated but also *repeated.* This repetition does not necessarily have to come in exactly the same words. The major points should fit well together. They should *add up to some overall main idea or thesis.* In addition, listen to check whether the speaker uses *summaries and previews.* Summaries are statements that list points already presented. Previews list points that will be presented.

Regarding *content of the body,* take note of what *data or reasons* the speaker gives to support major points. Are data or reasons *clear,* so that you can understand them? Does the speaker present *evidence* in the form of statistics or testimony from authoritative individuals or groups? What is the *quality of evidence* sources? For instance, a research article is probably better evidence than a story in a general newspaper. Does the speaker specifically *cite the source* of the evidence—author, qualifications of author, place published, and date? Finally, in evaluating content, consider whether the supporting materials have a *motivational power.* Do they command attention? Are they striking and powerful?

Criteria relating to speech *style* focus on the words used by the speaker. Is the style *clear?* That is, can you understand the words? Is the language specific? Do the words create pictures in your mind? Moreover, consider whether the speaker's style is *interesting.* The section on figures of style in chapter 10 gives specifics on how speakers make their language interesting.

Table 3.2 A speech critique form

Speaker: ______________________ Date: ______________________

Type of speech: ______________ Critic: ______________________

Ratings: 1 = good; 2 = OK; 3 = needs work

Criteria				Comments
Introduction:				
Created attention & interest	1	2	3	
Good orientation to subject	1	2	3	
Transition to body of speech	1	2	3	
Organization of body:				
Major points stated/repeated	1	2	3	
Gave 2–5 clear major points	1	2	3	
Focused on clear thesis	1	2	3	
Used summaries & previews	1	2	3	
Content of body:				
Compelling data & reasoning	1	2	3	
Clarity of ideas & reasons	1	2	3	
Good quality evidence	1	2	3	
Citation of evidence sources	1	2	3	
Material was motivating	1	2	3	
Style:				
Clear style of language	1	2	3	
Interesting figures of style	1	2	3	
Voice:				
Audible & crisp words	1	2	3	
Variety in voice	1	2	3	
Conversational & dynamic	1	2	3	
Other nonverbal factors:				
Essentially straight posture	1	2	3	
Used movement & gestures	1	2	3	
Direct eye contact	1	2	3	
Expressive face	1	2	3	
Sustained high energy	1	2	3	
A few notes briefly used	1	2	3	
Conclusion:				
Enhanced purpose	1	2	3	
Created feeling of closure	1	2	3	
Purpose:				
Emphasis on one purpose	1	2	3	
Achieved the purpose	1	2	3	
Kept listener's interest	1	2	3	

Next the speech critique sheet asks how effective the speaker's *vocal communication* was. Generally, a good speaking voice is one in which the speaker *articulates* speech sounds crisply, emphasizes appropriate words, and exhibits *variety* in volume and pitch. Vocal delivery is particularly good when the speaker manages to sound both *conversational and dynamic*. The speech should seem like a conversation; but at the same time the speaker should show energy.

The category of *other nonverbal factors* deals with elements of delivery excluding voice. Does the speaker maintain appropriate *posture?* The speaker should keep a straight posture with weight approximately equal on both feet (though not rigidly so), with no prolonged slouching or leaning. What about *movement?* From time to time, it is desirable for the speaker to move a few steps, perhaps out from behind a podium or sideways to use a chart. Movement should be purposeful. Movement is in order only when it contributes to the speech, for instance, by emphasizing a point or enhancing direct eye contact. Does the speaker use *gestures* effectively? Gestures are purposeful movements of the arms, shoulders, and hands. Successful speakers use gestures to punctuate content and to emphasize the important words and phrases.

How much *eye contact* does the speaker maintain? Effective eye contact occurs when the speaker gives attention to all parts of the audience and lingers a bit to look at individual listeners. Research consistently shows that direct eye contact between speaker and listener increases both comprehension of the message and credibility of the speaker. What is revealed by the speaker's *facial expression?* Speakers whose faces are lively and expressive are more interesting. Furthermore, smiles and head nods increase the attractiveness of the speaker.

An overall way of looking at delivery is to consider the speaker's *energy level*. Does the speaker seem energetic or lethargic? Another good general test of delivery is to look for how the speaker *uses notes*. The fewer notes, the better, so look to see whether the speaker fumbles with too many notes. Also, the less the speaker looks at notes, the better.

Finally, as you listen to *conclusions,* consider whether or not the speaker gives the impression that the speech really has ended. A good conclusion ties up the speech, giving it finality or the feeling of *closure*. Also, consider whether the conclusion does anything to enhance the speaker's purpose. For instance, a call for action may highlight the speaker's main idea.

The final set of criteria in the critique sheet pertains to *purpose*. Does the speech seem to have a clear purpose to inform, to persuade, to inspire, or to entertain? As an overall evaluation, would you say the speaker attained this purpose? Why or why not? Another general way to assess a speaker's success is to take note of whether the speaker *kept the audience's interest* throughout the speech.

As a speech critic you will be focusing on various criteria of good content and delivery. Remember to focus on just a few criteria in the first speeches—even experienced teachers find watching for everything hard work. Also, be sure not to become preoccupied with the several features of delivery. Granted, a speaker's lack of eye contact will stand out as a glaring omission. Factors of content, on the other hand, usually are less immediate and less obvious than those of delivery. Since criteria of content are harder to grasp, you should spend the most time and devote the most care to evaluating content.

Focusing on a Constructive Attitude

The expression "criticism" often carries the connotation of making negative comments about things done badly. Perhaps we all are too familiar with the newspaper and television entertainment critics who take apparent delight in panning a show. Sometimes critics take on a negative attitude to appear more knowledgeable and in control. Research does, in fact, show that negative comments make a critic appear more intelligent and competent—though less likable.[16] On the other hand, criticism can become an exercise in back-slapping, as when television interviewers seem to stand in awe of celebrities. Here the critic functions more as a promoter than an analyst.

Good speech criticism avoids the extremes of the sock-it-to-them or pat-on-the-back approaches. The critic plays basically a positive role, realizing that when a critic expects to find good (or bad) in a speech, he or she will actually tend to see things as initially expected.[17] One particular advantage to a positive outlook is that it helps build the speaker's confidence. But, while the sensitive critic desires to support the speaker, this listener also realizes that "negative" remarks are necessary if the speaker ever is to improve. Research shows that student speakers *want to know things they should have done differently.*[18] A critic helps when he says, "I think you needed to include in the introduction more hints about your ideas." What, then, is a constructive critical outlook? This outlook consists of a positive attitude coupled with a willingness to offer appropriate negative pointers.

Making specific suggestions for improvement requires some thoughtful practice. Your general objective is to focus remarks on the criteria of good speaking. Avoid presenting criticism as a personal reaction—"I don't like it when you. . . ." Instead, try the format mentioned above: report what you observed, give an evaluation, and supply reasons. Effective recommendations for change also are better received when centered on speech criteria than on the individual person speaking. Instead of saying, "You were a dull speaker, today," it is better to say, "I think you needed more vocal variety." Student speakers appreciate negative comments when they are focused, objectively, on the criteria of good speechmaking. Speakers

The speech critic plays an important role by giving constructive feedback focused on criteria.

want you to assess what they actually did. Speakers do not benefit from suggestions presented as generalities ("your delivery was poor") or comments given as personal reactions ("I don't like speeches on that subject").

Feeling apprehensive and hesitant about making suggestions for improvement is normal for student critics. As time passes, students find themselves better able to provide feedback to their peers. The following three suggestions are helpful to guide you in organizing your first comments as a speech critic.

1. Be sure to find something you liked about the speech. Do not simply throw in a one-line, token compliment and immediately add "but" or "however." Instead, develop your positive remarks separately and as fully as you convey your negative ones.
2. Be sure to make your negative comments in an objective fashion. If you follow the observation-evaluation-reasoning format mentioned above, you will have no problems here.

3. Start your analysis with a positive remark and, if appropriate, end with one. Some teachers recommend using a "criticism sandwich" in which comments are presented in a positive-negative-positive order. Use this format when appropriate, but do not strain to find a positive ending point—it will sound strained. Instead of concocting something artificially cheerful, perhaps it would be possible to close with a summary statement, such as "well, those are my observations."

In chapter 2, we observed that speakers always report some degree of apprehension about presenting their talks. Would you believe that researchers have discovered something called listener anxiety?[19] Because listening is a role with several corresponding duties, it represents a performance that, like speaking, tests our competence. The solution to listener anxiety is similar to that of speech anxiety—reflection and experience.[20] This chapter has worked to supply the first element of confidence in listening—that of increasing an understanding of how to receive messages. You will contribute good listening to your public speaking class when you (1) identify speech content and (2) critically analyze content according to specific criteria of evaluation. By knowing how to listen to, evaluate, and critique public speeches, you can increase both your own rhetorical competence as well as that of your classmates.

Concepts for Review

Can you summarize the meaning of these terms or expressions? How does each relate to speechmaking?

listening as a role
appreciative listening
content listening
exact correspondence
abstracting
main idea abstract
outlining
subpoints
critical listening
fact
opinion
assumptions
reputation
performance credibility
validity
ethics
quality
truth
effectiveness
critique sheet criteria
introduction
body of speech
thesis
summaries
previews
evidence
style
vocal delivery
movement
conclusions
purpose
constructive critical attitude

Things to Try

1. Identify one time when you listened effectively and one time when you listened ineffectively. Now compare your successful and unsuccessful listening. What kind of listening were you doing? Content listening? Critical listening? Appreciative listening? Listening to help someone with a problem? What made the difference between success and failure?
2. Observe a group of listeners—perhaps students in one of your classes. Who seems to be listening well and not as well? How can you tell?
3. See if you can find some ways speakers encourage good listening for content. Watch a speaker and, at the same time, note your own listening. What does the speaker do that increases your ability to listen? Does the speaker do anything that makes listening for content difficult for you?
4. Review the critique sheet given in table 3.2. Choose one or two criteria of effective speaking. During one of the class periods given to speeches, watch each speaker carefully, taking notes. Evaluate how well the speaker puts into practice the skills you have chosen to observe.

Endnotes

1. See Glen E. Heimstra and Ann Q. Staton-Spicer, "Communication Concerns of College Undergraduates in Basic Speech Communication Courses," *Communication Education 32* (1983): 33.
2. Karl R. Wallace, "Booker T. Washington," in *A History and Criticism of American Public Address,* ed. W. N. Brigance, 2 vols.; (New York: Russell & Russell, 1943), 1:418.
3. Michael J. Beatty and Michael W. Kruger, "The Effects of Heckling on Speaker Credibility and Attitude Change," *Communication Quarterly 26,* No. 2 (1978): 46–50.
4. Hans Sebald, "Limitations of Communication," *Journal of Communication 12* (1962): 147.
5. *Courier-Journal* [Louisville], 21 November 1979, A8.
6. Seymour Wishman, "A Lawyer's Guilty Secrets," *Newsweek,* 9 November 1981, 25.
7. All columns taken from the *Courier-Journal* [Louisville], 16 March 1983, A11.
8. See *Discover* magazine, June 1981, 8.
9. Wayne C. Minnick, "The Public Speaking Approach," *Southern Speech Journal 20* (1954): 165.

10. David Zarefsky, "The Lincoln-Douglas Debates Revisited: The Evolution of Public Argument," *Quarterly Journal of Speech 72* (1986): 162–184.

11. William D. Brooks, "A Field Study of the Johnson and Goldwater Campaign Speeches in Pittsburgh," *Southern Speech Journal 32* (1967): 273–281.

12. Stephen L. Young, "Student Perceptions of Helpfulness in Classroom Speech Criticism," *Speech Teacher 23* (1974): 222–234.

13. Howard Gilkinson, "Social Fears as Reported by Students in College Speech Classes," *Speech Monographs 9* (1942): 141–160; Donald Klopf, et al., "Comparative Studies of Students, Laymen, and Faculty Members as Judges of Speech Contests," *Speech Teacher 14* (1965): 314–318; David W. Shepard, "Students Judging Student Speeches," *Central States Speech Journal 21* (1970): 196–198.

14. Cassandra Book and Katrina W. Simmons, "Dimensions and Perceived Helpfulness of Student Speech Criticism," *Communication Education 29* (1980): 135–145.

15. Young, "Student Perceptions of Criticism"; Book and Simmons, "Dimensions and Helpfulness of Student Criticism."

16. Carin Rubenstein, "Impression Management: Nervous Nabobs of Negativism," *Psychology Today*, September 1981, 85–86.

17. Walter Combs and Gerald Miller, "The Effect of Audience Feedback on the Beginning Public Speaker, Continued: A Counter-view," *Speech Teacher 17* (1968): 229–231.

18. Young, "Student Perceptions of Criticism"; Book and Simmons, "Dimensions and Helpfulness of Student Criticism."

19. Lawrence R. Wheeless, "An Investigation of Receiver Apprehension and Social Context Dimensions of Communication Apprehension," *Speech Teacher 24* (1975): 261–268.

20. Michael J. Beatty and Steven K. Payne, "Receiver Apprehension and Cognitive Complexity," *Western Journal of Speech Communication 45* (1981): 363–369.

Part

II

Building Blocks of Speechmaking

Chapter

4

Purpose

Outline

The General Purposes of Speech
- To Inform
- To Persuade
- To Inspire
- To Entertain

Applying Purpose to the Topic and Situation
- List Potential Speech Topics
- Evaluate Speech Topics
- Focus on One General Purpose
- Draft a Specific Purpose Statement

Purpose and Ethics
- The Social Contract of Speechmaking
- Five Ethical Tests

In July, 1976, Barbara Jordan, congresswoman from Texas, was preparing a keynote address to be delivered at the Democratic National Convention. She faced a tough rhetorical situation—one that has baffled many eloquent speakers. Should she appeal primarily to the partisan sentiments of the delegates in Madison Square Garden? Or should her major purpose be to win over the television audience? Furthermore, who among the radio and television listeners should get the most attention? Should she strive to rally Democrats, to convert Republicans, or to soothe the uncommitted voter? And what about her own personal situation? Jordan needed to decide what comments, if any, to make regarding her role as the first woman and first African-American keynote speaker for the Democrats. In a word, *purpose* was the key to Barbara Jordan's keynote speech. Until she decided upon her purpose, her exact audience and her specific remarks would remain fuzzy.

Barbara Jordan's speech ultimately became another illustration of the principle that challenging circumstances may produce the best speeches. Jordan's ability to reconcile and fulfill all of the potential purposes of her speech won an enthusiastic response from delegates. At the same time, pollsters discovered that the broadcast audience approved of her speech by the unusually wide margin of 54 percent to 9 percent. What was the secret of her success? Jordan responded to her problem of purpose by opening the speech with reference to the obvious novelty of her position as a keynote speaker. She observed that Democrats had been gathering in convention since 1832, "but there is something different about tonight. . . . I, Barbara Jordan, am a keynote speaker." Then, using her own position in the Democratic party as a rhetorical lever, Jordan proceeded to discuss why so many different kinds of people identified with the Democrats. She focused on the general aims and values of her party, rather than on advocating specific items of policy. This choice allowed her simultaneously to inspire the delegates and to satisfy the diverse television audience composed of Democrats, Republicans, and independents.[1]

Like Barbara Jordan, most of us enter the public speaking situation in one or both of two ways. We may find ourselves called upon to speak—as in speech class. Furthermore, we may discover that a particular topic prompts us to speak. Like Jordan, our first response should be to establish clearly the purpose of our remarks. Put another way, we need to assemble our various thoughts and motivations into one clear statement of an objective. In this chapter, we will look both at how the speech purpose evolves and how it guides us in the preparation of the message. Beginning with a survey of the general purposes of public speaking, we will see how to develop a specific purpose statement and how to evaluate the ethics of our intentions.

The pep talk is a kind of speech that aims for inspiration or persuasion.

The General Purposes of Speech

Think about some of the speeches you have heard during the last few weeks. At first glance, these presentations may seem a mixed bag of lectures, sales talks, sermons, or explanations. But a bit more attention to the speeches would show that they can be organized into categories. Let's try to classify a group of speeches.

I frequently ask my classes to put together a list of the types of speeches. The items below are typical:

- sermon
- after-dinner speech
- lecture
- State of the Union Address
- pep talk
- presentation of award
- resignation speech
- commencement address
- celebrity roast
- comedy monologue

- sales talk
- campaign speech
- keynote address
- speech of welcome
- acceptance of an award
- dedication speech
- speech of introduction
- remark at business meeting

How do we arrange these speeches into some order? We might classify them as to whether or not the speech allowed advance preparation. A polished keynote address, for instance, may be contrasted to an impromptu exchange during a meeting. We might also consider whether the speech flowed from a job-related role, such as giving a sales talk, or whether the speech represented a social situation, such as accepting an award.

Box 4.1

For Some, Speechmaking Is a Way of Life

Indiana Govenor Robert D. Orr balked when he saw the form the Senate Commerce Committee wanted him to fill out before it voted on his nomination to become a director of Amtrak. Among other things, the form asked for a full accounting of the nominee's speeches, which Orr refused to provide. "To do so," he wrote on the form, "is not only impossible but your committee could make no use of at least 1,500 speeches." The committee approved his nomination.

Source: *Courier-Journal* (Louisville), 8 May 1982, A3.

Observations about the various circumstances and occasions of speaking led Aristotle to identify three major categories of speeches. A *deliberative* speech was Aristotle's label for addresses that helped a group make decisions on policy. Aristotle's second category included *ceremonial* speeches centering on giving praise or blame. Third was the category of *forensic* or legal speaking, which focused on attack and defense.[2] Unlike the Greeks of old, who had to defend themselves personally in court, we leave our legal speaking to lawyers. In contrast, the above list of speeches contains many types that clearly reflect deliberative or ceremonial speaking. In fact, modern speechmaking tends to blend the deliberative and ceremonial occasions. For instance, in Barbara Jordan's address, she not only inspired the delegates on the occasion of their convention but also won over, as in a deliberative address, the broadcast audience.

Because of the overlap of deliberative and ceremonial speaking, modern teachers focus more on the general purposes of speaking than on the general types of speeches. Modern speech education reflects the fact that every speaker must decide what aim shall direct the speech. Do we want listeners to learn new information or to adopt new attitudes or practices? Do we want to impress our hearers with the significance of the subject, or do we prefer to highlight amusing aspects of it? These four possible reactions by an audience make up the four *general purposes* of speaking: to inform, to persuade, to inspire, and to entertain. (See table 4.1, p. 101.)

To Inform

You will often find yourself aiming to impart knowledge or to increase understanding. Presenting information is the essence of academic lectures, for instance. Yet, we should not think of the informative purpose as being limited to the classroom. Explanations by supervisors, directions by group organizers, and reports at meetings all have the goal of increasing understanding. Robert Jeffrey and Owen Peterson summarized informative speaking as a rhetorical act that involves "explanations, analyses, descriptions, demonstrations, definitions, and narratives."[3]

The major characteristics of the informative speech are these three:

1. Emphasis falls on informative content about the subject. Less emphasis goes to the speaker's own point of view about the content.
2. The speaker analyzes the audience primarily to determine how much they know already about the topic. The speaker also considers the opinions of listeners to decide what, if any, audience attitudes may complicate the goal of getting across information.
3. The speaker seeks to make the subject interesting to the listeners. The aim here is to promote both attention to and retention of information.

A speech by Harold L. Enarson, former president of Ohio State University (reprinted on pp. 386–390), illustrates the essential character of the informative presentation. Speaking to the Ohio State University Senate on November 15, 1980, Enarson began by laying out the details of budget cuts imposed on the university by the state government. After some initial description, Enarson stated that his main aim would be to promote understanding:

> It is absolutely imperative that all of us—students, faculty, administrators, and particularly our many alumni and friends across Ohio—understand clearly what these cuts mean.

The remainder of the speech adhered to its informative agenda. Enarson described the history of budget cuts since 1976. He outlined the decisions his administration had now taken to meet the latest cut. Finally, he presented the implications of the cuts for the continued effectiveness of Ohio State.

Enarson's speech reflects the three distinguishing features of informative speaking. First, informative content is primary, and the speaker's point of view is secondary. Enarson's audience of students, faculty, and administrators shared his alarm at the cuts. Therefore, proving that the budget cuts were dangerous was not as important for Enarson as illustrating this agreed-upon point.

Enarson's speech exhibits the second distinguishing feature of informative speaking. Like all informative speakers, Enarson was primarily interested in the audience's level of knowledge about his topic. He began the speech by spelling out the new policies. Yet, Enarson was also aware of the power of information to focus existing attitudes by portraying the future. Because listeners agreed with Enarson that the cuts were bad, their prime interest was to know the implications of the cuts for present and future operations.

Finally, Enarson's speech shows how a speaker's success is linked to arousing and maintaining the interest of listeners. Enarson organized the speech, first, to present problems. Only then did he discuss solutions and implications. Enarson thereby followed a practice calculated to win early and favorable attention to his ideas.

To Persuade

When our purpose is chiefly informative, our aim is to add to what listeners know about the topic. In contrast, persuasion is an effort to modify the opinions of the audience—or to move hearers to action. Occasions for persuasive speaking occur when we try to sell a product or idea, when we seek contributions for a cause, or when we defend actions we have taken. In persuasive communication, the intent can be to *create,* to *maintain,* or to *alter* the attitudes or behaviors of listeners. Results of this kind can be achieved only when the speaker gives satisfying reasons

Persuasive speaking has two major characteristics:

1. The speaker takes a definite point of view concerning the subject and presents information needed to get across that point.
2. The speaker analyzes listeners to find their beliefs, attitudes, and values. The speaker then selects and arranges the material to appeal to the particular opinions of listeners.

Persuasive speaking is well exemplified by John F. Kennedy's speech to the Greater Houston Ministerial Association on September 12, 1960. In campaigning for the presidency, Kennedy had found the question of his Catholic faith to be both persistent and threatening to his cause. Though the 1960 election was ostensibly focused on issues of Cold War strategy and economic development, doubts festered concerning whether a Catholic president would be politically independent of his church. After deciding he had to meet this matter directly, Kennedy chose a conservative southern religious group as his immediate audience. Kennedy clearly intended his address to be his single major national statement on what he termed the "so-called religious issue" (see text of speech on pp. 418–421).

Kennedy's speech made two essential persuasive points. First, the Massachusetts senator contended that, contrary to a variety of out-of-context quotations from Catholic literature, his political actions would be free from church dictation. Second, he said that if Protestant leaders opposed his election because he was baptized a Catholic, then they were seeking to subvert Article VI of the Constitution by requiring a "religious test" for public office. Throughout the speech, Kennedy closely connected himself to the tradition of religious freedom in America.

The subtle difference between informative and persuasive speaking may be seen in Kennedy's remarks. First, as a persuasive speaker, Kennedy concentrated on moving his audience to take a particular point of view of information and issues. Kennedy's approach was to lay out relatively few specific facts but to connect those facts to widely-accepted values. In contrast, we saw how Enarson's informative speech emphasized how to understand budgetary figures.

Second, in persuasion, our viewpoint as speaker is central. To change attitudes or actions, we necessarily employ a more detailed level of audience analysis than when our aim is to inform. For instance, Enarson assumed that the audience shared his own view that state-imposed budget cuts were harmful. In contrast, Kennedy's audience analysis focused on changing opinion. He needed to find all beliefs, attitudes, and values of listeners that were relevant to the connection of politics and religion. Kennedy focused on aspects of audience opinion that were *un*favorable to his position. He sought to correct what he described as inaccurate *beliefs* about what Catholic Church authorities had said. Attacking an unfavorable *attitude,* Kennedy stated flatly that his political decisions would be independent of church "pressure or dictate." Finally, Kennedy organized his entire remarks to associate himself with desirable *values* of religious freedom and church-state separation. In sum, by specifically responding to the knowledge and attitudes of listeners, Kennedy was able to put his ideas in the best possible light.

Box 4.2

Purpose Motivates the Speaker

Theodore Roosevelt's campaign managers observed that the former president performed best when he was fired up about his persuasive purpose. "In the Progressive campaign of 1912, on the first long trip to the Coast, the speeches were stale, the party secretary thought, and lacking in news value, because Roosevelt was not sufficiently stimulated. On the second tour, through the Midwest, he was supplied with continuous reports on [Woodrow] Wilson's activities and with a history of his thinking on various problems. The result was that Roosevelt would leave the table after a vigorous discussion and dictate speeches far in advance."

Source: Richard Murphy, "Theodore Roosevelt," *A History and Criticism of American Public Address*, ed. M. K. Hochmuth [Nichols] (New York: Russell & Russell, 1955), 333.

To Inspire

According to its root meaning, to inspire means to breathe life into something. When our aim is inspirational, we build upon the existing knowledge and attitudes of listeners. Our aim is not to give information or prove a case. Rather, we strive to deepen an existing appreciation for particular ideas, persons, or events. Inspiration is the chief aim of eulogies, commencement addresses, and speeches of dedication. Inspirational remarks are almost always connected with a specific public event. A eulogy is a speech responding to a fact of death; a commencement talk accompanies graduation; a dedication focuses on the opening of a new facility or institution.

Inspirational speaking generally shows four characteristics:

1. Remarks are centered on a public event that is taking place or has recently occurred.
2. Audience analysis helps the speaker decide how the audience may respond to the event—what values listeners see reflected in the occasion.
3. The speaker organizes remarks to express accepted values that are represented by the event(s).
4. The speaker does not focus on explaining or gaining agreement for ideas, but rather works to enhance the appreciation of listeners for ideas already accepted.

Exemplifying the inspirational purpose is Ronald Reagan's "Welcome Home" address celebrating the return of the Americans held hostage in Iran during 1979–1980 (see text of speech on pp. 439–440). After greeting various dignitaries, Reagan addressed the released hostages: "You are home, and believe me, you're welcome." Throughout the speech, the episode of the hostage crisis dictated Reagan's thoughts and words. Although the occasion stood as the controlling principle of Reagan's remarks, his address centered on the ideas behind the events. Reagan praised the hostages for their determination, and he added that "you've represented under great stress the highest traditions of public service."

When we speak inspirationally, our central effort is to deepen the appreciation of listeners for some idea or viewpoint. To accomplish this, we employ rich, descriptive language, as well as apt quotations, seeking to dramatize the events or ideas being celebrated. We cite values and traditions that the particular group holds in reverence. Reagan's speech illustrates this effort. Little the president said was new to the audience. Reagan's effort was to point out the significance of the hostage crisis in terms of values accepted by Americans. His words were spoken in the mold of great inspirational addresses. Like Winston Churchill, who rallied England to war with spiritual calls to "be ye men of valor," Reagan cited the joyful 126th Psalm. Like John F. Kennedy, whose Inaugural Address asked for dedication to the values of freedom and liberty, Reagan spoke of the "courage, endurance and strength" exhibited by the hostages and their families.

To Entertain

When our purpose is to entertain, we want to captivate listeners. Yet we must not fall victim to the belief that a speech to entertain is nothing more than a comedy monologue. A monologue of jokes *is* one type of entertainment address, but few of us have the ability to win laugh after laugh. Our normal—and more modest—aim should be to relate interesting stories and to make exaggerated, amusing interpretations.

Two features set entertainment speaking apart from the other purposes of speechmaking:

1. Speakers rely on such options as tall tales and anecdotes, stressing the light side of a subject. Fidelity to facts is not crucial, as in the old folk saying "never let the truth stand in the way of a good story." The speaker has license to exaggerate because listeners understand that he or she is not seeking literal acceptance of the remarks.
2. The speech keeps a topical unity that connects and gives focus to the humor.

A classic instance of entertainment speaking is John F. Kennedy's after-dinner remarks at the 1960 Alfred E. Smith Memorial Dinner (see p. 452 for a text of the speech). The dinner is an annual event honoring Al Smith, the former New York governor and first Catholic to run as a major party candidate for president. Kennedy had initially been reluctant to attend this traditional dinner, hosted by Cardinal Spellman, believing that the resulting publicity might reinforce anti-Catholic feelings among voters.

Table 4.1 The general purposes of speaking

General Purpose	Characteristics
To Inform	Add to what listeners know
To Persuade	Find and change beliefs, attitudes, values
To Inspire	Deepen appreciation of values already held
To Entertain	Treat the light side of the subject

However, Kennedy finally decided to attend and take a light touch in his remarks. For instance, Kennedy used Harry Truman's reputation for salty language as an entry point for joking about the religious issue. Kennedy said:

> I have sent him [Truman] the following wire: "Dear Mr. President: I have noted with interest your suggestion as to where those who vote for my opponent should go. While I understand and sympathize with your deep motivation, I think it is important that our side try to refrain from raising the religious issue."

Kennedy's address at the Al Smith Dinner was consistent with two basic features of entertainment speaking. First, Kennedy's humor did not take the form of a string of miscellaneous jokes. Instead, Kennedy made exaggerated interpretations of current events. Further, consistent with its nature as a prepared speech, Kennedy's remarks kept a topical unity, in this case, events of fall 1960. Kennedy's light touch extended even to the serious religious issue, a subject that he had faced soberly in his Houston address mentioned earlier.

Applying Purpose to the Topic and Situation

When you volunteer to speak, or are drafted, your general human need to communicate becomes a specific set of concerns. What issues interest you? How can you get your audience to share your interests? What topics do you know about? Do you want to inform listeners about what you know? Do your goals require that you prepare a persuasive speech? What ideas would the audience like to hear? What can you say that would fit the time and place of the speech? These questions take you back to the concept of *speech situation* introduced in chapter 2. In other words, your speech will be successful only when you reconcile your own purpose with the needs of the audience in a given time and place.

Adapting your general purpose to a specific topic and audience is an important step in speech preparation. In the case of Barbara Jordan, this adaptation allowed her to build a speech that simultaneously built her own credibility, inspired the convention-hall delegates, and satisfied television viewers. A *statement of specific purpose* is the means by which you merge general purpose, topic, and audience. Such a statement serves as a useful road map for planning and preparation. A statement of specific purpose comes from a four-stage process: (1) list potential speech topics, (2) carefully evaluate possible topics, (3) focus on one general purpose, and (4) draft a statement that links details of the topic to the results you want to achieve.

List Potential Speech Topics

The most efficient way to begin looking for a topic is to start with what you know best—yourself. Seek topics by looking to your own experiences and interests. Below is a roster of twenty-three categories designed to stimulate your thinking about speech topics. To get the most benefit from these categories, take a blank sheet of paper—or your typewriter or word processor—and write down possible topics as you read each item in the list. Record each of your topic possibilities as a phrase or sentence rather than as a single word. For instance, "pricing policies of the campus bookstore" conveys a more fully developed thought than does "bookstore."

- Your social characteristics: age, sex, race, residence, occupation.
- Family experiences: home life, family history, family members.
- Opinions you hold: politics, sports, the economy, social conditions; what are some of your judgments?
- General experiences: school, clubs, growing up; things you like, dislike.
- Extraordinary experiences: what, when, how?
- Abilities: talents, special skills.
- Activities: campaigns, projects, groups, causes.
- Organization membership: social, religious, political.
- What you are curious about: science, history, relationships, people.
- Leisure: hobbies, sports, the arts.
- Travel: places you have visited or lived; how different or similar from where you live now?
- Vocations: jobs, skills, technology.
- College classes: subjects or ideas of special interest.
- What you read: books, magazines, newspapers.
- Future plans: career, residence, life-style, philosophy of life.
- History: events and people of the past that interest you.
- The future: what do you predict for society-at-large or for a smaller group or area?

Special interests and talents are reservoirs of speech topics.

- Human relations: family, social group, job, school.
- Human personality: fears, self-confidence.
- Contemporary issues: what encourages or worries you? Local, state, or national issues? Economic, political, social, religious, scientific, legal issues?
- Issues at your school: academic, economic, extra-curricular.
- Mass media: what you watch, listen to, like, dislike.
- Government: local, state, federal.

There is a saying that even a journey of a thousand miles begins with but a single step. Get a good start, now, on your speech education by developing the best list of topics that you can. The list can serve as a reservoir out of which you draw ideas for the duration of the course. Once you have gathered the largest possible list of topics, it is time to decide which are best suited to your needs.

Evaluate Speech Topics

The best speech topics are those that are appropriate not only for you, but also for listeners in a particular time and place.

Appropriate for speaker?

The first test of any topic must be whether it is appropriate to you. You may have selected a topic from an inventory of promising candidates. However, this fact does not in itself certify the topic as a good one. You should precisely consider whether your interest and experience are sufficient to carry you through the whole process of speech preparation. To place a topic on a list requires only a small amount of commitment. To spend hours preparing an address requires a higher level of enthusiasm.

One public speaking student began with a list of topics that included camping, water beds, and religion in the United States. Ultimately, the student chose to speak on restoring antique automobiles. This topic concerned a favorite hobby in which he had made major investments of time and money. The other subjects were of relatively passing interest to him.

When you are confident that the topic holds sufficient interest value, the next question to pose is how much you know, and want to know, about the subject. The rhetorically competent speaker appears to be—and *is*—an expert on the topic being addressed. Good speeches always rely on research conducted by the speaker, and often a speech includes references to personal experiences of the speaker. To decide if a topic is one about which you can become expert, you must question whether (1) you already have personal expertise with the topic and/or (2) you have a commitment to do research on a topic.

Consider the case of a public speaking student who listed such potential topics as smoking, volleyball, and solar energy. Ultimately, she gave a major speech on the disadvantages of such standardized exams as IQ tests and the Scholastic Aptitude Test. The topic she chose was one that arose from some unpleasant personal experiences. These experiences motivated her to search out and carefully examine studies on the validity and possible cultural bias of standardized tests.

Appropriate for audience?

Speeches are given to people, not to desks, chairs, or walls; thinking about listeners is vital to evaluating your topic. Ask yourself how you can make a particular issue important for the audience. A public speaking student once made this assessment of "passive smoking" as a topic appropriate for her audience:

> Most people have been in situations in which they were exposed to the smoke of others, like it or not. Because of their exposure, the subject would create audience attention. People will want to know how they have been and are being affected by others' smoke.

This prediction turned out to be right on the mark.

It is possible to *over*estimate how much a subject concerns other people.

Do not assume that because a topic is vital to you, the audience will share this outlook. If you find yourself commenting that listeners "should" be concerned by a topic, this is a sure sign that you are thinking less about the audience and more about your own interests.

Speakers sometimes *under*estimate the audience's interest. Securing attention from listeners does not require you to hit them over the head with a blockbuster topic such as "my first sexual experience" (probably a very unwise choice of topic). Even apparently dry or overworked subjects, such as "why you ought to vote," have aspects that can be made vital. This means that in evaluating the relevance-to-audience of a subject, you should not consider merely the subject as a whole. Give thought to various parts of the topic—things unfamiliar, unusual, newly important, recently changed, frequently misunderstood.

Do not be too quick to dismiss a subject as excessively difficult—or easy—for listeners. Careful selection, good organization, and specific research might make even nuclear arms control a manageable subject for a short talk. Something as commonplace as long-distance telephone calling could be well received if presented with lots of new details. You could focus on how calls are made to the different continents and how telephone companies actually connect the two parties during a call.

A final source of ideas about the appropriateness of a topic for listeners is to consider various objective characteristics of audience members. A student of mine once noted that his speech against nuclear power plants made a good match to the background of his young, college-educated audience. Such a group, he believed, possessed "the demographic characteristics associated with concern for environmental problems." Similarly, another student showed awareness that her anti-smoking message might cause smokers in the class "to feel uneasy, which would make the subject slightly inappropriate." She was right to say "slightly inappropriate," since discomfort sometimes serves a useful rhetorical purpose.

Box 4.3

Topics That Audiences Pay Big Bucks to Hear

These days, it is the corporations and trade associations that are paying fat fees for speakers, and it is the Washington political and media figure who is most eagerly sought—the men and women who can speak about trade and economic issues, who can analyze Soviet-American relations and Middle East problems, who can titillate audiences with inside stories of congressional machinations and political gossip.

Source: Barbara Gamarekian (*New York Times*), *San Francisco Chronicle*, 20 December 1988, B3.

Appropriate for time and place?

Give thought to the environment in which the speech is to be given. The immediate setting often reveals the mood or frame of mind that has taken hold of the audience. Even in a public speaking classroom—where speeches are required—factors of time and place have a bearing on your purpose, as shown below.

You should ask whether you can present the topic in the time given. This question relates to the manageability of a subject—whether it is narrow enough to be presented in the allotted number of minutes. If you are planning a five-minute talk on the State of Florida, perhaps you need to narrow the scope of the address. Perhaps it would be better to talk of Florida tourist attractions or the trek of northern college students to Florida during spring break.

Further, be sure to consider the connection between a topic and current events. Speeches need not be limited to today's front-page news, but you should be alert to possible links between your subject and current headlines. A student planning to speak on the U.S. space program made this observation about time and place:

> Time, in my opinion, would be in my favor. With the upcoming launch of NASA's space shuttle, it might tend to reinforce to my audience my belief in space exploration.

Not all speakers are sensitive to how current events relate to their topic, however. One student, who had prepared a speech on gun control, failed even to mention the handgun murder of John Lennon that had taken place earlier in the week. The result? His fellow students were asking him about the point even as he was returning to his seat.

A third consideration of time and place is to ask whether previous speeches might affect reception of your topic. Refer to earlier speeches if others have talked on the same or a related subject. Possibly you could modify your speech slightly to emphasize some aspect neglected by the other speakers. Perhaps you could mention the previous speaker(s), and use their remarks as points of comparison or of departure. You may find, to your surprise, that a speaker is talking on the very same subject as yours—in the same class period. In this case, you should make some specific mention of the earlier speech. By comparing some of your points to the earlier talk, you might turn a seemingly bad circumstance into an advantage.

When planning speeches to be given outside the classroom situation, a fourth question surfaces. Does the subject of the speech meet the requirements of the event? Whatever the situation or type of speech, a society shares assumptions about what should be said on an occasion. A dedication of a public facility would make a poor occasion to attack government spending. Similarly, if you have agreed to introduce another speaker, the assumption is that you feel able to be sincerely supportive of the upcoming speaker. For this reason, eyebrows were raised among President Reagan's advisers when Margaret Bush Wilson used these words to present the President to the convention of the National Association for the Advancement of Colored People: "The NAACP does not necessarily subscribe to the views which are about to be expressed."[4]

In choosing topics for speeches, be sure not to skip the evaluation step. Remember, you will be spending considerable time with each topic you choose. You must live with your choices—literally. Further, to borrow an expression from military life, your morale as a speaker will be affected by how much the subject excites you. If you can't wait to get your points across, then you will be motivated to prepare a better speech. When you attune your topic to the audience, you can be sure that your speech preparation is on target—right from the start.

Focus on One General Purpose

Clearly, we can identify differences among the general purposes of speech—to inform, to persuade, to inspire, and to entertain. Though the general purposes of speech *are* different, they are *not absolutely distinct.* Consider the speeches described in this chapter. Harold Enarson sought to promote understanding, but his remarks did support a particular attitude toward the budget cuts imposed by the state—they were bad. Similarly, the Houston speech saw John F. Kennedy implement his persuasive purpose of debunking anti-Catholic attitudes with an address having an inspirational flavor. Kennedy's remarks were calculated to deepen appreciation for the values of religious toleration and separation of church and state. Reversing Kennedy's approach of persuasion through inspiration was Ronald Reagan's speech of welcome. In addition to celebrating the return of the hostages, Reagan issued a political warning to terrorists. Finally, Kennedy's address at the Al Smith dinner used humor with a covert purpose of minimizing the religious issue. When a speaker can lead people to laugh at a prejudice, he or she is well on the way to persuading listeners to discount it.

Given the inevitable overlap among the general purposes of speech, it is vital that you emphasize one of the four purposes, keeping all other purposes secondary. If the speech has no clear sense of purpose, it is likely to be neither informative, nor persuasive, nor inspirational, nor funny—just confusing.

Draft a Specific Purpose Statement

Obviously, choice of a general aim points you in only a general direction. Your exact destination remains to be worked out. When you decide to inform, persuade, inspire, or entertain, the next step is to develop the *specific purpose*. Writing a statement to clearly detail your specific purpose is basic, but it is not easy.

Consider an example of a hypothetical student, Joe, who wants to speak on the Panama Canal. Joe is preparing the speech for an assignment in informative speaking as part of his public speaking class. Joe begins work on a specific purpose statement with two elements already known—topic and general purpose. Following is his first attempt to write out his specific purpose:

> To present information about the Panama Canal.

In this first attempt, Joe has clearly expressed the general purpose, but he has neither considered the audience, nor has he provided any specifics about the topic. Joe tries again:

> To inform the public speaking class about the nature of the Panama Canal.

The revised statement shows a clearer notion of the audience, but Joe remains a bit vague about what he wants classmates to understand. What exactly does Joe mean by "the nature of the Panama Canal?" Is he referring to construction of the canal, its operation, or the 1978 treaty between the United States and Panama? Joe must keep working.

> To get the public speaking class to understand the history of the Panama Canal.

To be sure, "history" is more specific than "nature," but Joe's statement of specific purpose still does not convey enough about his particular slant on the topic. The problem seems to be that Joe is seeking a single word to describe what he wants to say about his subject. Yet, a single word may not be able to express fully the important details of the subject. Joe must elaborate about those aspects of the canal that will serve as the center of his talk. He tries again:

> To get the public speaking class to understand how the Canal Zone was acquired by the United States and how the United States engineers overcame many obstacles in constructing the canal.

Joe's fourth attempt has produced a workable statement of specific purpose. He has not only identified his topic (the Panama Canal), his audience (the class), and his general purpose (to inform), but Joe has provided sufficient details about the topic to guide preparation of the speech. He has developed a road map that provides directions for his further work on the speech.

As the story of Joe shows, preparing a statement of specific purpose entails three steps. First, you decide what will be the topic and the general purpose. For instance, you might decide to present information about the university, persuade listeners to join an organization, or amuse them by relating a memorable experience. Second, you consider precisely the persons from whom you want the general response. For instance, you may want "to inform the alumni" or, put another way, "to get the alumni to understand." Third, you consider what can be said specifically about the subject. For instance, you might be impressed with the university's recent progress in recruiting students, improving physical facilities, and developing new academic programs. Putting together the three steps, you are probably ready to write a completely developed statement of specific purpose:

> To make the alumni aware of the progress the university has made during the last year in recruiting students, improving physical facilities, and developing new academic programs.

Statements of specific purpose are most useful in speech preparation when the statements are *audience-centered rather than subject-centered.* When your aim is to persuade, your goal is not simply to *transmit* arguments. Persuasion is an effect that must be *attained in listeners.* In other words, you will succeed as a persuasive speaker when you actually change the beliefs or behavior of people listening to you. Keep an audience-centered frame of mind when writing statements of specific purpose.

- *Instead of writing* "to inform the study club," *write* "to get the members to understand."
- *Instead of writing* "to persuade the class," *write* " to get classmembers to agree that" or "to get classmembers to sign up for."
- *Instead of writing* "to inspire the team members," *write* "to get the team to appreciate."
- *Instead of writing* "to entertain the class," *write* "to get my classmembers to enjoy," or "to smile," or "to laugh at."

When well-prepared, the statement of specific purpose will put you on the road to rhetorical competence by guiding your preparation of the speech. The statement is a kind of search beacon lighting your way to further work. Your purpose statement directs your attention to audience analysis (treated in chapter 5); it points to needed research about the topic (treated in chapters 6 and 7); and it gives the major points you need to organize (treated in Part III).

Purpose and Ethics

In chapter 3, we saw that ethical speakers take into account the true interests of listeners. In contrast, lapses of ethical communication commonly result when a speaker overemphasizes his or her needs to the neglect of others in society. The speaker's purpose is often the root of ethical problems in communication. Unethical speakers typically want to mislead or exploit listeners. Matters of ethics first enter the realm of rhetorical competence when we prepare our statement of specific purpose. We need to test whether our purpose as stated meets the requirements of ethical communication.

The Social Contract of Speechmaking

Questions of ethics figure in everyday life. A jury in Los Angeles awarded entertainer Carol Burnett 1.6 million dollars in a 1981 judgment against the *National Enquirer.* The jury accepted Ms. Burnett's claim that the *National Enquirer* knowingly had published a false story that she made a drunken scene at a restaurant. In 1987–1988, two leading television evangelists, Jim Bakker and Jimmy Swaggart, were forced to confess private sins long hidden. The disclosures contradicted the picture of righteousness the two preachers had been projecting over the television screen.

Common to episodes such as the above is the idea that communication ethics rest on a bond of trust between sender and receiver. Speech teachers traditionally agree that matters of ethics demand treatment in the public speaking classroom.[5] Why does speechmaking raise ethical questions? Thomas Nilsen helps us to understand the inherent place of ethics in public speaking when he points out that "every act of speech is essentially a social act . . . having an ethical component."[6] The ethical-moral aspect of speaking is inescapable. Whenever a speaker makes an assertion, he or she really is asking the receivers to accept three assumptions. First is the assumption of competence. The public speaker asks listeners to accept that he or she really understands what is being said. Speakers strive to appear well-informed and, until the contrary is proved, listeners are disposed to view the speaker as someone fully conversant with the subject. Second is the assumption of truthfulness. Basic honesty is taken for granted in all communication, including informal conversation. However, the formal nature of a public speech necessarily increases the responsibility of the talkative party to be truthful. Third is the assumption that the speaker gives information and advice consistent with the best interests of listeners. A public speech is an offer of help made in apparent good faith.

The three assumptions of a speaker's knowledge, truthfulness, and good faith make up *the social contract of speechmaking*. These assumptions delineate expectations of listeners and concomitant obligations placed on speakers. The ethics of speechmaking demand that speakers fulfill their contract with the audience by presenting messages based on careful analysis, truthful information, and explicit concern for the needs of the listeners.

Box 4.4

The Packaging of Speakers Can Hide Ethics

Since we have few public occasions in which the mind of the candidate or leader can be seen unshielded by speechwriters, it is now possible to elect someone whose primary qualifications are a knack for creating news McNuggets, a willingness to speak the thoughts of others, a talent for doing so with sincerity and conviction, and a tolerance for feigning enthusiasm when delivering the same stock stump speech for the seventh time in a single day.

Source: Kathleen H. Jamieson, *Eloquence in an Electronic Age* (New York: Oxford University Press, 1988), 237.

Five Ethical Tests

Judging the ethics of communication requires hard thinking on your part. Almost everyone would agree that the speeches of Adolf Hitler were unethical in view of Hitler's discredited Nazi regime. But what of contemporary persons whose proposals are not yet in effect? Further, can we assume that today's popular speakers always pursue ethical purposes? Below are five tests that you may apply to the problem of evaluating the ethics of speechmaking. (See table 4.2, p. 115.)

Intentions test

You may evaluate your purpose according to what you have in mind for listeners. This test focuses most directly on the social contract of speechmaking, the bond of trust that should exist between you and the receivers.

When a message fails the test of good intentions, most often the cause is that the communicator harbors some hidden and selfish motive. Jane Bryant Quinn, financial columnist, used the intentions test to doubt the motives of banks and savings and loan institutions in opposing the first money-market funds. One by one, Quinn examined the arguments of bankers, suggesting that the institutions were acting more in their own interest (no pun intended!) than that of the investing public. Quinn contended it was unethical for banks and S & Ls to demand that their money funds be "put in chains" (rather than asking for legal permission to offer more interest).[7]

When you apply the intentions test, you review your statement of specific purpose, asking who benefits most, and why, from your intention. A student speaking on antibiotics applied such a question to her purpose to persuade people to avoid indiscriminate use of the drugs. She judged that her intention was an ethical one because she wanted the audience "to save money and preserve their long term health as well as the health of future generations."

Values test

Values are notions of what is good and bad in life—what we seek or avoid. Value terms such as health, freedom, honesty, and sportsmanship describe positive goals that people want to attain. Negative terms such as poverty, bankruptcy, perjury, and laziness are concepts with which people would rather not be associated.

Every message is built upon an appeal to values. For instance, automobile commercials variously tout the economy, beauty, performance, or prestige of the product. Speeches also function by connecting ideas to values. If your persuasive purpose is to support an increase in taxes, you might want to connect your plan to the value of improved public services. If your intent is to oppose the tax, you would do well to link the increase to such concepts as government waste or undeserving recipients.

When you use the values test as the basis for ethical judgments, you question whether you are appealing to values considered good or bad by society. As an illustration, consider how one observer applied the values test to advertising for designer jeans. One critic argued that ads usually say nothing about the garments as useful clothing and, instead, "many show pre-teens wiggling their little bottoms. . . . That's more than sleazy. It's sick."[8]

Public speakers can use the values test, too. Consider what values are assumed by the arguments of your speech. A student who planned a speech on the importance of writing skills identified a number of values that underlay her arguments. She believed that her speech emphasized coherence, clarity, scholarship, intelligence, integrity, and wisdom.

Truth test

Untruthful communication breaks the bond of trust between speaker and receiver. Using the criterion of truthful communication, Dick Cavett once withdrew his name from an advertising campaign for a brand of rum. The advertisers paid a number of celebrities, including Cavett, for use of their names in testimonial stories about rum-and-soda cocktails. The resulting magazine ad campaign included pictures of beautiful couples with accompanying texts that stated X, Y, or Z celebrity had introduced the couple to the rum-and-soda drink. The ad featuring Cavett's name asserted that the rum drinker had met Cavett when "we were both in a whacky off-Broadway play in a theater so small the cast outnumbered the audience." "What whacky off-Broadway play?" asked Cavett, who added that "the fact that people took something to be true that isn't, disturbs me."[9]

The essential problem of truth in communication is well put by the media critic, A. J. Liebling. Liebling observed that reporters usually discovered only about half the truth of a situation; further, a given news story allowed them to communicate only about half of what they learned.[10] Liebling's description of the situation of writers applies equally well to that of speakers. What is a speaker to do? Two tests are helpful when you want to evaluate your speech's purpose according to truthfulness. First, you should consider whether your speech's purpose is based on any known deceptions. Second, you should judge whether you have made at least a reasonable effort to find the facts of a case. In this connection, a student planning a speech on restricting use of antibiotics noted that her persuasive purpose appeared ethical in view of the "sound statistical evidence to back my statements."

Means test

Speakers and writers can use many standard methods of explanation and persuasion—to be treated in later chapters. Some theorists of public speaking argue that techniques of persuasion, in themselves, are ethically neutral, or that "speech communication principles are amoral."[11] Contentions of this kind liken language to a tool such as a hammer, which is neutral unless someone uses it for good or ill. The difficulty in such a position is well-expressed by Socrates, the philosopher. He noted that some words, like iron or silver, induce people to "understand the same meaning." In contrast, he observed, terms such as "justice" or "goodness" caused folks to "veer off in different directions and dispute the meaning."[12]

The point is that no chemical process can separate ethical from unethical speaking. To evaluate speechmaking is more akin to deciding questions of justice and goodness than to separating iron from silver. Methods of persuasion are neutral only if we overlook the nature of speechmaking as execution of a social contract between sender and receiver. A speaker always asks that listeners accept the legitimacy of his or her intentions and proofs.

Since the time of Aristotle, scholars and teachers have identified several means of communication that always raise ethical doubts. When you check your speech purpose for ethical means, be aware of four representative unethical means of persuasion.

First, the argument that "everybody is doing it" suppresses ethical judgment. A speaker might assert that "The U.S.A. must ban capital punishment because Western European countries have done so." Here it would be more ethical to give and evaluate the reasons that the Europeans have abandoned the death penalty.

Second, *guilt by association* is a flimsy conclusion based on showing vague or coincidental links between one individual and an unpopular idea or person. Representative would be the argument that "Sally advocates a program of national health insurance, which is a long-standing policy of the Soviet Communist government." The Soviets support schools, too, so should Americans close theirs? The speaker needs to consider carefully the intellectual merits and demerits of national health insurance. A speaker acts unethically when suggesting that an idea can be condemned merely because it has been elsewhere adopted by an unpopular source.

Name-calling is a third disreputable tactic of persuasion. This argument not only represents a verbal assault, but it also usually distracts from issues at hand. For instance, in 1977, after Andrew Young called Presidents Richard Nixon and Gerald Ford "racists," he found himself apologizing for his evocative words. At the same time, Young vainly tried to get attention back to his main point that the United States was not sensitive enough to cultural differences in third world countries.[13]

Fourth, deceiving the audience about the intent of a message breaks the social contract of speechmaking. One of the oldest ploys of telephone marketing is to begin a sales pitch as if it were a survey to get information. This unethical tactic conceals the fact that the phone call comes from a business organization intending to sell its product. According to Ivy Lee, a founder of the field of public relations, when we conceal the biased source of a message, we become propagandists rather than communicators.[14]

Effects test

If a communicator's message brings about harmful effects, then we have grounds to doubt its ethical character. The effects test supplies grounds for the campaign against violent television program content by a group called

Table 4.2 Ethical tests of speaker purpose

Test	Criteria
Intentions	Does your purpose meet the needs of others?
Values	What value terms apply to your purpose?
Truth	Have you found the facts and avoided deceptions?
Means	Are you using acceptable tactics of persuasion?
Effects	What result does your purpose have for society?

Action for Children's Television. An ACT fund-raising letter argued that joining the group was one way that individuals "can stop the growth of more violence in our society." The letter cited findings that linked violent behavior in children and adults to the presentation of violence on television. The ACT campaign relied on the effects standard as a basis for condemning American television as ethically weak in view of its "shoddy, distorted, violent television fare."

In applying the effect test to speechmaking, you should examine your statement of specific purpose and pose this question: "What will be the effect for the listeners of what I am advocating?" In other words, if listeners followed the advice you give, what would happen to them? A student speaker applied this criterion to judge the ethics of her purpose to persuade listeners to stop indiscriminate use of antibiotics. She predicted that adoption of her views would bring two results. First, people would save money by not using antibiotics for minor ills that would rapidly go away without treatment. Second, she predicted that less use of antibiotics would reduce the problem of creating bacteria resistant to drugs, thus making antibiotics more effective when really needed. Because her purpose would bring social benefits, the speaker confidently believed that her speech passed the ethical test of effects.

Checking the ethics of your speech purpose is the final step in developing your rhetorical plan of action. The basic plan begins when you consider the four general purposes of public speaking and list potential topics. Your plan progresses further when you evaluate the appropriateness of speech topics for you, for the audience, and for the situation. Your plan becomes concrete when you draft a statement of specific purpose, merging your topic with your one general objective. Finally, when you have tested your plan of action for ethics, you are ready for the preparation steps explained in the next chapters.

Concepts for Review

Can you summarize the meaning of these terms or expressions? How does each relate to speechmaking?

purpose
deliberative speech
ceremonial speech
forensic (legal) speech
general speech purposes
informative speech
persuasive speech
inspirational speech
entertainment speech
speech situation
evaluating speech topics
appropriateness of topic
statement of specific purpose
social contract of speechmaking
assumption of competence
assumption of truthfulness
assumption of good faith
intentions test
values test
truth test
means test
effects test

Things to Try

1. Identify three speeches you recently have heard or that you find in an issue of *Vital Speeches.* Try to pick out which of the four general purposes of speech was most important in each speech. What did the speaker say that revealed his or her purpose? Did any of the other purposes also seem to figure significantly in the speaker's approach?
2. Develop a list of potential speech topics. Return to the categories listed on pages 102–103. Work to identify at least two topics for each category.
3. Test one of your speech topics for use in your speech class. Pick a topic and identify as many reasons as you can why the topic would be both appropriate and *in*appropriate for you. Similarly, write down reasons why the topic would be both appropriate and *in*appropriate for the audience and for the time and place. On the basis of these tests, do you think the topic will work well for an assignment in your speech class?
4. Pick a speech that you have recently heard, or consult the *New York Times* or an issue of *Vital Speeches* to find a recent speech. Evaluate the speech for ethics. How does the speech fare when measured against the tests of intentions, values, truth, means, and effects? A major failure of any one test or minor failures in several tests may require you to judge the speech as unethical.

Endnotes

1. See Wayne N. Thompson, "Barbara Jordan's Keynote Address: Fulfilling Dual and Conflicting Purposes," *Central States Speech Journal 30* (1979): 272–277.
2. *Rhetoric,* I. 3. 1358b.
3. Robert C. Jeffrey and Owen Peterson, *Speech,* 2nd ed. (New York: Harper and Row, 1975), 67–68.
4. *Courier-Journal* [Louisville], 30 June 1981, A8.
5. Robert C. Johnson, "Teaching Speech Ethics in the Beginning Speech Course," *Speech Teacher 19* (1970): 60.
6. Thomas R. Nilsen, *Ethics of Speech Communication* (Indianapolis, IN: Bobbs-Merrill, 1966), 12.
7. *Newsweek,* 16 March 1981, 80.
8. *Courier-Journal* [Louisville], 29 September 1980, C1.
9. *Newsweek,* 22 May 1978, 69.
10. A. J. Liebling, *The Press,* 2nd ed. (New York: Pantheon, 1964), 120.
11. Respectively, James C. McCroskey, *An Introduction to Rhetorical Communication,* 5th ed. (Englewood Cliffs, NJ: Prentice-Hall, 1986), 247–260; Bert E. Bradley, *Fundamentals of Speech Communication: The Credibility of Ideas,* 5th ed. (Dubuque, IA: Wm. C. Brown, 1988), 53.
12. Plato, *Phaedrus,* 263.
13. *New York Times* [City Edition], 7 June 1977, 1.
14. Ivy L. Lee, *Publicity* (New York: Industries Publishing, 1925), 23.

Chapter

5

Audience Analysis

Outline

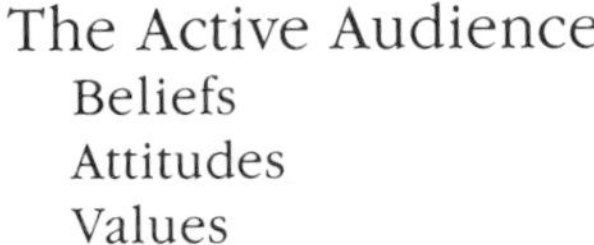

The Active Audience
- Beliefs
- Attitudes
- Values

Audience Selectivity
- Selective Exposure
- Selective Attention
- Selective Interpretation
- Selective Recall

Learning about Your Audience
- Demographic Generalizations
- The Speech Situation
- Questionnaires

Credibility Considerations
- Universal Factors of Credibility
- Situational Factors of Credibility

President Jimmy Carter never enjoyed a reputation as a great speaker. Wanting to avoid the exaggerated oratory he had heard as a child, Carter favored an understated type of delivery that frequently lacked the ability to inspire. However, in one of his most successful speeches, Carter used audience analysis effectively to overcome his wooden gestures and choppy vocal communication.

During a 1978 appearance before the Parliament of India, Carter organized his address around ideas that connected his own experience of growing up in Georgia to the world of his listeners. Central to Carter's speech were several links he drew between Martin Luther King, Jr., and Mahatma Gandhi, father of India's independence. Carter explained how King had used nonviolent protest to overcome the system of segregation. Making the connection to members of the Indian parliament, Carter portrayed King as "a son of Georgia and a spiritual son of Mahatma Gandhi." Carter told how King drew inspiration from Gandhi's campaign of nonviolent protest against British control of India. Carter's words struck home with his listeners. An American reporter observed the audience as Carter described the links between Gandhi and King. One member of Parliament "moved forward, nodding again and again as he [Carter] developed his points. When the president ended, she was sitting straight, her chin cradled deep into her hand, blinking back tears. All around her other expressions said, mutely but effectively, that Mr. Carter had touched them."[1]

Making our own ideas believable or persuasive to others is one of the basic problems of rhetoric. Now, as in classical times, rhetorical competence implies the ability to bridge the gap between our own views and ideas held dear by listeners. Some audiences are easy to please, as shown by the supportive listening of our parents or friends. Other situations confront us with obstacles to attaining our purpose. Chief among the impediments to automatic success in speechmaking are the existing beliefs, attitudes, and values of the audience. In this chapter we will begin by looking at how audiences respond to speeches. Next comes consideration of how to get information about our listeners. As you read the chapter, look for ways that audience analysis can help you prepare your upcoming speeches.

The Active Audience

In chapter 1, we observed that adaptation to our audience does not mean we surrender to whatever listeners want. Nor does adaptation mean that we search for weaknesses in listeners to manipulate them. As a component of rhetorical competence, audience adaptation is our effort to look for ways to win a fair hearing for our points. We look for ways to help our hearers better understand and better see the importance of what we are saying.

Effective adaptation to listeners requires *audience analysis.* We look carefully at characteristics of our listeners to predict how our ideas will fit in with theirs. Like Carter, we can make our ideas enter the world of listeners only when we connect our views and experiences to the beliefs and lives of others. The kind of audience analysis that supports rhetorical competence is illustrated by a talk that Theodore Roosevelt gave to a delegation of angry railroad workers. Roosevelt was alert to how he might connect his own ideas of industrial cooperation to the grievances of the railway employees. Spotting a Civil War veteran's badge worn by one of the engineers, Roosevelt emphasized that the railroad's need for good business leadership was analogous to the need of soldiers for good generals.[2]

Box 5.1

Democratic Life Is Based on Audience Adaptation

Socrates, the Greek philosopher, once asked Protagoras, a teacher of public speaking, how speechmaking could lead to good decisions. Socrates complained that anyone could address the public assembly—the ignorant as well as the enlightened. In answer, Protagoras told a story about the importance of toleration of diverse opinions (adaptation to audience) in the origins of political life. Protagoras speculated that the gods created man only after they had given animals most of the obvious advantages for survival and progress—great size, swiftness, thick fur, and the like. When the few relatively helpless people banded together in cities for survival, they began to quarrel among themselves. Zeus, fearing that mankind would perish, sent his messenger, Hermes, to bring humanity the qualities of reverence and justice, two sentiments necessary for social life in the city. These gifts were given to all—and not just to an elite—because the existence of a state requires that all its members share a willingness to cooperate.

Source: Plato, *Protagoras,* 321–322.

Herbert Blumer, an early sociologist of communication, characterized the human being as an "acting organism."[3] Blumer made the point that people are not entirely at the mercy of forces such as society, personal attitudes, human needs, or the mass media. People interpret what is going on around them, and then they work out a line of action appropriate to what they think. To take an immediate example, your decision to purchase a copy of this textbook (assuming that you did so) was not an automatic response caused either by the words "required text," or by your noticing that others had bought one. Probably you bought your text after deciding that your instructor was serious about using it and that other alternatives, such as borrowing, were either impossible or impractical.

The notion of people as actors who deliberate, think, and judge has implications for speechmaking. In the first place, such a view of the audience removes any notion that listeners will be under our control. All we can realistically expect is that listeners will weigh our words, compare what we say against their existing views, and then think or act in ways appropriate for them. A second implication of viewing listeners as active participants in communication is that we should be vitally interested in the process by which people interpret what they hear in speeches.

Putting the matter simply, listeners interpret a message by integrating the message into an existing image of the world. The term *image system* sometimes is used to designate the personal knowledge of life held by listeners. The image system is a storehouse of knowledge, consisting of various organized impressions. To Milton Rokeach, leading American psychologist, the image system consists of three kinds of thoughts: (1) beliefs, (2) attitudes, and (3) values.[4] Each of these three elements is important to understanding how our audience may respond to our speech. (See fig. 5.1, p. 124.)

Beliefs

Beliefs are thoughts about objects, events, or situations in the world. Beliefs seem to be of two types. *Verifiable beliefs* amount to factual knowledge of the world—for instance, when final exams begin. We may determine the truth of such beliefs by consulting outside sources—such as the school catalog. In contrast, *primitive beliefs* are assumptions that the future will resemble the present. Primitive beliefs do not provide specific factual information as much as they give us a view of how the world works. Our primitive beliefs include the faith that day will follow night and that the ground will remain solid while we walk on it. Primitive beliefs cannot be directly verified because they are a confidence in general experience. Unlike adults, who are prone to take their primitive beliefs for granted, babies delight in dropping an object several times to see if it *always* falls.

You should be concerned with the audience's store of verifiable and primitive beliefs that pertain to your speech topic. A student speaker planning an informative talk on earthquakes predicted that his California audience would be more likely than Ohioans to believe that an earthquake might occur in the near future. In other words, the speaker predicted that the audience's primitive assumption of a firm and solid earth would not present a major obstacle to his talk. However, since his classmates were not scientists, the speaker predicted that listeners would lack a detailed knowledge of what would happen to the San Francisco Bay Area during a major quake. Listeners lacked a store of verifiable beliefs about earthquake preparedness. The speaker planned to organize his talk to give a precise account of a monster earthquake.

Attitudes

An *attitude* is a tendency to approve or disapprove of an object, event, or condition. Rokeach views attitudes as overall judgments based on beliefs held by individuals. In Rokeach's scheme, beliefs accumulate to produce an attitude. For instance, if we believe the economy is improving and that the threat of war is lessening, then we are more likely to have a favorable attitude toward political leaders.

Unless the subject of your speech is a complete mystery to your audience, your listeners will hold attitudes toward some of the ideas you will present. For instance, Jimmy Carter knew that Mahatma Gandhi was the greatest hero of India. Carter could be confident that connections between Gandhi and America's Martin Luther King would build a bridge between the United States and India.

Consider how one student speaker analyzed her audience's attitude toward capital punishment and how she used this information to prepare her speech. The student wanted to persuade listeners that capital punishment was needed. However, she predicted that listeners would take the attitude that the death penalty conflicted with human rights. "We are in a period of time in which human rights are valued," she wrote. "Young people tend to want rights more strongly." Therefore, this student speaker considered how to respond to the expected unfavorable attitudes of the classroom audience toward her ideas. "In response, I will focus on the rights of victims to be protected from harm and the fact that criminals' rights are protected by laws."

Values

Rokeach presents beliefs and attitudes as thoughts about specific persons or things. In contrast, he defines *values* as deep-seated preferences that support various beliefs and attitudes. For instance, the value of honesty might support the belief that people should accurately report their income for tax purposes. Rokeach theorizes that people hold two types of values. The first kind, *terminal values,* deals with conditions in which people live, such as freedom or world peace. The second kind, *instrumental values,* deals with human conduct, such as courage or honesty.

Members of your audience hold values that pertain to your speech topic. These values serve as *sources of motivation* for listeners. For instance, a student speaker decided that her audience placed a high value on human rights and protection of children. She believed that these values would cause listeners to accept her thesis that pornography should be censored. Another public speaking student predicted that listeners valued health and good body appearance. She decided to use these two values as a basis for persuading her listeners to change their eating habits. "I will be able to use their desire for health to encourage them to follow my suggestions. Good nutrition is the key to avoiding illness. Nutrition can help achieve the result of thinness also."

Experimental research supports the notion of using values as motivational concepts in speechmaking. Researchers polled a group of students to find out what they viewed as the likely consequences (good or bad) of guaranteeing a minimum annual income to all citizens. For instance, reducing hunger and poverty would be a good consequence and, thus, a positive motivating concept. Reducing the incentive to work, a bad consequence, would be a negative motivating concept. Speakers were given the results of the survey to use in preparing messages. When the speakers based their remarks on consequences that listeners believed were likely, the speakers were more successful in achieving persuasion.[5]

Box 5.2

Values Are Doorways to Your Audience

"For where your treasure is, there will your heart be also." *Luke,* 12: 34.

The tendency of people to share images makes successful audience analysis possible for speakers. Each person's symbolic world contains a unique reservoir of beliefs, attitudes, and values. However, because people often experience events in common, many individuals may possess roughly the same image of a thing, idea, or event. We may term this the *shared public image,* which is a viewpoint held in common by a group of otherwise different persons.[6]

Audience Selectivity

The image system is useful because it functions as a sorting and selecting mechanism. All of us are bombarded with ideas from conversations, the electronic media, and our reading. Our image system helps us cope with this flood of data. For instance, our image of entertainers helps us select one movie in preference to another. In fact, Hollywood's star system began when movie makers realized the drawing power of "name" actors.

The sorting and selecting role of the image system has a bearing on your success as a speaker. Expect your ideas and arguments to be filtered through the image system of listeners. To take a particular case, if you intend to speak about nuclear power plants, what you say will be measured against things that listeners believe about nuclear safety. Research demonstrates

Figure 5.1 Speech, speaker, and audience.

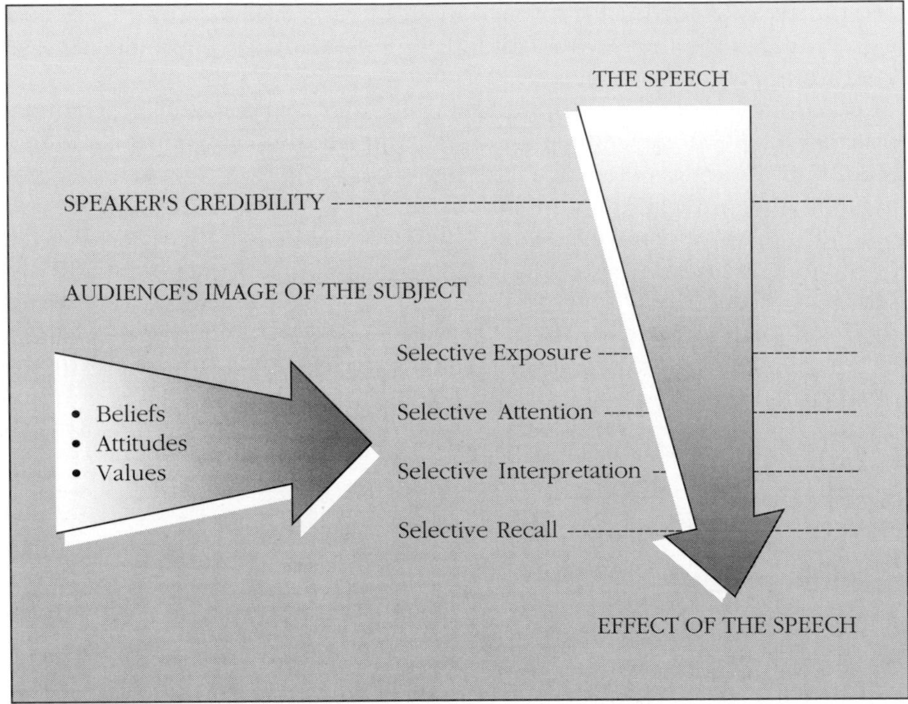

four ways that the image system makes people selective. People tend to show selectivity in their exposure to, attention to, interpretation of, and recall of messages. Each of these tendencies poses a special problem that demands actions by the rhetorically competent speaker.

Selective Exposure

Selective exposure means avoiding information inconsistent with an existing image and seeking out supportive information. Political discussions offer many classic examples of selective exposure. After the first Kennedy-Nixon television debate of 1960, most viewers later discussed the debate with persons who held the same political views as their own. Only eleven percent talked the debate over with an individual holding contrary views. Researchers who interviewed members of the audience of an anti-Vietnam War film, *Tell Me Lies,* similarly found a selective exposure effect. Only two of fifty-eight members of the audience expressed approval of the U.S. war policy in Vietnam. These findings show that audiences may select communication likely to reinforce their existing image.[7]

Public speakers tend to neglect the idea of selective exposure, considering listeners as somehow held captive for the duration of the talk. If you possess rhetorical competence, you will see beyond the myth that audiences come as gifts neatly wrapped. You will speak as if listeners might physically leave or mentally tune out at any point. For instance, one student speaker planned to address an audience of prospective adoptive parents, couples who had experienced the frustration of unsuccessfully trying to conceive a child. The speaker realized that if she "made the process of adoption seem equally frustrating," the couples might tune out.

To deal with selective exposure, set a goal to make the length and content of your talk so attractive that people wish you had said more—not that you had sat down sooner.

Selective Attention

Physically or mentally avoiding a message is not necessary for selectivity to occur. Listeners sometimes pay attention only to parts of a message consistent with their existing image, ignoring disagreeable ideas.

A graphic example of selective attention comes from a study of responses to newspaper stories about the 1968 presidential election. A researcher created a number of fictitious newspaper front pages. Each of these pages contained a prominent article that featured one of the major candidates (Richard Nixon, Hubert Humphrey, and George Wallace) and smaller stories about competitors. Readers were asked to look at the front pages and mark the stories according to their desire to read them. Predictably, readers were more interested in the stories that treated their favorite candidate—whether or not those articles were the most prominent.[8] Here a reader's initial image of the politician was a determining factor in attention.

Whether dealing with names on a list, faces in a picture, or articles on a page, people are likely to pay most attention to the items of greatest value for their existing image. This is the reason that Jimmy Carter held members of the Indian parliament in rapt attention when connecting Georgia's Martin Luther King and India's Mahatma Gandhi. Carter knew how to use selective attention as a resource for establishing common ground with his audience

Selective attention provides an ever-present challenge for public speakers. In preparing your speeches, consider the extent to which the subject *is* and *can be* a matter of interest to listeners. Sometimes you will find that the topic has almost automatic appeal. For instance, one student speaker planned a presentation on career opportunities for college graduates. His speech was prepared during the height of an economic recession when students faced unemployment. The speaker believed that he would keep attention by alerting the audience to areas in which job openings were on the rise.

Even when a topic does not hold automatic appeal for listeners, the rhetorically competent speaker looks for ways to make a topic come alive for listeners. Would you believe that one of the most dramatic speeches in American history was an address favoring changes in our nation's monetary policy? During the Democratic Convention of 1896, William Jennings Bryan, the Nebraska populist, brought delegates to their feet with an appeal to back the dollar with silver in addition to gold. Bryan's speech was powerful because he built his remarks on common resentments working people of the day harbored about the economic system. Bryan appealed to farmers' and workers' beliefs that the gold standard kept money scarce and out of the hands of laboring people. "We will answer their demand for a gold standard by saying to them: You shall not press down upon the brow of labor this crown of thorns, you shall not crucify mankind upon a cross of gold."[9]

Selective Interpretation

Even when we have overcome selective exposure and selective attention, we are yet faced with the tendency of listeners to make a message consistent with their existing views. Televised debates show how audience members selectively interpret the remarks of competing speakers. Researchers studying the 1976 Carter-Ford debates found that viewers "tended to see the candidate they had preferred before the debate as the winner." Similarly, the 1980 Carter-Reagan debate made viewers more supportive of the candidate they initially preferred; but watching the debate did nothing to make the audience more favorable to the opposing candidate.[10] In the Kennedy-Nixon debate, one Nixon supporter noticed that Vice-President Nixon seemed ill-at-ease and unsmiling. However, the viewer interpreted Nixon's performance to mean that he was "more careful, more subtle" and was "thinking over a problem."[11]

How can a speaker overcome selective interpretation? There is no easy solution to this tendency of listeners. However, rhetorically competent speakers work to address the problem directly. One student preparing a speech on the topic of smoking recognized that "those who are known smokers will feel a little embarrassed because my speech will show their smoking to do harm to others." She planned to overcome this tendency toward selective interpretation by arguing that, until recently, smokers did not have any reason to believe second-hand smoke was a harm to others.

Audiences are obstinate, and persuasion remains difficult even for advertisers who spend billions of dollars to win customers for new products. Rhetorically competent speakers, however, constantly search for ways to overcome mental blocks in listeners by making their remarks interesting, clear, and persuasive. Pay particular heed to suggestions for making your speeches clear through good style and organization. Look for ways to increase your credibility. Keep in mind that how you come across to audiences influences how they interpret your words.

Selective Recall

People are selective not only in how they first hear a message but also in what they later remember about it. After the Kennedy-Nixon debates, students who preferred Nixon remembered significantly more remarks by Nixon that they favored, and they remembered more disagreeable statements by Kennedy. Similarly, Kennedy supporters recalled more agreeable points made by Kennedy and more disagreeable arguments of Nixon.[12] A later experimental study found a tendency toward selective recall in the way students responded to news about presidential candidate Senator Barry Goldwater. Researchers gave students different news stories about Goldwater—one version showing him as successful and the other focusing on his problems. Students who were active supporters of Goldwater remembered better the message that showed Goldwater doing well.[13]

One student speaker directly considered the problem of selective recall as she prepared a speech on the subject of marriage for an audience of young singles. The speaker believed that her audience would have certain idealistic, but inaccurate, views about marriage. To help listeners retain a realistic view of what marriage demanded, the speaker decided to emphasize the principle of compromise as the key to success in marriage.

For specific tips on how to overcome selective memory in listeners, turn especially to the chapters on informative speaking (chapter 13), language style (chapter 10), and delivery (chapter 11).

Learning about Your Audience

Our view of the human image system shows that listeners are not passive receivers of what we have to say. The existing beliefs, attitudes, and values of audience members may set up barriers to achieving our purposes as speakers. Rhetorical competence means preparing the speech in ways that respond to what listeners think about our ideas. The first step in taking an audience-centered approach to speaking is to get information about listeners.

Analyzing the audience would present no problems if we could read the thoughts of others, or if, like George Gallup, we could employ our own staff of interviewers. Experienced speakers do not despair. Rather, they apply one or more of three commonly available resources for audience analysis: (1) demographic analysis, (2) analysis of the speaking environment, and (3) questionnaires.

Demographic Generalizations

Demographics are characteristics of a group of people. Applied to audience analysis, demography calls our attention to such features of our listeners as sex, age, education, income, and religious creed. Demography is useful to the public speaker because members of a particular group often have had certain experiences in common.[14] As a result, they may respond similarly to a message.

Since the time of Aristotle, writers on rhetoric have offered demographic characteristics as a consistent—though imperfect—help to speakers. Aristotle's system was based on the idea that impulses and preferences varied according to the age and wealth of listeners. For instance, Aristotle observed that youths tended to be confident and hot-tempered in contrast to the elderly, who were prone to hesitation and were more guided by reason.[15]

Modern demographic analysis is best illustrated by pollsters such as George Gallup, who survey the opinions of different groups of the population. For instance, if you were speaking on the topic of gun control, you would find useful the results of a *Gallup Report* of May 1986. The Gallup organization found that most Americans favored stricter controls on the sale of handguns. Specifically, of the men polled, 53 percent favored stricter control, whereas the percentage for women was 66. When opinions on gun control were tabulated according to race, Gallup found that those favoring stricter controls included 58 percent of whites, 76 percent of blacks, and 67 percent of Hispanic Americans.[16]

In your library, you can find poll data to help you assess the views of people similar to your own actual audience in sex, race, age, and income. More likely, you will use demographic analysis in the form of *generalizations* about your audience. Demographic analysis can help you prepare your speech by making you sensitive to links between the observable characteristics of listeners and how they might interpret your ideas.

You must be careful, however, in making and applying demographic generalizations. Differences between men and women, whites and blacks, young and old are usually subtle and are always matters of degree. Applied without discretion or common sense, demographic generalizations amount to crude *stereotypes* that all women, all racial minorities, or all rich people think and behave in the same way. Do not take an insensitive or patronizing attitude toward your audience by exaggerating small demographic differences. Instead, use demography with sensibleness and sensitivity so that it becomes another resource of rhetorical competence. You can benefit from social surveys that reveal how age, sex, education, residence, occupation, income, race, and religion may sometimes influence opinions.

Age

Age is related to values and life-styles. The young, especially those who are students, tend toward activity and self-discovery. Individuals under age twenty-five are heavily involved in sports and recreation. They are more health conscious than other groups, for instance, smoking less than other age groups. The young tend to read more than other groups but are less likely to think about significant public issues. Young people in the United States are more optimistic than are the elderly about the future.[17]

People between the ages of thirty and fifty tend to be either strongly oriented to personal achievement or are beginning to settle into identifying with one or more social groups.[18] People over age fifty tend to be more informed about current events but less optimistic. Perhaps because they are less optimistic, older persons tend to be less satisfied with social conditions.[19] Persons over the age of fifty are more than twice as likely as persons under thirty to have traditional views of sex, religion, and family life.[20] Persons over age sixty are less likely to be in debt but are more worried about money, since they feel less able to improve their finances. The elderly are more likely to believe that the world is changing too fast. They also show a tendency to be more cynical—for instance, they are less likely to believe in the basic honesty of people.[21] Further, with increasing age comes a tendency to value religion and salvation more. Older persons often put a higher premium on the value of friendship.[22]

Generalizations about the age of your listeners can help you prepare a speech. For instance, if you were planning to speak in favor of banning pornography, you might predict that an older audience would be more favorable to your views. Since older people favor traditional sex and family values, they would be likely to disapprove of explicit sexual material. Further, the elderly tend to be worried about social change, so you might expect them to be unhappy with today's increasingly prevalent pornography. Such predictions, based on demographic generalizations, are supported by actual survey data. The Gallup organization found that 71 percent of persons over the age of 65 favored a total ban on magazines that show adults engaged in sexual relations. In contrast, though those under thirty often favored curbing the public display of pornographic magazines (50 percent), they were relatively less supportive of a total ban (32 percent).[23]

Sex

We live in an era of changing sex roles, a fact that makes gender-based generalizations especially difficult and potentially controversial. Yet, research does offer some instances when the attitudes and values of men and women seem to diverge, albeit often only slightly. In general, women report less satisfaction with social conditions and trends in the United States than do men.[24] Women tend to be more likely than men to hold traditional values toward sex, family life, and religion.[25] When asked to rank various important values, women are more likely than men to rate religious salvation and forgiveness as crucial.[26] In 1987, 64 percent of women (versus 45 percent of men) reported that religion is important in their lives.[27] It is significant to note, in this connection, that women who are actively pursuing an outside-the-home career hold social opinions similar to those of men. In contrast, women who are homemakers, or who are retired, differ most in attitudes and values from men.[28]

Historically, American men have identified themselves more closely than have women with careers outside the home. For instance, when asked to rank important values, men typically have given greater preference than did women to the values of economic well-being and achieving competence and effectiveness.[29] Traditionally, more men than women have adopted to a lifestyle oriented to economic achievement.[30] Today, of course, various social factors have combined to make career concerns more central in the lives of women. Yet, young women appear to be more ambivalent than young men about the importance of economic advancement, perhaps because college women place greater emphasis than men on helping others and participating in community service.[31]

Can you see some ways that the demographic factor of sex might apply to speech preparation? Let's take the hypothetical topic of banning smoking in public places. Since women tend to take more of a nurturing-helping social role, you might predict that they would be more concerned about the health effects of smoking. So if your audience consisted predominantly of women, you might expect to have an easier time winning support for limitations on freedom to smoke in public. Such predictions are supported by poll data gathered in 1987—though the actual margin was small. Asked whether they favored or opposed a complete ban on smoking in public places, 59 percent of women responded in the affirmative versus 52 percent of men.[32]

Education

Level of education can serve as the basis for some rough predictions of how listeners will respond to speeches. Persons who did not complete high school tend to be more conservative on family issues, for instance, believing that a woman's place is in the home.[33] Persons of lower education seem to be relatively more worried about social change and about their personal finances. When persons of lower education hold stable jobs, they tend to (1) take conservative views on personal morality, (2) express satisfaction with society's leaders, and (3) report a high satisfaction with their job. In contrast, when persons of lower education lack job security, they tend to be rebellious and tend not to worry so much about conforming to traditional morality.[34]

As compared to those of lesser educational attainment, college-educated Americans tend to set high achievement goals. Their orientation is generally secular, with fewer reporting that religion is a central feature of their lives. The more a person has been exposed to formal education, the more likely he or she will be informed on issues of national policy. Individuals who are currently students tend to be above average in their desire for social recreation. For instance, they would rather go to a party than stay home. Also, students tend to be relatively permissive on social questions. They are more likely than the average American to favor premarital sex and legalization of marijuana.[35]

You could use generalizations about educational attainment as a basis for speech preparation. Assume you want to give a speech in favor of an agreement by the United States and Russia to abandon nuclear testing. If your audience consisted of people having at least some college education, you might predict that they would be less fearful about change and therefore more open to your plan. One survey indicated that college educated Americans were the most supportive of a test ban agreement. Another showed that 67 percent of college students believe that the United States government is not doing enough to promote disarmament.[36]

Residence

The attitudes and values of Americans vary somewhat according to place of residence. America's suburbs are home to most people who fall into the category of upper middle class achievers. These people are job-oriented and relatively optimistic about the future.[37] Compared to citizens of large cities, small town residents tend to be relatively more trusting of institutions. For instance, in a study of reactions to the Three Mile Island nuclear accident, Gallup reported that 50 percent of those living in communities of fewer than 2500 inhabitants believed that the Three Mile Island nuclear accident had been handled as well as possible. In contrast, 36 percent of those in cities of at least one million population held this opinion.[38]

Dividing the country into geographic regions also supplies useful information about audiences. The Northeast coast, the upper Midwest, and the Pacific coast regions contain the highest percentages of people who are socially conscious.[39] These individuals are more worried than other groups about such problems as pollution. Socially conscious Americans want to see more government money going to domestic social programs and are more skeptical about the military budget. Persons of strong social consciousness are also relatively more accepting than other groups of recent

Beliefs, attitudes, and values may vary due to sex, age, and education.

changes in family life and sexual freedom.[40] In contrast to the coast areas, the South is an area where relatively more people report that religion is important in their daily lives. Furthermore, people in the South are more likely than others to support traditional values on sex and family life.[41]

Using place of residence as a demographic predictor of attitudes, assume that you want to give a speech on cutting the federal budget. If your audience consisted of Californians, you might reason that your listeners consisted of people relatively high in social consciousness. You might predict that this type of audience would be relatively more supportive of cutting military spending than social security. This prediction would be consistent with actual survey data showing that Westerners are more likely than other groups to believe that military spending is too high.[42]

Occupation and income

Knowing the occupational status of listeners gives clues about their views of life. Because business and professional persons are managers or are self-employed, they tend to have relatively high initiative, drive, and optimism. Professionals are more likely than others to value accomplishment and to believe in personal responsibility. These achievers have relatively high incomes and a greater knowledge of social issues. Professionals who have attained the greatest income, however, tend to exhibit less social consciousness than those of middle income.[43]

In contrast to the professionals, skilled laborers and clerical workers tend to have relatively low employment satisfaction but are optimistic for improved income and jobs. Persons whose employment prospects are unstable or marginal have experienced tough financial burdens. They tend to express resentment about their situation, and they are less optimistic about the future.[44] Persons of low income report less satisfaction with life.[45] When ranking important values, they tend to put more store in religion and in being helpful to others.[46] Furthermore, they describe themselves as more traditional and conventional in life-style.[47] The attitudes and values of college students are influenced not only by their own incomes but also by their parents' income level.[48]

The demographic factors of occupation and income are obviously relevant to speeches given on the subject of the United States economy. You might expect listeners holding managerial positions to support current economic policy since they have relatively few worries about employment and income. In contrast, you might predict that an audience consisting of low income workers would be more favorable to discarding current economic policy. Survey findings support these generalizations. In 1987, 62 percent of persons with incomes greater than $40,000 approved of the administration's economic policies. In contrast, 65 percent of those earning less than $15,000 expressed disapproval of national economic policy.[49]

Box 5.3

How to Tell It to the Marines

President Reagan, facing an increasingly hostile Congress, took his case for a continued military buildup yesterday to an enthusiastic audience of 3,700 Marine recruits, who roared their approval of his program. . . .

"To all of those who say we must always cut defense first, that America can't afford a strong military, I have just one thing to say: Tell it to the Marines."

Source: *Courier-Journal* (Louisville), 5 June 1986, A6.

Race

Census data show that America is becoming a more racially diverse place to live as a result of immigration and the relatively higher birth rate for minorities. Blacks are concentrated in the South (18.6 percent of the population in the 1980 census) and are relatively less represented in the West (5.2 percent). Hispanic Americans are most often found in the population of the West (14.5 percent) and least likely to live in the North Central regions of the United States (2.2 percent of the population there). Americans of oriental descent are most often found in the Pacific coast states.[50]

The economic situation of minorities seems to be the most significant factor in causing minority attitudes to differ from those of whites. Many attitudinal differences between whites and minorities disappear when the groups are matched for education and income. African American and Hispanic Americans, in particular, are less often found in managerial positions and in high-paying professions, and they tend to express less satisfaction with social conditions and less trust of institutional leaders.[51]

The demographic characteristic of race can be useful for audience analysis, especially if you have no other information on the income level of your audience. If you were speaking on a topic related to economic policy, you might expect that blacks and Hispanics would be less approving of the government's economic policies. Hence, minority members of the audience might be more open to appeals for new economic policies. Survey data support this generalization. In 1987, 52 percent of whites generally approved of the Reagan administration's economic policies, versus 23 percent for all nonwhites and 14 percent for blacks in particular.[52]

Religion

Knowing the religious background of listeners probably is less useful to public speakers than several of the other demographic indicators already discussed. However, members of different religious groups do differ sometimes in opinion and outlook. For instance, members of mainline Protestant denominations often take more liberal social positions than do Catholics and fundamentalist Protestants.[53] In addition, surveys show some noticeable (though usually small) differences in the rankings given to certain value concepts by various religious groups.[54] Specifically, Baptists place relatively greater value on religious salvation than do Catholics, Jews, other Protestants, and nonbelievers. Compared to those who claim a religious affiliation, nonbelievers tend to place relatively greater importance on freedom, equality, being imaginative, and being self-controlled. Jews tend to ascribe relatively more importance than other groups to wisdom, inner harmony, and being logical—and less importance to freedom. Baptists and Catholics, compared to the others, agree in giving a lower ranking to the value of broadmindedness. Catholics tend to rank the value of national security higher than do other groups.

Religious demography allows only very general and very tentative insights into your audiences. Nevertheless, if you were speaking on the subject of abortion, you might rely on the generalization that the more conservative religious groups are less supportive of abortion on demand. A Gallup survey supports this prediction by showing that 25 percent of Catholics versus 17 percent of Protestants (a mixture of all denominations) believed that abortion should be banned under all circumstances.[55]

Demographic analysis has been a part of speechmaking since the time of the ancient Greeks. Modern surveys reinforce the idea that population groups can differ in beliefs, attitudes, and values. The great utility of demographic data is that you often know beforehand the characteristics of your audience. However, modern-day America is a far more complicated society than the city-state of Athens in which Aristotle derived his demography. Today, we must temper demographic analysis with a constant effort to avoid offensive or patronizing stereotypes. Do not engage in a fruitless search for settled and absolute differences between social groups. Rather, like Aristotle, cultivate your powers of observation as you grow in rhetorical competence.

The Speech Situation

Every speech takes place in a particular situation of time and place. Looking at the environment of your speech can supplement your analysis of demographic characteristics.

Time

Time can influence reception of your speech. First, consider the general influence of the clock and calendar. In speeches given for an early morning public speaking course, you may expect a higher percentage of distractions resulting from latecomers. On the other hand, people tend to be a bit sleepy after lunch. The classroom audience during the evening will be particularly unappreciative of speeches that run too long. Research as well as experience shows that time-of-day can affect listening comprehension.[56]

A particular time on the calendar can have special importance for listeners. Try to include reference to any significant date, local holiday, or anniversary. Speaking in favor of secession from the Union to an audience in Dadeville, Alabama, William L. Yancey took out his pocket watch, looked at it, and said: "By this time South Carolina has seceded from the Union." Yancey's timely remark touched off explosive applause.[57]

A second factor of time—the schedule—can be particularly useful for audience analysis when you are speaking outside the classroom setting. Will others be speaking? If you are the seventh speaker on the program, expect to shorten your remarks to compensate for others who have exceeded their allotted time. If yours is not the only speech, what other topics will the audience hear? What is scheduled for the time immediately after your speech? Avoid the error of one professor I watched, who gave a 45-minute address to students at an awards banquet. The listeners resented this long-winded talk because they knew the speech only delayed announcement of contest results. Also try to learn what nonspeech events are planned—music, refreshments, a question-and-answer session? Also keep in mind that alcohol consumption will reduce the persuasive impact of your speech.[58]

Finally, on the matter of schedule, discover the group norms that apply to a meeting. Are you speaking at the regular meeting of an established group? If your listeners belong to a homogeneous group, you will have an easier time planning the speech with their beliefs and attitudes in mind. If you are speaking during a regular meeting of a group, is attendance mandatory? What do listeners usually expect to happen at the meeting? Has the meeting and its agenda been circulated in advance? Should you expect any part of the audience to be particularly favorable or unfavorable to your message? Finally, is it common for listeners to respond outwardly to remarks? Research shows that when part of the audience demonstrates approval with smiles and head nods, the rest of the group becomes more positive. In contrast, overt negative reactions, such as frowns and inattentiveness, do not seem to reduce the general favorability of listeners to a speaker and speech.[59]

Place

In addition to time, consider the physical setting of your classroom. If just a few people are spread out in a large room, you will find it more difficult to create the feeling that you are communicating directly to them. Some classrooms suffer from distracting ventilation or street noise that can interrupt your train of thought.

For speeches given outside speech class, factors of place may vary considerably. Investigate distractions that may result from the particular indoor or outdoor location that is planned. Most speeches are delivered indoors, so what is the physical layout of the room? Is the speech to be delivered from a raised platform? Will you have use of a podium? How are conditions for use of visual aids? Is there a microphone?

Matters of place were significant during the first Kennedy-Nixon debate of 1960. This debate took place in a television studio in which the backdrop was painted gray. Kennedy's dark suit stood out well, whereas Nixon's gray suit caused him to fade more into the background. The effects of place tend to be contributory, rather than decisive, in matters of informative and persuasive speaking.[60] This was small consolation to Nixon's advisers, who fumed at the disadvantage their man faced in the studio setting.

Be sure to pay attention to every detail that may give you an advantage or put you in an uncomfortable position. Check in advance to see if sound equipment works. If distracting noises erupt during your speech, quickly ask someone to close a window or door.

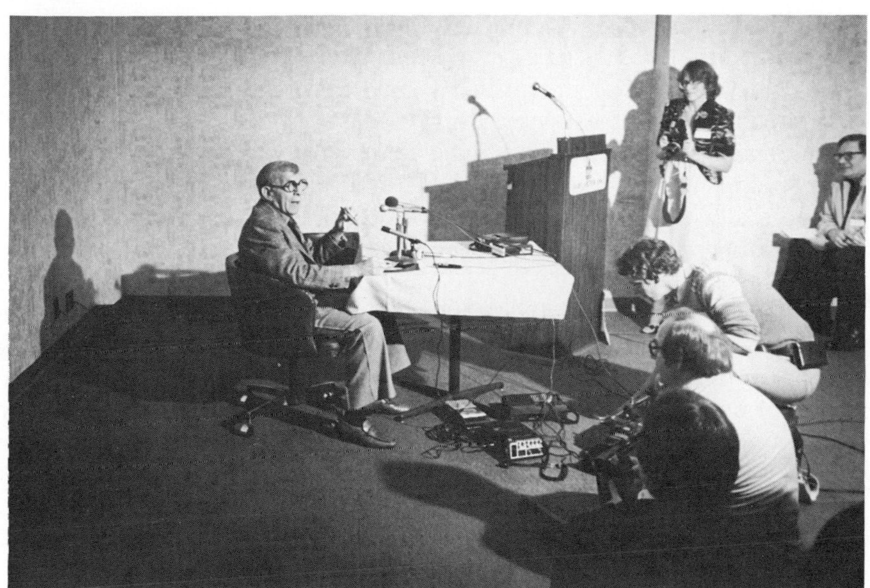

The place in which a speech is given influences the speaker's style and delivery.

Box 5.4

Place Can Be Vital for Your Topic

Governor Michael Dukakis came here [to Moog Automotive, Wellston, Missouri] yesterday to bemoan the rise of foreign investment in the United States. . . .

However, the candidate and at least some of his top aides were unaware that the site of his fiery speech, an automotive parts plant in this community near St. Louis, is owned by a foreign company.

Source: *San Francisco Chronicle,* 8 October 1988, A1.

Questionnaires

Neither advertiser nor national political manager would consider beginning a campaign without opinion poll data to give direct evidence of the public mind. For instance, when MCI Corporation decided to challenge the Bell System's virtual monopoly on long distance phone calls, MCI's lawyers hired opinion pollsters to learn the public image of American Telephone and Telegraph. Results of the polls showed that, despite the Bell System's long program of advertising, Americans were receptive to challengers of Ma Bell.[61]

Individual speakers do not have available the kind of opinion polling conducted by large institutions and major political figures. However, it is sometimes possible—and always desirable—for speakers to use questionnaires in advance of a speech. Every semester, a few students in my public speaking class accept the challenge to circulate a short questionnaire before class begins. The principle is the same for speeches given later in the so-called real world. For instance, the president of an organization might distribute and return to you questionnaires completed by members of the group.

A student planning to speak on the subject of the death penalty surveyed eighteen of her classmates, using two brief questions. First, she asked, "Should some crimes be punished by the death penalty?" Responses were 17 yes, 1 no, and 0 undecided. Second, she listed a number of crimes, asking whether capital punishment was appropriate for each. Of the eighteen students, sixteen responded that the death penalty was appropriate for premeditated murder. Seven accepted the death penalty as warranted for rape of a child, five for rape of an adult, and three each for unpremeditated murder and manslaughter. With these data, the student did not have to rely solely on hunches and predictions. She had direct information on several key ideas about the death penalty.

In analyzing your audience with a questionnaire, the most important tips are *simplicity* and *brevity.* Don't ask ten or twenty questions—narrow your list to three. Remember that your objective is to get a few specific insights into your listeners, not to collect and store census data for future generations. Anything that takes more than a minute to complete will be impractical for use in your speech class.

The needs of most public speakers will be met by a questionnaire containing three elements: (1) demographic questions, (2) awareness-oriented questions, and (3) attitude-oriented questions. If your audience is larger than twenty, it may help to have respondents list one or two key demographic characteristics, such as sex, age, or place of residence. You can then tabulate responses to see whether different demographic groups hold different views. A second type of question taps the awareness of respondents to the issues you will be raising. The Gallup organization often begins its surveys with questions probing whether an individual has heard or read about some event, person, or situation. If you were planning to speak on United States policy toward Central America, you could ask respondents to list three things they know about conditions there.

Finally, your questionnaire will include probes about the attitudes and values of listeners. What you need are a few brief questions that solicit important information and that do not tip your hand by revealing your own viewpoint. Alternatives for writing attitude questions include:

1. Open-ended question: What is your opinion about the space shuttle program?

2. List of response choices: Cigarette smoking is harmful to the health of nonsmokers in the vicinity (circle one): strongly agree; agree; no opinion; disagree; strongly disagree.
3. List of open-ended responses: What in your opinion are the most important and least important reasons for purchasing a new automobile?

Most Important	Least Important

Do not pass up the opportunity to use the questionnaire method. Take audience analysis seriously by using the questionnaire method for your next speech.

Learning about your audience is crucial if you are to win interest, attention, and support. Using demographic analysis, examining the speech situation, and using short questionnaires are proven methods for finding out about listeners.

Be sure that your audience analysis does not stop with learning how listeners respond to the ideas you will be presenting. Also consider how they evaluate *you*.

Credibility Considerations

Aristotle observed that credibility is established when a speaker's actions during the address show him or her to have good character, good sense, and trustworthy motives. Modern research has added details on how advance reputation figures in making a speaker believable.[62] Findings about credibility suggest that self-scrutiny can be an effective tool for audience analysis. Self-analysis of your own credibility calls for evaluation both of your *reputation* and your ability to *perform well* during the speech. In finding ways to boost your credibility, you should consider how you will fare according to (1) certain more or less universal factors of credibility and (2) situational factors of credibility.

Universal Factors of Credibility

Since the time of classical Greece, scholars of rhetoric have searched for reliable keys to what makes a speaker believable. Observing speakers in the agora, or market place, of ancient Athens, Aristotle identified three components of believability that seemed applicable to every situation of public speaking. Aristotle noted that audiences looked for signs that a speaker (1) exhibited good *moral character,* (2) showed *good sense* (competence) in discussing the subject, and (3) exhibited *trustworthy* motives. Social science researchers have generally confirmed Aristotle's view of credibility, although adding refinements. Statistical findings suggest that today's audiences also evaluate speakers according to two additional factors. First, is the speaker *dynamic* (that is, aggressive and energetic) instead of tired and meek? Second, is the speaker *objective* (that is, open-minded) instead of dogmatic?[63]

Your audience will be evaluating you on the basis of your apparent character, competence, good motives, dynamism, and objectivity. The ideal speaker would shine in regard to all universal factors of credibility. However, it is more often true that you will be strong in some areas and weak in others. Prepare your speeches to stress at least one, if not more, of the universal dimensions of credibility. For instance, mentioning your personal experience with a topic often boosts your believability by showing your competence. Also, if you have done considerable outside research, explicitly citing your sources can demonstrate competence and objectivity.

In addition to acting upon one or two possible strengths of credibility, be sure to consider what, if any, are your weak points. Gary Hart, Democratic candidate for president, learned during the 1988 presidential campaign that his reputation for extramarital infidelities fatally weakened his credibility. Voters decided that, whatever Hart's experience and ideas, they preferred not to support a candidate whose character had come under question. On the other hand, the career of Thomas Hart Benton of Missouri offers a classic instance of how perceived competence can overcome a flaw in character—in this case, vanity. Benton, one of the giants of the United States Senate before the Civil War, demonstrated an overwhelming competence for the job. His reputation of competence overcame his known tendency to treat his constituents in a condescending manner.[64]

Situational Factors of Credibility

Social science research shows that all factors of credibility are not equally important in every situation. What makes a speaker believable varies according to who is speaking and the topic of the address. In one study of 170 criteria for judging credibility, receivers applied none of the items in all situations.[65]

At least three conditions of a speaking situation influence how an audience rates the believability of a speaker. First, the sex of the speaker and listener may be relevant to judgments of credibility. Early social science research tended to document a general preference, by both males and females, for male sources of information. More recent evidence suggests that this bias toward men may be dissipating. One study found a consistent preference for male sources only on political topics. Researchers also found that women prefer female sources on some topics.[66] Be sure to ask yourself whether anything in your speech topic seems biased toward male or female speakers.

The attitude of listeners is a second situational factor of credibility. People tend to confer more credibility on those with whom they agree than on those who present disagreeable ideas.[67] For instance, polls consistently show that Republicans favor Republican candidates and Democrats give fellow Democrats a disproportionate benefit of the doubt. If you are presenting unpopular ideas, be sure to compensate by boosting your credibility in other ways.

Third, the similarity of speaker and listener can influence whether a speaker comes across as credible. When a decision involves an interpersonal relationship, such as whether to marry or live together, persons may prefer advice from someone similar to themselves. In contrast, when the topic concerns a technical question, such as whether or not to buy a particular used car, people prefer information from a *dis*similar source, one with objectively established expertise.[68] Ask yourself whether your speech topic favors appearing similar to listeners, or whether you will be better served by demonstrating objective expertise.

The idea of similarity and dissimilarity may be observed in political credibility. Voters want a candidate they can look up to, but not one whose life seems too removed from their own world. A West Virginia congressional campaign in 1982 illustrates how similar the ideal candidate should be to his constituents. One candidate accused the other of having graduated from Harvard Law School. Not so, his opponent protested; he held only a bachelor's degree from Harvard! The Harvard man won, showing that West Virginia voters felt confident about an office holder with ties to the elite Massachusetts school—as long as the ties were not too related to professional training.[69]

If you aspire to rhetorical competence, you should take note of how credibility may influence your chances for success as a speaker. First, give some thought to how you yourself measure up against various factors of credibility. One student speaker planning an informative talk on the role of the notary public focused on the credibility factor of competence. She planned to mention her eight years service as a notary to benefit from the credibility effect. A second way to use credibility as a tool in preparing the speech is to estimate the extent to which listeners will find your outside sources of information to be believable. The authorities, statistics, and examples you cite have the potential to strengthen the ideas you present—provided listeners hold your sources as credible. The subject of credible evidence in speechmaking is discussed in chapter 7.

This chapter has taken us from the general to the specific on the matter of analyzing audiences. When you speak, you face listeners who interpret your remarks according to an existing image system consisting of beliefs, attitudes, and values. Existing images make listeners selective in exposure to, attention to, interpretation of, and recall of information. To respond to the audience's existing image, you should consider the demographic background of listeners as well as the physical environment of the speech. The questionnaire method offers you the most direct look into the world of listeners. Audience analysis is a labor with immediate benefits. When you know what listeners think and expect, you will find it easier to construct the speech to win the fairest possible hearing for your ideas.

Concepts for Review

Can you summarize the meaning of these terms or expressions? How does each relate to speechmaking?

active audience
audience analysis
image system
beliefs
verifiable beliefs
primitive beliefs
attitudes
values
terminal values
instrumental values
values and motivation
shared public image
selective exposure
selective attention
selective interpretation
selective recall
demographics
stereotypes
age and image
sex and image
education and image
residence and image
occupation, income, and image
race and image
religion and image
time and the audience
place and the audience
preparing a questionnaire
universal factors of credibility
credibility and situation

Things to Try

1. Consider the audience for your next speech. Make a list of beliefs, attitudes, and values that your listeners probably hold about your topic. Pick two of the most important elements of the audience's image of your subject and identify what response you are making to it.

2. Look through a magazine to find an advertisement that seems interesting. Try to identify the implied audience. In other words, the advertisement is designed to have special appeal for some kinds of people. Is the ad pitched to the young or to the old? To men or women? Review the demographic characteristics discussed in this chapter and use them to describe the target audience for your advertisement.
3. Develop a questionnaire to help reveal how your audience views the topic of your next speech. Restrict your questions to no more than four. Complete the questionnaire yourself to be sure it can be finished in less than one minute. Have students fill out the questionnaire before speech class begins, or have some of your friends who are demographically similar to the actual class audience respond to your questions.
4. Identify one individual whom you find credible and another that you do not consider believable. Review the universal and situational factors of credibility to help you identify what makes the one person believable to you and the other not so. Show your analysis to someone else to see if he or she shares your assessments of credibility.

Endnotes

1. Haynes Johnson, *Courier-Journal* (Louisville), 3 January 1978, A4.
2. Richard Murphy, "Theodore Roosevelt," *A History and Criticism of American Public Address,* ed. M. K. Hochmuth [Nichols] (New York: Russell & Russell, 1955), 339.
3. Herbert Blumer, *Symbolic Interactionism* (Englewood Cliffs, NJ: Prentice-Hall, 1969), 15.
4. Milton Rokeach, *Beliefs, Attitudes, and Values* (San Francisco: Jossey-Bass, 1968).
5. Dominic A. Infante, "Cognitive Structure as a Predictor of Post Speech Attitude and Attitude Change," *Speech Monographs 39* (1972): 55–61.
6. Kenneth E. Boulding, *The Image* (Ann Arbor: University of Michigan Press, 1956), 14.
7. Paul J. Deutschmann, "Viewing, Conversation, and Voting Intentions," in *The Great Debates: Kennedy vs. Nixon, 1960,* ed. Sidney Kraus (Bloomington, IN: Indiana University Press, 1977), 236, and David L. Paletz, et al., "Selective Exposure: The Potential Boomerang Effect," *Journal of Communication 22* (1972): 48–53.

8. Charles K. Atkin, "How Imbalanced Campaign Coverage Affects Audience Exposure Patterns," *Journalism Quarterly 48* (1971): 235–244.
9. Quoted in William J. Bryan, *The First Battle* (Chicago: W. B. Conkey, 1896), 206.
10. David O. Sears and Steven H. Chaffee, "Uses and Effects of the 1976 Debates: An Overview of Empirical Studies," in *The Great Debates: Carter vs. Ford, 1976,* ed. Sidney Kraus (Bloomington, IN: Indiana University Press, 1979), 237, and David A. Leuthold and David C. Valentine, "How Reagan 'Won' The Cleveland Debate: Audience Predispositions and Presidential Debate 'Winners,' " *Speaker and Gavel 18,* No. 2 (1981): 63.
11. Kurt Lang and Gladys E. Lang, "Reactions of Viewers," in *Kennedy vs. Nixon,* ed. Kraus, 327.
12. Hans Sebald, "Limitations of Communication," *Journal of Communication 12* (1962): 142–149.
13. Lewis Donohew, "Decoder Behavior in Incongruent Political Material: A Pilot Study," *Journal of Communication 16* (1966): 133–142.
14. Theodore Clevenger, Jr., *Audience Analysis* (Indianapolis: Bobbs-Merrill, 1966), 56.
15. Aristotle, *Rhetoric,* II. 12–13. 1388b–1390a.
16. *The Gallup Report* (248), May 1986, 17.
17. See Arnold Mitchell, *The Nine American Lifestyles* (New York: Macmillan, 1983).
18. *Ibid.*
19. *The Gallup Report* (249), June 1986, 15.
20. *Ibid., 23.*
21. Mitchell, *Lifestyles.*
22. Milton Rokeach, *The Nature of Human Values* (New York: Free Press, 1973), 74–77.
23. *The Gallup Report* (251), August 1986, 7.
24. *Gallup Report 249,* 15.
25. *Ibid.*, 23.
26. Rokeach, *Human Values,* 57–59.
27. *The Gallup Report* (259), April 1987, 14.
28. Mitchell, *Lifestyles.*
29. Rokeach, *Human Values, 57–59.*
30. Mitchell, *Lifestyles.*
31. See *Chronicle of Higher Education,* 3 January 1990, A28 and *Chronicle of Higher Education Almanac,* 6 September 1989, 17.
32. *The Gallup Report* (258), March 1987, 5.
33. Mitchell, *Lifestyles.*
34. *Ibid.*
35. *Ibid.*
36. *Gallup Report 248,* 21; and *Chronicle of Higher Education,* 11 January 1989, A34.

37. Mitchell, *Lifestyles.*
38. George H. Gallup, *The Gallup Poll: Public Opinion 1979* (Wilmington, DE: Scholarly Resources, 1980), 14–15.
39. Mitchell, *Lifestyles.*
40. *Ibid.*
41. *Gallup Report 249,* 23; *Gallup Report 259,* 14.
42. *The Gallup Report* (260), May 1987, 3.
43. Mitchell, *Lifestyles.*
44. *Ibid.*
45. *Gallup Report 249,* 15.
46. Rokeach, *Human Values, 60–61.*
47. *Gallup Report 249,* 23.
48. *Chronicle of Higher Education,* 11 January 1989, A33.
49. *The Gallup Report* (261), June 1987, 24.
50. Jamshid A. Momeni, *Demography of Racial and Ethnic Minorities in the United States* (Westport, CT: Greenwood, 1984), 23.
51. *Gallup Report 249,* 15.
52. *Gallup Report 261,* 24.
53. Robert N. Bellah, et al., *Habits of the Heart* (New York: Harper and Row, 1985), 227–249.
54. Rokeach, *Human Values,* 82–83, 406–419.
55. Gallup, *Gallup Poll,* 14–15.
56. Charles R. Petrie, Jr., "Informative Speaking: A Summary and Bibliography of Related Research," *Speech Monographs 30* (1963): 85.
57. Rexford S. Mitchell, "William L. Yancey," *A History and Criticism of American Public Address,* ed. W. N. Brigance (2 vols.; New York: Russell & Russell, 1943), 2: 748.
58. Robert N. Bostrom and Noel D. White, "Does Drinking Reduce Resistance?" *Journal of Communication 29,* No. 3 (1979): 73–80.
59. Cal Hylton, "Intra-Audience Effects: Observable Audience Response," *Journal of Communication 21* (1971): 253–265.
60. Petrie, "Informative Speaking," 85; cf. Albert L. Furbay, "The Influence of Scattered Versus Compact Seating on Audience Response," *Speech Monographs 32* (1965): 144–148, and Gordon L. Thomas and David C. Ralph, "A Study of the Effect of Audience Proximity on Persuasion," *Speech Monographs 26* (1959): 300–307.
61. *Newsweek,* 9 March 1981, 84.
62. Aristotle, *Rhetoric,* I. 2. 1356a, II. 1. 1378a, and Carl I. Hovland, Irving L. Janis, and Harold H. Kelley, *Communication and Persuasion* (New Haven, CT: Yale University Press, 1953).
63. Gerald R. Miller and Murray A. Hewgill, "The Effect of Variations in Nonfluency on Audience Ratings of Source Credibility," *Quarterly Journal of Speech 50* (1964): 36–44, and Jack L. Whitehead, Jr., "Factors of Source Credibility," *Quarterly Journal of Speech 54* (1968): 59–63.

64. Norman W. Mattis, "Thomas Hart Benton," *A History and Criticism of American Public Address,* ed. M. K. Hochmuth [Nichols] (New York: Russell & Russell, 1955): 82, 84–86.

65. Gary Cronkhite and Jo Liska, "A Critique of Factor Analytic Approaches to the Study of Credibility," *Communication Monographs 43* (1976): 94; Jo Liska, "Situational and Topical Variations in Credibility Criteria," *Communication Monographs 45* (1978): 85–92; Ronald F. Applbaum and Karl W. E. Anatol, "The Factor Structure of Source Credibility as a Function of the Speaking Situation," *Speech Monographs 39* (1972): 216–222.

66. Virginia P. Richmond and James C. McCroskey, "Whose Opinion Do You Trust?" *Journal of Communication 23,* No. 3 (1975): 42–50.

67. Blaine Goss and Lee Williams, "The Effects of Equivocation on Perceived Source Credibility," *Central States Speech Journal 24* (1973): 162–167.

68. Stephen W. King, "Reconstructing the Concept of Source Perceptions: Toward a Paradigm of Source Appropriateness," *Western Speech Communication 40* (1976): 216–225.

69. *Chronicle of Higher Education,* 1 December 1982, 2.

Chapter

6

Investigating the Subject

Outline

The Thesis
- The Unifying Idea
- Connection of Key Concepts
- Stimulation of Research

Topoi and the Discovery of Ideas
- General *Topoi*
- Specific *Topoi*

Methods of Research
- Library Research
- Interviewing for Information
- Other Research Methods

Recording Information

"My recipe of life is curiosity," said the noted actor, critic, and lecturer, Vincent Price.[1] The formula for living recommended by Price makes a good motto for the public speaker. An active curiosity is a wellspring of rhetorical competence. When you possess a thirst for expertise about your subject, you have a positive attitude that powerfully boosts your ability to communicate.

The active curiosity that stands behind good communication skills is exemplified by Willard Wirtz, former United States Secretary of Labor, and personal adviser and speechwriter to Presidents Kennedy and Johnson. I once had occasion to escort Wirtz during a campus appearance. Wirtz was constantly observing—asking questions about students, the faculty, the school, things he saw in town. For Wirtz, observation and inquiry were continual activities. His constant curiosity was a means for gathering ideas to be used later on. Wirtz made quite a good impression on his audiences, partly because of his alert interest in everything that surrounded him. This rhetorical success contrasted markedly with the impact of other celebrity speakers who came to the university. Frequently, the speaker's apparent interest in the campus was centered on collecting the lecture fee. Such uninvolved speakers were satisfied to present canned talks delivered in the manner of a slightly bored tour guide.

Curiosity and interest in the speaking situation are important resources of rhetorical competence, providing a strong motive for thorough preparation. Vincent Price observed of his career as a lecturer that "I establish my integrity through preparation." Even though Price has lectured on theatre and art at more than 450 colleges, he still views each appearance as requiring a commitment to give his best. Between engagements, he is at work reading and adding to his scrapbooks. He gathers material to keep his lectures current and complete.

Chapter 6 is inquiry-oriented, treating skills of analysis and research. Investigative speechmaking allows us to make our thoughts and ideas substantive. In this chapter, we will work through four stages of rhetorical investigation. Beginning with a treatment of how you develop your thesis (main idea), we will look at your options for analyzing your speech topic, conducting research, and recording information.

The Thesis

Have you ever listened to someone talk and then wondered to yourself, "Exactly what was that individual trying to say?" If so, then you are already aware of the importance of having a clear thesis. A *thesis,* expressed in one sentence, is what you want your audience to understand or believe after the speech is over. The thesis sentence capsulizes your main idea; it is a thematic statement that summarizes the essence of what you want to get across. One student speaker expressed the thesis of her planned speech on physical fitness with this clear statement of a main idea: "People should get into shape, now, by a good diet and exercise program." Because she ultimately prepared her speech around this statement, no one had to wonder about the exact point she was trying to make.

Box 6.1

A Thesis Statement That Reassured a Nation

I am certain that my fellow Americans expect that on my induction into the Presidency I will address them with a candor and a decision which the present situation of our Nation impels. This is preeminently the time to speak the truth, the whole truth, frankly and boldly. Nor need we shrink from honestly facing conditions in our country today. This great Nation will endure as it has endured, will revive and will prosper. So, first of all, let me assert my firm belief *that the only thing we have to fear is fear itself—nameless, unreasoning, unjustified terror which paralyzes needed efforts to convert retreat into advance.* (italics added)

Source: Inaugural Address, Franklin D. Roosevelt, 4 March 1933, *Inaugural Addresses of the Presidents of the United States,* 82nd Cong., 2nd Session, House Document No. 540, 1952, 225.

A thesis serves three important functions in speechmaking. First, the thesis narrows the topic by specifying a unifying idea for the speech. Second, the thesis connects the key concepts of the speech. Third, the thesis acts as a stimulus for research.

The Unifying Idea

Most speakers begin work on a fairly broad topic such as physical fitness, capital punishment, or Agent Orange. If you followed the directions for writing a statement of specific purpose (chapter 4), you have begun the process of narrowing your subject. What you need now is to transform your purpose into a statement that clearly expresses and relates important details of your subject.

A well-worded thesis can help you overcome the problem of information overload. Your thesis transforms a wide-open idea such as "physical fitness" into a manageable topic focused on such aspects of health as diet and exercise. The thesis sets up boundary markers that specify who, what, and where. The idea is to construct a statement that narrows down an open-ended subject into *between two and five major points.*

Consider the case of one student speaker who chose to give a persuasive speech on the broad topic of capital punishment. She prepared a thesis that expressed her main idea that "capital punishment should be enforced to deter future murders and so protect the lives of innocent victims." This thesis statement indicated that her speech would be centered on two main points. First, she would argue that capital punishment deters crime. Second, she would claim the resulting advantage of her plan in protecting society.

When a speech is prepared with a clear thesis in mind, advantages result for audience and speaker. For listeners, the thesis unifies the speech, focusing attention and minimizing confusion. Antonia Brico, one of the first female symphony conductors, was often asked to lecture about her success in what had been an exclusively male profession. Brico herself had heard all too many autobiographical talks that seemed to lack coherence. To keep her audience from missing the point of her lecture, Brico would have listeners recite, in unison, her motto of life, which served as the thesis of her speech: "I will not be deflected from my course." No one exited Brico's lectures wondering what point she wanted to make.

Focusing a speech on a coherent, unified subject also brings benefits for the speaker. Because it aids listeners in comprehending information and arguments, a thesis helps overcome the problem of selective interpretation. Furthermore, putting our points together in a clearly unified theme can help in persuasion. The benefits of organizing speeches around a clear thesis was underscored in a study of the effective and ineffective campaign addresses of Governor Adlai E. Stevenson in his 1956 campaign for the presidency. A speech critic, Russel Windes, asked academic scholars, reporters, and political workers to identify those of Stevenson's campaign speeches that were most and least effective.[2] Windes then carefully compared the two sets of speeches. He found that each of Stevenson's effective speeches was a single-issue address. Stevenson organized his single-issue speeches around one weak point of the Eisenhower administration or a singular advantage in Stevenson's campaign platform. In contrast, five out of Stevenson's six ineffective speeches were addresses in which he jumped from one problem to another.

The unifying effect of a thesis serves ethical as well as practical purposes. Ethical speechmaking requires that we make clear exactly what position we are taking on a subject. The chief complaint of Socrates about the orators of his day was that they spoke on the basis of any number of ill-defined and sometimes inconsistent premises. Socrates contended that the lack of coherent talking helped transform discussion into a disorganized personal attack.[3] We can avoid a free-for-all of this kind when we organize our remarks around a clearly worded statement that expresses our position.

Connection of Key Concepts

Every subject of a speech involves potentially innumerable ideas and terms. For instance, the topic of Agent Orange calls our attention to the composition and toxicity of this chemical as well as facts of its production, sale, and use. Agent Orange further carries us to the Vietnam War, in which this defoliant was employed on a vast scale. Discussions of Agent Orange inevitably bring up the question of whether the chemical has ruined the health of Vietnam veterans and their children.

Against an inescapable backdrop of complexity, a thesis acts to link ideas and terms, putting otherwise miscellaneous material into a coherent whole. Because a thesis shows the relationship of concepts, it is identical with the main idea abstract described in chapter 3, except that a thesis should be written out as *one* sentence. If you write a thesis statement of this kind, it will assist you in several ways to pull together the ideas of your speech.

A thesis can show how concepts are related on the basis of *cause.* An example of a thesis oriented to causality is the following one prepared by a student of public speaking: "Pregnant women should avoid alcohol, tobacco, and caffeine, for these substances have been found to cause birth defects."

A thesis may connect ideas by *evaluating* them. A student once prepared an interesting informative talk centered on the idea that "American automobiles of the 1950s oftentimes were wastefully and outrageously styled."

Sometimes a speaker finds it useful to prepare a thesis that makes a *prediction* about concepts. One student speaker chose to tie together her remarks around the future of infant adoption. She told the class that "because of the increases in the numbers of unwed mothers who keep their babies, infant adoption is likely to decline significantly as an option for childless couples."

A thesis may function by *interpreting.* The kind of thesis that connects ideas through interpretation is exemplified by a student's assertion about illegal immigration. The student told the class that "illegal entry of aliens into the United States is not so great a social and economic problem as many commentators have suggested."

Stimulation of Research

You will find your thesis evolving as you analyze and research your subject, and as you arrange your ideas. Your final thesis statement may differ considerably from your earliest efforts to express your main idea. However, beginning statements of the thesis serve as a useful stimulus in speech preparation. Setting out a thesis encourages your attitude of curiosity, making the subject come alive. Furthermore, the thesis helps set specific goals for research.

Scientific research begins with a *hypothesis,* that is, with a statement of what the scientist believes will happen when certain experimental conditions are created. In like manner, the thesis serves as the research focus for the public speaker. Just as science is the process of testing a hypothesis, rhetorical analysis is the process of testing—and usually refining—the thesis.

The attitude of wanting to test a thesis is central to rhetorical competence, because your thesis marks out your very path of inquiry. John Dewey, the American pragmatist philosopher, observed that any systematic thinking begins with a perception that something is amiss.[4] Typically, we use such terms as problem, concern, issue, or question to express our feelings of puzzlement or difficulty. Lloyd Bitzer, the speech critic, uses the term *exigence* to label the tension associated with work on a thesis. Bitzer describes the exigence as "an imperfection marked by urgency . . . a defect, an obstacle, something wanting to be done, a thing which is other than it should be."[5]

No speaker stands in a vacuum of ideas when beginning work on a topic. Even before you have thought deeply about your subject, and before you have conducted research, you will find yourself favoring certain ideas. This initial presumption in favor of particular concepts—expressed in your thesis—is important because it provides the *motivation for analysis and research.* Advocates in the real world do not usually gather miscellaneous data and only then look for what can be concluded from the material. For instance, in analyzing and researching his speech on Agent Orange, the student speaker, Jack Dodds, began with the strong impression that the United States government had ungratefully ignored Vietnam veterans harmed by Agent Orange.

Although a thesis expresses our existing biases or assumptions about our topic, it inhibits critical thinking only if we begin research and analysis in a closed-minded fashion. True, when people know they must prepare a message, they do tend to become committed to their first impression of a topic.[6] Such a commitment could become an obstacle to speech preparation if we overlooked the attitude of the rhetorically competent speaker, who treats research as *the perfecting of knowledge.* As long as we keep an open mind, we need not fear the inevitable tendency of speakers (and writers) to seek material that supports an original thesis.[7]

In summary, why should you prepare a thesis statement? You will find that the thesis helps give you specific targets for research. The thesis ties together key concepts of your topic. Finally, since your mind inevitably will leap ahead to conclusions, a thesis guides systematic thought by putting your hunches into clear view.

Topoi and the Discovery of Ideas

Once you have developed your thesis, you are ready to probe more deeply into the details of your subject. Since the beginning of the rhetorical tradition in classical Greece, teachers have devised various ways for speakers to discover materials to use in the speech. The most influential of these methods has been the *topoi* system (pronounced TOW-pee), developed by Aristotle.[8] Aristotle based his method of analysis on his observation that a speaker could employ categories of thought to help stimulate ideas about the topic of a speech. Aristotle selected the term *topoi,* a Greek word meaning "places," to express the point that every category represented a region where the speaker could expect to find useful ideas. The *topoi* are a kind of index to useful information—a kind of Yellow Pages for public speakers. Each *topos* (TOW-pus, singular form of the word, *topoi*) shows you a place where you can find promising claims and arguments.

The theory of *topoi* relies on the fact that people store information by categorizing it. To identify ideas about a subject, you need only tap these places in the memory.[9] To see how the *topoi* system works, look at the following roster of categories developed by a student who was preparing to talk on the subject of nutrition. She examined her subject to identify what were some important facets of it—some *topoi.* As you browse through the *topoi* categories she used, consider how each *topos* might have helped the speaker identify specific things to say—specific arguments.

- health benefits
- food groups
- utensils
- methods of preparation
- costs
- seasonings

Each of these terms helped stimulate the speaker's thinking on her subject of nutritious foods. Each *topos* tapped recollections stored in memory. Each item on the list was a label or cue for a whole set of ideas about nutrition. For example, the category of "methods of preparation" caused the student to list such ideas as baking, broiling, deep frying, pan frying, boiling, steaming, peeling, slicing, dicing, and chopping. In this way the *topos* functioned as a collecting point for information.

You will find the *topoi* to be helpful as a first step in research. By causing you to list specific things known or needing to be known, the *topoi* categories effectively link the thesis to library research. In the example above, the *topos* of "methods of preparation" helped the student generate a list of ways to cook food. The student already knew what it meant to boil instead of broil. However, the student was not yet fully familiar with the relative nutritiousness of the various ways to prepare food. The list of methods generated by her *topoi* analysis gave her an agenda for research in books on nutrition.

Some *topoi* are more general than others. Look again at the student's list of six *topoi* given previously. How many of these categories would prove useful for analyzing the subject of nuclear power plants? Surely "food groups" and "seasonings" would be of little help. On the other hand, the *topoi* of "utensils" and "costs" might fit the topic of nuclear power about as well as the subject of nutrition. In fact, another student in the class used the two *topoi* of "cost to consumer" and "cost to producer" in investigating nuclear power. Since the *topos* of cost applies directly to more than one subject, we may term it a general *topos*. In contrast, *topoi* such as "seasonings" or "waste disposal" are useful only in relation to particular subjects.

Box 6.2

Topoi and the Public Speaker

The orator hunts for arguments as a hunter pursues game. Knowing where a particular kind of game (or argument) is to be found, he will hunt for it there, and not in some other place or places.

Source: Lane Cooper, trans., *The Rhetoric of Aristotle* (New York: Appleton-Century-Crofts, 1932), 155.

To best understand how the *topoi* method aids in speechmaking, we must distinguish between two levels of *topoi*: (1) the general (universal) *topoi* and (2) the particular (specific) *topoi*. Both kinds of *topoi* help you take stock of what you already know of your speech subject and what you need to know. By assessing your existing level of knowledge, you are in a better position to discover facts, interpretations, quotations, and visual materials of use in illustrating or proving your thesis.

General *Topoi*

Aristotle noticed that certain categories of analysis could serve the speaker no matter what the type of speech or subject of discussion.[10] One of the general *topoi* that he presented to his students was that of "consequences." Aristotle believed that a speaker might develop arguments by identifying what were the possible outcomes of an act. To take a modern example, the late Woody Hayes, long-time Ohio State University football coach, used to argue that only three things could happen when a football was thrown for a pass—and two of them were bad.

Perhaps the most familiar list of standard *topoi* is the journalists' categories of who, what, when, where, and how. Applied to an event, these categories call to mind a comprehensive range of points that might make up a good news report. With these categories in mind, the journalist would not fail to include in the story everything needing to be printed. To see how using general *topoi* can help in speech analysis, let's see how three such systems could help in analyzing particular speech subjects. We turn to: (1) the journalistic *topoi,* (2) a modern system developed by John Wilson and Carroll Arnold, two speech educators, and (3) the system of stock issues widely used in academic debating.

Journalistic topoi

The *topoi* of who, what, when, where, and how are components of basic newswriting. Each of these *topoi* points to elements of a story that may be crucial. The journalistic *topoi* also help the speaker ferret out ideas for every kind of speech. Whether your purpose is informative, persuasive, inspirational, or entertainment-oriented, the who-what-when questions can help.

A student speaker, preparing an informative talk on the age of the dinosaurs, used the journalist's *topoi* to draw out material about how dinosaurs became extinct.

When: When did dinosaurs become extinct? Check the fossil record.
What: What happened to bring about an end to the dinosaur? Possibly a collision of a giant asteroid with the surface of the Earth.
How: When the asteroid hits the Earth, it causes a colossal volcanic eruption, throwing up enough dust to block out the Sun's rays completely.
Where: Possibly anywhere on the face of the Earth. More probably in the ocean on a mid-ocean ridge, where the continental plates are pulling apart.

The Wilson-Arnold topoi

Wilson and Arnold have attempted to develop a comprehensive system of *topoi* for modern speakers. Like the journalist's *topoi,* Wilson and Arnold's two-part, sixteen-category system, shown in table 6.1, can be used for all types of speeches.

Let's see how the Wilson-Arnold categories would apply to an actual speech topic. Pick a subject on which you might give an informative or persuasive speech. Take a blank sheet of paper (or crank up your word processor), and begin by writing down the first category. Now, write a word or phrase to describe each idea that the category brings to mind about your subject. Say that the topic of your speech was advertising in the United States. Let's look at where the *topos* of "form" (item A.6) might lead you.

Table 6.1 The Wilson and Arnold system of *topoi*

A. Attributes commonly discussed

1. *Existence* or nonexistence of things
2. *Degree* or quantity of things, forces, etc.
3. *Spatial* attributes, including adjacency, distribution, place
4. Attributes of *time*
5. *Motion* or activity
6. *Form,* either physical or abstract
7. *Substance*: physical, abstract, psychophysical
8. *Capacity to change,* including predictability
9. *Potency*: power or energy, including capacity to further or hinder anything
10. *Desirability* in terms of rewards or punishments
11. *Feasibility*: workability or practicability

B. Basic relationships commonly asserted or argued

1. *Causality*: the relation of causes to effects, effects to causes, effects to effects, adequacy of causes, etc.
2. *Correlation*: coexistence or coordination of things, forces, etc.
3. *Genus-species* relationships
4. *Similarity* or dissimilarity
5. *Possibility* or impossibility

Source: John F. Wilson and Carroll C. Arnold, *Public Speaking as a Liberal Art,* 4th ed. (Boston: Allyn and Bacon, 1978), 94–95.

In what forms can we find advertisements? Ads can be divided according to those on television, on radio, in magazines. Ads may be examined according to their reliance on words, pictures, jingles, songs, or celebrity testimonials.

Once you have drawn out ideas with the single *topos* of "form," you can use these results as *topoi* for further and deeper analysis. One of the ideas stimulated by the category of "form" was "celebrity testimonials." Using this idea as another *topos,* you might write down the further ideas of particular kinds of testimonials: those by athletes, film stars, and television stars. Clearly, you could continue to work with the category of form until you ran out of paper or patience. And you would have fifteen categories remaining to give more ideas about the subject of advertising.

Would it really pay off for you to use the Wilson-Arnold system in your speech preparation? Yes. Research shows that students using the Wilson-Arnold system are able to identify between 10 and 17 percent more ideas about a speech subject than students using no system.[11] In a related study, speech researchers analyzed the *quality* of ideas generated by students using the Wilson-Arnold *topoi* to find solutions to an assigned problem. Results indicated that students employing the Wilson-Arnold system produced solutions of significantly higher quality than those students using no *topoi* categories.[12]

Stock issues topoi

The *topoi* of stock issues are designed for speakers who want to argue in favor of changes in public policy. The system is widely used in academic debating and is especially suited for persuasive speeches. The stock issues are six questions that might be asked about a new policy: (1) What *problem* calls for a change? (2) Is the problem so *significant* that it demands action? (3) To what extent is the problem an *inherent* part of present conditions? In other words, is the problem so closely tied to present conditions that it cannot be solved without completely changing present policy? (4) Will a new policy actually *solve the problem*? (5) Is the new policy *workable*? (6) Is the new policy free of serious *disadvantages*?

Consider how six lines of stock issues analysis might help a speaker analyze the policy of banning advertisements on television programs aimed at children.

Problem: How many children watch television? What kinds of advertisements are placed on children's television programs? Is it clear when the program ends and a commercial begins—or do they blend together? Is it fair to advertise to children who may not be able to resist advertising? Is it possible the ads perform a service by informing children about products? What is the nutritional value of food advertised on children's programs?

Significance: What evidence shows that advertising significantly harms children? Can children screen out ads? Do they quickly forget ads? Does the advertising play on their lack of sophistication? Could there be a psychological harm to children? Does advertising make children cynical? Is it appropriate for children of poor families to be exposed to ads for products their parents cannot afford to buy?

Inherency: What action is now being taken in regard to advertising on children's television? What are the laws? What policies do the networks have? Is there more or less advertising on kids' shows compared to programs prepared for adults? Why is the group, Action for Children's Television, opposed to advertising on kids' shows? Is it necessary to have advertising to pay for programming?

Solve the problem: Will a policy of banning the ads on children's television truly solve a problem? Wouldn't kids still be exposed to ads on adult programs? How can we measure the psychological benefits of eliminating the ads?

Workability: What details are involved in a plan to eliminate ads on children's television programs? Would the ban on ads apply only to direct selling pitches? Might advertisers still include simple announcements that a show was sponsored by a given product? What about television cartoon characters, such as Transformers, which are also available as toys in stores?

Disadvantages: Would the ban on advertising result in less free programming for children on the commercial networks? Would the ban lessen the chances for advertisers to tout products necessary for the well-being of children? Would the ban eliminate desirable children's products by interrupting the mass marketing of these items?

Each of the six stock issues categories calls our attention to a whole range of important questions. The stock issues *topoi* keep us from overlooking important aspects of a subject. They help us avoid becoming too quickly committed to a particular policy or plan.

Social science research shows the benefits of applying the stock issues to questions of policy. In one study, researchers trained students in a stock issues format similar to that given above. Other students in the experiment received only general instruction in how to analyze a subject. When students were later asked to list as many arguments as they could think of that opposed legalization of wiretapping, the students trained with the stock issues *topoi* identified significantly more arguments. A second study confirmed these results.[13]

Some people complain that a dictionary is no help in spelling because you can't find a word until you guess how it is spelled. Since the same limitation holds for library work, the *topoi* system helps by spelling out what you need to find. The result is that you save valuable time and minimize chances that you will gather irrelevant material. Research findings show that using a system of *topoi* gives you a head start over those who skip this beginning step of analysis and research. The *topoi* will start you along the process of inquiry with more and better ideas about your subject.

Specific *Topoi*

The journalistic, Wilson-Arnold, and stock issues *topoi* are general, prepared categories for analysis. An alternate way to use *topoi* is for you to prepare your own personal set of categories. We encountered this approach earlier in the case of the student who constructed six useful *topoi* for a speech on nutrition: health benefits, food groups, utensils, methods of preparation, costs, and seasonings.

There are two advantages to preparing specific *topoi*. First, each subject that you speak about has its own particular terminology. To experience this for yourself, listen to conversations going on around you in a crowded cafeteria or restaurant. To the right of you, two people may be discussing computers. On your left, a group might be talking about body building. In each case, you will find that one group is using terms and expressions different from the other. Just as you use the particular vocabulary of a subject when you chat about it, you likewise turn to special terms and expressions when you prepare a specific *topoi* list.

Stephen Toulmin, the philosopher, notes that different subjects of controversy call for different modes of analysis and argument.[14] The specific *topoi* help you respond to the tendency of each field to have its own ways of reasoning and analysis. Try to develop a special list of *topoi* every time you analyze a new speech topic. Reflect over the particular subject of your speech and identify important words and phrases that promise to call forth useful ideas. For instance, in preparing a speech on the subject of education, you will find that the *topoi* of age, grade, IQ, and methods are of help. More useful for a speech on safe driving would be speed limit, alcohol, and defensive driving.

Used as a supplement to the standard *topoi* systems, self-generated lists of *topoi* can deepen your powers of analysis on a subject. As an example of developing your own system of *topoi* for researching a subject, consider the list prepared by a student for her speech on drunk driving.

- definition of drunk
- blood alcohol count
- implied consent
- statistics
- cost
- arrest
- conviction
- sentence
- physiological effects
- solution
- Students Against Driving Drunk
- legal drinking age
- public awareness
- reputation
- fatalities
- Mothers Against Drunk Drivers
- prosecution
- safe highways

This student's list contains *topoi* that include certain general categories, such as "cost" or "solution" as well as concepts particular to the field of traffic safety. The result is to give her both a broad and a deep look at her subject.

Research findings show that developing your own *topoi* system may be even more beneficial than simply using prepared lists. In one study, researchers asked students to identify items of information about a subject.

Some students developed their own list of *topoi,* whereas others used one of four standard systems of *topoi.* Results showed that students using a self-generated list were able to think of more ideas than those using a standard roster.[15]

In your role of public speaker, you are in the same position as any traveler. You need some idea of where you are going before you set out. By helping you gather and organize your thoughts on a subject, the standard and self-generated *topoi* act as useful springboards for outside research. The standard *topoi* systems offer an ever-ready reservoir of ideas. But speakers who have attained a high level of rhetorical competence often prefer to create their own *topoi* systems. With practice, you too can develop personal *topoi* lists, either by modifying standard ones or by collecting key words that are particularly relevant to your needs.

Methods of Research

Research supplies the material that gives substance to your initial thoughts about a subject. When you aim to be a rhetorically competent speaker, you will follow Aristotle's advice that, "we must know some, if not all, of the facts about the subject on which we are to speak and argue."[16] Thomas Hart Benton, the longtime senator from Missouri, was one speaker who followed Aristotle's dictum. Throughout his thirty-year career in the United States Senate, Benton maintained a position of leadership with his familiar cry of "Give us the facts. What are the facts?"[17]

Facts relevant for your speeches include informative details, examples, statistics, and quotations from prominent authorities. On the subject of capital punishment, for example, the facts would include (1) where this punishment is now in effect, (2) laws and practices of capital punishment, (3) rates of murder in various places employing and not employing capital punishment, and (4) authoritative opinions on the morality and effect of the death penalty.

Research for speechmaking invariably means taking advantage of library resources. Other appropriate sources of information include personal interviews, questionnaires, and participant observation.

Library Research

Few persons are fully aware of the resources available at their libraries. A course in public speaking gives you a good opportunity to learn more about how the library can help you in your college education.

After the *topoi* analysis comes library research.

Getting started

Begin by learning how the major components of your library are organized and where they are located. Probably your library sponsors an orientation booklet or guide. Many university libraries sponsor tours or workshops in library research. Above all, ask questions. The librarians can advise you on their particular facilities, and they will help you find specific items.

Do you already know basically what your library offers? Check yourself against these test questions:

1. How does the library catalog the general collection of books? Most typically, books are listed in a card catalog, although some libraries use microfiche or on-line computer terminals. In many cases a library will retain a card catalog for old books and enter all new books in the computer.
2. How are the books shelved? Most university libraries use Library of Congress call numbers. Other libraries use the Dewey Decimal system or other format. Your library probably stocks several guidebooks that explain how the call number system works. These booklets give a list of various subject headings with their call numbers.

3. Where is the reference collection located? Several shelves, or a whole department, of your library will contain general materials such as dictionaries, almanacs, indexes, and public opinion polls—all limited to in-library use.
4. Where are the periodicals and newspapers located? How does your library summarize its holdings of periodicals?
5. Do you know where to look for each of these kinds of materials—pamphlet files, government documents, films, tapes, and phonograph records?
6. Where are the major library services located? Are you familiar with how to use the circulation desk, reserve materials, and use the reference desk, interlibrary loan system, and microforms?

While you learn about the major holdings and services of your library, take time to get acquainted with library personnel. The reference librarians can be of particular help to public speakers. They can give you general tips on how to research your subject area—for instance, how to find the journals and magazines likely to be of greatest help. Reference librarians also can help you find such specific items as the international treaties governing chemical warfare.

Do not take the attitude that a question only points up your ignorance. Everybody has to start somewhere in learning to use a particular library. A major part of a librarian's job is to answer questions from patrons. Although librarians are ready to help you, be sure to show your respect for them by having thought in advance about what you need. Do you want general help getting started in researching your subject? Do you need to know what are the best journals for your subject? Do you need a single fact? How much material do you need? How much time do you have? When do you need the material? Do you need to know how to use a particular kind of resource, for instance, microfilmed newspapers?

The resources of your library vary from books to topographical maps. For purposes of your speeches, you should be able to use at least these items: books, periodicals, newspapers, government documents, pamphlets, reference materials, and databases.

Books

The word library itself comes from the Latin term, *libri,* meaning books. Books still occupy most of the space in the modern library. Books may be found according to the name of their author or according to topical headings. If you wanted to consult books similar in nature to this textbook, you might try such headings as "public speaking," "speech," "oratory," or "rhetoric." Your earlier *topoi* analysis will help you use the card catalog or video display terminal to maximum effect.

Box 6.3

Computers Are Replacing Card Catalogues

On July 1 [1982] information about newly catalogued books and periodicals [at Ohio State University] will be available only on computer terminals, which are replacing the card catalogues as the source of information about current library acquisitions.

Source: *OSU On Campus*, 27 May 1982, 1.

Periodicals

Books frequently lack up-to-the-minute information because of the time lag involved in publishing. Periodicals can help bring speakers fully up to date. If you know which periodicals are most likely to be helpful, your first step might be to find where they are located. Most libraries have a book—usually a soft-bound photocopy—that lists all available magazines, scholarly journals, and newsletters.

It is possible that you may not have any idea, beforehand, which periodicals you want to consult. In this case, it helps to begin with one of the available periodical (serial) indexes. Familiar to many researchers is *Readers' Guide to Periodical Literature,* a source for a wide range of magazines. Do not be satisfied with a search of only one general index. Many specialized indexes can prove useful for particular topics of inquiry. For instance, if your subject pertains to government, politics, and economics, try *Public Affairs Information Service.* If your topic pertains to human relations, or to any aspect of psychology, you will find help in *Psychological Abstracts.* In the last several years, a number of new periodical indexing services have become available. One of these is *The Magazine Index.* This index is a self-contained microfilm reader that indexes hundreds of magazines.

Newspapers

Because newspapers record events on a day-to-day basis, they are invaluable not only for current goings-on but also as a way to see history through the eyes of the people who lived it. Newspapers usually provide a wide perspective on a topic, since they represent day-by-day efforts to report and interpret changing situations. The historical information in newspapers usually requires that you have a particular date in mind. Why not consult a newspaper to see what was happening on the day you were born? If you do not have specific dates in mind, your library is likely to have indexes either for local newspapers and/or for a few major newspapers such as the *New York Times* or the *Wall Street Journal.*

A relatively new newspaper reference service is *NewsBank*. This service collects major articles on current topics from over 100 United States papers. The articles are available on microfiche and can be found by using a microfiche reader that lists numerous subject headings. *NewsBank* emphasizes state and local stories rather than national ones.

Government documents

The United States government is the largest publisher in the world. The United States Government Printing Office supplies transcripts of Congressional committee hearings and reports, and it issues pamphlets on such topics of general interest as nutrition and child care. Whether the subject of your speech is child abuse or nuclear arms control, the documents division of your library may have something useful for your research.

Many libraries have large collections of federal publications. These may be listed in the general card catalog or on-line terminal. However, you may consult one or more special indexes for federal documents, including *Monthly Catalogue of United States Government Publications,* the *Congressional Information Service* index, and the *Publications Reference File* (on microfiche). In the case of recent publications, you may order them by mail, often at surprisingly low cost.

Pamphlets

Many libraries have an extensive collection of short booklets or pamphlets. Organizations (e.g., National Organization for Women), interest groups (e.g., Planned Parenthood), and agencies (e.g., the United States Department of Education) regularly send pamphlet materials to libraries. Also, a library may assemble a topical collection of short printed items. For instance, a number of libraries began collections of anti-war and other protest materials during the 1960s. Check to see how your library files its pamphlets. Also, check the *Vertical File Index* that lists many pamphlets offered by the government and private organizations.

Reference materials

The library's reference department is a repository of noncirculating items useful for finding basic facts. For instance, if you are looking for an interesting quotation to serve as an introduction to your speech, John Bartlett's *Familiar Quotations* would help. Find this work in the library's reference section, turn to the index, and see what you can locate under such categories as "freedom" and "spirit."

Bibliographies, biographies, organizations, and addresses may be found using the reference collection. Reference materials also include statistical summaries, abstracts, almanacs, dictionaries, fact books, and encyclopedias. The range of information found in books of this kind is enormous. The *Statistical Abstract of the United States* alone provides information summarized in forty pages of index listings. Entries in the general card catalog or on-line terminal may put you onto a useful item in the reference collection, or you may check with one of the librarians.

Databases

Database collections provide quick access to the information available in a particular field. An example is the ERIC database of the Educational Resources Information Center. This database contains thousands of documents or articles about education that are indexed in either *Resources in Education* (for documents) or *Current Index to Journals in Education* (for articles). Once you have identified the documents or articles you need, you may obtain them either in the form of microfiche (many libraries have the ERIC microfiche) or by ordering the item from the ERIC Document Reproduction Center.

In addition to ERIC, there are dozens of database collections representing a range of subjects. Examples include *Psychological Abstracts,* which indexes over 900 periodicals, and *Oceanic Abstracts,* which indexes 2000 sources dealing with marine-related subjects. Your reference librarian can point you to the databases most relevant to your topic.

Be sure to inquire about the possibilities for using a computer-based reference service. Such services store information from a variety of databases. Major service vendors include DIALOGUE Information Service, Systems Development Corporation (SDC) and Bibliographic Retrieval System (BRS).

The DIALOGUE system, for instance, contains the computerized records of ERIC, *Psychological Abstracts, Oceanic Abstracts,* and dozens of other databases representing areas of science, social science, humanities, and business. For a small charge—which possibly may be absorbed fully or partially by your library—you may use the DIALOGUE service to search one or more databases. The advantage is speed. The computer system can complete in minutes an amount of work that would take days by hand. Contact your reference librarian about using the computer databases.

Try to make the library a familiar place. Get started early. Avoid the end-of-term rush. Spend at least an hour or two each week gathering materials for speech class and for other courses.

Interviewing for Information

Although the library can put you in touch with an almost limitless amount of information, do not overlook the opportunity to interview local experts directly. If you were speaking on campus-related subjects, such as parking or the bookstore, then university officials and fellow students could give you important current and first-hand insights. Interviews would serve a similar purpose if you are preparing a speech on matters of city-wide concern. Following are some suggestions for preparing and conducting the information-seeking interview.

Preparing the interview

Socrates once observed the advantage of human conversation by noting that books always give the same answer no matter how many times you ask for a further explanation.[18] Still, though you may ask many different questions of your interview source, be sure to prepare in advance. You are likely to have only a brief amount of time with him or her.

To identify suitable persons for interview, consult campus or community telephone books or organizational directories. Libraries usually contain directories of this kind, and often the local chamber of commerce keeps a list of local organizations and their officers. Call the department, agency, or organization to ask about whom you might see.

Prepare for interviewing by reading about the relevant person or group.

Arrange in advance for the interview. Do not expect to walk in unannounced and have people be receptive to your needs. The people you want to see probably are busy individuals. Call or write in advance for an appointment. This courtesy will increase your chances to get agreement for a 15- or 30-minute session.

Well before your appointment, research the questions you will be asking. Your interview time is too precious to waste with matters you could resolve by reading available printed sources. Learn what you can about the person you will be meeting and the department or organization that he or she represents. Perhaps articles in the campus or local newspaper can give you useful ideas on preparing for your interview.

Box 6.4

Don't Be an Unprepared Interviewer

Today—28 years after his last game—Johnny Mize will stand in Cooperstown, New York, and be inducted into baseball's Hall of Fame, along with Bob Gibson and the late Andrew "Rube" Foster. . . .

As his date with the Hall of Fame has approached, there has been an increase in the number of interviews, some from people not too familiar with their subject. "I have had people call," he says, "and the first thing they ask me is, 'Well, let's see, what teams did you play for?' I tell them, 'Well, if you don't know that, let's just forget the whole thing. I just as soon you not do the story because I know you won't get it right.' The records are there, they can look them up."

Source: *Courier-Journal* (Louisville), 2 August 1981, C6.

Finally, be sure to develop a specific *interview plan*. This is your checklist of questions that you need to ask. Work on this list, revising it several times. Keep the list fairly short, however, because the conversation itself probably will go off in directions you cannot fully anticipate. Do not expect to follow rigidly a pre-planned set of questions; conversations just do not work that way. Instead, form a clear notion of what topics you need to cover, and be sure that you touch on each of these vital points during the interview.

Conducting the interview

Once the time for your interview is at hand, keep in mind some guidelines for getting the most out of your dialogue. First, be sure that the ground rules are clearly understood. Will you be allowed to take notes or use a tape recorder? Have you agreed on an endpoint for the interview session?

Provide orientation for the interview. Be sure to explain to the respondent why you are conducting the interview and what kinds of information you need. You might even summarize some of the major topics you want to cover. Remember that the respondent may be somewhat defensive. He or she may wonder why you want this information and what you will do with it. You might put your respondent at ease by commenting on your purposes.

Be sure to use appropriate types of questions. Different types of questions are appropriate for different objectives. At some point, you will want to use *closed* questions that specify precisely the information that you want. An example: "When did you become president of the chamber of commerce?" Closed questions are particularly useful when you want factual data and when you know, in advance, precisely the facts that are important. Sometimes, however, you are unsure of what you need to know. Issues may be highly complex, or you may be more interested in the respondent's attitude than in a fact itself. In such cases, *open* questions can better serve your purposes. An example: "What do you see as the future for enrollment on campus?" Finally, use *probing* questions to follow-up or to pursue points of interest. Probes usually are short questions such as "can you elaborate," or "how does this compare to."

An important reminder for interviewers is to *listen*. Do not lose sight of the fact that you have come to get information *from* the respondent, not to persuade him or her. Be sure that you spend most of your time listening, not talking. You may want to challenge the respondent to defend, clarify, or prove what he or she is saying. However, it does not serve your purpose to debate the respondent. One specific way to indicate that you are listening is use of *restatement* questions. A restatement question is one in which you paraphrase the essential point that you think the respondent has made. An example: "So you are saying that the university's parking fees probably will be raised next year?" Restatements of this type not only show that you have been listening, but they also allow your respondent a chance to clarify or elaborate.

Finally, when conducting the interview, seek and use feedback from the respondent. An interviewer is not only interested in what the respondent says, but also wants to get an overall impression of how the respondent is reacting to the interview. Nonverbal actions—eye contact, posture—will give clues about the respondent's credibility and attitude. Observing this feedback can help you get more out of your dialogue with the respondent. If you detect hostility, try to phrase questions in ways that will provoke less defensiveness. Instead of asking, "Why does the traffic department harass students so much?" word your question to be more descriptive and less opinionated. For instance: "A recent letter in the student newspaper complained that campus police go out of their way to harass students; what is your reaction to this?"

Properly used, the interview can be an important supplement to library work. For some topics, interviews can change a speaker's whole perspective. Many times a student speaker will begin work with the intention of blasting the campus parking department or bookstore. After some interview research, these students sometimes see the situation in an entirely different light.

Other Research Methods

In addition to library research and interviews, you have available two further sources of information about your speech—the questionnaire and participant observation.

Questionnaires typically contain questions that elicit information about the background, awareness, and attitudes of respondents. If you are giving a speech on graduation requirements, you might distribute to students questionnaires that would ask for attitudes toward specific requirements. If you also asked for some basic demographic information from your respondents, you could do some quick checks to see if opinions differed according to a respondent's academic major or sex.

In preparing questionnaires, try to observe two tips. First, avoid the common tendency to ask for too much information. Five questions probably will more than meet your needs. Second, be sure to word the questions in a neutral fashion. Do not write your questionnaire to suggest what answers you want or expect. Displaying your biases may cause respondents to modify answers in ways that distort their real opinions.

Speeches on topics of local significance often may be enriched by your own systematic *participant observation.* If you want to speak on campus sports, attend some of the games and make notes concerning attendance and participation. If you are preparing a speech on city streets, you can yourself note the potholes, time the stop lights, or count the cars passing through an intersection.

Because you will be speaking several times during your speech course, you may expect to find a use for every one of the research methods mentioned here. When preparing each speech, review the advice on library research, interviews, questionnaires, and participant observation. Consider ways that each method might help you.

Recording Information

Your research will be of greatest value if you have taken systematic notes on what you gather. Exactly how you organize the fruits of your research depends on both the amount of data and how much time you have to summarize it. Greater amounts of data and time necessitate greater care in storing information for easy access. If you are basing your speech on one book, notes from one interview, and an hour's personal observation, then probably you will not need to pay much attention to organizing your data. On the other hand, if you are using ten books, ten articles, and five interviews, then how you arrange your resources may help or hinder your speech preparation.

Why not think beyond your next speech assignments? Why not begin now to hone your skills for gathering materials that you might apply to all future speeches or college papers? A great way to advance your rhetorical competence is to begin a *speech materials file.* To keep such a file you would collect interesting clippings, copy down striking ideas, and make notes of useful remarks in books and magazines. By keeping a file of things of personal interest, you would have on tap a reservoir of materials for your present speech course and for later courses.

President Franklin D. Roosevelt was known for his care in keeping an ever-ready file of materials for speeches. FDR commented that "whenever anything catches my eye which I think will be of value to the preparation of a speech, I ask [my secretary] to put it away in the speech material file."[19] It is unlikely that your own collection will equal the twenty-four file boxes and sixty-three manila folders kept by President Roosevelt. The principle remains the same, nevertheless. If you collect items of interest on a daily basis, you will have at your fingertips a vast resource for speaking and writing.

In addition to keeping a general materials file for use in your speeches and papers, use the *file card method* of storage for your specific research on a particular topic. Not only will file cards enable you to find everything you have gathered, but learning this method can also help with later or longer projects. The file card method calls for a choice on the size of index card. Many researchers use 5 × 8 cards, the largest size, because much information can be stored on one side. If your handwriting is neat, or if you will be typing some of your cards, however, then the 4 × 6 or 3 × 5 card sizes may serve your purposes.

Consider each card a separate unit of information. Every time you have a good idea, every time you think of a good argument, every time you make a useful observation, write it out on a card. Do not consult books or periodicals without copying a few facts, statistics, and statements onto cards. After your interview sessions, also write out cards—one point to a card.

When preparing file cards, be sure to record all relevant information about the source of the data. For an interview, note the respondent's name as well as the place and time of the interview. When consulting printed material, carefully note a *complete source citation*—enough information that you could later return to the source and find the exact point. When taking notes from a *book,* list the author, the author's qualifications, title of book, location and name of publisher, copyright date, and page. For an *article* in a periodical, write down the author, qualifications, title of article, title of journal, volume, issue number or date, and page. Remember that your goal in writing source headings is twofold. Not only should you be able to return to the information, but you should also have a complete bibliographic citation in case you later use the information in a written term paper. If you are taking a large number of cards from a few sources, it may help to make one bibliographic card with all source information and then include on each note card the author's name, date, and page.

When writing out the information on your file cards, be accurate. If you are using a *paraphrase*—restating the source's information in your own words—indicate this fact. If you are taking the information exactly as it was presented, then be sure you use *quotation marks* for statements and that your statistical tables include all relevant information. Sometimes the information from printed sources will be too long or more complicated than you require. In these cases, you should edit the printed sources to shorten them without distorting their meaning. When editing the material, use *ellipses* (. . .) to indicate where you have deleted words, and use *brackets* [ ] to show that you have inserted something into the quotation to clarify it. Be sure that your editing of the material does not change the essential point that the author is trying to make.

Finally, in preparing file cards, write out each card to include three elements. At the top of the card, include a short heading that summarizes the content of the card. Below the heading, include the information about the source. Then paraphrase or quote the idea or fact that you have collected. A model of the index card is given in table 6.2.

This discussion of recording research data brings us full circle on the matter of investigating the speech subject. An active interest in the world is a wellspring of rhetorical competence. When you bring a curiosity about life to your research, you hold an attitude that will motivate you to look beyond your comfortable assumptions or prejudices. Begin your inquiry into a subject with a clearly stated thesis that can guide your search for speech material. Adopt the *topoi* method of analysis. Whenever you face a task of writing or speaking, let the *topoi* stimulate and organize your thoughts. Work to improve your skills as a researcher. Do not be content with whatever bits and pieces you cull from a magazine lying in a friend's room. Instead, dig in and learn as many relevant facts and opinions as possible. Finally, take care in storing the fruits of your research. Take the opportunity offered here to use the file card method. After your public speaking class is finished, save your cards. Make them part of a general speech materials file. Not only will your file cards enrich your speeches, but they also can help with later college projects.

Table 6.2 The index card

Heading:	Vietnam War Unpopular Despite Pro-War TV Coverage
Source Data:	Daniel C. Hallin (communication faculty, UC-San Diego), *The "Uncensored War,"* New York: Oxford University Press, 1986, 168.
Quotation:	"Late in 1965, when American troops were first committed to Vietnam in large numbers . . . there had been an initial surge of support for the war. But the initial rally was short-lived, and early in 1966 a steady erosion in public support began—at a time, it is important to note, when television was still strongly committed to the war."

Concepts for Review

Can you summarize the meaning of these terms or expressions? How does each relate to speechmaking?

thesis
2–5 main points
thesis stimulates research
hypothesis and thesis
exigence
topoi
topos
general *topoi*
journalists' *topoi*
Wilson-Arnold *topoi*
stock issues
specific *topoi*
library resources (list 5)
periodical index
government documents
reference department
databases
computer reference services
interview plan
closed questions
open questions
probing questions
restatement questions
questionnaire research
participant observation
speech materials file
file card method
complete source citation
paraphrase
ellipses
brackets

Things to Try

1. Consult a recent issue of *Vital Speeches* in your library. Read through the various speeches, and check to see if you can find at least one good example of a sentence that expresses the thesis of the speech. Sentences of this kind usually appear toward the beginning or end of the speech. As a model, use the speech of Franklin D. Roosevelt given in Box 6.1 (p. 150).
2. Identify a topic on which you might give a speech in the near future. Write a thesis for this topic, following the guidelines in this chapter. Now, consider how your audience might react to your thesis. Identify two perceptions they would have about your thesis—favorable or unfavorable. Do these perceptions suggest ways that you need to rewrite the thesis?
3. Apply *topoi* to the subject of one of your next speeches. Use at least three *topoi* taken from one of the general systems described in this chapter. Use at least three categories that you believe are particularly relevant to the specific subject of your speech. Write down each *topos,* and then list as many ideas as possible that the category helps uncover.
4. Identify a person to interview as part of your research for an upcoming speech. An official in the campus administration or in a local government office might be an appropriate source of information. Perhaps someone in business or on the faculty can help you. Do the preliminary research for the interview, and prepare a specific interview plan according to the directions in this chapter.

Endnotes

1. Public lecture, Indiana University Southeast, New Albany, Indiana, 28 September 1981.
2. Russel Windes, Jr., "A Study of Effective and Ineffective Presidential Campaign Speaking," *Speech Monographs 28* (1961): 43–45.
3. Plato, *Gorgias,* 457.
4. John Dewey, *How We Think* (Boston: D.C. Heath, 1910), 72.
5. Lloyd F. Bitzer, "The Rhetorical Situation," *Philosophy and Rhetoric 1* (1968): 6.

6. Gerald R. Miller and Richard L. McGraw, "Justification and Self-Persuasion Following Commitment to Encode, and Actual Encoding of Counterattitudinal Communication," *Speech Monographs 36* (1969): 443–451, and Fredric A. Powell, "Cognitive Tuning and Differentiation of Arguments in Communication," *Human Communication Research 1* (1974): 53–61.
7. Thomas M. Conley, "'Logical Hylomorphism' and Aristotle's Koinoi Topoi," *Central States Speech Journal 29* (1978): 94.
8. Aristotle, *Rhetoric,* II. 18–23. For a useful presentation of Aristotle's system, see Robert C. Dick, "Topoi: An Approach to Inventing Arguments," *Speech Teacher 13* (1964): 313–319.
9. William F. Nelson, "Topoi: Functional in Human Recall," *Speech Monographs 37* (1970): 121–126.
10. Aristotle, *Rhetoric,* II. 18. 1391b.
11. Nelson, "Topoi," 121–126.
12. William Nelson, John L. Petelle, and Craig Monroe, "A Revised Strategy for Idea Generation in Small Group Decision Making," *Speech Teacher 23* (1974): 191–196.
13. Dominic A. Infante, "The Influence of a Topical System on the Discovery of Arguments," *Speech Monographs 38* (1971): 125–128, and Infante and Robin A. Grimmett, "Attitudinal Effects of Utilizing a Critical Method of Analysis," *Central States Speech Journal 22* (1971): 213–217.
14. Stephen E. Toulmin, *The Uses of Argument* (Cambridge: Cambridge University Press, 1958), 14–15.
15. John L. Petelle and Richard Maybee, "Items of Information Retrieved as a Function of Cue System and Topical Area," *Central States Speech Journal 25* (1974): 190–197.
16. Aristotle, *Rhetoric,* II. 22. 1396a.
17. Charles F. Hunter, "Thomas Hart Benton: An Evaluation," *Quarterly Journal of Speech 30* (1944): 284.
18. Plato, *Phaedrus,* 275.
19. Earnest Brandenburg and Waldo W. Braden, "Franklin Delano Roosevelt," *A History and Criticism of American Public Address,* ed. M. K. Hochmuth [Nichols] (New York: Russell and Russell, 1955), 471.

Chapter

7

Speech Materials: Verbal and Visual

Outline

Campaigning in Texas in September 1960, John F. Kennedy planned to confront head-on the suggestion of many Protestant leaders that a Catholic president could not act independently of the dictates of his church. During his visit to San Antonio's historic Alamo, John F. Kennedy thought about his upcoming speech before the Greater Houston Ministerial Association. Kennedy wondered how many Catholics had died during the legendary defense of the Alamo Mission. Kennedy's staff rushed the question to the Library of Congress. While the librarians could find a list of the dead, the religious affiliations of the fallen were not available. Kennedy incorporated this research into his evening address, for the findings illustrated well his thesis that religious creed should not be a test for entry into public service.[1]

As he stood before the Protestant ministers in Houston's Rice Hotel, Kennedy contended that the fight for separation of church and state had been an important principle of the war for Independence as well as in the struggle to establish the Constitution and the Bill of Rights. Kennedy added that the principle could also be seen in the defense of the Alamo. "For side by side with Bowie and Crockett died Fuentes and McCafferty and Bailey and Bedillio and Carey—but no one knows whether they were Catholics or not. For there was no religious test there" (full text of speech given at the end of chapter 14).

Kennedy's telling use of the names of Alamo defenders illustrates an important principle of rhetorical competence. Good speeches are fashioned out of good speech materials. Effective speakers see to it that their remarks are centered on powerful ideas, decisive arguments, compelling evidence, and striking visual elements gathered through research. Kennedy's Houston speech reflects well a principle of superior speechmaking held by Theodore Parker, one of the last century's greatest American preachers. Parker believed that to be a *permanently impressive* speaker, the advocate needed to acquire the habit of basing communication on the superior ideas reflected in strong speech materials.[2] This chapter shows how to acquire the habits of permanently impressive speaking. Our focus is on building the speech through arguments, evidence, and visuals, with special attention to matters of persuasive effect and logical validity.

Arguments

Considered as a unit of speech, an *argument* may be defined as reasoning by the speaker that presents, explains, and/or proves a point in the speech. When Jack Dodds, student speaker, recommends that listeners support a compensation fund for Vietnam veterans exposed to Agent Orange, he is *presenting* an argument. When he contends that "Agent Orange was a herbicide used during the Vietnam war to defoliate over five million acres of land to destroy enemy cover,'' he is arguing by *explanation.* When Jack cites a study on the toxic character of Agent Orange, he is supplying *proof* regarding the health harms to veterans. These arguments represent statements created by one speaker to win understanding and support for his ideas.

When you have attained rhetorical competence, you will be able to examine and select arguments according to the major issues they raise. According to the Roman rhetoricians Cicero and Quintilian, an *issue* marks the point or points at which the controversy lies. An issue is something in question. Typically, an argument raises one or more of three kinds of issues. First is the issue of *fact;* did something happen or does it exist? Second is the issue of *definition;* what is the meaning of the happening or thing? Third is the issue of *value;* shall we consider the event or thing to be good or bad? Your powers of analysis and reasoning will grow when you examine arguments on the basis of issues they raise—fact, definition, and value.[3]

Cicero, who not only wrote on rhetoric but also practiced the arts of speech in the Roman Senate, used this three-fold division of arguments in his defense of Milo. Milo, a prominent Roman politician, was charged with the murder of his political opponent, Clodius. In his defense of Milo, Cicero conceded the issue of *fact;* it so happened that Milo did kill Clodius. Instead, Cicero defended Milo by organizing his arguments around the issues of *definition* and *value.* Cicero focused his case on the *definition* of murder, contending that Milo killed Clodius only in self-defense. Cicero emphasized that Clodius had laid in ambush, planning to kill Milo; therefore it was right for the attacked man to defend himself to the point of slaying his assailant. In addition, Cicero defended Milo through use of the issue of *value.* At several moments in his speech for Milo, Cicero noted that Clodius was held in disrepute by Romans. Cicero observed that many Senators expressed relief when learning of the death of Clodius. Romans praised Milo for rendering a valuable service by removing an enemy of the state.[4]

The issues of fact, definition, and value correspond to three major forms of arguments. *Descriptions* are speech materials that supply basic facts. *Interpretations* are speech materials that define facts by placing them into categories. *Evaluations* are speech materials that emphasize one value over others. As you prepare your speeches, look for arguments falling into each of these three categories. If you follow this advice, you will be likely to hit upon all decisive ideas available for use.

Descriptions

A *description* is a statement that points to something observable or potentially observable; it sets out a fact that can be independently verified to the satisfaction of all reasonable people. To say that George Bush was elected President of the United States in 1988 is to raise a point that can be conclusively checked by you, by me, or by anyone else who took the trouble.

Descriptions can make powerful arguments. Paul Rosenthal contends that a descriptive claim creates a favorable impression precisely because of its openness to verification. Rosenthal observes that a descriptive statement invites the listener to test it, thereby creating "a psychological presumption of its own truth."[5] Tamara Carbone tested Rosenthal's theory by studying how listeners respond to tape-recorded extemporaneous speeches. She found that listeners rated a speaker as more credible when the speech contained specific points that could be checked.[6]

Descriptions frequently come in the form of *examples.* To argue by example is to cite a particular instance as support for a generalization. Sometimes termed an illustration or an anecdote, the argument of example adds an important feeling of reality to what we say. The details provided by examples create an important bond of mutual knowledge between speaker and listener. There is an old saying that "if you speak for more than two minutes without an illustration, the chances are that neither you nor your audience knows what you are talking about."[7]

Not only does the example improve understanding of an idea, but the example is a strong form of proof as well. Instances *are* important, as Aristotle noted, for "in practical life, particular facts count more than generalizations."[8] Modern research bears out the benefits of using examples in speechmaking. One experiment showed the example to be the type of argument least vulnerable to refutation by an opponent.[9] Examples seemingly give us a direct tap into reality.

The desirability of examples is well understood by the speakers whose addresses are reprinted in this textbook. Harold Enarson's informative address, reprinted at the end of chapter 13, is built largely on examples. He gives instances of cuts in university support by the State of Ohio; he gives illustrations of what is meant by quality in education; and he gives examples of regrettable cuts in programs that might come in the future. Similarly, the address of Martin Luther King, Jr. at the Lincoln Memorial (reprinted at the end of chapter 10) lists a roster of grievances that must be solved before blacks can be satisfied. He cites police brutality, segregated facilities, and lack of the vote.

Examples function particularly well to establish generalizations. In his speech to the Greater Houston Ministerial Association, John F. Kennedy wanted to make the point that *all* religious groups—not just Catholics—were vulnerable to religious prejudice if society allowed discrimination against *any* one creed. Kennedy clinched his contention by pointing to Baptists, who were harassed by establishment churches in eighteenth century Virginia. Similarly, in his greeting to the American hostages released from Iran, Ronald Reagan wanted to make the point that the Americans had exhibited strength throughout their ordeal. Reagan cited the instance of how Sergeant Lopez defied his Iranian captors (see full text in chapter 15).

Take a cue from these speakers. Be sure to include examples in your speeches. Research can give you particular instances to support each point in your speech. Although library work can supply a host of compelling examples, do not overlook the potential power of *personal examples.* As a case in point, consider the speech of Connecticut State Representative Robert Sorenson, who supported a bill to legalize use of marijuana for those undergoing chemotherapy. When Sorenson disclosed his own treatment for cancer, he brought an attentive hush to the chamber of the Connecticut House.[10]

Interpretations

Descriptive arguments are focused on facts; in contrast, interpretations are efforts to generalize from facts. To interpret is to make particular facts meaningful by showing how they support general conclusions. William F. Buckley, Jr. gives an interpretation when he argues that the $60 million cost of the Panama Canal treaties is minor *in comparison* to the monies spent by the United States to rent military bases from Spain, Turkey, and Greece (see full text in chapter 14). Buckley's argument is based less on simple dollar figures and more on a judgment about these figures.

Life—and speechmaking—would be simpler if every fact spoke for itself. But any single piece of information is tied to a host of other relevant facts. As a result, every detail becomes meaningful only when examined against other things known. Interpretations always amount to exercises in *emphasis.* The speaker maximizes certain data and minimizes other information. Buckley minimizes the figure of 60 million dollars, not only by arguing that the United States spends more elsewhere, but also by contending that we will get some of our money back through canal fees.

Buckley's interpretive argument was based on comparison of one figure to others. We need to examine not only interpretations based on comparison, but also generalizations drawn from causes, signs, consequences, humor, and dilemmas.

Comparisons

To argue by means of comparison, you interpret an event or object by showing its similarity to other relevant situations and things. Instances of comparative argument abound in the speeches reprinted in this textbook. Jack Dodds argues that assistance for Agent Orange victims should be handled "as done in the past for black lung exposure, radioactive exposure or PCB contamination" (text at end of chapter 2). Dodds compares a present controversy to past solutions. Martin Luther King, Jr. uses the metaphor of a promissory note to show how black people have been denied their expected rights as citizens. King argues that blacks now have come to take possession of the freedom, equality, and justice granted all citizens by the Declaration of Independence and United States Constitution. Here King interprets a present situation by showing its connections to statements made in the official documents of American history.

Arguments of cause

When we argue by means of cause, we contend that one object or situation has brought about another. An alternative is to cite an effect and work back to discover its origins.

Causes and effects reveal much about the meaning of an object or situation. In an informative presentation in her speech class, Jacquelyn Flanigan reasoned by means of cause when she related the origins of the Mafia. She pointed out that the roots of Mafia culture explain the irony that this criminal group shares many traditional American values (full text at end of chapter 13). Similarly, William F. Buckley offered a causal argument in support of turning over control of the Panama Canal to Panama. Buckley argued that national pride could cause the Panamanians to sabotage the Canal, even though their country would suffer losses of revenue.

Arguments of sign

To reason from sign is to claim that something we observe leads directly and logically to a conclusion—as smoke brings us to a fire. For instance, John F. Kennedy inferred that Catholics died alongside Protestants at the Alamo on the basis of the names of the fallen—Fuentes, McCafferty, Bailey, Bedillio, and Carey. In the same speech, Kennedy argued from sign to refute the charge that Catholics had a divided loyalty to the United States, or that Catholics did not believe in freedom. Kennedy offered his own combat record in the Pacific, as well as his brother's death fighting Nazi Germany, to generalize on the deep loyalty of Catholics.

Arguments of consequences

Speechmaking often aims to show and to shape the future. Three common types of interpretation seek to forecast the consequences of action: the argument of direction, the fear appeal, and the effort to reduce things to an absurd result (*reductio ad absurdum*).

In the *argument of direction,* we contend that a present action necessarily sets us on a course that, once begun, will be difficult or impossible to change. A typical argument of this kind is the assertion that the registration of handguns would quickly lead to confiscating rifles from hunters and sportsmen.

To use a *fear appeal* is to arouse concern by showing the terrible results that are in store for listeners. Most of us have encountered fear appeals of one kind or another. High school students, in particular, frequently are treated to gory films and pamphlets detailing the results of careless driving, cigarette smoking, and unsafe sexual practices.

When using a *reductio ad absurdum* argument, we make an idea seem ridiculous by taking the point to its extreme case. When *Newsweek* quoted the opinions of John Hinckley, Jr., would-be assassin of Ronald Reagan, on national questions, a reader responded with a *reductio.* "Perhaps next you could give us . . . Charlie Manson's feelings about family life."[11] John F. Kennedy used a *reductio* argument when he contended that attacks on his Catholic faith represented an effort to "subvert Article VI of the Constitution by requiring a religious test" for public office.

Humor as argument

Effective speakers have long recognized the power of humor to undermine or refute an opponent's case. Ronald Reagan used humor effectively in his second debate with Walter Mondale in 1984. Reagan's stumbling performance in the first Louisville debate had put the issue of his age on page one. Reagan planned to use humor to defuse the issue in Kansas City two weeks later. Asked whether he still felt up to the job of president, Reagan replied in the affirmative. Reagan added: "I want you to know that also I will not make age an issue in this campaign; I am not going to exploit for political purposes my opponent's youth and inexperience."[12]

Box 7.1

Humor Can Make a Vivid Argument

Americans of the early 1930s were wondering what our country should do about Europe's new conflicts and squabbles. Will Rogers, the Oklahoma folk humorist, wrote in his newspaper column this advice to President Franklin Roosevelt: "Mr. Franklin D., shut your front door to all foreign ambassadors running to you with news. Just send 'em these words: 'Boys, it's your cats that's fighting. You pull 'em apart.' "

What to do about military preparedness? Rogers wrote: "To reduce your navy in these times is exactly like a man who is not doing so well financially canceling all his life insurance, figuring it's a dead loss because he hasn't died yet."

Source: William R. Brown, *Imagemaker: Will Rogers and the American Dream* (Columbia, MO: University of Missouri Press, 1970), 20.

Dilemma argument

Frequently, you will want to interpret an event or situation by showing its possible outcomes or results. In a dilemma argument, you would identify two possibilities and show that one is superior to the other. For instance, William F. Buckley used a dilemma to argue that America should turn over operating control of the Panama Canal. Buckley suggested that Americans had two spiritual choices relative to the Panama Canal treaties. On the one hand Americans could support the treaties. This alternative would find Americans taking legitimate satisfaction in affirming the ideal that even small nations should control their national territory. The other alternative was to engage in "prideful excesses" by trying to maintain full control of a strip of territory in Panama.

Interpretations function as midwives to facts. Our interpretations give life to facts, making particular details meaningful as part of important conclusions. By keeping aware of the common types of interpretive arguments, you will be ever ready to minimize or maximize effectively the facts relating to a topic.

Evaluations

Examine the persuasive message of any magazine advertisement or television commercial. You will not fail to notice that advertising works by connecting a consumer product to something desirable. One brand of car supposedly brings prestige or luxury. A particular deodorant spray enables people to remain socially attractive. Just as values serve as grounding for advertisements, value-based arguments furnish important materials for speeches. Like an advertisement, your speech promotes a product in the form of a thesis or main point. One way of gaining support for your rhetorical product is to link your idea with something favored by listeners.

Obviously, evaluative arguments contribute significantly to the speeches reprinted in this textbook. For instance, in his speech on the Challenger disaster, Ronald Reagan assured Americans that the space program would continue. Reagan stressed the value of "exploration and discovery," arguing that the deaths of the seven astronauts were "part of taking a chance and expanding man's horizons" (see text in chapter 15). In a similar way, Douglas MacArthur's commencement speech at West Point was built around three essential values that served as the foundation for military service. "Duty, honor, country: Those three hallowed words reverently dictate what you want to be, what you can be, what you will be" (see text at end of chapter 10).

In these and all cases of speechmaking, values serve as the foundation for arguments. As the ground for claims, values have a twofold usefulness in public speaking. First, an appeal to values makes us think about what is

Table 7.1 Value terms

Positive value terms (goods)	Negative value terms (bads)
balanced budget	losing
equality	pollution
family	discrimination
health	unemployment
loyalty	weakness
morality	dictatorship
success	censorship

most important—what must be emphasized—in a given situation. Ronald Reagan worked to convince Americans that the need for scientific progress meant that we must bear the risk of death that comes with space exploration. Reagan argued that Americans must aim for discovery and accept the danger. "The future doesn't belong to the fainthearted. It belongs to the brave." Because value arguments focus on important goals or ways of living, Richard Weaver calls them "ultimate terms." Weaver, a significant modern writer on rhetoric, believes that a value term can help us understand what is of greatest significance in a particular case.[13]

Beyond helping us see what is most important, value arguments are useful in view of the motivational power they carry. Values are *sources of motivation.* When you connect an action or an idea to a particular value, you provide a stimulus which makes the action or idea seem more attractive. For instance, by showing that space exploration is part of the destiny of mankind, Ronald Reagan helped overcome second thoughts about the space program. Similarly, by making concessions to Panama appear consistent with American ideals, William F. Buckley helped his audience feel better about surrendering control of a national achievement.

Many writers have recognized the importance of value argumentation, as shown by the effort to compile lists of values held by Americans.[14] The rhetorically competent speaker works to gain a sense for what people value, not only generally, but for each particular speech situation. Look at the list of values in table 7.1. Read through the positive and negative terms listed; then try to add to the list. If you have trouble finding some additional value terms, consider some of the values stated or implied in speech topics you have heard recently in class.

Descriptions, interpretations, and evaluations—these three forms of argument represent your options for getting across your main idea. Closely linked to arguing is using evidence. Your own claims gain force when you bolster them with data taken from outside sources.

Box 7.2

"Mr. Lincoln, You Have One Minute to Reply."

Do today's television debates allow speakers to prepare and employ coherent arguments? Reflecting on his campaign for convention delegates during the 1988 presidential primaries, Senator Paul Simon of Illinois wrote this analysis of American political debating:

"The campaign was marked by far more debates than in any previous presidential campaign. But 'debate' is really the wrong word to describe these multicandidate encounters. They were as different from the Lincoln-Douglas debates as a Beethoven symphony is from a radio jingle. Journalists asked questions, and our answers generally had to be kept to one minute or less.

The brief replies tended toward sloganeering and prepackaged answers that were great for television-news 'bites' but provided only minimal understanding of either the candidates or the issues."

Source: Paul Simon, *San Francisco Chronicle*, 5 July 1988, A8.

Evidence

Arguments function as *evidence* when their force depends on the credibility of an outside thing, an outside reference source, or a person other than the speaker.[15] Thus, a picture, a definition taken from an encyclopedia, or an opinion from an outside expert would amount to argument through evidence. Social science research shows that evidence functions differently from statements originating from the speaker. Therefore, we must understand important forms of evidence, the persuasive power of evidence, and the best ways to use evidence in speeches.

Forms of Evidence

Testimony and statistics are two particularly important forms of evidence available to modern speakers.

Testimony

When you quote statements from a third party, you are using testimonial argument. Social life would be impossible if we were required personally to verify every fact. For this reason, we commonly resolve many factual issues through testimony. Using testimony is not merely a matter of convenience, however. When you cite outside sources, you are asking listeners to accept a claim or reasoning partly because of the qualifications of the expert making the statement.

Testimony is particularly useful for student speakers who usually have no personal reputation as an expert on the subject of a speech. For instance, in the informative speech she prepared for her public speaking class, Jacquelyn Flanigan used testimony to establish the major values held by Americans. She mentions six important values, noting that "in his book, *The Art of Persuasion,* W. C. Minnick categorizes a summary of these values." In his classroom persuasive speech, Jack Dodds cited testimony to establish such critical facts as the harms of dioxin, the use of Agent Orange in Vietnam, and claims by veterans that dioxin harmed their health.

Testimony adds luster and credibility even to prominent speakers. In his address at the conclusion of the Iran-Contra hearings in 1987, Representative Lee Hamilton chastised Colonel Oliver North for believing that his loyalty to the president sanctioned lies to Congress.

> So often during these hearings—not just during your testimony, but others as well, I have been reminded of President Thomas Jefferson's statement. "The whole art of government consists in the art of being honest."[16]

Experimental research further shows the benefits of using testimony in speeches. Audiences perceive speakers as more reasonable, and their arguments as stronger, when the speaker uses highly credible sources of testimony. Research is inconclusive on the matter of whether credible testimony necessarily produces significantly greater attitude change among listeners.[17] However, receivers clearly prefer unbiased sources of evidence.[18] Credible testimony is best for speakers, not only psychologically, but also logically.

How can we tell if our testimony has credibility? The first consideration is the reputation of (1) the people we cite and/or (2) the publications from which we obtain the quoted statements of our witnesses. Testimony of medical authorities taken from a medical journal possesses greater credibility than a story in a general newspaper. As to the *internal* credibility of testimonial statements themselves, the eighteenth century philosopher, David Hume, provided guidelines still valid for today. Hume observed that:

> We entertain a suspicion concerning any matter of fact, when the witnesses contradict each other; when they are but few, or of a doubtful character; when they have an interest in what they affirm; when they deliver their testimony with hesitation, or on the contrary, with too violent asseverations [assertions].[19]

Beyond the question of whether our sources of testimony are believable, there is the issue of whether we are quoting the sources accurately. Principles of ethics and quality in speechmaking require that we do not misrepresent the witnesses we cite. The temptation to distort evidence is strong for beginning speakers. In a classic study of a championship college debate, researchers found that only about half of the evidence citations were free of misrepresentation, inaccuracy, or fabrication.[20] Unethical speakers usually defend their distorted evidence with a self-serving rationalization. For instance, one debater claimed that by faking a quotation he was "only making explicit" what seemed to be true from his other reading. More disturbing than ethical lapses among student speakers is a report by Bryn Mawr psychologist, June Tangney, on fakery of evidence in scientific research. Her survey found that 32 percent of scientists suspect that one or more of their colleagues has falsified research data.[21]

Pressures to win debates or to publish impressive scientific findings are ever-present motivations for distorting or faking evidence. You will know you are on the road to rhetorical competence when you overcome such temptations, taking an attitude of personal pride in your research work. When you have a thirst really to understand the subject of your speech, fakery becomes less alluring. Furthermore, if you hold a strong research ethic, you will remember that distorted evidence can create skeletons that may later become embarrassing. In 1988, one of the final blows against Senator Joseph Biden's campaign for the presidency was the leaked report that he had plagiarized a law school paper some *twenty-three* years earlier.

Statistics

To argue with statistics, you cite quantitative data or numbers to show comparative size or to indicate relationships. Whereas the example amounts to a single case, statistics summarize many cases into a single figure. We should consider two forms of statistical proof: descriptive statistics and inferential statistics.

Descriptive statistics represent an effort to count every member of a relevant category, from members of the United Nations Organization to automobiles produced in the United States during 1990. In today's complex society, statistical summaries do much of the work formerly assigned to examples. Part of the reason for the shift from examples to statistics is that modern people have so much information at their beck and call that examples become almost too easy—too cheap. In an atmosphere where examples rain down in torrents, statistics function to put examples into order and perspective.[22] The ability of statistics to correct the defects of examples is reflected in a *Newsweek* story about police investigations. "Every cop has a tale of smoking guns or dramatic confessions suppressed because of picky rules of police conduct. . . . But . . . recent studies show that only a handful of cases are dismissed because of evidence problems."[23]

Probably you will find obtaining good descriptive statistics more difficult than collecting one or two telling examples. But if you are aiming for rhetorical competence, the effort to secure descriptive statistics is rewarding.

In fact, statistics serve as the foundation of many examples used by Harold Enarson in his informative speech to the Ohio State University Senate. When Enarson wanted to establish the generalization that "Federal funding for the general support of University programs also has declined," he cited a "prime example" based on statistics. Speaking of grants for the health sciences, Enarson noted that "in 1973–74 we received $4.8 million, and in today's dollars it would take $8.8 million to meet those same commitments." Similarly, William F. Buckley relied on statistics to clinch his point that the United States would be better off militarily by ratifying the Panama Canal treaties. Buckley noted that since 75 percent of the employees of the Canal are Panamanian, removing local resentment about total United States control of the canal would be helpful in time of war.

Occasionally, your statistical data will be of a second type—*inferential.* Whereas a descriptive statistic counts each member of a class of objects, an inferential statistic is a measure taken of a *sample* of a whole class. If a representative sample has been chosen, findings about the sample may be taken (with a small margin of error) to provide information about the entire class or population. For instance, *USA Today* and Cable News Network conducted a poll of 1,005 voters "randomly selected from across the USA" to learn the personal characteristics that voters found desirable in a candidate for president. Results of this October 1987 poll included the finding that 51 percent of voters would oppose a candidate who had had an extramarital affair. Eighty percent of voters stated they would vote against someone "caught failing to report income to IRS." The pollsters employed statistical methods to compute a likely margin of error of plus or minus three percent in taking results from the sample to represent the opinions of the whole population.[24]

Obviously it takes more work to find outside testimony and statistics than simply to make claims on our own authority. Inevitably, therefore, we come to the question: Why use evidence?

The Power of Evidence

The reason to use evidence may be summarized briefly: *it works.* Modern research findings show that when a speaker cites outside sources concretely, the speaker appears more credible and achieves greater persuasive effect.[25] While evidence generally produces belief, it is not true that evidence affects every listener in a uniform manner. Nor does evidence bring the same effects on all speech topics.[26] However, the benefits of evidence are so well established that the chief issue for the rhetorically competent speaker is *how* to use evidence rather than whether to use it.

In a pioneer study of evidence in speechmaking, William Dresser raised the question of why a speaker would expect to be more persuasive by citing an outside source than by simply making the point in his or her own words.[27] The answer seems to be that evidence adds *authority* and *specificity* to a speech.

When you are not known personally as an expert on the subject, evidence can help you by surrounding your remarks with the aura of authority. Consider the case of Jack Dodds, student speaker, who argued that Dow Chemical Company had advance knowledge that Agent Orange was toxic to humans. Jack wisely decided not to rely on his own credibility as an undergraduate student. He turned to the expertise of Samuel S. Epstein, biochemist.

For speakers known to be authorities, evidence still adds the impression of objectivity and reliability. A classic instance of the importance of specific evidence citations comes from the famous Lincoln-Douglas debates that took place in Illinois in 1858. In his debates with Abraham Lincoln, Senator Stephen A. Douglas, known as the Little Giant, usually failed to cite the exact sources and dates of his evidence. Even when pressed by Lincoln, Douglas did not abandon this characteristic vagueness. Douglas's imprecise evidence was not fatal, since Douglas was still able to build effective arguments on facts already known to the audience. However, the Little Giant's habit of omitting concrete evidence citations reduced his ability to neutralize suspicions about him held by pro-Lincoln voters.[28]

Even disreputable speakers know the advantage of offering authoritative-sounding, seemingly testable evidence. When speaking in the United States Senate, Senator Joseph McCarthy once made a show of apparently reading from an official "document" to support one of his charges about disloyalty in America. McCarthy insisted on the absolute validity of his evidence, and he offered to show the material to any senator present. Much to McCarthy's astonishment, Senator Herbert Lehman stepped across the senate aisle to inspect the supposed document. McCarthy quickly withdrew his offer—"I yield no further," he said. It later became clear that McCarthy had been ad-libbing while pretending to be quoting. Joe McCarthy realized that bogus and misrepresented evidence often served as well as accurate data. The senator knew that few people trouble themselves to check references, but that all are impressed by an invitation to do so.[29]

Research bears out what public speakers know by intuition: listeners are quite sensitive to how specific a source citation is. In one experiment, speakers used either vague or detailed citations. When using vague source documentation, the speakers would describe their remarks as being based upon material obtained from "a study" or "in the newspaper." When citing evidence more precisely, the speakers mentioned exact names and affiliations. Results showed that listeners rated speakers and speech content significantly more favorably when source documentation was concrete.[30]

How to Use Evidence

Modern research findings do more than establish the overall effectiveness of supplementing arguments with citations from outside sources. Experimental studies further show us how we may best capitalize on evidence. Following are tips on presenting evidence to the best advantage.

1. If you have no personal reputation for expertise on the subject, be sure to cite outside evidence. In the absence of reputation, evidence boosts credibility and persuasiveness.[31] This is the reason that public speaking teachers emphasize the need to use evidence in student speeches.
2. Be sure to cite evidence if you are addressing listeners who hold strong opinions on the subject of your speech. Evidence boosts persuasion more when listeners have firmly fixed opinions than when they are relatively neutral.[32]
3. If other speakers are using evidence, then you are strongly advised also to cite evidence to support your arguments. Experimental findings suggest that when a preceding speaker has presented evidence, a following speaker will lose credibility by not also including evidence. This item of advice flows from the general finding that evidence protects a speaker's long-range persuasiveness by reducing the impact of later opposing messages.[33]
4. In general, cite only evidence sources viewed as credible by the audience. Your own credibility and persuasiveness will increase in proportion to the extent to which your sources of evidence are favorably perceived.[34] In fact, evidence having extremely low credibility with receivers can *reduce* your persuasiveness. If your source is viewed as having very low credibility, your argument would be more persuasive if you omitted the evidence and merely asserted the point in your own words.[35] Furthermore, your credibility suffers when you use evidence that comes from publications disliked by listeners.[36]
5. Look for sources who appear objective. Evidence boosts credibility most when sources are not making statements that serve their own self-interest. For instance, a television industry executive would be perceived as having a self-serving motive to assert that television programming is of high quality.[37]

6. Make an effort to quote evidence that contains facts and opinions previously unknown to listeners. Research suggests that novel facts and opinions have the most value in boosting your credibility and persuasiveness.[38] Be sure that your quoted evidence is relevant; irrelevant material can hurt your credibility and persuasiveness.[39]
7. To boost your credibility most, cite the evidence source specifically. Listeners take as more believable those citations that specifically mention the name and qualifications of the author(s).[40] Such a finding flows naturally from the nature of evidence as proof by outside authority. Listeners are understandably less impressed when they are asked to take on faith the identity and expertise of an alleged authority.
8. Vary the placement of your source citations to adapt to the credibility of your source. If your audience views the evidence source as highly credible, it is better to name the source before reading the quotation. Conversely, if the source is perceived as less credible, cite him or her after reading the quotation.[41]
9. Be sure not to rush the presentation of your source citations and quotations. When presented with poor delivery, evidence will still boost your credibility. However, experimental findings suggest that poor delivery reduces the persuasive impact of evidence.[42] Therefore, practice presenting your evidence until your source citations and quotations become smooth and natural parts of your talk.

Validity of Materials

Arguments and evidence give substance to a speech only to the extent that they are *valid*. For a speech to be valid, it must be founded on straightforward materials that are (1) free from trickery and (2) establish the major claims of the speech directly and relevantly.

Checking our speech materials for validity is vital because of the human tendencies toward selective perception and interpretation. Temptations to distort and misrepresent show up early in the rhetorical process. First, when we begin to research a speech topic, we become more committed to our initial thesis.[43] We risk following the example of the college debater who believed faked evidence was OK because it coincided with his general impressions. Second, preparing the speech for presentation puts us in a frame of mind in which we recall more arguments consistent with our thesis.[44] Consequently, we are more apt to overlook relevant opposing arguments. Finally, we should heed the finding that the stronger our attitude on a topic, the greater the tendency for us to exaggerate the validity of our arguments.[45]

To help overcome a distorted view of our arguments and evidence, we need to measure them against principles of valid argumentation. Two general kinds of tests help us assess the validity of our speech materials. One type of test reveals possible distortions in our speech materials. A second kind of test shows whether we have misused or misapplied our materials.

Tests of Distortion

When suffering from distortion, speech materials are fabricated or contain some hidden element of trickery. A significant instance of fabricating an argument occurred in 1985 when President Reagan's press spokesman, Larry Speakes, made up two Presidential "quotations." Speakes was worried that Soviet leader, Mikhail Gorbachev, was appearing in press reports to be more committed to the peace negotiations in Geneva than was President Reagan. Speakes issued a press release that featured two supposed comments of Reagan to Gorbachev. One faked quote had the president commenting that "there is much that divides us, but I believe the world breathes easier because we are talking here together." When the Russians did not dispute the two manufactured quotations, Speakes attained his short-term objective of polishing the President's image. Just as the press secretary had expected, American news reports on the Geneva Summit featured the carefully-crafted fake quotations. The pitfalls of distortion were shown three years later when Speakes revealed this episode in his memoirs. Not only did the revelation embarrass the White House, but Speakes himself was pressured to resign his lucrative public relations job with Merrill Lynch.[46]

In addition to trickery in testimony, statistical arguments are subject to distortion. A classic case occurred when Pepsi Cola ran ads in which consumers taste-tested brands labeled "M" (Pepsi) and "Q" (Coca-Cola). The tests showed that consumers preferred brand "M" over "Q." Spokesmen for Coke charged that the tests were biased since their own research revealed that people liked the letter M better than Q. Did people really prefer Pepsi, or did they pick the preferred letter?[47]

The above two instances represent cases of *distortion by commission.* In each case, the advocates included in their assertions elements of fakery or exaggeration. It is also possible to distort *by omission,* that is, by failing to include details that are necessary to understand the true meaning of supporting materials. In her campaign for mayor of New York City, Congresswoman Bella Abzug ran a newspaper advertisement that asserted: "1976: The U.S. House of Representatives votes Bella Abzug one of its three most influential members!" The advertisement implied that the survey had been authoritative and comprehensive. Omitted from the ad was the crucial information that only 20 of 435 members of the House had responded to the questionnaire. The results could have been a fluke rather than a representative finding.[48]

Tests of Misapplication

Related to matters of trickery is the problem of invalid links between supporting materials and conclusions. Speech materials may be misapplied on several accounts: (1) the materials may be irrelevant to a conclusion, (2) the relationship of the materials to the conclusion may be exaggerated, or (3) the materials may have only an ambiguous connection to a conclusion.

A letter to the editor in *Newsweek* illustrates how an advocate may fall into the trap of using an ***irrelevant reason*** to support a point. One writer wanted to comment on an earlier article about United States veterans who, during a tour of duty in Japan, were exposed to radiation from the atomic bombs dropped on Hiroshima and Nagasaki. The writer supported the idea that the United States government should aid the veterans, and probably this sentiment was shared by many *Newsweek* readers. However, the *Newsweek* writer based the case for government aid to the veterans with an analogy far removed from the matter under consideration. Federal help was justified, the writer asserted, because "our government should be taking care of its own before playing doctor to a man like the Shah [of Iran]."[49] This comment made for an interesting comparison, but it was essentially irrelevant to the needs and claims of the World War II veterans.

In addition to using irrelevant arguments, advocates may misapply speech materials by ***exaggerating*** the extent to which the materials supply actual proof. We are all familiar with the automobile gas mileage ratings supplied by the Environmental Protection Agency (EPA). To assess the relevancy of the EPA statistics to arguments about auto mileage, one must note that the ratings are gathered in unrealistic operating conditions. Professional drivers operate the cars on laboratory treadmill-like devices. For this reason, the EPA figures are valid only as *comparisons* among cars. Automobile commercials, however, usually cite the figures to establish the merits of a *single* type of car. One may find in small print the notation that actual mileage "may" vary. It certainly will!

Another way that speech materials may be misapplied is through ***ambiguity*** in the connection between proof and conclusion. When colleges in California were faced with funding cuts, among the proposals being considered by the legislature was a limitation in the salaries of college administrators. Testifying against the proposal, one college dean argued that the limitations would harm higher education. "We need competent academic leadership to get through these times," contended the dean.[50] The problem in this particular argument is that "competent" does not necessarily mean "more highly paid." The ambiguous relationship between competence and pay has always been a prominent feature of higher education, since few enter college teaching with the expectation of attaining a high salary. The dean's argument had an equivocal validity in view of the ambiguous connection between his claim and proof.

Box 7.3

Ambiguity: It May be Smart—But is it Valid?

In 1968, media advisers for Richard Nixon prepared a television spot that showed scenes of wounded American and South Vietnamese soldiers. In a voice-over, Nixon stated: "Never has so much military, economic, and diplomatic power been used as ineffectively as in Vietnam."

The solution? Nixon concluded: "I pledge to you: we will have an honorable end to the war in Vietnam."

What kind of end? Military? Diplomatic?

Why was he so vague? A Gallup Poll of May 1968 showed that 41 percent of the public wanted to use more aggressive military tactics in Vietnam. On the other hand, 41 percent wanted reduced military efforts (with 18 percent expressing no preference).

Nixon wanted votes from "hawks" and "doves."

Effective? Valid?

The tests of rhetorical validity given above supply no easy answer to the problem of selective perception in gathering and using speech materials. Research shows that people are only about fifty percent successful in applying tests to assess whether evidence actually proves an assertion.[51] Furthermore, training in critical analysis does not immunize students against fallacious arguments when the students already have an attitude about the subject.[52] Though tests of evidence supply no pat answer to the problem of validity, they provide a starting point for rhetorical competence. They help us overcome the specific problems of distorting or misapplying speech materials.

When you take on the attitudes of the rhetorically competent speaker, you will seek valid speech materials as a matter of principle. However, validity is not simply a matter of politeness. History shows that invalid arguments can reduce an advocate's long-term persuasiveness. A classic illustration of the relationship between invalid arguments and failed persuasion may be observed in the case of the Johnson Administration's effort to win support for its policy of military intervention in Vietnam. The Administration denied vehemently that the conflict between North and South Vietnam could be considered a civil war. Washington insisted that the Saigon government represented true democracy versus the dictatorial nature of the enemy. Finally, the White House argued that failure to support Saigon would inevitably lead to a wider war in Asia, possibly even to World War III.

As members of Congress and the general public gradually came to learn more about the Vietnam War, assertions by the Administration were increasingly seen as distorted and exaggerated. The early protests against

Vietnam policy came from Congressmen, college teachers, and clergy who believed the Administration had used propaganda rather than proof.[53] News reporters, too, began to report less favorably on the war when the Tet Offensive of 1968 seemed to give lie to the Administration's claim that the enemy was close to defeat.[54] By relying on claims whose validity was exaggerated, the Johnson Administration set the stage for a credibility gap that fatally undermined support for the Administration's war policies.

Questions of persuasiveness and validity in speech materials bring us to the essential point of this chapter. To be effective, we must deliver speeches *of substance*. Arguments, evidence, and visual aids supply the stuff of which good speeches are crafted. Rhetorically competent speakers should be alert to gathering arguments and evidence that fall under the categories of description, interpretation, and evaluation. Because these forms of argument correspond to the issues of fact, definition, and value, these categories take you through the full range of questions that may be raised about a topic. A further resource is the chance to supplement words with visuals. Visuals can help transform any one of your points into the kind of striking idea that is remembered and that serves as a basis for action.

Visuals

Arguments and evidence typically are things heard but not seen—just the opposite of the ideal child in the era of our grandparents. Though many speakers can safely omit visual aids, some situations call for—even require—visuals. In business presentations, for example, the speaker is often expected to organize remarks around slides or transparencies. In short, there are reasons that you will want to consider the potential contributions of visual aids. Beginning with the available range of visual materials, let us consider the possible advantages of visuals in speechmaking.

Visuals Available to the Speaker

Visual materials run along a continuum beginning with real objects and ending with words on a chart. Speakers may take up any element in the gamut of visual support: (1) real action by the speaker or participation by the audience, (2) an object itself, (3) scale models, (4) motion pictures, (5) still pictures, (6) maps, (7) diagrams, (8) graphs, or (9) printed handouts.

Table 7.2 Visual aids

Type	Examples of use	Advantages
Real action	Show exercise method; Use audience participation	Gives vivid impression; Makes point memorable
An object itself	Carving equipment; Art object	Gets attention; Gives reality to words
Model	Model of human body (small scale model); Model of atomic particle (large scale model)	Shows relationship among parts of object or steps of a process
Motion pictures (film or VCR)	Show the action of making a carving	Presents live action to clarify explanation; Shows action that cannot be done during speech
Still pictures (paper or film)	Picture of injuries of abused children	Creates strong mental image of events, persons, situations
Map	Map of Europe to accompany talk on travel	Shows comparative location
Diagram	Architect's plans; Table of organization of a business	Shows physical layout of organization, system, or object
Graph	*Pie graph* on various sources of electrical power; *Bar graph* on United States trade balance; *Line graph* of rise in cost of living	Makes comparisons and shows relationships—especially those involving statistics
Printed handout	Brochure; Directions for assembling something	Gives quick reference to supplement oral explanation; Can use to collect information from audience

Figure 7.1 lists these common types of visual aids, showing their use and summarizing their advantages. Below, we will consider how every kind of visual material can help your speech. For instance, one student speaker giving a talk on modern dancing asked for *audience participation*. When classmembers stood and walked through some of the steps, the speaker not only held their attention but helped them translate words into movement.

Figure 7.1a
Real action gives a vivid impression and makes a memorable point.

Figure 7.1b
Showing actual equipment adds directness to a speech on fitness.

Figure 7.1c A small model shows detail and yet is manageable.

Figure 7.1d The videocassette recorder is a readily available way to show live action.

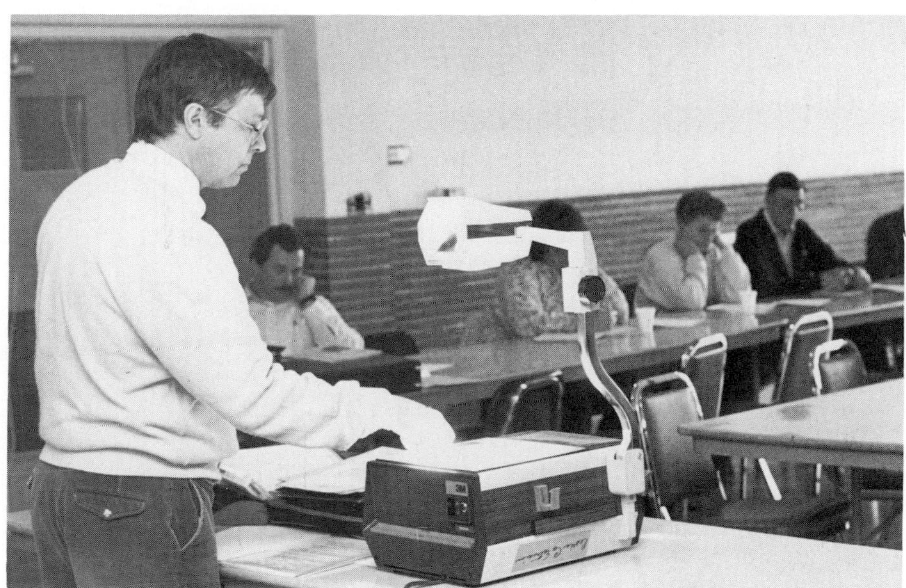

Figure 7.1e Pictures can be shown with slides or an overhead projector.

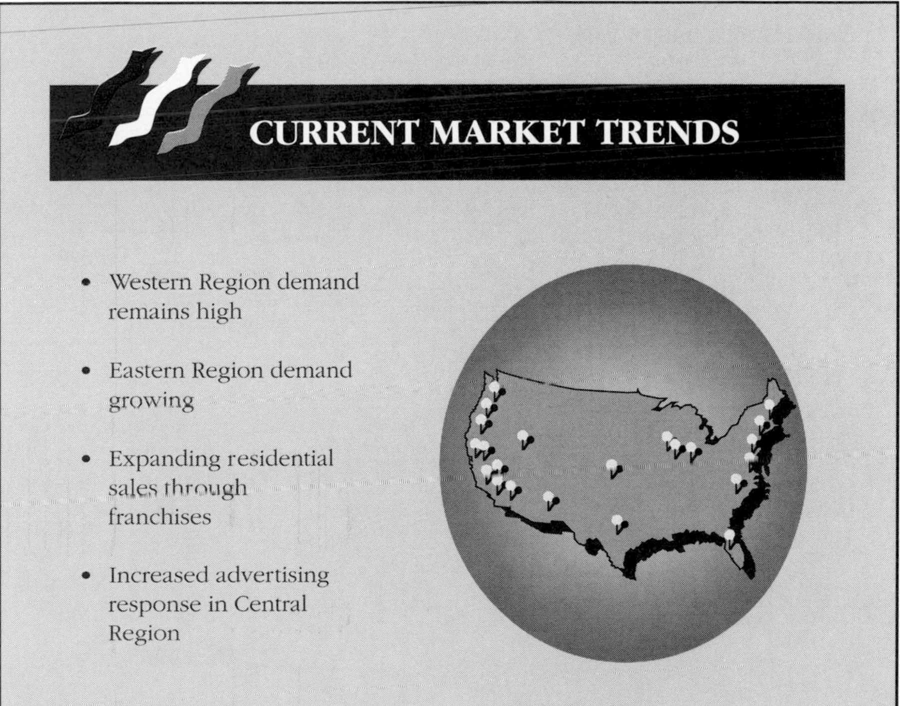

Figure 7.1f Maps show comparative location.

Originally printed on an HP PaintJet Series color graphics printer with the HP Color PrintKit for Macintosh Computers using Aldus Persuasion 1.0 software.

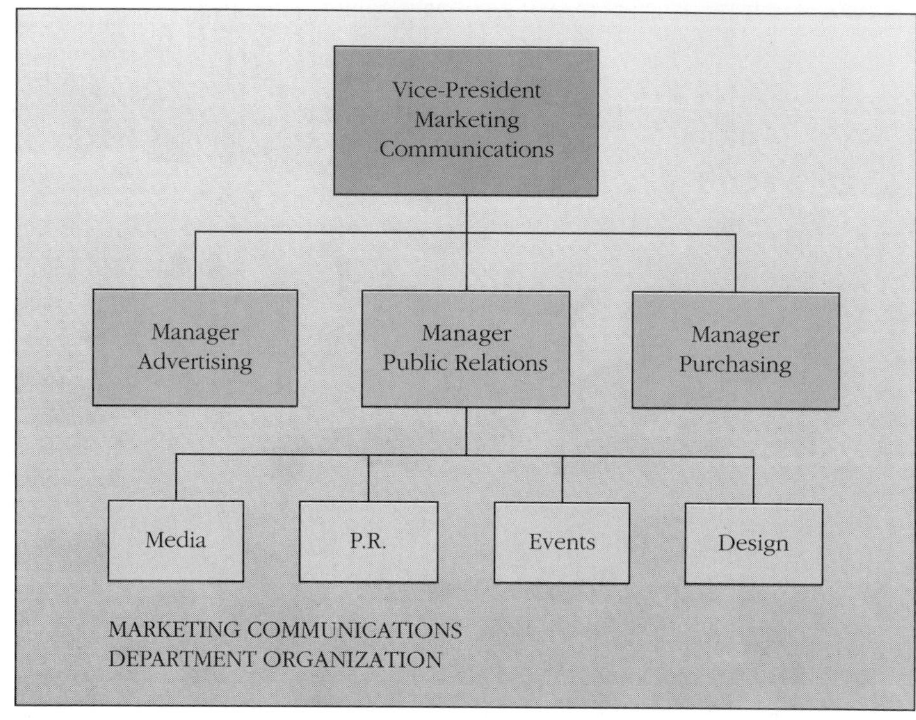

Figure 7.1g
A diagram shows the physical layout of an organization, system, or object.

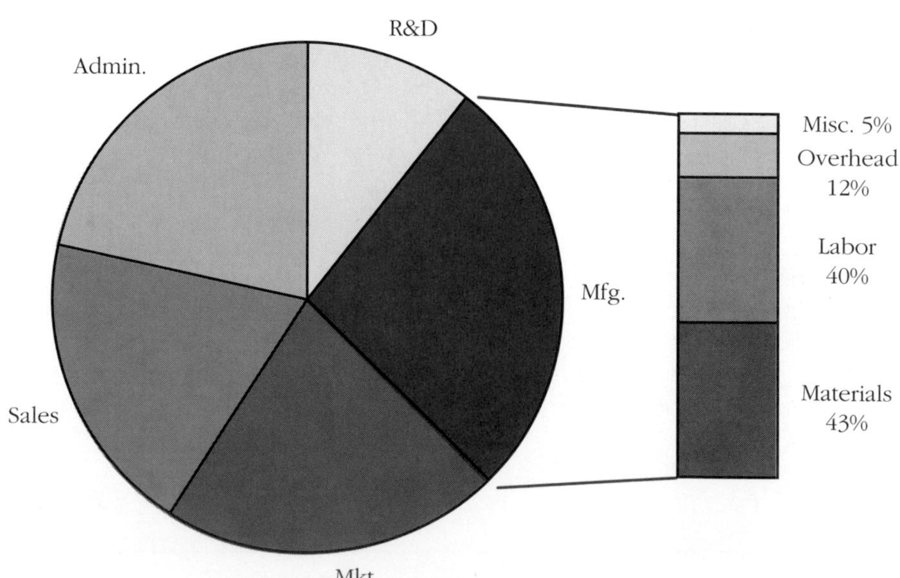

Figure 7.1h
A graph, especially one involving statistics, makes comparisons and shows relations.

Figure 7.1i
Properly used, a printed handout gives quick reference to supplement oral explanation.

Reasons to Use Visuals

It is possible to list several advantages of adding visual materials to the speech. Visuals can help hold and control attention, add clarity, aid retention of information, increase credibility, and enhance persuasiveness.

Visuals materials help win attention. Visuals appeal to our sense of sight, thereby offering you a second channel into the minds of listeners. As you alternately state and show, you create a sense of contrast that helps capture and control the awareness of listeners. Visuals may make a point more vividly than words. The anti-slavery preacher, Henry Ward Beecher, capitalized on this effect. Delivering an abolitionist sermon, Beecher brought a slave girl, still in manacles, into his pulpit.[55] Visuals may also help create a sense of surprise or suspense. A case in point occurred when cartoonist Milton Caniff spoke to an Ohio State University alumni group. Caniff asked a confederate in the audience to come forward. She did so, and Caniff promptly asked her to take off her dress. The student complied—to reveal a T-shirt with the caption "Yea Ohio, Beat Michigan."[56]

Box 7.4

Audience Participation Makes a Point Memorable

National-security adviser Zbigniew Brzezinski wanted to know how many of the student leaders gathered at the White House thought the nation should rely entirely on volunteers for its armed forces.

Almost every one of the more than 250 student-body presidents attending a private briefing yesterday raised a hand.

And how many, Brzezinski then asked, would volunteer themselves?

All but a few of the hands went down.

"That's why we need [draft] registration," the students quoted Brzezinski as saying just before he left the briefing room.

Source: *Louisville Times,* 16 February 1980.

Visuals impart clarity to the speech. Visuals make the speech seem more real by exhibiting what otherwise would merely be heard. Words represent what is called a digital code, that is, a system in which each symbol gradually builds up an idea. In contrast, when showing objects, charts, or slides, the speaker creates an immediate, full-scale impression. Edward Everett, the past century's greatest ceremonial speaker (who spoke ahead of Lincoln at Gettysburg) often used physical objects to enhance reality. In one speech, he held up a powder horn to fix the minds of listeners more closely on his account of the Battle of Lexington. In another, he hoisted an ear of corn to exhibit the contrast between Indian maize and California's gold.[57] Following the example of Everett, the student speaker, Jack Dodds, used a citrus orange to set up the contrast between the beauties of nature and the toxic man-made chemical, Agent Orange.

Visual aids have been found to help people *remember* the content of a speech. Testifying in House hearings, Joseph Duffey, of the National Endowment for the Humanities, spoke in favor of government support for the preservation of library books. To give a memorable impression of this seemingly dull problem, Duffey held up several deteriorating volumes from the Library of Congress. The books fell apart in his hands, creating a vivid image that legislators remembered.[58] Research shows that graphs, charts, and pictures can assist in retention of information. Research studies are inconsistent on the question of whether visuals *always* make the ideas of the speech significantly more memorable.[59] However, the findings generally support using visuals to convey the gist of your major ideas.

Finally, visual materials may enhance both credibility and persuasiveness. Visuals do not automatically make a speaker more credible and persuasive; but this beneficial effect has been documented on some occasions.[60]

It is not difficult to understand why visual materials would help in the performance of communication skills. The effect is apparent when public speaking students deliver a speech to demonstrate how something works. When speakers present the steps in making something, or when they use charts and diagrams to summarize components of a system, visual materials keep things organized, often making notes unnecessary. Students also find that handling visuals helps reduce anxiety by keeping focus on the message itself instead of on personal feelings.

Guidelines for Using Visuals

Minding the proper use of visuals is the key to success with them. Following are some handy tips for successfully incorporating visual aids into your speech.

1. Keep visual materials simple. For instance, a rule of thumb for an overhead projector transparency is to limit the information to six words per line and six lines per sheet.
2. Be sure that each visual makes just one point. Work for focus and avoid clutter. Use everything in the visuals you present; presenting a complicated visual and treating just part of it is distracting.
3. Remember that the criteria for choosing visual materials are the same as for selecting good arguments and evidence. Does the visual advance the thesis? Does it support an important point in the speech? Is the visual aid appropriate for use for a particular audience, location, and time limit?
4. Use advance planning. If you will be using videotape or slide materials, be sure that you or someone else are able to provide the necessary equipment. Make sure that the room will accommodate your materials.
5. Practice your speech using the visual materials. Do not wait until the time of the speech to integrate visuals with your other arguments and evidence. Modify your speaking or your visuals until the two fit well together.
6. Remember that visuals can distract the audience from points you are making orally. In some cases, you can prevent distraction by keeping visual aids out of view until you use them. Circulating material to listeners while you speak may distract the audience from what you are saying. Unless you are referring to the handouts frequently, perhaps you could distribute them after the speech.
7. Practice until you can skillfully create or modify your visuals during the speech. If you write on the blackboard, avoid breaking eye contact with listeners for more than a few moments. When using slides, look at the screen briefly, then turn, face listeners, and direct the rest of your remarks to them.

Your class in public speaking is a chance to get some new speech experiences at relatively low risk and cost. If you have never used visual materials, make it a point to include them in at least one of your classroom presentations. Don't treat visuals as something to be ignored unless specifically required for a speech assignment. Use visual materials in each speech.

Chapter 7 is your introduction to the basic stuff of which speeches are fashioned. If you take to heart the importance of selecting and using strong speech materials, you will be well on the way to becoming a permanently impressive speaker. Using arguments, evidence, and visuals in your speech is not simply a matter of technical skill, however. You must acquire the underlying knowledge about and attitudes toward valid and impressive evidence. Senator Thomas Hart Benton's passion for strong speech materials once led him to hire a teacher to instruct him in Spanish. Benton wanted to gain a first-hand understanding of western land grants, and so he learned how to read the documents in the original.[61] Like Benton, you should aim to gather specific and authoritative materials. With this attitude, you will be all the more likely to apply credible evidence to best effect in your speeches.

Concepts for Review

Can you summarize the meaning of these terms or expressions? How does each relate to speechmaking?

permanently impressive speaker
argument
issue
issue of fact
issue of definition
issue of value
description
example
personal example
interpretation
comparison
argument of cause
argument of sign
argument of consequences
fear appeal
reductio ad absurdum
humor as argument
dilemma
evaluations
values and motivation
evidence
testimony
credibility of witnesses
descriptive statistics
inferential statistics
evidence & authoritativeness
when to use evidence
how to use evidence
valid speech materials
distortion by commission
distortion by omission
irrelevant reason
exaggerated reason
ambiguous reason
types of visual aids
benefits of visual aids
how to use visual aids

Things to Try

1. Construct a thesis statement and identify two arguments for it and two arguments against it. Now, classify these four arguments as to type. Are the arguments chiefly descriptive, interpretative, or evaluative? Can you be more specific in classifying the arguments? Are they comparisons, fear appeals, etc?
2. Select an argument or an item of evidence that you might use in a persuasive speech. Test this sample speech material according to the standard of validity, applying (a) the tests of distortion and (b) those of misapplication. Now, reflect a bit on the persuasiveness of the speech material for your audience. Is your argument or evidence more persuasive than it is valid?
3. To see how speakers use evidence, select a sample printed speech for analysis, consulting such sources as *Vital Speeches* or the index for the *New York Times.* As you read the speech, note where the speaker uses evidence to support a point. Take two of the most significant instances of evidence and evaluate them. According to the advice on using evidence given in this textbook, does the speaker use evidence well?
4. Consider how visual aids might apply to a speech you are planning to give. Identify at least two places in your speech where visual aids would help. What type of aid? What does the visual help you achieve: attention, clarity, memorableness, credibility, persuasiveness?

Endnotes

1. From a public lecture by David Powers, aide to John F. Kennedy, John F. Kennedy Library, Columbia Point, MA, 5 November 1987.
2. Roy C. McCall, "Theodore Parker," *A History and Criticism of American Public Address,* ed. W. N. Brigance, 2 vols. (New York: Russell and Russell, 1943), 1: 242.
3. Cicero, *De Inventione,* I. viii, 10; Quintilian, *Institutio Oratoria,* III, vi, 1–104.
4. Cicero, *The Oration of M. Tullius Cicero for T. Annius Milo,* 2, 5, 9, 10, 21, 28, 38, especially.
5. Paul I. Rosenthal, "Specificity, Verifiability, and Message Credibility," *Quarterly Journal of Speech 57* (1971): 399.
6. Tamara Carbone, "Stylistic Variables as Related to Source Credibility: A Content Analysis Approach," *Speech Monographs 42* (1975): 99–106.
7. Lionel Crocker, "Make the Illustration Linger," *Today's Speech 4,* No. 1 (1956): 5.

8. Aristotle, *Rhetoric,* II. 19. 1393a.
9. Dick A. Bridges and John C. Reinard, Jr., "The Effects of Refutational Techniques on Attitude Change," *Journal of the American Forensic Association 10* (1974): 203–212.
10. *Courier-Journal* [Louisville], 23 May 1981, A2.
11. *Newsweek,* 26 October 1981, 6.
12. *Newsweek,* November-December 1984 issue on "The Fall Campaign," 109.
13. Richard Weaver, *The Ethics of Rhetoric* (Chicago: Henry Regnery, 1953), 211ff.
14. Weaver, *Ethics;* Edward D. Steele and W. Charles Redding, "The American Value System: Premises for Persuasion," *Western Speech 26* (1962): 83–91; Jurgen Ruesch and Gregory Bateson, *Communication: The Social Matrix of Psychiatry* (New York: W. W. Norton, 1968), 94–134; Robert N. Bellah, et al., *Habits of the Heart* (New York: Harper and Row, 1985).
15. See James C. McCroskey, "A Summary of Experimental Research on the Effects of Evidence in Persuasive Communication," *Quarterly Journal of Speech 55* (1969): 170 and John C. Reinard, "The Empirical Study of the Persuasive Effects of Evidence: The Status After Fifty Years of Research," *Human Communication Research 15* (1988): 5–8.
16. *San Francisco Chronicle,* 15 July 1987, 10.
17. Irving D. Warren, "The Effect of Credibility in Sources of Testimony on Audience Attitudes Toward Speaker and Message," *Speech Monographs 36* (1969): 456–458.
18. Reinard, "Persuasive Effects of Evidence," 34.
19. David Hume, *Enquiries Concerning the Human Understanding and Concerning the Principles of Morals,* ed. L. A. Selby-Bigge, 2nd ed. (Oxford: Clarendon, 1902), 112–113. Reprinted from the edition of 1777.
20. Robert P. Newman and Keith R. Sanders, "A Study in the Integrity of Evidence," *Journal of the American Forensic Association 2* (1965): 8.
21. *Peninsula Times Tribune,* 30 August 1987, A7.
22. Reinard, "Persuasive Effects of Evidence," 24–25.
23. *Newsweek,* 23 March 1981, 53.
24. *USA Today,* 6 November 1987, 5A.
25. McCroskey, "Effects of Evidence"; Robert N. Bostrom and Raymond K. Tucker, "Evidence, Personality, and Attitude Change," *Speech Monographs 36* (1969): 22–27; B. Thomas Florence, "An Empirical Test of the Relationship of Evidence to Belief Systems and Attitude Change," *Human Communication Research 1* (1975): 145–158; Helen Fleshler, Joseph Ilardo, and Joan Demoretcky, "The Influence of Field Dependence, Speaker Credibility Set, and Message Documentation on Evaluations of Speaker and Message Credibility," *Southern Speech Communication Journal 39* (1974): 389–402; Reinard, "Persuasive Effects of Evidence."
26. John A. Kline, "Dogmatism of the Speaker and Selection of Evidence," *Speech Monographs 38* (1971): 345–355; Kathy Kellermann, "The Concept of Evidence: A Critical Review," *Journal of the American Forensic Association 16* (1980): 159–172; Reinard, "Persuasive Effects of Evidence," 40–46.

27. William R. Dresser, "The Impact of Evidence on Decision Making," *Journal of the American Forensic Association 3* (1966): 47.
28. Forest L. Whan, "Stephen A. Douglas," *A History and Criticism of American Public Address,* ed. W. N. Brigance, 2 vols. (New York: Russell and Russell, 1943), 1: 818.
29. Richard H. Rovere, *Senator Joe McCarthy* (New York: Harper, 1959), 169–170.
30. Fleshler, *et al.,* "Speaker and Message Credibility."
31. McCroskey, "Effects of Evidence," and Joseph A. Luchok and James C. McCroskey, "The Effect of Quality of Evidence on Attitude Change and Source Credibility," *Southern Speech Communication Journal 43* (1978): 371–383.
32. Thomas B. Harte, "The Effects of Evidence in Persuasive Communication," *Central States Speech Journal 27* (1976): 42–46.
33. James C. McCroskey, "The Effects of Evidence as an Inhibitor of Counter-Persuasion," *Speech Monographs 37* (1970): 188–194.
34. Warren, "Credibility in Sources."
35. Bradley S. Greenberg and Gerald R. Miller, "The Effects of Low-Credible Sources on Message Acceptance," *Speech Monographs 33* (1966): 127–136.
36. Luchok & McCroskey, "Quality of Evidence."
37. William E. Arnold and James C. McCroskey, "The Credibility of Reluctant Testimony," *Central States Speech Journal 18* (1967): 97–103; McCroskey, "Effects of Evidence"; Loren Anderson, "An Experimental Study of Reluctant and Biased Authority-Based Assertions," *Journal of the American Forensic Association 7* (1970): 79–84.
38. McCroskey, "Effects of Evidence."
39. Luchok & McCroskey, "Quality of Evidence."
40. Fleshler, *et al.,* "Speaker and Message Credibility."
41. Greenberg & Miller, "Low-Credible Sources."
42. McCroskey, "Effects of Evidence."
43. Stanley E. Jones, "Attitude Changes of Public Speakers During the Investigative and Expressive Stages of Advocacy," *Speech Monographs 33* (1966): 137–146, and Keith Jensen and David A. Carter, "Self-Persuasion: The Effects of Public Speaking on Speakers," *Southern Speech Communication Journal 46* (1981): 163–174.
44. Frederic A. Powell, "Cognitive Tuning and Differentiation of Arguments in Communication," *Human Communication Research 1* (1974): 53–61.
45. Gerald R. Miller, "Some Factors Influencing Judgments of the Logical Validity of Arguments: A Research Review," *Quarterly Journal of Speech 55* (1969): 276–286.
46. *San Francisco Chronicle,* 12 April 1988, A14.
47. *Newsweek,* 30 August 1976, 67.
48. *New York Times* (City Edition), 12 July 1977, 26M, and George Will, *Courier-Journal* [Louisville], 20 February 1978, A7.
49. *Newsweek,* 17 December 1979, 5.
50. *Chronicle of Higher Education,* 26 June 1978, 5.
51. Thomas B. Harte, "Audience Ability to Apply Tests of Evidence," *Journal of the American Forensic Association 8* (1971): 109–115.

52. Roy V. Wood, James J. Bradac, Sara A. Barnhart, and Edward Kraft, "The Effect of Learning About Techniques of Propaganda on Subsequent Reaction to Propagandistic Communications," *Speech Teacher 19* (1970): 49–53.
53. Marie E. Rosenwasser, "Six Senate War Critics and Their Appeals for Gaining Audience Response," *Today's Speech 17,* No. 3 (1969): 43–50; Jess Yoder, "The Protest of the American Clergy in Opposition to the War in Vietnam," *Today's Speech 17,* No. 3 (1969): 51–59; Howard Martin, "The Rhetoric of Academic Protest," *Central States Speech Journal 17* (1966): 244–250.
54. Edward J. Epstein, *Between Fact and Fiction* (New York: Vintage Books, 1975), 220–223.
55. Lionel Crocker, "Henry Ward Beecher," *A History and Criticism of American Public Address,* ed. W. N. Brigance, 2 vols. (New York: Russell and Russell, 1943), 1: 282.
56. *Ohio State University Monthly,* June 1979, 3.
57. Ronald F. Reid, "Edward Everett: Rhetorician of Nationalism, 1824–1855," *Quarterly Journal of Speech 42* (1956): 280.
58. *Chronicle of Higher Education,* 28 April 1980, 11.
59. William J. Seiler, "The Conjunctive Influence of Source Credibility and the Use of Visual Materials on Communication Effectiveness," *Southern Speech Communication Journal 37* (1971a): 174–185; Seiler, "The Effects of Visual Materials on Attitudes, Credibility, and Retention," *Speech Monographs 38* (1971b): 331–334; Seiler, "Audiovisual Materials in Classroom Instruction: A Theoretical Approach," *Speech Teacher 21* (1972): 197–204.
60. Seiler, "Credibility and Visual Materials," and Seiler, "Effects of Visual Materials."
61. Norman W. Mattis, "Thomas Hart Benton," *A History and Criticism of American Public Address,* ed. M. K. Hochmuth [Nichols] (New York: Russell and Russell, 1955), 77.

Part III

Arranging the Materials

Chapter

8

Putting Materials into Sequence

Outline

> The cabinet meeting, scheduled for ten o'clock that morning, had been postponed to eleven because the President was not up at ten.
>
> On the hour, Nixon walked into the room and took his seat at the center of the oval table. There wasn't the usual applause. . . .
>
> "I would like to discuss the most important issue confronting this nation," the President began, "and confronting us internationally too—inflation."
>
> Cabinet members looked about in mild astonishment.
>
> But Nixon quickly shifted to what was on everybody's mind. "I want the facts out," he said. He described Watergate as "one the most asinine things that was ever done. I'll take whatever lumps are involved."[1]

How we arrange our ideas makes a difference. The scene in the White House cabinet room occurred just two days before Richard M. Nixon became the first to resign from the presidency. When Nixon began his talk to the cabinet on the topic of inflation, heads turned in bewilderment. The cabinet officers wondered about a more fundamental matter—who would be president? Would Nixon resign or would he fight for office by undergoing an impeachment trial? When President Nixon organized his remarks to the cabinet as if the meeting were a routine session, he called attention to a key principle of rhetorical competence. The order of our ideas must respond appropriately to the demands of subject and situation.

In chapter 2 we observed that *structure* referred to the ideas and words of the speech, together with how those ideas and words were arranged. This chapter marks our first comprehensive look at sequencing ideas for a speech. We begin with a general view of the skill of organization. Next, our attention turns to the steps for developing an outline. We conclude with a look at using transitions to make sure the audience follows the arrangement of points we have prepared.

Organizing Your Ideas

When is your speech well-organized? As applied to speechmaking, *organization* encompasses several related skills of preparation and execution.

1. You develop an outline of important points.
2. You make minor ideas subordinate to major ones.
3. You use *transitions*—statements that highlight or tie together points on the outline.

Every one of these three elements of organization can contribute to your success in conveying the content of your speech, but before looking at these individual components of organization, we should consider the skill in general.

Exactly how does organization figure in speechmaking? First of all, remember that organization is something basic both to people and to speeches. Organization is an act of categorizing things, and so this skill is closely related to thinking itself.[2] Furthermore, organization is a bedrock element of speaking. Early experimental research established that, when questioned about a speech, listeners are fully able to discuss whether the message is well- or poorly-organized.[3]

Since organization is a fundamental part of thinking and speaking, we have reason to believe that effective arrangement contributes to effectiveness in public speaking. Research bears out this common sense assumption. A number of studies show that organization not only helps in getting listeners to remember your speech, but it also helps win support for your thesis.

Box 8.1

Poor Organization Helped Keep the Democrats Out of the White House

In 1984

Associated Press—WASHINGTON—Walter F. Mondale, looking back on his landslide defeat in the 1984 presidential election, said yesterday that he "fundamentally mishandled" the case he tried to make to the American people by failing to emphasize the positive side of his message.

"They heard opportunity from the other side; they didn't hear it from me," the former Democratic presidential nominee said on NBC-TV's "Meet the Press."

Source: Associated Press–Washington (*Courier-Journal,* [Louisville], April 8, 1985, p. A2).

In 1988

John Sasso, who headed the presidential campaign of Michael S. Dukakis, commented on the causes for the defeat. Sasso placed blame directly on Dukakis and his staff for failing to establish "a central and sustained theme." This mistake "created a vacuum" in which the Republicans could win points with television ads stressing the American flag and the Massachusetts furlough program for convicts.

Source: (*Times-Tribune,* [Palo Alto], January 25, 1989, p. A15).

First, good organization increases the extent to which listeners understand and remember your message. This effect does not always occur, but reviews of the research literature reveal a strong general connection between speech organization and comprehension.[4] Even relatively minor changes in speech structure can increase or decrease how much listeners remember about it. To test the impact of organization, researchers sometimes take a well-organized speech and randomly rearrange sentences in the introduction, body, or conclusion. Findings show that listeners are less able to recall if the sequence of sentences has been rearranged.[5] Similarly, when researchers randomly rearrange the paragraphs in a speech text, listeners remember significantly less about it.[6]

Second, good organization increases the ability of listeners to use effectively the ideas you present in a speech. In one study, researchers gave students a number of facts about a World War II battle. Listeners received the facts in messages that varied in quality of organization. After listening to the well-organized message, receivers were better able to generalize, that is, identify patterns or trends in the message. Also, students hearing the well-organized message were better able to use information to solve specific problems later presented to them.[7]

Finally, you can expect that a well-organized speech will markedly improve your credibility and persuasiveness—two important benchmarks of speech success. Research shows a connection between good organization and improved speaker credibility. Correspondingly, disorganization leaves a bad impression. In some cases, disorganization will cause members of a student audience to think less favorably of a speaker than before. In other cases, a disorganized speaker does not lose credibility but merely fails to receive the normal credibility boost that accompanies a well-put-together speech.[8] Good organization not only helps credibility; it can increase your persuasiveness. Studies show that when your presentation is well-organized, you are significantly more likely to move listeners to your point of view.[9]

Abraham Lincoln was particularly effective in making sure that his speeches were clearly organized around his thesis. In debates with Stephen Douglas, Lincoln was careful to subordinate minor points to his dominant theme that slavery should not be extended into the territories. Because Lincoln kept all remarks tightly connected to this one main point, his speeches probably carried more long-term effectiveness than those of his opponent, Douglas.[10]

In sum, expect that your speeches will be more effective as you improve your ability to organize. What's more, when you acquire the skill of organization, you will reap benefits in situations other than public speaking. Research shows that people skilled in organization gain four additional benefits.

1. They recall more details when they listen to a message.[11]
2. They better use details to form generalizations.[12]
3. They better use information to solve related problems.[13]
4. They comprehend more when reading.[14]

These findings show that organization is a skill well worth cultivating. By acquiring this aspect of rhetorical competence, you will function better as a thinker, writer, and speaker.

Up to this point we have considered organization *in general.* Now it is time for us to consider the several different dimensions that, together, make up this skill. In the next two sections of the chapter, we will examine how to build the speech outline and, further, how to be sure your important points actually get across to listeners.

Preparing by Outlining

Reduced to its basic elements, a speech is a set of points, put in logical order, that supports a thesis. The logical arrangement of your points amounts to your *outline,* the skeleton of your presentation.

Basic Rules of Outlining

It is difficult to overstate the importance of preparing a written outline as an early step in speechmaking. Putting across your thesis effectively *requires* outlining. Only by using an outline are you able to organize the materials of the speech into a coherent format ready for presentation. For reference as you prepare your upcoming speeches, pay attention to these four essential guidelines for outlining.

1. Write out each idea in the outline as a complete sentence. A sentence is the basic unit of argument, so only by using sentences will your outline clearly state the ideas that illustrate or prove your thesis.
2. To make the outline logical and easy to follow, adopt a consistent pattern of symbols to designate major points and subpoints. The common practice is to use the following order of symbols: I, A, 1, a, (1), (a).

3. Be sure that each point on the outline expresses only one idea.
4. Make an effort to have at least two points at every level of the outline. For instance, if you wish to elaborate either or both of your major points, I and II, be sure to have at least two subpoints, A and B. If you want to elaborate either or both of your A and B points, have at least two ideas, 1 and 2, and so on. If you want to express only one point at a particular level of your outline, consider placing this idea somewhere else.

Just as knowing traffic laws is only a first step in getting a driver's license, the rules of outlining are mere preliminaries in helping you arrange points in the speech.

Box 8.2

The Bottom Line of Organization

A speech has two parts. You must state your case, and you must prove it.

Source: Aristotle, *Rhetoric,* III. 13. 30.

Structure of an Outline

Building an outline requires finding the important ideas to be presented and putting these points in the most appropriate order. The resulting outline of your speech divides itself naturally into three parts: (1) the introduction, (2) the body, and (3) the conclusion. In idealized form, your speech outline will follow the pattern shown in table 8.1.

Since the body of the speech holds around 80 percent of speech content, most of your outlining work will pertain to the body. The body of the speech is the place where you present the *major points* that you will use to get across your thesis (main idea). Your major points are the two to five theme ideas that, taken together, lead listeners to your overall thesis. As table 8.1 shows, each of your major points, in turn, may be supported by one, two, or three levels of *subpoints.* Subpoints are subsidiary ideas on your outline. You enter subpoints on your outline beneath the more important points they clarify, support, prove, or elaborate.

Let's take a close look at how major points and subpoints function in the bodies of actual informative and persuasive speeches.

Table 8.1 The speech outline

Introduction	
You give one or more short points to introduce the topic of your speech.	
Body	
I. Major point	[two to five in speech]
A. First level subpoint	[at least one level of
1. Second level subpoint	subpoints—but possibly two or
2. Second level subpoint	three]
B. First level subpoint	
1. Second level subpoint	
2. Second level subpoint	
II. Major point	[plus subpoints]
III. Major point	[plus subpoints]
Conclusion	
One or more short points to conclude the speech.	

Major points

Your major points are the two to five ideas in the body of your speech that, taken together, illustrate or prove your thesis. As an example of an outline for an informative speech, we turn to the speech prepared by Jacquelyn Flanigan, an undergraduate student. Jacquelyn's informative treatment of the Mafia focused on the ironic finding that Mafia criminals share many of the traditional values held by Americans. To convey this thesis, Jacquelyn developed these major points. (See the text of this speech on pp. 384–386.)

I. Americans traditionally hold six important values.
II. The Mafia value system developed in Italy and was refined with Italian immigration to the United States.
III. The Mafia value system focuses on security, family, and religion.

These three major points give details about the comparative values held by Americans and the Mafia. The result is to elaborate and clarify Jacquelyn's thesis that the two are ironically similar.

In an informative speech, such as that by Jacquelyn Flanigan, the major points act to clarify or elaborate the thesis. On the other hand, in the persuasive speech, major points more often act to prove or defend the thesis. We turn now to a sample persuasive speech, that by William F. Buckley, Jr. (reprinted on pp. 421–426). Buckley's thesis is that the United States Senate should ratify two treaties that gradually turn over operations of the Panama Canal to the nation of Panama. Since Buckley's purpose is persuasive, he wants to do more than clarify the meaning of his thesis. He wants listeners to agree with his main idea. Therefore the three major points he presents function also to establish and prove his case.

I. Many conservative anti-communists support the treaties.
II. Supporters of the treaties are neither weak nor naive.
III. The United States will be better off militarily, economically, and spiritually by ratifying the treaties.

The informative speech by Jacquelyn Flanigan and the persuasive address by William Buckley each present three major points. This is well, for a rhetorical rule of thumb is to have at least two and no more than five contentions. Listeners cannot remember everything you say in the speech, so they will take away more ideas if you center on a few important themes.[15] Your audience will better understand and remember your message when you organize it around a few well-developed key ideas.[16]

One useful way to keep focus on your major points is to use *capsule statements* to introduce them. Receivers comprehend more when you begin each key point with a clear sentence, such as when Jack Dodds argued "We can help the victims of Agent Orange." Listeners understand and retain less when general, fuzzy material precedes the statement of a major point.[17]

Once you have developed between two and five major points, you are ready to develop subpoints for each of your key supporting ideas.

Subpoints

To make your major points compelling, you must present subsidiary ideas that elaborate, clarify, prove, explain, and/or support the major points. These subsidiary ideas are your *subpoints.*

To illustrate subpoints in an informative speech, we turn to Jacquelyn Flanigan's speech. For two of her three major points, Jacquelyn presents subpoints:

I. Americans traditionally hold several important values— family, freedom, liberty, and church.
II. The Mafia value system developed in Italy and was refined with Italian immigration to the United States.
    A. The Mafia began during the Napoleonic Wars.
    B. The Don acted as leader for Italian immigrants.
III. The Mafia value system focuses on security, family, and religion.
    A. The vow of silence is the root of security and freedom.
    B. Mafia members have strong family bonds.
    C. Mafia members are devout Roman Catholics.

Jacquelyn developed subpoints for only two of her three major points. In the case of the first major point—a listing of values held by Americans—she simply enumerated the values rather than develop each one. Her second and third major points more directly expressed her thesis, so she spent time elaborating each with specific historical narration or informative details. Taken together, Jacquelyn's major points and her subpoints establish her thesis about "the truly ironic relationship between the American value system and that of the Mafia."

To observe how subpoints function in the persuasive speech, we turn again to the speech of William F. Buckley, Jr. Like Jacquelyn, Buckley develops subpoints for two of his three major points:

I. Many conservative anti-communists support the treaties— James Burnham, Admiral Zumwalt, Ellsworth Bunker.
II. Supporters of the treaties are neither weak nor naive.
    A. To ratify is not to apologize for our history.
    B. To ratify is not to try to curry favor with other nations.
III. The United States will be better off militarily, economically, and spiritually by ratifying the treaties.
    A. We will be better off militarily to ratify the treaties.
        1. The Panama Canal is useless in nuclear war.
        2. In conventional war, we would need the cooperation of the Panamanian people.
        3. The treaties give the United States a continuing role in defending the canal.
    B. We will be better off economically to ratify the treaties.
        1. We retain much of the canal revenues.
        2. The economic aid given to Panama under the treaty is small compared to the billions we spend elsewhere.
    C. We will be better off spiritually to ratify the treaties.
        1. We are not trying to gain grace in the eyes of foreign countries.
        2. We simply endorse the principle that small nations should have sovereignty the same as powerful ones.

As with Jacquelyn's informative speech, Buckley's persuasive speech has major points, designated by Roman numerals, followed by subpoints that are entered with capital letters or Arabic numbers.

Considering the substance of Buckley's outline, his three major points are clearly developed in varying ways. In giving his first major point, Buckley essentially lists names. For his second major point, Buckley states and supports two subpoints. But for his third major point—the advantages of the treaties—Buckley introduces two levels of subpoints. He develops each of his military, economic, and spiritual subpoints to the extent that he presents a second level of subpoints for each. Buckley's speech outline is heavily oriented to the refutation approach discussed in chapter 14. In other words, he frequently identifies and then refutes prominent arguments used by his opponents.

Research shows the benefits of clearly organizing your subpoints around the major points. In a classic psychological study, George Miller found that people remember only a limited number of points from a message. To help people recall details, Miller suggested, communicators should keep individual items closely connected to major points by "chunking" the details. *Chunking* means to link particulars to your general ideas. The result is that you transform your major points into memorable single "chunks" of information.[18]

To this point, we have treated outlining as a matter of putting points on paper. The question inevitably arises of how to make sure that listeners notice the sequence of points you have planned.

Sounding Organized

As you use them in speechmaking, outlines are not entirely or even chiefly creatures of paper. In sequencing your important ideas, your goal is not to achieve an outline that looks nice. Your intention is larger—you want to sound organized when you give the speech. How do you sound organized? The key to sounding organized is to use transitions skillfully. What are *transitions?* They are words, phrases, and patterns of speech that alert listeners to key parts of your speech outline. Transitions are useful to state a point in your outline or to move from one point in the outline to another.

Functions of Transitions

Transitions generally serve to unify the speech. Specifically, transitions perform three interrelated functions: (1) they highlight points, (2) they subordinate points, and (3) they coordinate points.

Box 8.3

Transitions Highlight Your Thesis

Jack Seiler, Senior Vice President of Liberty National Bank and Trust Company, Louisville, Kentucky, teaches a class for people who are planning to begin small businesses. He wants his listeners to remember the point that starting a small business is difficult and risky, so Seiler begins by putting across his thesis clearly—so clearly that it hurts.

Seiler tells his audience of aspiring small businesspersons: "Ninety percent of you are going to fail. It's a fact. I'm sorry, but that's the way it is."

Source: *Courier-Journal* (Louisville), 20 February 1983, E1.

Transitions ***highlight*** or emphasize the important content of your outline, notably the two to five major points you make in the body. The function of highlighting content can be accomplished in various ways. One useful way to highlight a point on your outline is to *repeat* a point more than once, perhaps in slightly different words. In his 1989 Inaugural Address, President Bush several times referred to the idea of unity. At one point, Bush said "unity; in important things," and at another time, he returned to the idea: "In crucial things, unity."[19] You may also highlight by giving a *preview* of points. For instance, William F. Buckley gives a preview of the three subpoints that belonged to his third major point.

> What we are maintaining is that the United States, by signing these treaties, is better off militarily, is better off economically, and is better off spiritually.

Transitional statements often are accompanied by appropriate gesture and movement.

A preview introduces points, whereas a *summary* transition reviews them. For instance, after discussing various values central to Mafia culture, Jacquelyn Flanigan reviewed them with this summary: "Religion—family—security—freedom—these are all values listed under Minnick's six categories of American values."

The second function of transitions is to *subordinate* material in your speech by connecting major points to related minor ones. Subordinating transitions would include any statement linking thesis to major points or major points to subpoints. Thus, Buckley's preview statement—that the United States is better off militarily, economically, and spiritually—also functions to subordinate each of these subpoints to the larger idea that the treaties are beneficial. Subordinating transitions also include those that link evidence to a point that it supports. For instance, Jacquelyn Flanigan says she will "take a brief look at some values Americans traditionally hold." Her next statement gives a transition into her evidence. "In his book, *The Art of Persuasion,* W. C. Minnick categorizes a summary of these values into six headings." Finally, a transition may subordinate ideas by linking any point in the speech to the overall thesis. For instance, Jacquelyn Flanigan states that "the most conclusive illustration of the truly ironic relationship between the American value system and that of the Mafia can be seen in the name of a man who is at present a prominent Mafia leader."

The third function of transitions is to *coordinate* material in the speech. A coordinating transition connects two or more points of an outline that are parallel, that is, appear on the same level. Coordinating transitions include statements that connect two major points, two subpoints, or two evidence citations. Representative of this type of transition would be George Bush's movement from his treatment of domestic problems to international ones in his 1989 Inaugural Address. "To the world, too, we offer new engagement and a renewed vow: We will stay strong to protect the peace."

The general effect of transitions is to boost comprehension.[20] This result is only natural if we look back to Miller's idea that "chunking" together details makes them more memorable. Obviously, your transitions will help in "chunking" specific information around major points. This finding applies directly to your present situation as a student of public speaking. One study showed that students were better able to outline a speech when the speaker previewed major points at the beginning, and then reiterated them in the conclusion.[21]

Keeping in mind that transitions always function to highlight, subordinate, and/or coordinate, we turn now to specific kinds of transitions.

Kinds of Transitions

Transitions usually fall into one or more of three categories: (1) transition words, (2) signpost-type transitions, and (3) transitional patterns.

Transition words and phrases

Probably you can already name many of the familiar transition words and phrases. Try it. How about "next," "also," or "for example?" But don't rest on your laurels. You will improve your ability to communicate a sense of organization if you study the various words or phrases that alert listeners to a shift from one idea to another.

Thirty-six stock expressions that signal transition within the speech are:

accordingly	in addition	on the one hand/other hand
again	in fact	the one/the other
also	in other words	since
although	in short	so
and	let us/it/the	still
because	likewise	then
but	moreover	there
clearly	more important	therefore
finally	next	they say
for example	now	while
furthermore	no doubt	yet
however	not only	
if		

To become familiar with using these words and phrases, look over a couple of the speeches reprinted in this book. Pay particular attention to first words in paragraphs.

When you want to highlight an important point or keep focus on its relationship to other ideas, you may need more than a single transitional word or phrase. In such a situation, you want to combine a transition word with either a signpost or a larger transitional pattern—both discussed below.

Signposts

A signpost is a statement that, almost literally, holds up for view one or more points in your outline. For instance, when you say "I am going to make four points in this speech" (and perhaps mention each one, briefly), you are giving out advance word of your major points. The effect is almost the same as if you held up a sign with each of the four points printed on it. Some speakers actually employ visual signposts, projecting the points onto a screen by means of slides or transparencies.

We may identify five general types of signposts: (1) the preview, (2) the summary, (3) the summary-preview combination, (4) the capsule statement of a major point, and (5) enumeration.

Preview statements give advance notice of upcoming content. Previews are particularly important in informative speeches, in which the speaker uses a general topical heading to lead into the next point on the outline. In Harold L. Enarson's speech on cutting back the Ohio State University budget, he used a preview to launch into examples of quality in education:

> Let's see if we can't identify some of the elements of quality.

Another type of preview is one that actually lists the subpoints to follow. This approach may be observed in Jacquelyn Flanigan's informative speech.

> My speech will be broken down into two main points: (1) the origin and development of the Mafia value system and (2) examples of these values as they exist today.

What about the complaint that previews seem mechanical or artificial? Speakers often experience awkwardness when they first attempt to use previews. Do not let such feelings deter you! You will be able to use previews effectively with practice. And good previews can come *only* when you actually practice using them. The payoff is clear if we turn to research findings showing that preview statements sometimes increase what listeners remember about our speech.[22]

A *summary statement* is a signpost that reviews content. You may use a summary to review either the theme of your speech, the major contentions, or a particular level of points on your outline. Use of the general summary is illustrated by Harold L. Enarson's conclusion to his argument about what quality in education means. "I need not continue my list," Enarson said. "The point has been made. In higher education as in everything else, you get what you pay for."

As an instance of the listing-type summary, we may turn to a speech given by Richard D. Lamm, former Governor of Colorado.

> In conclusion, let me summarize what I've said. America finds itself in an international marketplace and one in which we are *not* winning. The international marketplace will eventually force us to restructure

> much of what we do to make it more efficient and effective. We must ask cost benefit questions of all our societal institutions. One of these institutions—and one high on the list—will be the legal profession.[23]

Summaries, particularly when you summarize in the conclusion, can significantly increase comprehension of the speech.[24]

The *summary-preview combination* is a signpost-type transition that combines a summary with a preview of the following point on the outline. Harold Enarson's informative speech on Ohio State budget cuts included this typical summary-preview transition.

> You have heard the bad news. Now let's talk a moment about exactly what is at stake, as the State of Ohio continues its budget-cutting course of recent years.

In Jack Dodds' persuasive speech, we find him using a summary-preview transition to move from the characteristics of Agent Orange to the results of its use in Vietnam. "That's the cause. What are the effects of this spraying?"

Another kind of signpost is the *capsule statement.* Here you simply state your point in a single phrase, one that is direct and easy to remember. In his 1989 Inaugural Address, President George Bush used the capsulizing phrase "a thousand points of light" to describe his Administration's approach to meeting national goals.

> I have spoken of a "thousand points of light"—of all the community organizations that are spread like stars throughout the nation, doing good.[25]

This idea, or metaphor, expressed Bush's preference for a partnership of government and private groups in solving problems. When you introduce your major points with capsule statements, listeners are more likely to understand and remember them.[26]

Enumeration is a signpost in which you use numbers to list contentions and subpoints. Enumerative transitions work particularly well in situations where you are giving impromptu speeches. Consider the situation of Tom Doyle, student speaker, who took first place in a national speech contest with his extemporaneous talk on United States trade with Japan. Tom was assigned to speak on the question, "Will tariffs on Japanese products stem the United States trade deficit?" He began by repeating the question assigned to him. Then he quickly used enumeration as the entry point into his specific arguments: "And the answer to this to me is clearly, 'No.' And I have two reasons to support this answer."[27]

Box 8.4

Authoritative Speakers Use Clear Transitions

Alexander Hamilton, architect of the United States Constitution and author of the *Federalist Papers,* was not only a disciplined writer. He was also a speaker who used transitions to make his points distinct and powerful.

"In appearing before an audience, Hamilton never relied solely on his charming presence and engaging manner. His speeches uniformly demonstrated an active intelligence energetically at work. . . .

Hamilton's speeches reveal many instances of clear transitions. If the line of the argument was not immediately perspicuous [clear], he introduced such a phrase as 'Without dwelling any longer on this subject, I shall proceed to the question immediately before the committee. . . .' On still another occasion he provided a characteristic transition simply by announcing the new subject: 'I now proceed to consider the objection with regard to the number of representatives, as it now stands.' "

Source: Bower Aly, "Alexander Hamilton," in *A History and Criticism of American Public Address,* ed. M. K. Hochmuth [Nichols] (New York: Russell & Russell, 1955), 34–35.

Transition patterns

Many times you will want to put transition words and signposts into a larger frame of thought. Here you make the points on your outline part of a general theme. Useful transitional patterns include repetition, metaphorical themes, reference to situation, and rhetorical questions.

Repeating a point—your thesis, a major point, a subpoint—brings the dual benefits of emphasis and coordination. The most common form of repetition is using a single phrase several times. For instance, in his speech to the Protestant ministers in Houston, John F. Kennedy says he will describe the kind of America he believes in. Kennedy then alternates between "I believe in an America where" and "this is the kind of America I believe in." Repetition of the phrase gives unity to Kennedy's various ideas on how to promote religious tolerance and church-state separation.

Repetition is often found in truly memorable speeches. It is no accident that the most famous modern instance of repetition comes in one of our era's greatest speeches. Martin Luther King's refrain of "I have a dream" occurs in a string of inspiring visions as King sets out an image of American brotherhood. The usefulness of the repetition approach is borne out in research. Repetitions make the ideas of the speech more memorable, particularly when three or four repetitions of a point are concentrated in a single section of a speech.[28]

Another useful transitional pattern is the *metaphorical theme.* Metaphors are comparisons in which the speaker describes one kind of object in words that are usually applied to another. Thus, the much-overused football theme could serve as a metaphor for a fund raising campaign: "It's fourth down and goal-to-go in meeting our objectives in this year's drive." George Bush used the metaphor of "a new breeze" as an organizing pattern to connect several points in his 1989 Inaugural Address. Early in the speech, Bush commented on changes in governments around the world, saying that the breeze of freedom now refreshed the world. Later, Bush stated that a new breeze of cooperation between Republican and Democrat seemed to stir in Washington. Finally, Bush incorporated the metaphor into his conclusion: "The new breeze blows, a page turns, the story unfolds."

When you make specific *references to the speech situation,* you rely upon a proven way to unify points in your speech. You may develop transitions that refer to yourself, to time, to events, or to the audience. George Bush used a reference to *self* early in his Inaugural Address. "I have just repeated word-for-word the oath taken by George Washington 200 years ago." Ronald Reagan's eulogy on the Challenger astronauts relied heavily on references to *time.* For instance, Reagan remarked on the coincidence that "on this day 390 years ago, the great explorer Sir Francis Drake died aboard ship off the coast of Panama."

In one of his first speeches as president, Ronald Reagan effectively used a reference to *events* in commemorating the spirit of resistance of the American hostages held by Iran.

> I'm told that Sergeant Lopez here put up a sign in his cell . . . and his guards didn't know that "*Viva la roja, blanco, y azul*" means "Long live the red, white and blue."

In the same speech, Reagan employed a reference to *audience.* Reagan told those assembled on the White House lawn that:

> I'm sure that you'll want to know that with us here today are families of the eight heroic men who gave their lives in the attempt to effect your rescue.

Rhetorical questions are arguments phrased in the form of questions. Since they contain the kernel of an argument, rhetorical questions are especially useful in keeping focus on a thesis, a major point, or a subpoint. Consider an example. Explaining how Ohio State University is menaced by state-imposed budget cuts, Harold L. Enarson comments that people ordinarily accept the idea that "we get what we pay for." He continues: "When it comes to the services provided by a university, however, the public apparently thinks that different rules apply." Enarson then states his rhetorical question: "Why should this be so?" The question helps call attention to the links that Enarson then makes between funding and the quality of a university.

Visual materials can serve as signpost transitions.

Transition words, signposts, and transition patterns are available to help unify your speech, but be sure not to treat your transitions as simple pegs to hammer into a board. Making effective transitions requires thought. As you practice your speeches, keep asking two questions.

1. Is it clear how each point I am making relates to the ideas that precede and follow it?
2. Is it clear how each point in my speech relates to the thesis?

If you can answer yes to both questions, then you can be sure that each point in the speech advances your purpose and aims.

Transitions come into play when you begin to flesh out the skeleton of your speech—your outline. As you first deliver a true speech from your outline, you will naturally grab for transitions to link individual points. Specific directions are given in chapter 12 on how to transform your speech outline into notes for use during delivery of your speech. Remember: rhetorical competence in organization means making a paper outline into a well-arranged, living speech.

"But is *all this* really necessary?" speakers sometimes ask. "Couldn't I just rough out my points without actually outlining my speech?" Roughing out your points with a quick once-over before class will boost your speech effectiveness somewhat. If your goal is rhetorical competence in speech class and in post-college days, however, then you should make the outline method a habit. Heed the research findings that show organization to be an important skill. Prepare outlines; then practice with them to make sure that you sound organized. Your goal should not be merely to *have* an outline but, rather, to *use* the outline to make your points to the audience.

Concepts for Review

Can you summarize the meaning of these terms or expressions? How does each relate to speechmaking?

structure
organization
effects of organization
outlining
three parts of the speech
major points
subpoints
chunking
transitions
transitions highlight
transitions subordinate
transitions coordinate
transitions boost comprehension
transition words
signposts
previews
summaries
summary-preview combination
capsule statements
enumeration
transition patterns
pattern of repetition
metaphorical theme
reference to speech situation
rhetorical questions

Things to Try

1. Look at five speeches reprinted in a copy of *Vital Speeches.* Note the break points between introduction, body, and conclusion for each speech. Count the number of lines taken up by the introductions, bodies, and conclusions. Figure the percentage of lines devoted to the body of each speech. Do the percentages vary widely for the different speeches?
2. Select a speech reprinted in *Vital Speeches.* Review the four basic rules for outlining, and prepare your own sentence outline of the speech. Be sure to divide your outline into the three major categories of introduction, body, and conclusion. For the body of

the speech, list only the major points, rather than all subpoints. Is the speech easy to outline? If not, it may be that you need to sharpen your skills. On the other hand, if the speech is difficult to outline, it may be a sign that the speaker did not give sufficient care to organization.

3. Look at the body of the speech you chose for exercise 2. Now that you have identified the two to five major points in the speech, pay attention to the transitions that highlight, subordinate, or coordinate these major points. Review the kinds of transitions listed in this chapter. Which ones does the speaker use? Which ones do not appear? What improvements, if any, could the speaker make in using transitions?
4. Prepare an outline for a speech you are planning to give in class. Follow the rules for outlining given in this chapter.

Endnotes

1. Bob Woodward and Carl Bernstein, *The Final Days* (New York: Simon and Schuster, 1976), 386.
2. Jerome S. Bruner, Jacqueline J. Goodnow, and George A. Austin, *A Study of Thinking* (N.Y.: John Wiley, 1956) and George A. Miller, "The Magical Number Seven, Plus or Minus Two: Some Limits of Our Capacity for Processing Information," *Psychological Review 63* (1956): 81–97.
3. Raymond G. Smith, "An Experimental Study of the Effects of Speech Organization Upon Attitudes of College Students," *Speech Monographs 18* (1951): 292–301.
4. Charles R. Petrie, Jr., "Informative Speaking: A Summary and Bibliography of Related Research," *Speech Monographs 30* (1963): 79–91, and Richard F. Whitman and John H. Timmis, "The Influence of Verbal Organizational Structure and Verbal Organizing Skills on Select Measures of Learning," *Human Communication Research 1* (1975): 293–301.
5. Ernest Thompson, "An Experimental Investigation of the Relative Effectiveness of Organizational Structure in Oral Communication," *Southern Speech Journal 26* (1960): 59–69; Donald K. Darnell, "The Relation Between Sentence Order and Comprehension," *Speech Monographs 30* (1963): 97–100; Ernest Thompson, "Some Effects of Message Structure on Listeners' Comprehension," *Speech Monographs 34* (1967): 51–57; John E. Baird, Jr., "The Effects of Speech Summaries Upon Audience Comprehension of Expository Speeches of Varying Quality and Complexity," *Central States Speech Journal 25* (1974): 119–127; Whitman and Timmis, "Verbal Organizational Structure,"; Tom D. Daniels and Richard F. Whitman, "The Effects of Message Introduction, Message Structure, and Verbal Organizing Ability Upon Learning of Message Information," *Human Communication Research 7* (1981): 147–160.

6. Arlee Johnson, "A Preliminary Investigation of the Relationship Between Message Organization and Listener Comprehension," *Central States Speech Journal 21* (1970): 104–107, and Baird, "Speech Summaries."
7. Whitman and Timmis, "Verbal Organizational Structure."
8. James C. McCroskey and R. Samuel Mehrley, "The Effects of Disorganization and Nonfluency on Attitude Change and Source Credibility," *Speech Monographs 36* (1969): 13–21; Harry Sharp, Jr. and Thomas McClung, "Effect of Organization on the Speaker's Ethos," *Speech Monographs 33* (1966): 182–183; Eldon E. Baker, "The Immediate Effects of Perceived Speaker Disorganization on Speaker Credibility and Audience Attitude Change in Persuasive Speaking," *Western Speech 29* (1965): 148–161.
9. Smith, "Effects Upon Attitudes," and McCroskey and Mehrley, "Effects of Disorganization."
10. Jeanette Anderson, "Man of the Hour or Man of the Ages? The Honorable Stephen A. Douglas," *Quarterly Journal of Speech 25* (1939): 82–83.
11. Thompson, "Organizational Structure," and "Message Structure"; Arnold G. Abrams, "The Relation of Listening and Reading Comprehension to Skill in Message Structuralization," *Journal of Communication 16* (1966): 116–125; Whitman and Timmis, "Verbal Organizational Structure"; Daniels and Whitman, "Learning of Information."
12. Whitman and Timmis, "Verbal Organizational Structure."
13. Whitman and Timmis, "Verbal Organizational Structure."
14. Abrams, "Listening and Reading Comprehension."
15. Miller, "Magical Number," and Petrie, "Informative Speaking."
16. Petrie, "Informative Speaking."
17. Darnell, "Order and Comprehension."
18. Miller, "Magical Number."
19. *San Jose Mercury News,* 21 January 1989, 20A.
20. Petrie, "Informative Speaking," and Thompson, "Message Structure."
21. Phillip K. Tompkins, "Organizing the Speech to Inform," *Today's Speech 7,* No. 3 (1959): 21–22.
22. Thompson, "Message Structure."
23. Richard D. Lamm, "Lawyers and Lawyering: The Legal System and Its Cost to American Society," *Vital Speeches,* 15 January 1989, 209.
24. Thompson, "Message Structure."
25. *San Jose Mercury News,* 21 January 1989, 20A.
26. Darnell, "Order and Comprehension."
27. In *Championship Debates and Speeches,* ed. John K. Boaz and James R. Brey (n.p.: Speech Communication Association and American Forensic Association, 1987), 110.
28. Ray Ehrensberger, "An Experimental Study of the Relative Effectiveness of Certain Forms of Emphasis in Public Speaking," *Speech Monographs 12* (1945): 94–111; Warner Wilson and Howard Miller, "Repetition, Order of Presentation, and Timing of Arguments and Measures as Determinants of Opinion Change," *Journal of Personality and Social Psychology, 9* (1968), 184–188; Petrie, "Informative Speaking."

Chapter

9

Beginning and Ending

Outline

Patrick Henry, orator of the revolution.

One speaker begins:

> Yesterday, December 7, 1941—a date which will live in infamy—the United States of America was suddenly and deliberately attacked by the naval and air forces of the Empire of Japan.[1]

Another concludes:

> I know not what course others may take; but as for me, give me liberty or give me death![2]

Do you recognize the speakers? The first is Franklin D. Roosevelt, proposing a declaration of war against Japan. The second is Patrick Henry, demanding that Virginians take up arms against British forces in the American colonies.

It is no accident that a great speech is sometimes known by its introduction or conclusion. Beginnings and endings mark the two points when the audience is most attentive. Good speakers recognize this fact of human perception—and make the most of it. Experienced speakers often prepare introductions and conclusions *last*—after the rest of the speech is completed. This way, they are sure to begin and end the speech with material that both highlights and reflects the body.

In chapter 8, we looked at organization as a whole process—through the vehicle of the outline. Now it is time to give thought to two special opportunities of speechmaking: introductions and conclusions. Viewed in a less optimistic light, however, introductions and conclusions mark special problems of public speaking. If you are like most beginning speakers, you will feel somewhat awkward beginning and ending your speeches. Why? Starting a speech, or concluding one, can be likened to learning to drive a car equipped with a standard transmission—a "stick shift." Your ride starts out a bit rough and jerky as you attempt to get going—as in a speech introduction. Once you are in gear, however, things proceed pretty smoothly. You are OK as long as you keep up speed. But when you shift down in preparation to stop, the car may become balky again—just like a speech conclusion.

When we begin and end our speeches, we inevitably come into contact with two principles of rhetorical competence. First, we must understand the functions of introductions and conclusions. Second, we must know our options for beginning and ending our speeches. These two principles set our agenda for this chapter.

Functions of the Introduction

Introductions can be worrisome. After all, from your point of view as a speaker, the start of the speech is when self-consciousness may be greatest. But viewed from the perspective of the audience, the introduction can be seen as a point of promise. The first few moments of a presentation finds the audience primed to listen, so the problem of beginning the speech is essentially one of overcoming *your* self-consciousness and capitalizing on *their* early attention.

How? Let's turn to three general functions of the introduction: (1) to win attention, (2) to promote good will, and (3) to prepare the way for your ideas. These functions set your goals for the first part of the speech. Notice that they correspond to three key elements of the speech situation—audience, speaker, and message. You are aiming to win attention from the audience, credibility for yourself, and a favorable hearing for your views.

When you set out to speak, one of your first aims is to win the *attention* of the audience. Expect that your listeners will have a natural receptiveness to your opening remarks. This means that your task in the introduction is to confirm their hope that listening to you will be rewarding. Ways to promote favorable attention include:

- using a startling statement
- referring to something that is on people's minds
- quoting an apt saying or anecdote
- asking for a response, such as a show of hands

Creating good will and respect for you, the *speaker,* is the second function of the introduction. Credibility is important in speechmaking. The introduction is an occasion in which the audience pays special attention to you as a person. Your character, motives, competence, and personality are on display. You must remember this fact and consider whether your opening remarks put you in a good light. For instance, using appropriate humor may help show your personality in a favorable light. Also, discussing personal experiences may reveal your links with the audience.

Finally, when introducing the speech, you want to prepare the way for the *message* itself. A well-worded introduction may, even without seeming to, help push you ahead in making your case, because the introduction helps set up a *psychological context for listener's attention.* When Chief Logan spoke to Lord Dunmore, Royal Governor of Virginia, he began by describing his efforts to keep good relations with whites.

> I appeal to any white man to say if ever he entered Logan's cabin hungry, and he gave him not meat; if ever he came cold and naked, and he clothed him not.[3]

Logan's beginning words placed blame on whites for frontier warfare without actually stating the point explicitly.

In using your introduction to pave the way for your ideas, you may want to be more explicit than Logan about your information or claims. To achieve this purpose, you might use a *preview* to list some of your major points. Do not be alarmed if your first efforts to use the preview approach seem somewhat stiff or mechanical. Even if your early efforts at previews do not sound smooth and comfortable, don't give up. When you get the hang of this method, you will be able to increase your long-term effectiveness. Previews sometimes significantly increase how much listeners comprehend.[4]

To prepare the way for the message, your introduction must be relevant. Canned jokes, even if they happen to be funny on their own terms, tend to skirt the points you are making in the body of the speech. Second, avoid the trite introduction. Triteness often is signaled by such overused phrases as "it is both a privilege and a pleasure. . . ." Be careful about resorting to gimmicks, also. A gimmicky introduction creates unfavorable attention by diverting the audience's attention from you and your message. Profit from the poor example of one student speaker who began a speech on gun control by suddenly pointing a pistol at the class and firing a blank cartridge. The student was not only guilty of poor firearms safety, but he also shocked the class to such an extent that people could not listen to what he had to say.

Gaining attention, enhancing your credibility, and getting out some of your thoughts—these are your major goals in beginning your speech. To find out how to attain these objectives, we turn to several customary ways to introduce speeches.

Techniques of Introduction

If you are like most speakers, you will welcome specific suggestions about how to begin your speech. Below are six categories of introductions for speeches. Under each of the categories you will find several options for starting your remarks. The several kinds of introductions listed below will not fit your needs equally well. Some are particularly useful for getting attention, others for boosting credibility, still others for leading into the subject. All, though, are proven methods for making your introduction purposive and effective. Remember, however, that any introduction serves many functions, and that the categories below overlap to a certain extent.

Introductions Using Speech Structure

You may begin your speech by commenting on the structure of it. Introductions of this kind include stating your thesis, previewing major points of the speech, and identifying the purposes of the speech.

Stating the thesis

Starting the speech by mentioning your thesis has the effect of focusing attention immediately on your subject. The use of thesis statement as an introduction is shown in a speech by Justin Synnestvedt of the humanities faculty of Moraine Valley Community College.

> I am going to argue that we should all simply stop watching commercial television. That's right, completely.[5]

Previewing major points

In the preview method—sometimes called the method of partition or division—you give more than your basic thesis. You mention the major chunks of content you will be presenting. Earlier we observed the effectiveness of the preview in stimulating recall. The preview method finds a place in both informative and persuasive speaking. For instance, in his address to the Town Hall of Los Angeles, California, Robert T. Parry, President of the Federal Reserve Bank of San Francisco, used this preview introduction. Parry greeted the audience, stated his general focus on the economic issues of 1989, and finally, previewed specific major points:

> I'll begin with a brief review of the economy's recent performance. This sets the stage for a discussion of the key concerns I have as we stand on the threshold of a new year. Then I'll sum up with my view of what this means for the economy and monetary policy in 1989.[6]

Stating your purpose

You identified your specific speech purpose early in the process of preparing your talk. Stating your purpose makes a simple, straight-forward introduction for many kinds of speeches. For instance, in his speech to present an award, Karl Wallace, a revered teacher of speech communication, began with these words:

> Professor Braden, at this time I have the special privilege of presenting to the Speech Association of America a volume of studies which I trust is not only symbolic of the long and honorable history of our subject in centuries past, but signalizes the maturity of our subject today and prophesies our scholarship in the decades to come. (See full text in chapter 15.)

Introductions by the Topic of the Speech

You may begin by telling listeners something about the *topic* of your speech as well as saying something about its structure. Familiar approaches of this type include defining terms, giving a historical review, and referring to the title of the speech.

Defining terms

Defining one or more key terms of your topic may suit you as a way to get started with clarity. Usually the tactic is to define the one term that best capsulizes the speech, or to define a term that the audience must understand to comprehend the speech. To this end, after relating the case of a kindergarten student named David, Sallie Jo Hart explained:

> . . . In fact dyslexia is a condition, not a disease, which results from certain chemical or physical makeups which cause the child or adult not to have the right-left perception.[7]

Reviewing history

Many topics are best begun with a review of past history. After briefly greeting his audience, Martin Luther King, Jr., launched into his "I Have a Dream" address in this way:

> Five score years ago, a great American, in whose symbolic shadow we stand, signed the Emancipation Proclamation. . . . But one hundred years later, the Negro still is not free. (Full text at end of chapter 10.)

Giving the title of your speech

If the title of your speech has been published in advance, or if the title has been assigned to you, then it may be appropriate to begin with reference to it. This is how Phyllis J. Springen began her address to the Danforth Foundation on the topic "The Dimensions of the Oppression of Women."

> When I was asked to speak on "The Dimensions of the Oppression of Women," I laughed. "Oppression" is such an ugly word. Our chairman must have been thinking of those Arab countries where women can't vote and where a woman can be forced to marry any man her father selects, but in the United States women are hardly "oppressed." But as I began to do my research, I quit laughing. There exists a tremendous amount of legal and economic discrimination against the American woman. Much of it is subtle and, therefore, hard to recognize.[8]

Introductions to Get Attention

Sometimes your main purpose in the introduction will be to capture attention. If this is the primary goal, then three useful approaches are to make a startling statement, to use suspense, or to use a visual aid.

Making a startling statement

You may win attention and get the audience thinking about your subject when you state a fact or opinion that surprises or shocks the group. Thus, in her informative speech, Jacquelyn Flanigan leads off with an Italian battle cry: *"Morte alle Francia Italia anelo."* She then explained the significance of her opening:

> "It's not a greeting, it's a battle cry. But listen and look closer at the first letter of each of the five words: M-A-F-I-A." (Full text at end of chapter 13.)

Using suspense

An introduction contains suspense when it makes the audience ask the question, "I wonder what that speaker is up to?" In her national championship informative speech, student speaker Theresa Buescher used the approach of suspense to peek the curiosity of listeners.

> Forty-three million tons settle over the United States each year. Irving Addler says that we may inhale up to four hundred thousand million particles of this per day. No, it's not second hand smoke. Irving Addler is the author of a book entitled *Dust.*[9]

Box 9.1

Suspense as Introduction

The scene was Boston, October 1988. Michael Dukakis, Democratic candidate for president began a news conference. In just a few hours his running-mate, Senator Lloyd Bentsen, would begin a crucial nationally-televised debate with Republican vice-presidential candidate, Senator Dan Quayle. Dukakis opened his news conference by addressing these words to reporters:

> This is, as I guess all of you know, a day we've been waiting for a long, long time.
> It's a very big day for us. There's a lot of media speculation about it. I'll frankly say I'm concerned myself and a little nervous.
> The Red Sox are going to win today.

(Actually, the Sox lost this American League playoff game to the Oakland A's, 2–1.)

Source: *New York Times* (National Edition), 6 October 1988, A12.

Using visual aids

Occasionally it will be possible to begin your remarks with a diagram, audio-visual image, or object. This approach can be used to good effect in catching attention, not only because the visual stimulates several senses at once, but also because it can raise questions. Recall how student Jack Dodds displayed a citrus orange as a way of leading into his subject of Agent Orange.

Introductions by Speech Situation

Things familiar often make convenient points of entry into your speech topic. And what is more familiar than the immediate situation at hand? Your options for using surrounding circumstances include (1) referring to a current social situation, problem, or issue, (2) referring to the immediate occasion of the speech—its place, time, audience, or previous speaker, or (3) making a personal reference.

Referring to current situation

Current events often are at the forefront of people's thoughts. You may take advantage of this fact by using a timely reference to launch the speech. In his eulogy for John F. Kennedy, delivered before the United Nations, Adlai Stevenson began simply:

> My privilege in this sad hour is to convey to you, Mr. President [of the General Assembly], Mr. Secretary General, and to you, the assembled delegates of the world, the profound gratitude of the people of my country for what has been done and for what has been said here today. Our grief is the more bearable because it is so widely and so genuinely shared. . . .[10]

Referring to present occasion

References to the occasion sometimes are demanded by etiquette, as in the case of thanking someone for introducing you. As an example, Betty Ann Welchel accepted her scholarship award from Chi Omega sorority with these words:

> First I would like to say thank you to all of you. Without the support of Chi Omegas, the Mary Love Collins Memorial Scholarship and its tribute to the ideas Mary Love represented would not exist. (Full text in chapter 15.)

In other speeches, alluding to time, place, audience, or previous speaker may be a convenient way to get from what is happening to what you want to say. A visiting scholar at Stanford University's Hoover Institution, Vladislav Krasnov, began his remarks to a conference of political scientists by referring to a recent speech given by the President of the USSR:

> Since Gorbachev's Vladivostock speech on July 28, 1986, it has become apparent that the Soviet approach to the Asian-Pacific region was about to change.[11]

Making a personal reference

Sharing your immediate thoughts with the audience is a natural and appropriate way to begin your remarks. After thanking the audience of Army officials at The United States Military Academy, General Douglas MacArthur shared with the cadets his feelings at receiving the award.

> No human being could fail to be deeply moved by such a tribute as this. Coming from a profession I have served so long, and a people I have loved so well, it fills me with an emotion I cannot express. (Full text at end of chapter 10.)

The speech situation can serve as your introduction when you build upon current events, a present moment, or a personal reference, but beware of the temptation to make a weak apology. Do not apologize for your lack of preparation, for a change in the program, for the lateness of the hour, and so on. If these problems require some response, use some other method, such as a short speech, to compensate for them. Your listeners deserve more than lame apologies followed by half-hearted efforts.

Introductions Using Literary Material

You may want to follow the example of many speakers and draw from a wealth of literary material to begin a speech. You may transform anecdotes, quotations, and humor into an introduction.

Using anecdotes

Anecdotal introductions narrate the theme of your speech. The anecdote may be real or hypothetical, although a real-life example frequently is more impressive. One student speaker won a national speech contest with an extemporaneous speech that began:

> In 1853, U.S. Naval Commander William Perry brought a fleet of ships into a harbor in Japan and demanded that they open up their economy to international trade. Oh, Commander Perry, where are you today?[12]

Using quotations

Chances are good that some poet or politician has coined a phrase or written a passage that aptly puts your point. Books of sayings and quotations are available in the library. Better yet, work to develop your own library of quotations by jotting down useful passages as you encounter them in your reading. A century ago it was common for educated people to keep what was called a commonplace book. This was a notebook filled with ideas, observations, and sayings. One of today's leading speech coaches, Jack Valenti, advises speakers to develop a deep sense for literary matter: "Disregard books of quotations. Too often a quotation from Bartlett's sounds exactly as if you had lifted it."[13] In other words, start with Bartlett but don't end there. Buy your own copy of significant literature, and mark interesting passages for later reference.

No contemporary American speaker used quotations more effectively than Sam Ervin, Senator from South Carolina. For instance, this is how Ervin began his remarks as moderator of a televised debate between Ronald Reagan and William F. Buckley.

> John Milton, who knew much about the power of words and the ideas they express, said, "Give me the liberty to know, to utter, and to argue freely according to conscience above all liberties."

Ervin continued (see full text in chapter 15) with this theme, providing a fitting opening to a public exercise of free speech.

Using humor

Humor sometimes boosts speaker credibility, so it can provide a good opening for your remarks.[14] Use humor as your opening when it possesses these four characteristics. First, be original. Personal experiences and spontaneous observations are better than familiar jokes. Next comes the consideration of good taste. For instance, do not joke at the expense of a person who introduced you. Err on the side of caution by avoiding humor focusing on ethnic differences, male-female stereotypes, and human body functions. A third characteristic of good humor is relevance. Ask first whether the humor relates to your thesis and only then if it is funny. Finally, mind the appropriateness of your humor. Be sure your humor fits the mood of the speech situation. Some occasions just do not call for humor.

Contrary to popular myth, not all speeches must begin with a joke. In fact, students frequently tell me they are afraid to begin with a joke—after all, people might *not* laugh. Then, too, there is the problem of taste in humor as baseball great Johnny Bench once learned. During an appearance

Mark Twain captivated audiences with his store of anecdotes.

at Cincinnati's Music Hall, Bench made jokes about Jews, blacks, and Poles, prompting twenty listeners to walk out and another thirty to write letters of complaint.[15] More in the true spirit of humorous introductions was actor Kirk Douglas in his toast to former Secretary of State Henry Kissinger. "I lift my glass to Henry Kissinger, who is as American as apple strudel."[16]

Introductions Focusing on Audience

Extemporaneous speaking often resembles a friendly conversation. Therefore, a natural option for beginning speeches is to speak directly to your listeners. You can ask a question, appeal to the self-interest of the audience, or ask for some unison audience response such as a show of hands, applause, or standing.

Asking a question

Questions are a good way of quickly drawing attention to your topic and thesis. Rhetorical questions are those that imply their own answers. They put your beliefs into the form of a question, more than they actually invite a direct answer from listeners. Questions of this kind often can put light directly on your thesis. One student speaker began his remarks by asking

"Did your unmarried sister have a child when she was fifteen?" In quick succession, he posed eleven other questions that illustrated the range of information about people that may be stored in computer data banks.[17]

Appealing to audience's self-interest

Showing how a subject pertains to the lives of listeners is a good way to build interest in and attention to your message. One student speaker effectively used the principle of audience self-interest to make the otherwise mundane topic of bridge repair strike home. After relating an incident of a bridge collapse, she continued:

> Does this example sound like something that happens to someone else somewhere else? Well it could very easily happen to you. How many bridges do you cross each day on your way to school or work? According to the Federal Highway Administration "one out of five bridges in the United States is unsafe."[18]

Box 9.2

Appealing to Self-Interest

Consumers are resistant to direct mail advertising. Advertisers know that the first few words of their letters make all the difference. Appeals to self-interest are common in direct mail advertising.

A PITCH ON INSURANCE RATES: SEPTEMBER 1988

Dear Friend,

Have your auto insurance rates skyrocketed in the last few years?

AN APPEAL TO STOP AN EXCISE TAX ON BEER: FEBRUARY 1989

300 percent federal tax increase on beer. They wouldn't dare . . . or would they?

Dear Fellow Beer Drinker:

You bet they would . . . and they will greatly increase the price of every beer you drink—unless you help me stop them.

Asking for unison audience response

Asking the audience to raise hands, applaud, or stand is a quick way to relate the subject to the hearers. Joseph A. Califano, former United States Secretary of Health and Human Services, once used this method in a talk to junior high school students. Wanting to promote his anti-smoking campaign, Califano asked the class how many of them smoked cigarettes. Only one of fifty sixteen-year-olds raised her hand; but Califano was able to build on the question by offering the Houston, Texas, student a trip to Washington, D.C. as a reward for quitting the habit.[19]

Califano's question is one that implied some small amount of risk for respondents, since minors are not legally able to buy cigarettes. Try to avoid putting your audience in an embarrassing position with such questions as "how many of you have cheated on college exams." Threatening questions cause self-preoccupation among listeners and, thus, detract attention from your thesis, so stick to the straightforward question, unless you have good reason to try a risky one.

Armed with knowledge of the common ways to begin a speech, you should be able to manage the frequent worry of speakers who comment, "I know what I want to say, but I don't know how to get started." To be sure that you have chosen the most effective method of launching your subject, experiment with several of the types of introductions. Many speakers begin their speeches by combining two or more of the standard introductions. For instance, you might combine a question with a preview of points. Remember: the introduction sets the tone for your speech, so work to put your best speaking forward.

Functions of the Conclusion

Like introductions, conclusions are important but tricky. Now that you have gotten your momentum, how do you stop? To answer this question, we should begin with a look at functions and then techniques for concluding the speech.

Your conclusions will be effective when they meet three objectives. First, your introduction should complete or tie together the contents of the speech. Second, the introduction should successfully close the speech. That is, your final remarks should convey a clear impression that the end has indeed come. Finally, the conclusion should leave the listeners in a psychological state appropriate both to your purpose and to the general occasion of the speech.

Capsulizing the content of the speech represents what we may term the logical function of the conclusion. To test your conclusion as a summary of content, ask yourself whether your last few comments effectively highlight the theme or thesis of your speech. If so, then the conclusion is an apt ending that leaves your main idea fresh in the minds of the hearers.

Although the first function of the conclusion focused on the message itself, the next two functions concern how the audience perceives the message. A good conclusion not only wraps things up, but it conveys the clear impression that all *is* completed. We may term such an impression the feeling of *closure.* It is difficult, if not impossible, precisely to describe what makes listeners believe a speech is neatly wrapped up. Generally, we may say that closure conveys a feeling of ease and relaxation. Its opposite is a nagging concern or irritation that things still seem at loose ends. Suffice it to say that you and your listeners both will recognize the presence or absence of closure. That is all the more reason to pay close attention to the techniques to be presented below for concluding speeches.

Finally, as for function, we may say that the conclusion should put the audience in the proper state of mind. Your concluding remarks should communicate an emotional or mental state that fits not only the type of speech you are giving but also your own particular speaking purpose. As you look over the various methods to conclude the speech, notice that they do not always communicate the same mood. In his eulogy for John F. Kennedy, Adlai Stevenson closed by putting listeners in a mood of quiet repose:

> So, my friends, we shall honor him in the best way that lies open to us—and the way he would want it to be—by getting on with the everlasting search for peace and justice for which all mankind is praying.[20]

In contrast, Robert Ingersoll created an exciting climax in concluding his nominating speech for James Blaine:

> Gentlemen of the convention, in the name of the Great Republic, the only republic that ever existed upon this earth; to the name of all her defenders and of all her supporters; in the name of all her soldiers living; in the name of all her soldiers dead upon the field of battle, and in the name of those who perished in the skeleton clutch of famine at Andersonville and Libby, whose sufferings he so vividly remembers, Illinois—Illinois nominates for the next President of this country, that prince of parliamentarians—that leader of leaders—James G. Blaine. (Full text in chapter 15.)

Concluding a speech by describing an ideal future communicates satisfaction. In contrast, an appeal for action provides stimulation.

Box 9.3

Functions of the Conclusion

The epilogue has four parts. You must (1) make the audience well-disposed towards yourself and ill-disposed towards your opponent, (2) magnify or minimize the leading facts, (3) excite the required state of emotion in your hearers, and (4) refresh their memories.

Source: Aristotle, *Rhetoric*, III. 19. 1419b.

Techniques for Concluding

There is no perfect conclusion that fits equally well every speech situation. Generally, where persuasion is your goal, you will be better served by including an *explicit conclusion,* that is, a specific statement of what you want listeners to remember. Research findings suggest that you may expect to achieve less attitude change when listeners are vitally concerned about the topic and you allow them to draw their own conclusions from arguments and evidence.[21]

A second general finding about conclusions is that more persuasion results when the conclusion includes some metaphorical language. Researchers compared the effect of two speeches, identical except in their conclusions. Both speech conclusions summarized the case against giving federal aid to needy students. One of the two conclusions included metaphorical language to portray aid to students as harmful to human initiative. These metaphors were that federal aid would "strangle" individuality leading to a "murder" of values and the "death rattle" of liberty. Listeners were more persuaded by the version of the speech that concluded with these metaphors of death.[22]

Although research shows the general advantage of explicit conclusions using metaphorical language, your choice of conclusions always requires individual judgment and taste. One major consideration is whether your conclusion should review specific points or merely reiterate the general theme of the speech. Minor decisions about your conclusion include whether the conclusion should be a serious or a humorous one, a declarative or an interrogative one, and a logical or an emotional one.

It is impossible to specify in advance what will be the best conclusion for any of your future speeches. However, we may review a wide range of choices. Speakers typically use conclusions that fit one of four categories: (1) conclusions relying on the structure of the speech, (2) conclusions focusing on the future, (3) conclusions using literary material, such as quotations, and (4) conclusions focusing on the audience.

Conclusions by Speech Structure

Your speech is well-organized when you keep focus on the outline of your major points. Therefore, citing the important points in your speech makes a convenient way to conclude. You may summarize your major points, reiterate your thesis, or return to the method you used to introduce the speech.

Summarizing major points

Sometimes called the *review* method, the summary-type conclusion finds you repeating the major points you have made. Research shows that concluding summaries can significantly boost comprehension by receivers.[23]

As was the case with *pre*views, however, reviews do not always increase comprehension, nor do they affect all persons in exactly the same way.[24]

An instance of the summary method is shown in a speech by Donald P. Rogers, professor of management, to the Rochester, New York, chapter of the National Association of Accountants. Rogers preached the advantages of voluntary disclosure of information by business organizations. He concluded:

> . . . I hope that you will consider the points I've discussed tonight: (1) The effects of disclosure are not as terrible as we fear, (2) Public attitudes strongly support disclosure, and (3) Public policy will promote more disclosure in the future. After you have considered these points, I think you will decide that the best disclosure strategy is one of deliberate, voluntary disclosure and aggressive, honest communication.[25]

Reiterating thesis

You may conclude by repeating the theme of the speech as an alternative to running through the individual major points made. The conclusion to Jack Dodds' persuasive speech illustrates this way of ending.

> The war for many vets did not end when they left Vietnam; but it continues to be fought here in the United States against the government that sent them there: a war to survive both psychologically and physically. The question being asked by them today is "I was there when my country needed me, where is my country now that *I* need help?"

Returning to introduction

In concluding a speech you may find it helpful to return to the method you used to begin the speech. When you use your introductory method as your mode of concluding, you help create a sense of completeness. For example, in a national contest in persuasive speaking, one student used these words to begin a speech on American policy toward South Africa: "Pontius Pilate. You remember him." The speaker continued, noting that Pilate washed his hands of Jesus, leaving others to arrange His crucifixion. The speaker then called for direct United States actions to encourage democratic reforms in South Africa instead of using the punishment approach of economic sanctions. In the conclusion, the speaker returned to the opening remarks. "Let's not be Pontius Pilates."[26]

Conclusions Looking to the Future

Speeches often deal with the future, suggesting how things could be or should be. The forward thrust of speechmaking provides you with another

Martin Luther King's vision of equality is an important statement of democracy.

convenient avenue for concluding. In this vein, you may (1) help listeners visualize conditions after your thesis is accepted, (2) make a prophecy, (3) refer to a following speaker, or (4) state your own intentions or actions.

Visualization

To conclude by visualizing is to use descriptive language to portray conditions after your thesis is put into practice. Martin Luther King, Jr., has given us the most famous modern example of conclusion by visualization:

> And when this happens, when we allow freedom ring—when we let it ring from every village and every hamlet, from every state and every city, we will be able to speed up that day when all of God's children, black men and white men, Jews and Gentiles, Protestants and Catholics, will be able to join hands and to sing in the words of the old Negro spiritual, "Free at last! Free at last! Thank God almighty, we are free at last."

Prophecy

Many speakers conclude by pointing to the likely future. Here is how Donald E. Petersen, president of Ford Motor Company, concluded a speech about the automobile industry:

> Tough tasks ahead for all of us—Unquestionably! Lots of risks and short term disappointments—Certainly! A real need to manage better—You bet! An opportunity for all of us to have a positive impact on the well-being of millions of people—Absolutely!
>
> You can count on it![27]

Reference to following speaker

If your speech is part of a program, it can be useful to conclude by mentioning or introducing the next speaker. In his speech welcoming the American hostages returned from Iranian captivity, President Ronald Reagan concluded with reference to the following speaker.

> And now, ladies and gentlemen, I call on, to speak for this wonderful group of returnees, Bruce Laingen, Deputy Chief of Mission in Tehran, Mr. Laingen. (Full text in chapter 15.)

Expression of your own intentions

"I know not what course others may take, but as for me, give me liberty or give me death!" Patrick Henry's declaration probably is the most famous example of self-intention and self-action used as the conclusion of a speech. So memorable were these words that they lived on in Virginia folklore for years until written down by Henry's biographer, William Wirt.

Conclusions Using Literary Material

The standard materials useful for opening the speech also may be used to close addresses. Anecdotes, metaphors, quotations, and humor are commonly-used options of this kind.

Anecdotes

A concluding anecdote often can serve to illustrate the theme or thesis of your speech. In her informative speech, Jacquelyn Flanigan takes this approach.

> The most conclusive illustration of the truly ironic relationship between the American value system and that of the Mafia can be seen in

> the name of a man who is at present a prominent Mafia leader. This man was once an assassin for Albert Anastasia's Murder, Inc., a group of hired hit-men who murdered on contract. He is the graying and grandfatherly, the gruesome and gory Aniello Dellacroce—"little Lamb of the Cross." His contradictory characteristics remind us of the admonition to "Judge not, lest you be judged." (Full text at end of chapter 13.)

Metaphors

Earlier we saw that metaphors can serve as unifying transitions. They can capsulize speeches, also. In his now-classic address to the Democratic National Convention in 1896, William Jennings Bryan used metaphors of Good Friday to argue that American workers suffered by having the money supply backed solely by gold:

> Having behind us the producing masses of this nation and the world, supported by the commercial interests, the laboring interests, and the toilers everywhere, we will answer their demand for a gold standard by saying to them: You shall not press down upon the brow of labor this crown of thorns, you shall not crucify mankind upon a cross of gold.[28]

Quotations

Quotations serve as conclusions as well as for introductions. Concluding his speech to the Houston ministers, John F. Kennedy quoted from the oath taken by the United States presidents and stated in the Constitution:

> But if, on the other hand, I should win this election, I shall devote every effort of mind and spirit to fulfilling the oath of the Presidency—practically identical, I might add, with the oath I have taken for fourteen years in the Congress. For, without reservation, I can, and I quote "solemnly swear that I will faithfully execute the office of the President of the United States and will to the best of my ability preserve, protect and defend the Constitution, so help me God." (Full text at end of chapter 14.)

Humor

Although many speeches begin with humor, few conclude with it. Perhaps speakers fear that a humorous conclusion will cause the audience to think less of the thesis, but if you look at humor as being a slight variation of the anecdotal conclusion, then it may be appropriate for your situation.

In a commencement address at Hastings College, Professor Benjamin A. Rogge concluded on this note:

> This favorite heroine of mine is a little girl in an old cartoon in the *New Yorker* magazine. She is being force-fed by her mother, but is obviously rejecting whatever it is that is being offered her. Finally in desperation, her mother says to her "But dear, it's broccoli." At this, the little three-year-old girl in her high chair looks her mother in the eye and replies, "I say it's spinach and I say the hell with it!"
>
> May the next years be exciting and productive for you, and as you go on through life, may you gradually come to the knowledge of the difference between broccoli and spinach, and may you acquire the courage to challenge those who confuse the two.[29]

Conclusions Focusing on Audience

Concluding the speech is akin to saying goodbye to your listeners. Why not bring your speech to an end by directly making a point? Ways to address your audience directly include questions, challenges, appeals for action, and appeals to the self-interest of listeners.

Questions

Questions are an effective way to point up a key theme of your speech. William F. Buckley concludes by posing a series of interrogatives:

> We have great tests ahead of us. Are we going to disarm unilaterally? Is our word to our allies a reliable covenant? Do we really believe in human rights? Do we believe in sovereignty—even in sovereignty for little countries whose natural resources, where and when necessary, we are entitled to use but not to abuse? The kind of satisfaction, a nation truly consistent in the practice of its ideals, seeks for itself is the kind of satisfaction, at this moment in history, we can have by ratifying treaties that at once enhance our security and our self-esteem. Thank you. (Full text at end of chapter 14.)

Challenges

Frequently, your goal as a speaker is to persuade. In such a case, you may benefit by challenging listeners to accept the views you have advocated. In an address to the National Catholic Education Association, Virgil C. Blum issued this challenge:

> This is the challenge I propose to you: to adopt a new vision of your teaching apostolate; to make radical changes in your perception of your duties as teachers and administrators. . . .

Begin and conclude speeches with a look of confidence.

If you accept this challenge, you will not only continue to influence the intellectual, religious and moral development of generations of students, you will be architects of the future of both the Church and American society. . . .

The challenge is clear—how you respond is crucial to the future of Catholic education in America.[30]

Appeals for action

Closely related to the challenge is the appeal for action. Challenges may require thought or behavior; but the call for action usually demands immediate steps, such as donating or volunteering. Loret M. Ruppe, Director of the Peace Corps, made this final appeal in a speech at Los Angeles: "Join us, Support us, Be a volunteer for Peace."[31]

Appeals to audience's self-interest

Reminding listeners that "this affects you!" can be a good way to cap a speech. In a winning entry in a national speech contest, one student used the self-interest approach. She stressed the health dangers posed by electromagnetic radiation emanating from modern electronic conveniences.

> Right now the harms of electromagnetic radiation have been proven. How much longer can we allow ourselves to be test animals? Because if the facts continue to be ignored, there is no telling when you, a family member, a friend, might become a Becky Krismon or a Thomas Montgomery. Can we continue to afford the risk?[32]

The conclusion provides a lingering image of your speech effectiveness—an impression far greater than the relative length of the conclusion. Be sure to end on a strong note. Spend time planning, selecting, and polishing the conclusion. Read over the conclusions of the speeches reprinted in this text, particularly the large number of speeches given in chapter 15. Note how many of the speakers combine several of the types of conclusion to accomplish several objectives. Your work will be time well spent.

Box 9.4

Forceful Conclusions

Susan B. Anthony, speaker for women's suffrage, was known for her forceful conclusions. Here is a sample:

> Forget conventionalisms; forget what the world will say, whether you are in your place or out of your place; think your best thoughts, speak your best words, do your best works, looking to your own conscience for approval.

And another:

> There is an old saying that if you give a woman an inch, she'll take an ell [an arm's length].
>
> Women of Maryland—we've got the inch.

Source: Doris Y. Twichell, "Susan B. Anthony," in *A History and Criticism of American Public Address*, ed. M. K. Hochmuth [Nichols] (New York: Russell and Russell, 1955), 120–121.

The methods for concluding a speech bring us to the conclusion of this chapter. As a speaker desiring rhetorical competence, you will want to master the techniques for starting a speech strongly and for stepping confidently away from the lectern. Introductions and conclusions take up relatively little time in your speech, but they mark the two places where you can be sure the audience's curiosity is greatest. As you plan each of your speeches, review the several techniques for beginning and ending. These methods will contribute to your credibility, making it possible for you to get and maintain the image of a prepared, competent speaker.

Concepts for Review

Can you summarize the meaning of these terms or expressions? How does each relate to speechmaking?

functions of introduction:
- create attention
- give good will
- set psychological context

preview
gimmicky introduction
techniques of introduction:
- using speech structure
- using speech topic
- getting attention
- using speech situation
- using literary material
- focusing on audience

functions of conclusions:
- create feeling of closure
- capsulize content
- create frame of mind

explicit conclusion
metaphorical language
techniques of conclusion:
- using speech structure
- focusing on future
- using literary material
- focusing on audience

Things to Try

1. Consult a recent issue of *Vital Speeches* in your library. Look at the introductions and conclusions of the speeches, noting what options the speakers have used. Which speakers combine any of the various methods for introducing and concluding the speech? Can you find any introductions or conclusions that do not fit the options listed in this chapter?

2. Save your junk mail for a week or two. Now, look at the opening and closing sentences of these advertising letters. What techniques of introduction and conclusion do you find? Do the introductions and conclusions accomplish all the functions listed in this chapter?
3. Plan the introduction for your next speech. First, which of the six general methods for introducing a speech best fits your needs? Do you need or want to combine two of the methods? Now consider and use appropriate specific tactics for introducing speeches listed under each of the six major categories. Prepare and rehearse your introduction.
4. Plan and rehearse the conclusion for your next speech. Using the same method as in item three, above, consult the four general techniques for concluding speeches and the various tactics listed under each.

Endnotes

1. Franklin D. Roosevelt, "War Message," in *Three Centuries of American Rhetorical Discourse,* ed. R. F. Reid (Prospect Heights, IL: Waveland, 1988), 699.
2. Patrick Henry, "The 'Give Me Liberty or Give Me Death' Speech," in *The World's Famous Orations,* ed. W. J. Bryan, 10 vols. (New York: Funk and Wagnalls, 1906), 8:67.
3. "Logan to Lord Dunmore," *World's Famous Orations,* 8:3; P. X. Knoll, "Presumption in the Introduction to the Argumentative Speech," *Quarterly Journal of Speech 18* (1932): 637–642.
4. John P. Parker, "Some Organizational Variables and Their Effect Upon Comprehension," *Journal of Communication 12* (1962): 27–32; Ernest Thompson, "Some Effects of Message Structure on Listeners' Comprehension," *Speech Monographs 34* (1967): 51–57; John E. Baird, Jr., "The Effects of Speech Summaries Upon Audience Comprehension of Expository Speeches of Varying Quality and Complexity," *Central States Speech Journal 25* (1974): 119–127.
5. "TV—No!" *Vital Speeches,* 15 January 1989, 209.
6. "Issues Shaping the U.S. Economic Outlook in 1989," *Vital Speeches,* 15 January 1989, 197.
7. "Is It 'B' Or 'D'?" *Winning Orations of the Interstate Oratorical Association 1971,* ed. D. L. Aschenbrenner (Omaha, NB: Interstate Oratorical Association, 1971), 40.
8. Phyllis J. Springen, "The Dimensions of the Oppression of Women," *Vital Speeches,* 15 February 1971, 265.

9. *1987 Championship Debates and Speeches,* ed. J. K. Boaz and J. R. Brey (Annandale, VA: Speech Communication Association, 1987), 142.
10. *Representative American Speeches: 1963–1964,* ed. L. Thonssen (New York: H. W. Wilson, 1964), 31.
11. "The Soviet Union and the Asian-Pacific Region in the 1990s," *Vital Speeches,* 1 January 1989, 164.
12. *Championship Speeches 1987,* 110.
13. Jack Valenti, *Speak Up With Confidence* (New York: William Morrow, 1982), 98.
14. Charles R. Gruner and William E. Lampton, "Effects of Including Humorous Material in a Persuasive Sermon," *Southern Speech Communication Journal 38* (1972): 188–196.
15. *Courier-Journal* (Louisville), 12 January 1978, D1.
16. Valenti, *Speak Up,* 85.
17. David J. Walsh, "Jungle of Judgments," *Winning Orations 1971,* 98.
18. Betsy Mallison, "America's Bridges Are Falling," *Winning Orations of the Interstate Oratorical Association 1979,* ed. L. Schnoor (Mankato, MN: Interstate Oratorical Association, 1979), 88–89.
19. *Courier-Journal* (Louisville), 4 March 1979, B14.
20. *Representative American Speeches: 1963–1964,* 33.
21. Stewart L. Tubbs, "Explicit Versus Implicit Conclusions and Audience Commitment," *Speech Monographs 35* (1968): 14–19.
22. John W. Bowers and Michael M. Osborn, "Attitudinal Effects of Selected Types of Concluding Metaphors in Persuasive Speeches," *Speech Monographs 33* (1966): 147–155.
23. Parker, "Organizational Variables," and Baird, "Speech Summaries."
24. See Frederick H. Turner, Jr., "The Effects of Speech Summaries on Audience Comprehension," *Central States Speech Journal 21* (1970): 24–29; James F. Vickery, Jr., "An Experimental Investigation of the Effect of 'Previews' and 'Reviews' on Retention of Orally Presented Information," *Southern Speech Journal 36* (1971): 209–219; Parker, "Organizational Variables."
25. Donald P. Rogers, "The Disclosure of Information: A Challenge to Corporations in the 80s," *Vital Speeches,* 1 May 1980, 433.
26. *1986 Championship Debates and Speeches,* ed. J. K. Boaz and J. R. Brey (Annandale, VA: Speech Communication Association, 1986), 129, 131.
27. Donald E. Petersen, "The Future Task of the Worldwide Auto Industry," *Vital Speeches,* 15 August 1981, 665.
28. Text in William J. Bryan, *The First Battle: A Story of the Campaign of 1896* (Chicago: W. B. Conkey, 1896), 206.
29. Benjamin A. Rogge, " 'Well, So You're a College Graduate?' What Tricks Can You Do?" *Vital Speeches,* 1 August 1980, 614.
30. Virgil C. Blum, "Should Catholic School Teachers and Parents be Involved in Education Politics?" *Vital Speeches,* 15 July 1981, 584.
31. Loret M. Ruppe, "Why a Peace Corps in the 1980s?" *Vital Speeches,* 15 September 1981, 723.
32. Elighie Wilson, "Before It's Too Late," *Winning Orations 1979,* 20–21.

Part

IV

The Speech As Presented

Chapter

10

Style in the Speech

Outline

What is the greatest speech in American history? An early survey of speech anthologies showed Abraham Lincoln's Gettysburg Address to be the most frequently reprinted speech.[1] Many of the other entries on this 1930s list, such as Henry Grady's "New South" address, are today almost forgotten. However, Lincoln's speech has a staying power from age to age. E. D. Hirsch includes the Gettysburg Address in his 1988 index of items that every educated American should know.[2]

Why does Lincoln's address stand as a classic today as yesterday? Certainly the ideas in the speech are great and inspiring ones. In fact, early newspaper comments on Lincoln's speech were focused on the president's ideas.[3] However, the continuing vitality of the Gettysburg Address cannot be explained simply by Lincoln's treatment of the crucial values of equality, freedom, and national unity. We must consider also the power of style. Lincoln's social and political theories continue to strike home because of how Lincoln expressed them. President Lincoln's simple but impressive style gives ideas an importance and freshness that keeps them alive against the passage of decades. Lincoln's concluding remark that our nation struggled to preserve "government of the people, by the people, and for the people" lives as one of the most important summaries of America's democratic objectives.

Style is important in speechmaking precisely because of the inevitable effect of good style in improving the ideas of a speech. Hirsch's list of "what literate Americans know" makes clear that an idea must be well put to become part of America's common cultural knowledge. For instance, Hirsch's roster of vital knowledge for Americans includes the final words of Patrick Henry's speech calling for armed resistance against British encroachment: "Give me liberty or give me death!" Suppose, instead, that Henry had said, "Friends, I really think we ought to stop writing letters of complaint." Such a less notable phrase would have conveyed a less powerful thought; it would have rightly passed unremembered.

What exactly does *style* mean, anyway? If you are like most students, you will have no trouble finding things to say about the style of a song or a car. But the style of *a speech?* In classroom discussions, students (and teachers) often fumble for words when asked to comment upon the style of language used by a speaker. Sometimes the concept of style conjures up the image of fussy academic exercises or artificial ornamentation. Instead, think of style as language that communicates your ideas in a clear and interesting manner. Rhetorical competence in matters of style means to select words, phrases, and sentences that clearly, appropriately, and powerfully express your ideas.

For modern speakers, style represents an often untapped source of rhetorical success. Since the 1920s, when the modern "plain speech" approach came into vogue, Americans have made a habit of ignoring the style of speeches. Campaigning for the presidency in 1988, Michael Dukakis expressed no concern that the style of his language was less commanding than that of Jesse Jackson. "I am what I am," Dukakis said. Fair enough—all speakers have different strengths. But this remark also seems to suggest that style is a trivial trait, one that cannot be improved because it is a natural gift.[4] That is not so, as we will shortly observe.

If we now give so little everyday attention to speech style, isn't it strange and paradoxical, then, that our own generation's favorite speeches are those of powerful style? When E. D. Hirsch asked 100 experts to list great ideas that all Americans should know, the panelists took the key phrase, "I have a dream," from Martin Luther King's address at the Lincoln Memorial as well as John F. Kennedy's call to "ask not what your country can do for you" (inaugural address). The continuing legacy of American speechmaking suggests that knowing something about style is worthwhile.

What does style add to speaking? This chapter begins with a look at how style serves as a powerful aid to argument and persuasion. When you take the attitude that style is important in rhetorical competence, you are ready to review key differences between oral and written style. Next comes a look at the basic criteria for a good speaking style. Finally, on the matter of skill in style, we turn to certain stylistic figures that supply specific doorways to better language.

The Power of Style

To tap the power of style, you must *want* to attain a good style. You must believe that style makes a difference. You need to understand how style advances and strengthens the ideas and arguments in your speech.

Style and Substance

One common myth makes sensing the power of style difficult for speakers. This is the view that style in language amounts to only a fancy juggling of words. This myth stands as a legacy of the 1600s and 1700s, a time when people saw style as a mere dressing up of ideas.[5] The view of style as ornament assumes that a person first invents an argument and then, in a separate act, uses devices of style to embellish it. If this were true, then style would have little to do with thought and argument.

Against the view of style as decoration, the writings of Aristotle show style as closely related to direct, real communication.[6] Modern writers, too, are rediscovering the idea that style deepens our analysis and, at the same time, allows us to better impress ideas into the minds of others.[7] Any doubt that stylistic figures are important today may be banished by looking at modern advertising. Ads are built around rhythmic words that build interest in a product. Ads use carefully styled phrases, jingles, and slogans. For instance, a 1988 ad for Merit cigarettes claims: "You won't miss what you'll miss" (i.e., tar); here the same word, miss, is used in two different senses. Or "It's perfect, it's Perrier"—a repetition of sound.

Box 10.1

Getting Applause with Style

In speeches, conversations and most other forms of communication, the most commonly used type of list contains *three* items. . . . One of the main attractions of three-part lists is that they have an air of unity or completeness about them. . . . [Audiences] treat the completion of a third item as the place to start clapping.

> "Soviet marxism is ideologically, politically, and morally bankrupt" (Margaret Thatcher, British Prime Minister, 1980).

Source: Max Atkinson, *Our Masters' Voices* (London: Methuen, 1984), 57, 61, 63.

Some who follow the Aristotelian tradition argue that the study of style can be merged with the study of argument, organization, and delivery.[8] This extreme position has its merits. But there is much to be said for retaining style as a separate compartment of rhetorical competence. Working on our word choices is a good rhetorical practice that helps give greater power to our argument and delivery.

Jeremiah S. Black, one of the nineteenth century's great attorneys, was a master of style as tool of argument. Black's speeches were always marked by a solid train of reasoning from premise to conclusion, but Black also phrased his logic to show its close connection to values and goals held dear by the audience. Black's style highlighted his reasoning by making people *want* to accept the results of his train of thought. Speaking before the United States Supreme Court (an expert, logical audience), Black described one Congressional act that weakened local courts as a "sheer, naked, flat breach of the Constitution." (Note the *repetition* of synonyms.) Black advised the court to set aside the law because it would destroy state courts. If the law were applied, he argued, all trials would take place in far-off Federal courts.

Using a reference (allusion) to ancient times, Black drove home his point, saying that Federal prosecutors would rule with a heavy hand like the Roman proconsuls of old. Black's effort to prove the danger of the act owed much to the power of his style.[9]

Style gives force to argument; thus the various devices of style—which we will consider later—directly relate to enhancing the substance of our speeches. Harry Emerson Fosdick's use of opposites (antithesis) stands as a case in point. Fosdick, the Baptist preacher, often built his sermons around incidents in the lives of famous people. Fosdick liked to use these episodes to highlight differences between the atheist and the person of faith. For instance, whereas Paul once lay in prison at the order of the Emperor Nero, the saint now towered above the tyrant in the verdict of time. Similarly, Fosdick contrasted Tamerlane, the powerful warrior, and Gutenberg, the

Abraham Lincoln's remarks at Gettysburg showed a simple yet powerful use of language.

German printer. While Tamerlane was terrorizing Eastern Europe—only to be forgotten later—Gutenberg was quietly revolutionizing the world by producing the first printed copies of the Bible.[10]

Without good style, public speaking lacks much of its wit and weaponry. If you still don't believe it, compare the Gettysburg Address, as Lincoln delivered it in 1863, to a parody of the great Emancipator's masterpiece, rewritten to reflect today's all-too-common vague, rambling, or bureaucratic speech.

Sample Speech

Gettysburg Address
By Abraham Lincoln

Fourscore and seven years ago our fathers brought forth upon this continent a new nation, conceived in Liberty, and dedicated to the proposition that all men are created equal.

Now we are engaged in a great civil war, testing whether that nation, or any nation so conceived and so dedicated, can long endure. We are met on a great battlefield of that war. We have come to dedicate a portion of that field, as a final resting-place for those who here gave their lives that that nation might live. It is altogether fitting and proper that we should do this.

But in a larger sense, we can not dedicate—we can not consecrate—we cannot hallow—this ground. The brave men, living and dead, who struggled here, have consecrated it, far above our poor power to add or detract. The world will little note, nor long remember, what we say here, but it can never forget what they did here. It is for us, the living, rather, to be dedicated here to this unfinished work which they who fought here thus far so nobly advanced. It is rather for us to be here dedicated to the great task remaining before us—that from these honored dead we take increased devotion to that cause for which they gave the last full measure of devotion—that we here highly resolve that these dead shall not have died in vain—that this nation, under God, shall have a new birth of freedom—and that government of the people, by the people, and for the people, shall not perish from the earth.

Sample Speech

Gettysburg Address in Modernese
By Oliver Jensen

I haven't checked these figures but 87 years ago, I think it was, a number of individuals organized a governmental set-up here in this country. I believe it covered certain Eastern areas, with this idea they were following up based on a sort of national independence arrangement and the program that every individual is just as good as every other individual. Well, now, of course, we are dealing with this big difference of opinion, civil disturbance you might say, although I don't like to appear to take sides or name any individuals, and the point is naturally to check up, by actual experience in the field, to see whether any governmental set-up with a basis like the one I was mentioning has any validity and find out whether that dedication by those early individuals will pay off in lasting values and things of that kind.

Well, here we are, at the scene where one of these disturbances between different sides got going. We want to pay our tribute to those loved ones, those departed individuals who made the supreme sacrifice here on the basis of their opinions about how this thing ought to be handled. And I would say this. It is absolutely in order to do this.

But if you look at the overall-picture of this, we can't pay any tribute—we can't sanctify this area, you might say—we can't hallow according to whatever individual creeds or faiths or sort of religious outlooks are involved like I said about this particular area. It was those individuals themselves, including the enlisted men, very brave individuals, who have given this religious character to the area. The way I see it, the rest of the world will not remember any statements issued here but it will never forget how these men put their shoulders to the wheel and carried this idea down the fairway.

Now frankly, our job, the living individuals' job here, is to pick up the burden and sink the putt they made these big efforts here for. It is our job to get on with the assignment—and from those deceased fine individuals to take extra inspiration, you could call it, for the same theories about the set-up for which they made such a big contribution. We have to make up our minds right here and now, as I see it, that they didn't put out all that blood, perspiration, and—well—that they didn't just make a dry run here, and that all of us here, under God, that is, the God of our choice, shall beef up this idea about freedom and liberty and those kind of arrangements, and that government of all individuals, by all individuals and for the individuals, shall not pass out of the world-picture.

Source:

"The Gettysburg Address in Eisenhowerese," by Oliver Jensen, in *Parodies,* ed. D. MacDonald (New York: Random House, 1960), 447–448.

Style is not mere ornamentation. When you view style and argument as helpmates, you are taking on the attitude of a rhetorically competent speaker.

Style and Your Audience

One important reason that style gives power is that it helps you build a close relationship with your listeners. Your style is what merges your mind to the minds of listeners, cementing a close communicative bond. Style strengthens the rhetorical relationship in two ways. On the one hand, your stylistic choices actually channel the thinking of receivers. On the other hand, if you are like most speakers, you will find yourself modifying your word choices to accommodate the beliefs and attitudes of your audience.

According to the *Sapir-Whorf hypothesis,* the style of expression can affect thought itself. Edward Sapir asked, "What if language is not so much a garment as a prepared road or groove?"[11] In other words, he believed, style marks out a path of thought. As an example of how style channels thought, consider the psychological theory of Eric Berne. Berne, author of *Games People Play,* argued that neurotic behavior is a sign that someone is playing a game to win power or attention. For instance, a person might "accidentally" destroy another individual's property. When we view someone's neurotic actions as a part of a "game," rather than as a symptom of the "disease" of mental illness, we are less likely to look for a medical solution.

An even more striking case of where style became the very substance of communication occurred during World War II. In 1943, the Allied leaders proclaimed the policy of "Unconditional Surrender"; that is, there would be no negotiation until Germany and Japan had first surrendered. Some believe that the expression "Unconditional Surrender" caused the United States to ignore peace overtures from Japan—since United States officials were waiting only for a total capitulation. It is possible, therefore, that the diplomatic slogan of "Unconditional Surrender" led directly to the decision to use the atomic bomb as a way of forcing the Japanese to give up the fight abruptly.[12]

The importance of style in setting the rhetorical relationship is further shown in findings that speakers adjust style to fit the listeners. Most of us intuitively realize that our style reveals our attitudes.[13] Furthermore, at the time we speak, we usually have some clues about whether our audience agrees or disagrees with us. Research shows that when we face an audience that opposes our main idea, we tend to use language that is significantly less intense or opinionated.[14] In other words, if we are like most people, we will adjust our style to keep hostile groups from tuning out our ideas.

Since listeners are sensitive to how we phrase our arguments, we should consider how to use style to avoid giving needless offense. First, many listeners are put off by the generic "he." Better to say "a historian must carefully choose *his or her* evidence." Also, some listeners are likely to give negative marks to a speaker who uses nonstandard English grammar. Finally, remember that listeners usually are offended by mudslinging, that is, when a speaker intensely attacks an opponent on a personal level.[15] The point is: We must consider audience sensibilities when we want to convert people to new ideas.

Style is important in making your ideas powerful and in impressing your points on listeners. If you have the attitude of the rhetorically competent speaker, you want to incorporate good style into your speaking. You accept the probability that style will stimulate thought, invigorate argument, and enhance effectiveness. We turn now to the best kind of style for a public speaker—an oral style.

Oral Style

The ancient Greeks were the first to develop a full alphabet (by advancing the work of the early Phoenicians). The Greeks were also the first to appreciate the difference in style between written and spoken language. Today, we have little sense of the tension between written and oral style that came with the discovery of writing in Greece. The Greek experience therefore gives important lessons for speakers and writers of the present.

The Role of Style in Oral Communication

In ancient Greece, as everywhere, oral speech preceded written language. Having no writing, the earliest Greeks developed methods of recitation to transmit stories orally. The traveling bards who spoke the stories of Homer provided the Greeks with their first literature. These tales of the heroes of the Trojan War existed for centuries in only oral form, before they were gradually put into writing.

The style of the Homeric legends gives a clue to some important ingredients of oral style. If the Homeric speakers wanted to discuss the concept of courage, they would *not* follow the modern practice of giving an analytic definition. Today, we would probably define courage by putting it into the class of virtuous acts, then list specific characteristics of courage. Instead of constructing a formal, analytic definition of courage, the Greek bards would relate a story about someone who was courageous—someone such as Ulysses, the king who overcame obstacles human and divine to return to Ithaca. In other words, the early Greeks would rely on the stylistic device of *personification,* associating an attribute with the actions of a particular human agent. To make stories more memorable, and thus insure their transmission across the generations, the Homeric story tellers would use *rhyme* and *rhythm.* Just as the litany "thirty days hath September" helps us recall days of the month, so too would Homer take advantage of the natural human capacity to remember poetry better than prose.[16]

As the Greeks developed writing skills, they found themselves able to discuss concepts independent of oral stylistic devices. The Greeks found that analytic writing brought into play a new kind of language. Unlike spoken messages, written communication did not need to be instantly memorable, since the reader could, at leisure, consult the text again. Similarly, the Greeks observed that continuous interest value was not as crucial for a written composition as for a spoken one. Words on a page lost none of their essential power even if the reader's attention should lapse for a moment. Nor did written messages need to be as personal as did oral tales. Unlike the story teller, whose audience was ever before him, many individuals unknown to the author would later consult a work communicated in writing.

Not only could written communication avoid the need for phrases instantly memorable, constantly interesting, and intimately personal, writing offered unique stylistic possibilities. Because manuscripts were held, seen, and studied, written sentences could be longer and more complicated. In fact, long sentences were needed to provide visual variety. For the same reasons, longer words were both possible and advantageous for writers. Further, in organizing the written composition, the author found it easier to arrange ideas according to the logic of the particular topic. The topical organization of written sentences differed from methods for arranging oral stories. Ideas transmitted through stories almost invariably demanded chronological arrangement. Finally, compared to the speaker, the writer had to be more precise, because written remarks were permanent. Instead of saying "many" or "a few," a writer felt more pressure to specify precise facts and figures.

The traditional thinkers of ancient Greece, the sophists, had effectively used oral style in their method of education. The sophists helped make Athenian democracy possible by teaching middle class artisans how to speak in public, and, thus, how to participate in politics as equals to aristocrats. For political speakers in ancient Athens, the nature of oral style as something entertaining and occasionally vague posed no problems. However, the emerging profession of philosophy, represented by Socrates and Plato, came to rely on the new analytic style of communication with its precision and impersonality. Rejecting the view of the sophists that truth emerged in a free-for-all debate among citizens, Socrates and Plato held that truth was objective and known through personal discovery and step-by-step analysis. They favored an analytic style of dialogue, focused on the rational dimension of humanity, in which concepts were defined and tested carefully. Plato wished to purge the Greek language of its action words and to reshape it into a less flexible vehicle, one more suited for communicating the eternal truths of philosophy.[17]

Aristotle, the pupil of Plato, saw merit in applying elements of the analytic style to public speaking. But in contrast to Plato, Aristotle believed that traditional oral style also provided advantages to speakers. Aristotle took a more organic view of people as beings who gained real knowledge through feelings as well as thoughts. The effective speaker, Aristotle believed, could merge the precise analytic style, associated with the Socratic method, with the interesting and intimate features of the oral tradition. In this view, speeches before large public assemblies required repetition and a preponderance of emotion over specific detail. In contrast, when speaking before an audience of experts, the speaker needed to avoid seeking a dramatic effect, since experts must reach a logical decision.[18]

The theory and practice of the ancient Greeks teach us that style is an important dimension of rhetorical competence. Stylistic competence requires us to learn what features of style best serve a particular rhetorical purpose. The basic idea is to use an oral style structured by disciplined analysis. This lesson is a crucial one in twentieth century America, where a high literacy rate accompanies our immersion in the oral idiom of radio and television. Franklin D. Roosevelt, the first great speaker of the media age, was fully aware of the need for his speeches to have an oral flavor. Most of FDR's presidential addresses were from manuscript. However, he often practiced the speeches aloud, judging every word by its sound, not merely its appearance.[19]

Box 10.2

A Speech Is Not an Essay Standing on Its Hind Legs

These are shocking things for teachers to admit; but the fact remains that some of the "essentials" of speaking in old textbooks are not essentials on the platform. Many a man, elated with the audience response to his extemporaneous speech, has been astonished to find, upon reading a stenographic report, that the speech was not fit to print. Yet there need be no mystery about that: the speech was not *meant* for print. All this does not justify carelessness on the part of a student. It should encourage him, however, to take account in his own speaking of the differences between effective speech and effective writing.

Source: William T. Foster, "Random Notes on Public Speaking," *Quarterly Journal of Speech 33* (1947): 140.

Features of Oral Style

Aristotle was one of the first to spell out several of the differences between oral and written style. Social science researchers have used modern techniques to elaborate Aristotle's relatively brief suggestions about style. You may take advantage of several findings based on detailed comparisons of written and oral language. As you practice your speeches aloud, why not tape record them? Listen to your words, consulting the following guidelines. Decide if your speech contains these necessary touches of oral style.

1. An oral style promotes understanding and interest through a simple vocabulary. Speakers normally use fewer different words than do writers.[20] This means that repetition of words is greater in oral communication.[21] At the same time, speakers use a greater number of familiar, easier words.[22] Furthermore, compared to writing, oral language is made up of shorter words having fewer syllables.[23] The essence of oral style is to use words having the most direct punch. This does not mean you should hide a well-developed vocabulary. You can include unusual words to create interest, but do not rely on unfamiliar or obscure words that leave listeners hanging.
2. An oral style is based on simpler sentences than a written style. Oral sentences tend to be shorter in length.[24] Furthermore, oral sentences tend to involve simpler grammatical construction.[25] This follows from the need of oral style to be instantly understandable. The complexity found in academic writing does not usually serve your purposes as a speaker.
3. An oral style is more active, favoring action words (verbs and adverbs) over static nouns and adjectives.[26] One way to check your style is to select a few sentences and count the number of verbs and adjectives. Typically an oral style contains more verbs for each adjective.[27] Another way that oral style creates a sense of action is through use of questioning sentences and sentences of exclamation.[28]
4. An oral style is more interpersonal, containing more direct references to the speaker, audience, and immediate situation.[29] Oral language contains more self-reference words, that is, phrases such as "I think" or "I say."[30] The personal nature of oral style further comes across when you use more personal pronouns. Oral style means more first-person pronouns (I, me, my) as well as second-person pronouns (you, yours).[31] Because oral language is directly addressed to listeners, the speaker is more likely than the writer to mention specific people.[32] Also, an oral style makes clear its connection to a given time and place. Oral language contains more references "to the particular situation in which the speech is being delivered."[33] Finally, the language includes more filler words, such as "now" or "you know."[34] Words of this type often make a connection with people or present time.

5. An oral style is more likely to generalize by using what may be called *allness terms*: all, none, every, always, never.[35] Similarly, an oral style uses more pseudo-quantitative terms—much, many, a lot, very.[36] The generality of the oral does not mean that orality cannot express distinctions. In fact, oral language includes more terms that qualify or limit a generalization. Examples of qualification terms are: if, however, but, except.[37] Similarly, an oral style contains more terms that show your awareness that you are projecting opinions onto listeners. When you speak (as compared to when you write), you are more likely to use such expressions as "it seems to be" or "it appears."[38]

In sum, we may say that an oral style attains clarity through familiar vocabulary and grammar. In addition, oral style imparts vitality and freshness to communication by means of action words, personalness, and generalizing. The hallmark of a good speaking style is keeping to the features of orality, but you will attain the most effective style of speechmaking when you discipline oral language with some of the analytic precision associated with writing.

The Effective Style

Style in speechmaking is so often neglected in modern days that it offers modern speakers a special path to rhetorical competence. As noted above, the essential style of public speaking is oral. The features of oral language impart freshness, interest, and directness to what you have to say. Though orality in language is a *necessary* ingredient of rhetorical competence, oral style may not always be *sufficient* to insure success. Recall Aristotle's observation that analysis and precision are important when we are speaking to an audience of experts. The kind of precision we associate with written style may also be necessary when we speak on a topic of great complexity. Therefore, we modern speakers must keep an essentially oral style; but, at the same time, we should be open to adding a dimension of disciplined reasoning.

The advice given in the remainder of this chapter will help you merge an essentially oral style with useful elements of precise argument. A good speaking style begins with clarity and appropriateness. In addition, the effective speech style joins concreteness with variety, merges personalness with analysis, and wins attention without being excessively intense.

Essentials of Good Style

For a speaking style to be called effective, it must possess clarity and appropriateness.

Clarity

Clarity is the bedrock requirement of effective style in speechmaking. Clear speaking means (1) using words that are meaningful and simple, (2) framing sentences that are easy to follow, and (3) putting sentences into groups that are unified. William Brigance, a famous speech teacher, always emphasized that oral speech must be clear in the sense of being "instantly intelligible" to the audience. Listeners cannot visually review what they hear in a speech.[39]

President Franklin Roosevelt was a master of the straight forward, instantly intelligible style. Roosevelt once asked his Secretary of Labor, Frances Perkins, to give him some materials for a speech on the social security program. Perkins summed up one section of her draft with the words "we are trying to construct a more inclusive society." When Perkins heard the speech over the radio some weeks later, Roosevelt had altered the phrase to give it more of the punch of simple oral speech. Roosevelt told his listeners that "we are going to make a country in which no one is left out."[40]

The speeches by Douglas MacArthur and Martin Luther King, Jr., reprinted in this chapter, also contain examples of clear and effective style. Douglas MacArthur explains in simple but elegant language how those who wear the military uniform abhor war:

> This does not mean that you are warmongers. On the contrary, the soldier above all other people prays for peace, for he must suffer and bear the deepest wounds and scars of war.

Martin Luther King's metaphor of the bad check gives clear voice to the issue of incomplete citizenship:

> It is obvious today that America has defaulted on this promissory note insofar as her citizens of color are concerned. Instead of honoring this sacred obligation, America has given the Negro people a bad check; a check which has come back marked "insufficient funds."

Such models of clarity did not come without effort. Like MacArthur and King, we must ever fight against several temptations of cloudy language. These include passive voice, triteness, jargon, pompous language, euphemisms, and vagueness.

1. Passive voice: "It has been asserted that. . . ." Who did the asserting? If someone by the name of Campbell made the point, then use the active voice: "Campbell likes to say."
2. Trite, puffed up language: Be careful about exaggerated and overused phrases, such as those used to hawk new books: "wild and wonderful," "a story for the ages," and "a totally unique book."[41]
3. Jargon: Today's communicators frequently replace ordinary language with a specialized professional jargon. Susan Sontag contends that the effort to rename everything helps bring on today's literacy crisis. For instance, teachers become "language skills coordinators."[42]
4. Pompous, confusing language: Former Secretary of State Alexander Haig once won a "Doublespeak Award" from the National Council of Teachers of English for his description of the murder of three American nuns in El Salvador. Seeking to minimize the responsibility of the United States-backed Salvadorian government, Haig presented this cloudy "explanation": "And this [the murder] could have been at a very low level of both competence and motivation in the context of the issue itself."[43]
5. Euphemisms: Taking second prize to Haig in the NCTE awards was the Environmental Protection Agency. Its entry was an effort to ban the word "hazard" and replace this term with "mitigation of risk." Such a euphemism would disguise the reality of harmful chemicals.
6. Vague slang words: Granted, a speech cannot compete with an encyclopedia article for precision; but words such as "stuff" and "things" convey little meaning.

In public speaking, then, style may fall victim to such enemies of clarity as the passive voice, triteness, jargon, pompousness, euphemisms, and vague slang. Research shows that people do notice when a speaker's language is murky.[44] Vagueness generally reduces the speaker's credibility and ability to make the speech memorable.[45] There is some evidence that unclear language occasionally helps win short-term rhetorical success. Vagueness may help when the only other alternative is clearly to state ideas that listeners find objectionable.[46] For instance, in 1968, Richard Nixon knew that the American people were divided on the issue of what to do in Vietnam. In his campaign for president, Nixon wanted to get votes from both hawks and doves. In a major television spot, Nixon asserted that "never has so much military, economic, and diplomatic power been used as ineffectively as in Vietnam." The solution he offered, however, did not make clear whether he favored a military or diplomatic solution to the Vietnam War. "We will have an honorable end to the war in Vietnam."[47] Though vagueness on

Vietnam may have helped Nixon win the election, this murky style did not build up his image as an honest speaker. Deliberate vagueness constitutes a breach of faith with listeners, and the benefits are likely to be only fleeting.

Appropriateness

Language should fit the circumstances in which we give our speech. An appropriate style is one in keeping with the nature of the audience, speech topic, and setting. The inspirational cast of Martin Luther King's "I Have a Dream" address was appropriate given his audience of marchers who needed an uplifting message. King's style also fit both the place of the speech, the Lincoln Memorial, and his themes of equality and fair play. Similarly, Douglas MacArthur's inspiring treatment of the words "duty, honor, country" were a good match for the May ceremonies at West Point.

Just as inspirational language fit the purposes of King and MacArthur, so too does a plainer descriptive language suit the needs of an informative speaker. For instance, Jacquelyn Flanigan used a simple but still impressive narration to get across information about the early Italian immigrant in the United States.

> With very little money and a pronounced language barrier, many of the Italians were forced to seek help. Help was often a wealthier, more established "paesano," a fellow countryman. The "paesano" would see to it that his own people were cared for. He arranged employment; he dealt with relentless landlords; he guaranteed passports for family members still in Italy.

In addition to finding models of good persuasive, inspirational, and informative style, we may locate elements of style that are generally *in*appropriate. Research shows that in the normal speech situation profane and obscene language lessen both the speaker's credibility and persuasiveness.[48] In like manner, humor directed to sexual, racial, and ethnic differences is prone to provoke offense. Humor of this kind is risky even when you yourself are a member of the group serving as the butt of the joke. Finally, there is evidence that stating your points in an intense fashion may be dangerous. To say that somebody "squandered"—rather than "spent"—money may be out of place unless you have initially high credibility with the listeners or unless they agree strongly with your ideas.[49] Granted, you may succeed with risky ethnic humor or with intense language, but remember that these choices always carry higher-than-average risks.

Although the appropriateness of style may be predicted, the only sure way to tell if language works is to look for actual audience reactions. During the 1976 presidential campaign, Jimmy Carter committed two major offenses against standards of appropriate style in speaking. Early in the campaign, Carter used the unfortunate phrase "ethnic purity" to describe his opposition to government programs that imposed changes on existing neighborhoods. This phrase immediately provoked criticism. Not only did the words conjure up memories of Nazi theories of racial purity, but they sounded like code words for segregation. Forced on the defensive for his language, Carter tried, without much success, to explain his intentions. Finally he publicly apologized. Later in the campaign, Carter found himself under attack for the informal style he used in an interview printed in *Playboy* magazine. During most of the infamous interview, Carter used the careful and guarded language typical of a public figure speaking for the mass audience. However, in discussing contemporary morality, Carter shifted to an informal and personal style. He emphasized that Christians should not proudly scorn a person who "shacks up" and "screws a whole bunch of women." Carter's style violated expectations about the proper language of public figures and became, briefly, the talk of the time.[50]

The question raised by Carter's experiences is whether he could have predicted these problems in advance. Granted, saying something meaningful and striking while at the same time guarding against giving offense is difficult. Yet, a large part of the attack on Carter came because of individual words. Had he changed just two or three words, he could have avoided much bad publicity.

Factors of Balance in Good Style

Good style is not simply a matter of being clear and seeking appropriate language. Human experience and academic research show a number of contradictory and paradoxical links between style and success. Getting results through speech requires us to balance three tricky and sometimes inconsistent aspects of language. We must balance concrete words with those giving variety to our remarks. We must speak in a way that is simultaneously personal and analytic. We must get attention without expressing our points too intensely.

Concreteness with variety

Successful speakers cultivate a style that provides variety within the framework of concrete and specific words. A *concrete* style of talking is one that makes ideas specific and real. According to political speech writer Aram Bakshian, today's audiences demand speeches that are "short and graphic." Bakshian, who worked as a speechwriter for President Nixon, explained that the effective speech has "almost got to be visual." As an example, Bakshian explained that "rather than saying X thousand school children today are being bused, speak of a little seven-year old girl in Boston who has got to go five miles to the other side of town."[51]

Bakshian's point underscores the value of using real examples. Employ specific descriptive materials that give a good mental picture of actual conditions. Martin Luther King conveyed concreteness when he gave a litany of conditions to be met before blacks would be satisfied.

> We can never be satisfied as long as the Negro is the victim of the unspeakable horrors of police brutality. We can never be satisfied as long as our bodies, heavy with the fatigue of travel, cannot gain lodging in the motels of the highways and the hotels of the cities. We cannot be satisfied as long as the Negro's basic mobility is from a smaller ghetto to a larger one. We can never be satisfied as long as our children are stripped of their selfhood and robbed of their dignity by signs stating "For Whites Only." We cannot be satisfied as long as a Negro in Mississippi cannot vote and a Negro in New York believes he has nothing for which to vote.

King's list is long—but not wordy. The sentences provide specific details to clinch his claim.

Although you gain clarity by using simpler words and sentences, you will find that *diversity in vocabulary and sentence structure* can boost your credibility. Keeping balance is the key to the paradox of simplicity and diversity. Rhetorically competent speakers seek variety within the framework of a concrete style. Social science findings validate this approach, showing that a wider vocabulary makes a speaker appear more credible.[52] Why? Variety in vocabulary creates a good impression because it adds interest.

An example of an arresting style is that of Rufus Choate, the great nineteenth century lawyer and political speaker. People sought opportunities to hear Choate, who was called "the wizard of the bar." Choate captured audiences, surprising listeners with understandable words used in unpredictable ways. One critic, commenting on Choate's "ingenious pairings of words," cites a typical sentence:

> I say that there is not an occupation of civilized life, from the making of laws and poems and histories, down to the opening of New Jersey oysters with a broken jack-knife, that is not better done by a bright than a dull man, by a quick than a slow mind, by an instructed man than a gross and simple man, by a prudent, thoughtful, and careful man than by a light and foolish one.[53]

A long sentence! But Choate keeps up interest by giving a rhythm to his sentence and by using unexpected but immediately vivid words.

Unpredictability in the use of words similarly helped Winston Churchill to balance concreteness with variety. In an experimental study, researchers gave students part of a Churchill sentence, along with several possible words to complete it. Results showed that the words Churchill actually chose were frequently not what people predicted—but were nevertheless completely clear. For instance:

- "I do not grudge our loyal, brave people . . . who never *flinched* under the strain of last week. . . ." Only 3 percent of students predicted the word "flinched."
- ". . . unless by a supreme recovery of moral health and martial vigor, we arise again and take our stand for freedom as in the olden *time*." Ninety-five percent of students predicted that Churchill would use the word "days" instead of "time."

Churchill's sentences were neither longer nor more difficult than those of other speakers of his day. And Churchill's words were just as familiar. Churchill's genius as a stylist stemmed from his ability to be unpredictable while remaining fully understandable.[54]

Variety in sentence structure as well as variety in phrasing serves as a source of rhetorical competence. Research shows that sentence variety can boost the speaker's credibility.[55] Franklin D. Roosevelt understood how to construct sentences that balanced concreteness with variety. Roosevelt alternated long sentences with short ones to make his points doubly clear. In FDR's speeches, a lengthy narrative passage typically is followed by a short, pungent statement giving the crux of his argument. For instance, "There lies the road to peace," or "I do not share those illusions."[56]

Douglas MacArthur, too, balanced concreteness and variety through alternating simple and complex sentences. In his address to the cadets, he typically introduced a new idea with a simple sentence:

- "But these are some of the things they do."
- "Their story is known to all of you."
- "You now face a new world—a world of change."
- "This does not mean that you are warmongers."

These simple constructions usually were followed by sentences of greater length.

Even MacArthur's longest sentences, however, were easy to follow because they contained unifying devices. For instance, one of MacArthur's sentences narrated for the cadets the meaning of the words "duty," "honor," and "country":

> They teach you to be proud and unbending in honest failure, but humble and gentle in success; not to substitute words for action. . . .

Continuing his sentence, the General drew fully *nine* more contrasts. MacArthur held this long sentence together with parallel construction. He welded together the separate clauses with either the words "not to," or "to

Winston Churchill's speeches serve as models of eloquence.

be." Other of the General's long sentences tended to have a rhythmic flow. Some of them were built of short units spoken in a staccato pace. For instance:

> They give you a temper of the will, a quality of the imagination, a vigor of the emotions, a freshness of the deep springs of life, a temperamental predominance of courage over timidity, an appetite for adventure over love of ease.

All in all, MacArthur's style conveyed a feeling of variety. Short, pithy statements were mixed with longer, flowing sentences and with long sentences composed of short units.

Personality with precision

In addition to balancing concreteness and variety, a good public speaking style merges intimacy with precision. You want to speak in ways that move people personally but at the same time convey powerful ideas.

To make your speech intimate and personal, refer directly to yourself and to others. Follow the pattern of oral style and include references to "I" and "you." Instead of speaking in generalities, name relevant persons, places, and things that are close at hand. Using familiar names helps identify you with the audience. Did you ever notice that politicians make an effort to name the local mayor and high school during a campaign stop? Just before arriving in a particular locality, aides brief the candidates so that they can use all-important local names.

Mentioning familiar names is a good rhetorical tactic. Research shows that people are aroused by words that have close personal association. An experiment involving college students found that the most involving words were these: names of family members, names of specific academic majors, name of the university, and terms such as freshman, sophomore, junior, or senior. Other research demonstrates the advantage of making words and sentences personal. When speakers mention the first names of listeners, the audience views the speech as more interesting. This effect is useful, because a speech rated as interesting is more likely to be remembered. Furthermore, an interesting speech leads to higher marks on credibility for the speaker.[57]

Wayne Thompson describes the ideal speech as one that links the personal and conceptual aspects of language. He advises us that "the best speeches usually are a combination of personal materials with facts, statistics, examples, and authoritative quotations derived through research." Thompson adds: "Without library work the speech is likely to be vague and general; without the individual's own ideas and experiences, it is likely to be dull and impersonal."[58] Thompson's advice is borne out in statistical research by Tamara Carbone. She found that a speaker's credibility increased when the speaker included more personal pronouns (I, we, you), and referred to more specific individuals.[59]

Attention without excessive intensity

Your effort to use oral style gives you many ways to gain and sustain the attention of listeners. This is fortunate, because *any* loss of attentiveness imperils effective speaking. Aspiring to rhetorical competence, you will want to check your language against several ways to *win attention.*

1. Help listeners see action. When Douglas MacArthur describes the World War I soldier, he builds on the tendency of human eyes and ears to follow action:

   > I could see those staggering columns of the first World War, bending under soggy packs on many a weary march, from dripping dusk to drizzling dawn, slogging ankle deep through mire of shell-pocked roads; to form grimly for the attack, blue-lipped, covered with sludge and mud, chilled by the wind and rain.

2. Describe sizeable things. In his speech to the Houston ministers, John F. Kennedy showed the massive effect for American society if he were branded unfit for office on the basis of his religious affiliation.

> But if this election is decided on the basis that 40,000,000 Americans lost their chance of being President on the day they were baptized, then it is the whole nation that will be the loser.

3. Mention things that are concrete. John F. Kennedy cited the name of the fallen at the Alamo: "For side by side with Bowie and Crockett died Fuentes and McCafferty and Bailey and Bedillio and Carey."
4. Mention things that are familiar: Martin Luther King cited the common signs that stated "for whites only."
5. Call attention to things close at hand. Harold L. Enarson listed Ohio State University programs threatened by budget cuts:

> Here are some of the possibilities that have been suggested to me—*all bad:* sell one or both of the OSU golf courses . . . eliminate the student health service . . . disband the marching band for a year or two. . . .

6. Make it personal. In his opening words, Douglas MacArthur describes his pleasure at the tributes he has received during his visit to West Point: "It fills me with an emotion I cannot express."
7. State unusual ideas. William F. Buckley sarcastically refers to Pandit Nehru, long-time prime minister of India, as "the great ethical heart throb of the century."
8. Use contrast. This is how Congressman Lee Hamilton criticized Colonel Oliver North during the 1987 Iran-Contra hearings:

> In your opening statement you said that these hearings have caused serious damage to our national interests. But I wonder whether the damage has been caused by these hearings or by the acts which prompted these hearings.[60]

9. Use suspense. "Don't you think it strange that people have become so apathetic over it?" Virgil Phinney, a student speaker, continued to refer the problem as "it," until, in the sixty-first word of his speech, he explained that he was speaking on the subject of divorce.[61]
10. Mention conflict. Lee Hamilton chastises Colonel North, arguing that "your testimony points up confusion throughout the foreign policy-making process."
11. Use humor. William F. Buckley admits "I fully expect that someday I'll be wrong about something."

12. Include the promise of reward. Martin Luther King gives his vision of Americans joining hands and singing "in the words of the old Negro spiritual, 'Free at last! Free at last! Thank God almighty, we are free at last!' "

People listen to us when we speak in personal terms, make strong contrasts, and express wit. Though intensity creates an image of power, we nevertheless run risks when we use vivid language to arrest the attention of listeners. Why? A style that commands attention frequently relies on language of great intensity. *Intense language* strongly states an opinion or evaluation, showing we are opinionated.[62] Speaking with intensity, we say we were "ripped off" rather than "overcharged." We complain that an opponent "lied" rather than "made a factual error." Intense language makes us look powerful, but it also may provoke offense, making for another dilemma of style.[63]

The models of style by Martin Luther King, Jr. and Douglas MacArthur, reprinted in this chapter, represent speaking of a fairly intense kind. King talks of black children "stripped of their selfhood" by segregation and discrimination. King draws picture of attacks by "vicious racists." Similarly intense is the language of General MacArthur, who uses such terms as "pedant," "demagogue," "cynic," "hypocrite," and "troublemaker" to describe those who criticize the military tradition. MacArthur attacks "Federal paternalism" and the violence by "extremists."

We may say that the language of King and MacArthur is appropriately intense because their attacks fit the temper and expectations of their audiences. King shares the passions and articulates the demands of civil rights marchers. MacArthur plays the same role for West Point cadets. In both cases, intensity of style creates an agreeable atmosphere of sound while adding force to argument. Balanced intensity means to secure attention with powerful language that matches the audience and situation.

Eloquent speakers know how to use intense language appropriately. In his debates with Abraham Lincoln, Stephen A. Douglas carefully adjusted intensity of language according to whether his audience was favorable to him. In localities where Lincoln was the more popular, Douglas moderated his tone, stating his arguments clearly and not attacking Lincoln directly. Where Douglas enjoyed greater popularity, he was more likely to ridicule both Lincoln's views and Lincoln himself.[64] Franklin Roosevelt similarly was sensitive to when intense language could serve his purposes. As he guided the nation toward war preparedness in 1940, Roosevelt branded his isolationist opponents as "ostriches" and "appeasers." Roosevelt asserted that their "loose talking and loose thinking" followed the same line as the "Axis bureau of propaganda."[65]

The history of American public address suggests that the climate of opinion is what makes intense language appropriate or inappropriate. Experimental studies indicate specific conditions *when you should use intense language with extreme care.* First, avoid intense language when you have initially low credibility with your audience. A second time to avoid intensity is when listeners initially disagree with your thesis. Finally, intense language will not contribute much to your speech when listeners are in a highly emotional state at the time you begin to speak. In these three situations, experimental researchers found evidence that intense language decreased the persuasiveness of speeches.[66] In related studies, researchers found that you may lose credibility and persuasiveness by insisting that listeners have no choice but to agree with your claims.[67] One study also found that women may be generally less successful in using intense language.[68] However, social evolution may be rendering his finding obsolete. In her keynote address at the 1988 Democratic National Convention, Ann Richards of Texas seemed successful in a speech that, for example, ridiculed Bush for being born with "a silver foot in his mouth."[69]

A rhetorically competent speaker uses language that is clear and appropriate. At the same time, the effective stylist blends concreteness with variety, mixes personality with analysis, and wins attention without excess intensity. Clarity, appropriateness, balance—these hallmarks of effective speech style represent the strategic goals of rhetorical language. Now we turn to some useful tactics of good style—the stylistic figures.

Figures of Style

Figures of style are ways to phrase your points to add clarity, appropriateness, and balance. They represent specific *skills of style* that you will want to cultivate in your quest for rhetorical competence.

Sometimes the term "figure of speech" is used as a negative expression to separate what is said (the figure) versus what is meant (the "pure" idea). Such a view harkens back to the old idea that style is something merely ornamental. Frankly, an unhealthy preoccupation with figures of speech can hamper communication. For instance, some speakers of the early 1800s practiced a stylistic overkill. William Wirt, a prominent Virginia politician and writer, criticized the speakers of his day for their tendency to "encrust" and "bury" their arguments with a "concert of sounds."[70] In today's era of plainness in speaking, however, figures of style may be a resource for bringing both clarity and interest to public speaking. The figures serve as microscopic techniques of language that make possible an effective balance of orality and analysis.

Since classical times, teachers have offered lists of the figures of style. Each figure of style has several possible uses, but it is helpful to group them into six (overlapping) categories of use. Figures of style can (1) give perspective, (2) provide description, (3) facilitate comparison, (4) dramatize, (5) emphasize through grammar and semantics, and (6) emphasize through sound.

Figures of Perspective

Figures of speech let us communicate our point of view or perspective in a clear and striking fashion. Five figures are particularly useful in making our points more understandable and memorable.

1. Maxim. A maxim is a brief argument presented as a principle of life. William F. Buckley uses the figure of maxim in developing his policy of negotiation with Panama over the Canal Zone. "I happen to believe that the surest road to international prestige is to pay absolutely no heed whatever to foreign opinion."
2. Understatement. We use understatement when we minimize the significance of something to such a degree that we actually make the idea more striking. Understatement is characteristic of British speakers and writers. For instance, scientists Watson and Crick developed a model for DNA (deoxyribose nucleic acid) that they described in private as "perhaps the most famous event in biology since Darwin's book." To close associates the two presented their finding as something that would "revolutionize biology." However, in the article announcing their model, the authors stated that "we wish to suggest a structure [having] novel features which are of considerable biological interest."[71]
3. Exaggeration. In his speech of nomination for James G. Blaine at the Republican National Convention of 1876, Robert Ingersoll uses metaphor (comparison) to present an exaggerated but striking picture of James G. Blaine speaking to defend himself against charges of political corruption.

   > Like an armed warrior, like a plumed knight, James G. Blaine marched down the halls of the American Congress and threw his shining lance full and fair against the brazen foreheads of the defamers of his country and the maligners of his honor.

4. Irony. Irony puts together opposite impressions in one of two ways. One kind of irony is to identify circumstances that are opposite to what one would expect. For instance, in his eulogy of John F. Kennedy, Adlai Stevenson remarks "he who gave all to contain violence, lost his all—to violence."[72] Another form of irony is to use a word in a way opposite to its normal meaning. When we label a good thing as "bad" we speak ironically.
5. Reversal. In the figure of reversal, we turn a phrase around. One ancient, but still familiar, example of reversal is this one: "You must eat to live, not live to eat." Jesse Jackson phrased a memorable argument in his 1988 address at the Democratic National Convention using the figure of reversal: "I was born in the slum, but the slum wasn't born in me."[73]

Figures of Description

Speakers sometimes describe the world with short, concise, sentences. Other times they use detailed description. The figures of conciseness and vividness help us work a good balance between clarity and variety.

1. Conciseness. Adlai Stevenson uses concise sentences to impress his listeners with the stark fact of John F. Kennedy's sudden death by assassin's bullet. "Now he is gone. Today we mourn him. Tomorrow and tomorrow we shall miss him."
2. Vividness. Douglas MacArthur provides a detailed picture in words of the World War I soldier. "I could see those staggering columns of the First World War, bending under soggy packs on many a weary march. . . ."

Figures of Comparison

Comparison represents a fundamental kind of argument, as noted in chapter 7. Four figures of style directly help us in stating effective comparisons.

1. Metaphor. A metaphor is a description of one thing in terms usually applied to another. Jesse Jackson used the metaphor of making a quilt to argue that different groups in the Democratic party would not win until they joined their individual patches into a larger covering.[74] Jackson's metaphor minimized the disappointment of his supporters at the same time maximizing the importance of party unity.[75]

Box 10.3

Build Your Metaphors on the Familiar

A society for which the horse was so necessary [frontier Missouri] naturally based its metaphors on the animal and its management. A man who spoke without success was "singing songs to a dead horse"; . . . a speaker who presented proof had "the documents in his saddle bags". . . .

(Source: Frances L. McCurdy, *Stump, Bar, and Pulpit* [Columbia, MO: University of Missouri Press, 1969], 19.)

What are some good sources of metaphors for your audience? Could you base your metaphors on school, automobiles, religion, or sports?

2. Simile. A simile is a shortened metaphor often in the form "X is like Y." "Your guidepost stands out like a tenfold beacon in the night—duty—honor—country" (Douglas MacArthur).
3. Antithesis. To use antithesis is to emphasize the contrast of opposing ideas. "The world will little note, nor long remember, what we say here, but it can never forget what they did here" (Lincoln). "I come to bury Caesar, not to praise him," says Marc Anthony in Shakespeare's play, *Julius Caesar*.
4. Allusion. An allusion is a reference to some striking event or past person in history. In his speech to the 1988 Democratic National Convention, Jesse Jackson reminded his listeners of the murder of white and black civil rights workers during the 1960s. He also referred directly to well-known phrases from Martin Luther King's "I Have a Dream" speech, for instance King's hope that the "sons of former slaves and sons of former slave holders will be able to sit down together."

Figures of Dramatizing

A number of rhetorical figures put ideas into dramatic form as in a stage play.

1. Dialogue. Jesse Jackson, in one portion of his 1988 Democratic Convention speech, spoke directly to the downtrodden. He used dialogue to get across what people watching the speech from street corners might say to him: "Jesse, you be on TV"; "you don't understand my situation." Jackson then related his own origins in poverty, adding "I understand."

2. Personification. To represent an idea or a thing as living, speaking, or acting is to use personification. In his first Inaugural Address, Franklin Roosevelt put personal blame on Wall Street financiers for the nation's economic collapse. "The money changers have fled from their high seats in the temple of our civilization. We may now restore that temple to the ancient truths."[76] (Note also the allusion to Jesus cleansing the Temple in Jerusalem.)
3. Rhetorical question. As a prelude to argument, a speaker sometimes asks a question. "We have great tests ahead of us," asserted William F. Buckley. "Are we going to disarm unilaterally? Is our word to our allies a reliable covenant? Do we really believe in human rights? Do we believe in sovereignty—even for little countries?"
4. Apostrophe. Apostrophe is a short expression of deep grief or indignation. "Oh injustice!"

Jesse Jackson's speech in Atlanta was memorable for its style.

Figures of Grammar

Several tactics for arranging words and sentences can help create interest and clarity.

1. Substitution. Speakers can add variety by substituting unusual words for ones normally used. Martin Luther King substitutes a phrase for a word when he uses "citizens of color" instead of the then-familiar term, Negro. The phrase "this collection of arguments" used in place of the word "speech" is a substitution of the part for the whole. Substitution of the whole for the part occurs in news stories in which the phrase "the government ordered" replaces a particular department. To say "The White House denied"—instead of "President Bush denied"—is to substitute a related name for the person or thing itself.
2. Parallel structure. When a speaker presents a series of sentences or clauses stated in the same form, we have a case of parallel structure. Martin Luther King's "I Have a Dream" address concludes in this way:

    > I have a dream that one day this nation will rise up and live out the true meaning of its creed. . . .
    >
    > I have a dream that one day on the red hills of Georgia. . . .
    >
    > I have a dream that one day even the state of Mississippi. . . .
    >
    > I have a dream—that my four little children. . . .
    >
    > I have a dream that one day, down in Alabama. . . .
    >
    > I have a dream that one day every valley shall be exalted. . . .

3. Unusual word order. Speakers sometimes want to put words of a sentence into a surprising order. Instead of saying "Morning came and we went ahead," a speaker might say: "Came the morning and ahead we went."
4. Short clauses. Sometimes speakers compose a sentence made up of short units that are presented with pauses. One of Douglas MacArthur's most striking sentences is a long one that presents a series of lessons. Speaking of the words duty, honor, and country, MacArthur argues that:

    > They teach you to be proud and unbending in honest failure, but humble and gentle in success; not to substitute words for action; not to seek the path of comfort, but to face the stress and spur of difficulty and challenge; to learn to stand up in the storm, but to have compassion on those who fall; to master yourself before you seek to master others; to have a heart that is clean,

> a goal that is high; to learn to laugh, and never forget how to weep; to reach into the future, yet never neglect the past; to be serious, yet never take yourself too seriously; to be modest so that you will remember the simplicity of true greatness.

Figures of Sound

Certain figures capitalize on sounds of speech in getting across a point.

1. Alliteration. Speakers frequently create a phrase that contains words repeating the same sound:
   - "*d*ark and *d*esolate valley" (Martin Luther King)
   - "*f*laming *f*orges" (Robert Ingersoll)
   - "the strange, *m*ournful *m*utter of the battlefield" (Douglas MacArthur)
2. Repetition. Speakers may create a useful rhythm in their speeches by repetitions. One kind of repetition is of the first or last word in a series. Speaking to reporters at a rally late in his 1988 campaign for the presidency, Jesse Jackson emphasized that he was going ahead despite setbacks.

   > We intend to get our share of delegates based on popular votes. Write that down. We intend to come out of California, then New Jersey, in search of a management team and a running mate to go against George Bush. Write that down.[77]

   Another form of repetition is of the endings of words, for instance, "they died unquestioning, uncomplaining" (Douglas MacArthur). One may also repeat ideas by using synonyms instead of the same word, as in this example taught to Roman students: "You have impiously beaten your father; you have criminally laid hands upon your parent."[78]
3. Onomatopoeia. Onomatopoeia is a stylistic figure that finds the speaker using words whose sound is like the thing being described. For instance: "the *whoosh* of the evening tide."

Figures are short units of style. These many skillful uses of language promote both deeper analysis and fuller persuasion. Most of us will never become a great stylist of speech in the manner of Franklin Roosevelt, Douglas MacArthur, Martin Luther King, John F. Kennedy, William F. Buckley, or Jesse Jackson. But everyone can benefit from an effort to include several stylistic figures in a speech. The rhetorically competent speaker knows that style can be a powerful help in speech effectiveness.

Jack Valenti attributes much of today's shortage of wit in public speaking to a disregard of speaking style. Valenti, former speechwriter for Lyndon Johnson, also serves as a widely-known public speaker and speech consultant. Valenti argues that if we survey the vital issues of our time "it appears that the most serious shortage in America today is that of political wit." Today's speakers, committed to the idea that speaking style contributes little to success, often see no reason to demand arresting language of themselves—or of their speech writers. When, years ago, great speakers cultivated their language, witty remarks—and the devastating rebuttals they provided—came naturally to the tongue. Hearing a windy colleague proclaim on the floor of the United States House that he "would rather be right than president," Thomas Reed of Maine replied that "the gentleman need not be disturbed; he will never be either."[79]

You will not take up the challenge of style unless you believe that style makes a difference, so observe the style of the speeches you hear. Work to understand and appreciate oral style. Seek to make your own speaking clear, appropriate, and balanced. Turn to the figures of speech as sources for a striking and powerful style.

Sample Speech

"I Have A Dream"

By Martin Luther King, Jr.

I am happy to join with you today in what will go down in history as the greatest demonstration for freedom in the history of our nation.

Five score years ago, a great American, in whose symbolic shadow we stand, signed the Emancipation Proclamation. This momentous decree came as a great beacon light of hope to millions of Negro slaves who had been seared in the flames of withering injustice. It came as a joyous daybreak to end the long night of captivity.

But one hundred years later, the Negro still is not free. One hundred years later, the life of the Negro is still sadly crippled by the manacles of segregation and the chains of discrimination. One hundred years later, the Negro lives on a lonely island of poverty in the midst of a vast ocean of material prosperity. One hundred years later, the Negro is still languished in the corners of American society and finds himself an exile in his own land. So we've come here today, to dramatize a shameful condition.

In a sense we've come to our nation's Capital to cash a check. When the architects of our republic wrote the magnificent words of the Constitution and the Declaration of Independence, they were signing a promissory note to which every American was to fall heir. This note was a promise that all men—yes, black men as well as white men—would be guaranteed the unalienable rights of life, liberty, and the pursuit of happiness.

It is obvious today that America has defaulted on this promissory note insofar as her citizens of color are concerned. Instead of honoring this sacred obligation, America has given the Negro people a bad check; a check which has come back marked "insufficient funds." But we refuse to believe that the bank of justice is bankrupt. We refuse to believe that there are insufficient funds in the great vaults of opportunity of this nation. And so we have come to cash this check—a check that will give us upon demand the riches of freedom and the security of justice. We have also come to this hallowed spot to remind America of the fierce urgency of *now*. This is no time to engage in the luxury of cooling off or to take the tranquilizing drug of gradualism. *Now* is the time to make real the promises of Democracy. *Now* is the time to rise from the dark and desolate valley of segregation to the sunlit path of racial justice. *Now* is the time to lift our nation from the quicksands of racial injustice to the solid rock of brotherhood. *Now* is the time to make justice a reality for all of God's children.

It would be fatal for the nation to overlook the urgency of the moment. This sweltering summer of the Negro's legitimate discontent will not pass until there is an invigorating autumn of freedom and equality. 1963 is not an end, but a beginning. Those who hope that the Negro needed to blow off steam and will now be content will have a rude awakening if the nation returns to business as usual. There will be neither rest nor tranquility in America until the Negro is granted his citizenship rights. The whirlwinds of revolt will continue to shake the foundations of our nation until the bright day of justice emerges.

But there is something that I must say to my people who stand on the warm threshold which leads into the palace of justice. In the process of gaining our rightful place we must not be guilty of wrongful deeds. Let us not seek to satisfy our thirst for freedom by drinking from the cup of bitterness and hatred. We must forever conduct our struggle on the high plane of dignity and discipline. We must not allow our creative protest to degenerate into physical violence. Again and again we must rise to the majestic heights of meeting physical force with soul force. The marvelous new militancy which has engulfed the Negro community must not lead us to a distrust of all white people, for many of our white brothers, as evidenced by their presence here today, have come to realize that their destiny is tied up with our destiny. They have come to realize that their freedom is inextricably bound to our freedom. We cannot walk alone.

As we walk, we must make the pledge that we shall march ahead. We cannot turn back. There are those who are asking the devotees of civil rights, "When will you be satisfied?" We can never be satisfied as long as the Negro is the victim of the unspeakable horrors of police brutality. We can never be satisfied as long as our bodies, heavy with the fatigue of travel, cannot gain lodging in the motels of the highways and the hotels of the cities. We cannot be satisfied as long as the Negro's basic mobility is from a smaller ghetto to a larger one. We can never be satisfied as long as our children are stripped of their selfhood and robbed of their dignity by signs stating "For Whites Only." We cannot be satisfied as long as a Negro in Mississippi cannot vote and a Negro in New York believes he has nothing for which to vote. No, no, we are not satisfied, and we will not be satisfied until justice rolls down like waters and righteousness like a mighty stream.

I am not unmindful that some of you have come here out of great trials and tribulations. Some of you have come fresh from narrow jail cells. Some of you have come from areas where your quest for freedom left you battered by the storms of persecution and staggered by the winds of police brutality. You have been the veterans of creative suffering. Continue to work with the faith that unearned suffering is redemptive.

Go back to Mississippi, go back to Alabama, go back to South Carolina, go back to Georgia, go back to Louisiana, go back to the slums and ghettos of our northern cities, knowing that somehow this situation can and will be changed. Let us not wallow in the valley of despair.

I say to you today, my friends, that in spite of the difficulties and frustrations of the moment I still have a dream. It is a dream deeply rooted in the American dream.

I have a dream that one day this nation will rise up and live out the true meaning of its creed: "We hold these truths to be self evident; that all men are created equal."

I have a dream that one day on the red hills of Georgia the sons of former slaves and the sons of former slaveowners will be able to sit down together at the table of brotherhood.

I have a dream that one day even the state of Mississippi, a state sweltering with the heat of injustice, sweltering with the heat of oppression, will be transformed into an oasis of freedom and justice.

I have a dream—that my four little children will one day live in a nation where they will not be judged by the color of their skin but by the content of their character. I have a dream today.

I have a dream that one day, down in Alabama, with its vicious racists, with its governor having his lips dripping with the words of interposition and nullification, one day right there in Alabama little black boys and black girls will be able to join hands with little white boys and white girls and walk together as sisters and brothers. I have a dream today.

I have a dream that one day every valley shall be exalted, every hill and mountain shall be made low, the rough places will be made plane, and the crooked places will be made straight, and the glory of the Lord shall be revealed, and all flesh shall see it together.

This is our hope. This is the faith that I go back to the South with. With this faith we will be able to hew out of the mountain of despair a stone of hope. With this faith we will be able to transform the jangling discords of our nation into a beautiful symphony of brotherhood. With this faith we will be able to work together, to pray together, to struggle together, to go to jail together, to stand up for freedom together, knowing that we will be free one day.

This will be the day—this will be the day when all of God's children will be able to sing with new meaning: "My country, 'tis of thee, Sweet land of liberty, Of thee I sing: Land where my fathers died, Land of the pilgrims' pride, From every mountain-side, Let freedom ring."

And if America is to be a great nation this must become true. So let freedom ring from the prodigious hilltops of New Hampshire. Let freedom ring from the mighty mountains of New York. Let freedom ring from the heightening Alleghenies of Pennsylvania!

Let freedom ring from the snowcapped Rockies of Colorado!

Let freedom ring from the curvaceous slopes of California!

But not only that; let freedom ring from Stone Mountain of Georgia!

Let freedom ring from Lookout Mountain of Tennessee!

Let freedom ring from every hill and molehill of Mississippi. From every mountainside, let freedom ring.

And when this happens, when we allow freedom ring—when we let it ring from every village and every hamlet, from every state and every city, we will be able to speed up that day when all of God's children, black men and white men, Jews and Gentiles, Protestants and Catholics, will be able to join hands and sing in the words of the old Negro spiritual, "Free at last! Free at last! Thank God almighty, we are free at last!"

Sample Speech

Speech at West Point
By Douglas MacArthur

General Westmoreland, General Groves, distinguished guests, and gentlemen of the corps: As I was leaving the hotel this morning, a doorman asked me, "Where are you bound for, General?" and when I replied, "West Point," he remarked, "Beautiful place, have you ever been there before?"

No human being could fail to be deeply moved by such a tribute as this [Sylvanus Thayer Award]. Coming from a profession I have served so long, and a people I have loved so well, it fills me with an emotion I cannot express. But this award is not intended primarily to honor a personality, but to symbolize a great moral code—the code of conduct and chivalry of those who guard this beloved land of culture and ancient descent. That is the meaning of this medallion. For all eyes and for all time, it is an expression of the ethics of the American soldier. That I should be integrated in this way with so noble an ideal arouses a sense of pride and yet of humility which will be with me always.

Duty—honor—country: These three hallowed words reverently dictate what you ought to be, what you can be, what you will be. They are your rallying points: to build courage when courage seems to fail; to regain faith when there seems to be little cause for faith; to create hope when hope becomes forlorn. Unhappily, I possess neither that eloquence of diction, that poetry of imagination, nor that brilliance of metaphor to tell you all that they mean. The unbelievers will say they are but words, but a slogan, but a flamboyant phrase. Every pedant, every demagogue, every cynic, every hypocrite, every troublemaker, and I am sorry to say, some others of an entirely different character, will try to downgrade them even to the extent of mockery and ridicule.

But these are some of the things they do. They build your basic character, they mold you for your future roles as the custodians of the nation's defense, they make you strong enough to know when you are weak, and brave enough to face yourself when you are afraid. They teach you to be proud and unbending in honest failure, but humble and gentle in success; not to substitute words for actions, nor to seek the path of comfort, but to face the stress and spur of difficulty and challenge; to learn to stand up in the storm but to have compassion on those who fail; to master yourself before you seek to master others; to have a heart that is clean, a goal that is high; to learn to laugh yet

Source: Congressional Record, May 31, 1962, pp. A4008–A4009.

never forget how to weep, to reach into the future yet never neglect the past; to be serious yet never to take yourself too seriously; to be modest so that you will remember the simplicity of true greatness, the open mind of true wisdom, the meekness of true strength. They give you a temper of the will, a quality of the imagination, a vigor of the emotions, a freshness of the deep springs of life, a temperamental predominance of courage over timidity, an appetite for adventure over love of ease. They create in your heart the sense of wonder, the unfailing hope of what next, and the joy and inspiration of life. They teach you in this way to be an officer and a gentleman.

And what sort of soldiers are those you are to lead: Are they reliable, are they brave, are they capable of victory? Their story is known to all of you: it is the story of the American man-at-arms. My estimate of him was formed on the battlefield many, many, years ago, and has never changed. I regarded him then as I regard him now—as one of the world's noblest figures, not only as one of the finest military characters but also as one of the most stainless. His name and fame are the birthright of every American citizen. In his youth and strength, his love and loyalty he gave—all that mortality can give. He needs no eulogy from me or from any other man. He has written his own history and written it in red on his enemy's breast. But when I think of his patience under adversity, of his courage under fire, and of his modesty in victory, I am filled with an emotion of admiration I cannot put into words. He belongs to history as furnishing one of the greatest examples of successful patriotism; he belongs to posterity as the instructor of future generations in the principles of liberty and freedom; he belongs to the present, to us, by his virtues and by his achievements. In twenty campaigns, on a hundred battlefields, around a thousand campfires, I have witnessed that enduring fortitude, that patriotic self-abnegation, and that invincible determination which have carved his statue in the hearts of his people. From one end of the world to the other he has drained deep the chalice of courage.

As I listened to those songs of the glee club, in memory's eye I could see those staggering columns of the First World War, bending under soggy packs, on many a weary march from dripping dusk to drizzling dawn, slogging ankle deep through the mire of shell-shocked roads, to form grimly for the attack, blue-lipped, covered with sludge and mud, chilled by the wind and rain; driving home to their objective, and, for many, to the judgment seat of God. I do not know the dignity of their birth but I do know the glory of their death. They died unquestioning, uncomplaining, with faith in their hearts, and on their lips the hope that we would go on to victory. Always for them—duty—honor—country; always their blood and sweat and tears as we sought the way and the light and the truth.

And twenty years after, on the other side of the globe, again the filth of murky foxholes, the stench of ghostly trenches, the slime of dripping dugouts; those boiling suns of relentless heat; those torrential rains of devastating storms; the loneliness and utter desolation of jungle trails, the bitterness of long separation from those they loved and cherished, the deadly pestilence of tropical disease, the horror of stricken areas of war; their resolute and determined defense, their swift and sure attack, their indomitable purpose, their complete and decisive victory—always victory. Always through the bloody haze of their last reverberating shot, the vision of gaunt, ghastly men reverently following your password of duty—honor—country.

The code which these words perpetuate embraces the highest moral laws and will stand the test of any ethics or philosophies ever promulgated for the uplift of mankind. Its requirements are for the things that are right, and its restraints are from the things that are wrong. The soldier, above all other men, is required to practice the greatest act of religious training—sacrifice. In battle and in the face of danger and death, he discloses those divine attributes which his Maker gave when He created man in His own image. No physical courage and no brute instinct can take the place of the divine help which alone can sustain him. However horrible the incidents of war may be, the soldier who is called upon to offer and to give his life for his country, is the noblest development of mankind.

You now face a new world—a world of change. The thrust into outer space of the satellite, spheres and missiles marked the beginning of another epoch of the long story of mankind—the chapter of the space age. In the five or more billions of years the scientists tell us it has taken to form the earth, in the three or more million years of development of the human race, there has never been a greater, a more abrupt or staggering evolution. We deal now not with things of this world alone, but with the illimitable distances and as yet unfathomed mysteries of the universe. We are reaching out for a new and boundless frontier. We speak in strange terms: of harnessing the cosmic energy; of making winds and tides work for us; of creating unheard synthetic materials to supplement or even replace our old standard basics; of purifying sea water for our drink; of mining ocean floors for new fields of wealth and food; of disease preventatives to expand life into the hundred of years; of controlling the weather for a more equitable distribution of heat and cold, of rain and shine; of spaceships to the moon; of the primary target in war, no longer limited to the armed forces of an enemy, but instead to include his civil populations;

of ultimate conflict between a united human race and the sinister forces of some other planetary galaxy; of such dreams and fantasies as to make life the most exciting of all time.

And through all this welter of change and development, your mission remains fixed, determined, inviolable—it is to win our wars. Everything else in your professional career is but corollary to this vital dedication. All other public purposes, all other public projects, all other public needs, great or small, will find others for their accomplishment; but you are the ones who are trained to fight: yours is the profession of arms—the will to win, the sure knowledge that in war there is no substitute for victory; that if you lose, the nation will be destroyed; that the very obsession of your public service must be duty—honor—country. Others will debate the controversial issues, national and international, which divide men's minds; but serene, calm, aloof, you stand as the nation's war-guardian, as its lifeguard from the raging tides of international conflict, as its gladiator in the arena of battle. For a century and a half you have defended, guarded, and protected its hallowed traditions of liberty and freedom, of right and justice. Let civilian voices argue the merits or demerits of our processes of government; whether our strength is being sapped by deficit financing, indulged in too long, by Federal paternalism grown too mighty, by power groups grown too arrogant, by political groups grown too corrupt, by crime grown too rampant, by morals grown too low, by taxes grown too high, by extremists grown too violent; whether our personal liberties are so thorough and complete as they should be. These great national problems are not for your professional participation or military solution. Your guidepost stands out like a tenfold beacon in the night—duty—honor—country.

You are the leaven which binds together the entire fabric of our national system of defense. From your ranks come the great captains who hold the nation's destiny in their hands the moment the war tocsin sounds. The long grey line has never failed us. Were you to do so, a million ghosts in olive drab, in brown khaki, in blue and gray, would rise from their white crosses thundering those magic words—duty—honor—country.

This does not mean that you are warmongers. On the contrary, the soldier, above all other people, prays for peace, for he must suffer and bear the deepest wounds and scars of war. But always in our ears ring the ominous words of Plato that wisest of all philosophers, "Only the dead have seen the end of war."

The shadows are lengthening for me. The twilight is here. My days of old have vanished tone and tint; they have gone glimmering through the dreams of things that were. Their memory is one of wondrous beauty, watered by tears and coaxed and caressed by the smiles of yesterday. Listen vainly for the witching melody of faint bugles blowing reveille, of the far drums beating the long roll. In my dreams I hear again the crash of guns, the rattle of musketry, the strange, mournful mutter of the battlefield.

But in the evening of my memory, always I come back to West Point. Always there echoes and reechoes duty—honor—country.

Today marks my final rollcall with you, but I want you to know that when I cross the river my last conspicuous thoughts will be of the corps, and the corps, and the corps.

I bid you farewell.

Concepts for Review

Can you summarize the meaning of these terms or expressions? How does each relate to speechmaking?

style gives force to argument
Sapir-Worf hypothesis
oral style is more active
oral style is more personal
allness terms
clarity of style
jargon
euphemisms
appropriateness
concrete style
variety in vocabulary
mixing personal and conceptual
style creates attention
intense language
figures
maxim
understatement
exaggeration
irony
reversal
conciseness
vividness
metaphor
simile
antithesis
allusion
dialogue
personification
rhetorical question
apostrophe
substitution
parallel structure
unusual word order
short clauses
alliteration
repetition
onomatopoeia

Things to Try

1. To see how style figures in modern life, leaf through a couple of magazines, noting what seems to be interesting language in the advertisements. Review the list of rhetorical figures given in this chapter. Look for these figures in the ads.
2. Consult a recent issue of *Vital Speeches.* Xerox two or three of the speeches. Try to decide what makes the language either impressive or unimpressive. Read through the speeches, marking places where the style seems striking and interesting. Is the speaker using a figure of style? Also mark some places where the language is particularly unclear or dull. Does the speaker use any jargon that blocks your understanding of the speech?
3. Taking one speech you marked in exercise 2, above, review the figures of style given in this chapter. Look again at where the language seems particularly interesting. Can you find any of the figures treated in this chapter? Look at places where the language seems confusing or dull. Try to freshen these places by rewriting the speech, using a figure of style.
4. Apply the figures of style to your classroom speeches. For your next speech, select two figures of style and practice including them in your speech. Experiment with new figures in every following speech.

Endnotes

1. Hugo E. Hellman, "The Greatest American Oratory," *Quarterly Journal of Speech 24* (1938):36–39.
2. E. D. Hirsch, Jr., *Cultural Literacy* (New York: Vintage, 1988), 174.
3. Ronald F. Reid, "Newspaper Response to the Gettysburg Addresses," *Quarterly Journal of Speech 53* (1967), 50–60.
4. *San Francisco Chronicle,* 31 March 1988, A13.
5. Peter France, *Rhetoric and Truth in France: Descartes to Diderot* (Oxford: Oxford University Press, 1972), 15–16, 20–27.
6. Walter R. Fisher, "The Importance of Style in Systems of Rhetoric," *Southern Speech Journal 27* (1962): 173–182.
7. John Kozy, Jr., "The Argumentative Use of Rhetorical Figures," *Philosophy and Rhetoric 3* (1970): 141–151, and Chaim Perelman and L. Olbrechts-Tyteca, *The New Rhetoric,* trans. by J. Wilkinson and P. Weaver (Notre Dame, IN: University of Notre Dame Press, 1969), 167.

8. Haig Bosmajian, "Rhetoricians Against Style," *Western Speech 25* (1961): 33–36.
9. William N. Brigance, "Jeremiah S. Black," *A History and Criticism of American Public Address,* ed. W. N. Brigance, 2 vols. (New York: Russell & Russell, 1943), 1:476.
10. Robert D. Clark, "Harry Emerson Fosdick," *A History and Criticism of American Public Address,* ed. M. K. Hochmuth [Nichols] (New York: Russell & Russell, 1955), 447.
11. Edward Sapir, *Language* (New York: Harcourt Brace Jovanovich, 1921), 15.
12. Arthur Hastings, "Metaphor in Rhetoric," *Western Speech 34* (1970): 181–193, and James W. Hikins, "The Rhetoric of 'Unconditional Surrender' and the Decision to Drop the Atomic Bomb," *Quarterly Journal of Speech 69* (1983): 379–400.
13. See Jerry D. Feezel, "A Qualified Certainty: Verbal Probability in Arguments," *Speech Monographs 41* (1974): 348–356, and James J. Bradac, John W. Bowers, and John A. Courtright, "Three Language Variables in Communication Research: Intensity, Immediacy, and Diversity," *Human Communication Research 5* (1979): 257–269.
14. Helen H. Franzawa, "Psychological Factors Influencing Use of 'Evaluative-Dynamic' Language," *Speech Monographs 36* (1969): 103–109.
15. Barbara Bate, "Nonsexist Language Use in Transition," *Journal of Communication 28,* No. 1 (1978): 139–149; Brenda Bochner and Arthur Bochner, "The Effects of Social Status and Social Dialect on Listener Responses," *Central States Speech Journal 24* (1973): 75–82; Charles J. Stewart, "Voter Perception of Mud-Slinging in Political Communication," *Central States Speech Journal 26* (1975): 279–286; Judee K. Burgoon, Miriam Wilkinson, and Ralph Partridge, "The Relative Effectiveness of Praise and Derogation as Persuasive Strategies," *Journal of the American Forensic Association 16* (1979): 10–20.
16. David R. Olson, "Oral and Written Language and the Cognitive Processes of Children," *Journal of Communication 27,* No. 3 (1977): 10–26, and Eric A. Havelock, "The Coming of Literate Communication to Western Culture," *Journal of Communication 30,* No. 1 (1980): 90–98.
17. Compare Protagoras's description of the nature of human deliberation (in Plato, *Protagoras,* 320–328) and Socrates's views (shared by Plato) in Plato, *Phraedrus,* 258–268.
18. Aristotle, *Rhetoric,* III. 12. 1413b–1414a.
19. Earnest Brandenburg and Waldo W. Braden, "Franklin Delano Roosevelt," *History and Criticism,* ed. M. K. Hochmuth [Nichols], 509.
20. James W. Gibson, Charles R. Gruner, Robert J. Kibler, and Francis J. Kelly, "A Quantitative Examination of Differences and Similarities in Written and Spoken Messages," *Speech Monographs 33* (1966): 444–451; Joseph A. DeVito, "The Encoding of Speech and Writing," *Speech Teacher 15* (1966b): 55–60; Jane Blankenship, "The Influence of Mode, Sub-Mode, and Speaker Predilection on Style," *Speech Monographs 41* (1974): 85–118; Lois Einhorn, "Oral and Written Style: An Examination of Differences," *Southern Speech Communication Journal 43* (1978): 302–311.

21. John B. Newman and Milton W. Horowitz, "Speaking and Writing," *Today's Speech 13,* No. 1 (1965): 2–4, 16.
22. Joseph A. DeVito, "Comprehension Factors in Oral and Written Discourse of Skilled Communicators," *Speech Monographs 32* (1965): 124–128, and Einhorn, "Oral and Written."
23. DeVito, "Factors in Oral and Written"; Gibson, et al., "Written and Spoken Messages"; DeVito, "Speech and Writing"; Blankenship, "Influence on Style"; Einhorn, "Oral and Written."
24. Gibson, et al., "Written and Spoken Messages"; Einhorn, "Oral and Written"; Edward C. Carterette and Margaret H. Jones, *Informal Speech* (Berkeley: University of California Press, 1974), 33; Tamara Carbone, "Stylistic Variables as Related to Source Credibility: A Content Analysis Approach," *Speech Monographs 42* (1975): 99–106. Note, however, that Jane Blankenship, "A Linguistic Analysis of Oral and Written Style, *Quarterly Journal of Speech 48* (1962): 419–422, and DeVito, "Factors in Oral and Written," found no major differences between the length of oral and written sentences.
25. DeVito, "Factors in Oral and Written"; DeVito, "Speech and Writing"; Carterette & Jones, *Informal Speech 33;* Carbone, "Stylistic Variables."
26. Joseph A. DeVito, "A Linguistic Analysis of Spoken and Written Language," *Central States Speech Journal 18* (1967): 81–85.
27. DeVito, "Spoken and Written Language," and Blankenship, "Influence on Style."
28. Gladys Borchers, "An Approach to the Problem of Oral Style," *Quarterly Journal of Speech 22* (1936): 114–117.
29. Olson, "Language and Cognitive."
30. Joseph A. DeVito, "Psychogrammatical Factors in Oral and Written Discourse by Skilled Communicators," *Speech Monographs 33* (1966a): 73–76, and Blankenship, "Influence on Style."
31. Borchers, "Problem of Oral Style"; Kenneth Berger, "Conversational English of University Students," *Speech Monographs 34* (1967): 65–73; Einhorn, "Oral and Written."
32. Borchers, "Problem of Oral Style," and Einhorn, "Oral and Written."
33. Borchers, "Problem of Oral Style," 116.
34. Newman & Horowitz, "Speaking and Writing"; DeVito, "Psychogrammatical Factors"; Carterette & Jones, *Informal Speech,* 26.
35. DeVito, "Psychogrammatical Factors," and Blankenship, "Influence on Style."
36. DeVito, "Psychogrammatical Factors."
37. DeVito, "Psychogrammatical Factors."
38. DeVito, "Psychogrammatical Factors," and Blankenship, "Influence on Style."
39. William N. Brigance, *Speech Composition,* 2nd ed. (New York: Appleton-Century-Crofts, 1953), 203.
40. Brandenburg & Braden, "Franklin Delano Roosevelt," 505.
41. *Newsweek,* 21 July 1975, 64.
42. *Chronicle of Higher Education,* 2 February 1981, 3.
43. *Chronicle of Higher Education,* 2 December 1981, 11.

44. M. Lee Williams and Blaine Goss, "Equivocation: Character Insurance," *Human Communication Research 1* (1975): 265–270.
45. Carbone, "Stylistic Variables"; C. Jack Orr and Karen E. Burkins, "The Endorsement of Evasive Leaders: An Exploratory Study," *Central States Speech Journal 27* (1976): 230–239; G. Wayne Shamo and John R. Bittner, "Recall as a Function of Language Style," *Southern Speech Communication Journal 38* (1972): 181–187.
46. Blaine Goss and Lee Williams, "The Effects of Equivocation on Perceived Source Credibility," *Central States Speech Journal 24* (1973): 162–167; Williams & Goss, "Character Insurance"; Orr & Burkins, "Evasive Leaders"; M. Lee Williams, "The Effect of Deliberate Vagueness on Receiver Recall and Agreement," *Central States Speech Journal 31* (1980): 30–41.
47. Joe McGinniss, *The Selling of the President 1968* (New York: Trident, 1969), 90.
48. Robert N. Bostrom, John R. Baseheart, and Charles M. Rossiter, Jr., "The Effects of Three Types of Profane Language in Persuasive Messages," *Journal of Communication 23* (1973): 461–475; Anthony Mulac, "Effects of Obscene Language Upon Three Dimensions of Listener Attitude," *Communication Monographs 43* (1976): 300–307; Bradac, Bowers & Courtright, "Three Language Variables."
49. William J. McEwen and Bradley S. Greenberg, "The Effects of Message Intensity on Receiver Evaluation of Source, Message and Topic," *Journal of Communication 20* (1970): 340–350; Michael Burgoon, Stephen B. Jones, and Diane Stewart, "Toward a Message-Centered Theory of Persuasion: Three Empirical Investigations of Language Intensity," *Human Communication Research 1* (1975): 240–256; Bradac, Bowers & Courtright, "Three Language Variables."
50. *Playboy,* November 1976, 86; Martha Solomon, "Jimmy Carter and *Playboy:* A Sociolinguistic Perspective on Style, *Quarterly Journal of Speech 64* (1978): 173–182; Ellen R. Gold, "Political Apologia: The Ritual of Self-Defense," *Communication Monographs 45* (1978): 312–313.
51. Gage W. Chapel, "Speechwriting in the Nixon Administration," *Journal of Communication 26,* No. 2 (1976): 71.
52. Carbone, "Stylistic Variables"; James J. Bradac, Catherine W. Konsky, and Robert A. Davies, "Two Studies of the Effects of Linguistic Diversity Upon Judgments of Communicator Attributes and Message Effectiveness," *Communication Monographs 43* (1976): 71–79; James J. Bradac, Roger J. Desmond, and Johnny I. Murdock, "Diversity and Density: Lexically Determined Evaluative and Informational Consequences of Linguistic Complexity," *Communication Monographs 44* (1977): 273–283; Bradac, Bowers & Courtright, "Three Language Variables."
53. John W. Black, "Predictability as Related to Style," *Speech Monographs 40* (1973): 103.
54. John H. Timmis, III, "Textual and Information-Theoretic Indexes of Style as Discriminators Between Message Sources," *Communication Monographs 52* (1985); 136–155.

55. Bradac, Konsky & Davis, "Two Studies of Linguistic Diversity."
56. Brandenburg & Braden, "Franklin Delano Roosevelt," 506–507.
57. Loren D. Crane, Richard J. Dieker, and Charles T. Brown, "The Physiological Response to the Communication Modes: Reading, Listening, Writing, Speaking, and Evaluating," *Journal of Communication 20* (1970): 231–240, and Charles R. Gruner, "The Effect of Humor in Dull and Interesting Informative Speeches," *Central States Speech Journal 21* (1970): 160–166.
58. Wayne N. Thompson, *Responsible and Effective Communication* (Boston: Houghton Mifflin, 1978), 25.
59. Carbone, "Stylistic Variables," 104–105.
60. *San Francisco Chronicle,* 15 July 1987, 10.
61. "A Contract in Crisis," *Winning Orations of the Interstate Oratorical Association 1979,* ed. L. Schnoor (Mankato, MN: Mankato State University, 1979), 14.
62. John W. Bowers, "Language Intensity, Social Introversion, and Attitude Change," *Speech Monographs 30* (1963): 345.
63. Michael Burgoon and Lawrence J. Chase, "The Effects of Differential Linguistic Patterns in Messages Attempting to Induce Resistance to Persuasion," *Speech Monographs 40* (1973): 1–7, and Dominic A. Infante, "Effects of Opinionated Language on Communicator Image and in Conferring Resistance to Persuasion," *Western Speech Communication 39* (1975): 112–119.
64. Forest L. Whan, "Stephen A. Douglas," *A History and Criticism of American Public Address,* ed. W. N. Brigance, 2 vols (New York: Russell & Russell, 1943), 2:810.
65. Brandenburg & Braden, "Franklin Delano Roosevelt," 493.
66. R. Samuel Mehrley and James C. McCroskey, "Opinionated Statements and Attitude Intensity as Predictors of Attitude Change and Source Credibility," *Speech Monographs 37* (1970); Burgoon, Jones & Stewart, "Message Centered Theory of Persuasion"; Bradac, Bowers & Courtright, "Three Language Variables."
67. Mary J. Smith, "The Effects of Threats to Attitudinal Freedom as a Function of Message Quality and Initial Receiver Attitude," *Communication Monographs 44* (1977): 196–206, and Smith, "Discrepancy and the Importance of Attitudinal Freedom," *Human Communication Research 4* (1978): 308–314.
68. Burgoon, Jones & Stewart, "Message Centered Theory of Persuasion."
69. *San Francisco Chronicle,* 19 July 1988, A12.
70. Judy G. Hample, "William Wirt's Familiar Essays: Criticism of Virginia Oratory," *Southern Speech Communication Journal 44* (1978): 38. Also see Howard H. Martin, " 'Style' in the Golden Age," *Quarterly Journal of Speech 43* (1957): 374–382.
71. James D. Watson, *The Double Helix* (New York: New American Library, 1968), 127, 140.

72. *Representative American Speeches: 1963–1964,* ed. L. Thonssen (N.Y.: H. W. Wilson, 1964), 32.
73. *Rhetorica ad Herennium,* IV. 28. 39; *San Francisco Chronicle,* 20 July 1988, A1.
74. *New York Times* (national edition), 20 July 1988, A12.
75. See Michael M. Osborn, "The Evolution of the Theory of Metaphor in Rhetoric," *Western Speech 31* (1967): 121–130.
76. "Inaugural Address," Franklin D. Roosevelt, 4 March 1933, in *Inaugural Addresses of the Presidents of the United States,* House Document No. 540, 82nd Cong., 2nd sess., 1952, 226.
77. *San Francisco Chronicle,* 29 April 1988, A9.
78. *Rhetorica ad Herrennium,* IV. 28. 39.
79. Jack Valenti, *Courier-Journal* (Louisville), 10 February 1980, D3.

Chapter

11

Delivery: Voice and Movement in Speaking

Outline

Asked to list the three keys to effective speaking, Demosthenes, the Athenian leader, replied "delivery, delivery, delivery."[1] In assigning delivery such a high place in rhetorical competence, Demosthenes did not mean to ignore the importance of good content in speechmaking. Instead, Demosthenes was drawing a lesson from his long practical experience in the political debates of ancient Athens. He knew that even the best of ideas and arguments carried little weight when presented with a dull or distracting delivery. From the beginning of his career, Demosthenes was concerned with good expression. As a young man, he vowed to hide away in a cave until he had overcome certain awkward habits of voice and movement. To hold himself to his oath, Demosthenes shaved half his head so that shame would prevent him from rejoining society before he had mastered the arts of good rhetorical presentation.[2]

The cases of two recent presidents, Jimmy Carter and Ronald Reagan, illustrate the importance of complementing good content with good delivery. One of the frequent problems of the Carter administration was not as much *what* the president said—but *how* he said it. Carter, trained as an engineer, always had a good command of facts and information. However, seeking to avoid the rhetorical excesses of ministers he observed in his youth, Carter overcompensated with a flat delivery. Eugene McCarthy, the former senator and current political gadfly, said that Carter spoke like an "oratorical mortician." The president's ideas often lacked punch.[3] No wonder Carter had trouble when debating Ronald Reagan, the genial actor, narrator, and program host.

If the successes of Ronald Reagan prove anything, they show that a good delivery puts listeners into a frame of mind that helps a speaker's cause. That is not to say that beginning speakers should strive to sound exactly like Reagan, whose folksy style worked partly because of his status as President. As a speech student, your aim should be to combine the factual precision of Carter, the engineer, with the friendly manner of Reagan, the actor. But how? Our objective in this chapter will be to search out the specifics of what constitutes rhetorical competence in delivery. The chapter divides itself naturally into the basics of good vocal communication and good body movement. The treatments of voice and movement both culminate in sections dealing with essential skills. Vocal variety represents the essence of a speaking voice skillfully trained. The conversational manner constitutes the natural form of body action best suited to complement vocal variety.

In matters of delivery, skills are important, but *attitude* counts for all. No other aspect of rhetorical competence is as personal as delivery. Our ways of speaking are tied up with our very personalities. To change habits of speech delivery requires an attitude of determination and human commitment. To acquire an attitude of wanting better delivery, pay attention to the evidence that voice and movement are *independent sources of effectiveness* —over and above content.[4] Look for and underline these findings as you read the chapter. If you remember this evidence, you are more likely to modify your "speech personality" in the direction of skillful delivery.

Voice and Credibility

Your voice is the channel of transmission for most of your speech content. If you take care of your voice, it will reflect well on you. George Bush, in his acceptance speech at the Republican National Convention of 1988, impressed commentators by speaking "confidently and emphatically."[5] Although sometimes criticized for being too wishy-washy, on this occasion Bush used his voice to sound a note of strong leadership. The speech marked a turning point in Bush's successful campaign for the presidency. In like manner, as you begin your education in vocal effectiveness, take specific action to mend any weaknesses of voice. First, make sure your voice produces clear sounds. Second, study how vocal cues convey an impression of you.

Vocal Clarity

"Excuse me?" "What was that?" Ever hear someone ask for words to be repeated? When you give a public presentation, your listeners are not able to ask you to restate points. This means that clarity must be the basic characteristic of the good speaking voice—as was true of style. Does your speech possess *instant* clarity? To check yourself, consider whether you possess the two key components of vocal clarity: articulation and fluency.

Articulation

When we produce speech sounds clearly, we show good articulation. To influence others we must be heard; but in practice, we sometimes neglect articulation. Imagine that you are at a meeting. Turn your head to one side of the room, and you may hear someone mumble. "Hi mynaymz Samu-Churz." Perhaps our friend meant to say "Hi, my name is Samuel Church." Look ahead and you may see a speaker earnestly look up from the podium and say, "nowlemme-moovonto-mynex poin." Take apart the sounds and you might unscramble this code as, "Now, let me move on to my next point."

Teachers of speech often use the term "lip laziness" to remind us that poor articulation—unseparated sounds—usually may be corrected simply by taking pride and care in one's speech. Although poor articulation is a general problem of human life, lapses of voice clarity are particularly troublesome when we stand before a group. When we talk informally with others, we can always ask people to repeat, to clarify, or to speak up. On the other hand, when we speak to a large group, our listeners cannot ask for such individual help. Furthermore, in a public presentation, we usually experience a greater separation from our listeners than in ordinary conversation. Where we must project sounds over a wide area, lip laziness is a significant barrier to rhetorical competence. Because of poor articulation, William Casey of the CIA, known privately for his brilliant mind, conveyed the speaking image of a fumbler. Hearing Casey mumble references to "Nicowawa" (Nicaragua), Democrats in Congress jibed that they would not approve funds to overthrow any government Casey couldn't pronounce. Even President Reagan joked that Casey was the first head of CIA who did not need a scrambler on his telephone.[6]

Sometimes we may be prone to think of clear articulation as sounding artificial or mechanical. Frankly, there is some truth to this impression that a clear voice is foreign to ordinary speech. A theater director once coached me for a role by explaining that a way to "sound British" was to articulate clearly. However, a clipped sound is an extreme of articulation. The essential element of good articulation is to avoid such extremes while at the same time producing sounds more distinctly. Fight the temptation to hurry your words, to run words together, to mumble. Practice your articulation by whispering to someone standing at some distance from you. Since you cannot use volume to make yourself heard, you will have to form the speech sounds distinctly.

Besides making your speeches more understandable, good articulation will benefit your credibility. Think of people *you* hold as credible. These folks are likely to have better-than-average abilities in articulating their speech. Social science research provides evidence that faulty articulation can lower a public speaker's credibility.[7] Prevent this loss by practicing the clear production of speech sounds.

Fluency

As the term is used by speech professionals, fluency is a complex of many factors, including voice, words, and body action. In fact, one researcher identified no less than forty-six attributes of fluency.[8] For our purposes, however, we may define fluency as a lack of interruption in the flow of speech.

Fluency is often defined by its opposite—nonfluency. Typical kinds of nonfluencies include:

- Needless *repetition*: "The Post Office will—Post Office will be able to. . . ."
- *Interjections*: "ah," "uh," "um."
- *Corrections*: Of his years working with President Reagan, George Bush said, "We've had triumphs, we've made mistakes, we've had sex—setbacks. We've had setbacks."[9]
- *Stutter*: "The c-cost. . . ."
- *Excessive filler words*: "now," "you know," "OK," "see."
- *Unintelligible sounds*: "I, ah you, a zee, seeeee."
- *Empty pauses*: "Yes, I (pause) I can say that. . . ."

Nonfluencies are not desirable, but they are nevertheless inevitable in spontaneous speech. Attaining a realistic level of good fluency does not mean to eliminate episodes of nonfluency, but rather to improve fluency through practice. The speech transcripts reprinted in this book are somewhat misleading in regard to fluency, because oral errors are normally edited out of published speeches. A specially prepared transcript of the 1976 Carter-Ford debates showed that nearly every other sentence contained some form of nonfluency. With preparation and experience, however, you can expect to become more fluent. For instance, Jimmy Carter's nonfluencies were much more numerous in the first debate than in the second, probably a result of Carter's greater tension during his first encounter with President Ford.[10] Research does show that anxiety can increase the number of nonfluencies.[11]

The prevalence of nonfluencies in your speaking generally will decline with experience, especially when you are well into the content of your remarks, but do not wait for nature to take its course. Maximize your chances for fluency by practicing your delivery. Your effort will repay itself. Experimental findings suggest that as your nonfluencies decrease, you may expect to find your credibility increasing.[12] As a general rule, it is better to pause briefly in silence—with a thoughtful smile—than to produce a string of meaningless filler words and sounds.

Your first step in using your voice successfully is to attain vocal clarity through clear articulation and fluent statements. The next, more complicated step is to make sure your voice gives the best possible impression of you.

Voice and Rhetorical Impressions

Your voice talks not only about ideas, but also *about you*. If you want to give the impression of being stable, competent, energetic, and trustworthy, then you will be wise to pay attention to your voice. Your voice may send out signals that contradict the very purpose of your speech. Many a macho star of the silent screen failed as a speaker in the "talkies" because the voice just didn't match the heroic movie role. During the 1988 political season, speech experts listed Michael Dukakis's voice as one factor in his favor. In contrast to Dukakis's baritone, the experts rated George Bush's voice as too high-pitched.[13] That Bush won the election shows that vocal quality is not judged in isolation from other factors of rhetorical competence. Still, consideration of the exercises for vocal improvement offered in this chapter is worthwhile.

Specifically, what do listeners pick up from our voices? First, our voices communicate our emotional states. Studies show that listeners can accurately identify whether a speaker is happy or sad, nervous or depressed, simply by hearing the speaker's voice.[14] This tell-tale power of the voice to communicate emotions does not depend on the actual words being spoken. In two studies, listeners were able to judge emotion from voice recordings filtered to obscure the actual words said.[15] Listeners can tell how you feel, so put yourself into an emotional state appropriate to your purpose.

In addition to revealing our emotional state, voice cues provide an accurate insight into our personality. Experimental findings show that listeners are often able to match voices to a variety of personal characteristics. These include age, general appearance, vocation, factors of personality (such as extroversion-introversion and dominance-submission), values held as important, and overall personality traits.[16] Your voice is a powerful source of the impression you make on people.

Finally, our voices give an accurate indication of our social and economic standings. In two experimental studies, researchers arranged for audiences to listen to tape-recorded voices. The listeners then (1) predicted the social and economic status of the speakers and (2) rated the speakers for credibility. In both studies, listeners correctly pegged the socioeconomic position of the speakers (as objectively measured by income and education). Furthermore, listeners rated persons of higher social standing as more credible.[17] If you want to be taken as a responsible member of the community, it helps to sound like one.

Of course, in real life, voice and words are united. In producing an image of our total speech personality, *how we sound* combines with the content of *what we say.* One researcher specifically examined the intermingling of voice and content. He found that speech content (words) were chiefly responsible for conveying an impression of a person's sincerity. In contrast, voice was dominant in getting across the social attractiveness of the speaker, that is, whether the speaker would be likable and sociable. Voice and content combined to produce an impression of the speaker's competence.[18] These results confirm the common sense notion that our total believability as a speaker is a marriage of impressions given by our delivery and content.

The close connection of *what we say* and *how we say it* leads to the question of whether the *what* is more important than the *how.* Suppose our voice gives a different impression than our words? Findings on this question are inconclusive. On the one hand, the research listed above showed that audiences may judge sincerity primarily through content. This suggests that listeners may rely on content more than vocal cues to resolve a contradiction between the two, but other research suggests that voice plays a more important role than content.[19] Probably the relative importance of voice and content differs in varying situations. However, the general point is crucial for speakers: *Voice conveys an impression of you that may reinforce or contradict your statements.*

Box 11.1

Delivery Shows You Mean It

For two years, Ms. [Karen] Ludwig, an actress, has taught women how to be effective in the courtroom. In a profession that prizes reason and has often been accused of sexual stereotyping, she counsels women to be emotional.

"Women have been taught to cut out emotionality because they're afraid of being thought of as too feminine, overly emotional, hysterical, unable to make a good point," Ms. Ludwig said. But to be convincing, she went on, "you have to find what you have at stake so that you can personalize the issue—you have to learn to mean it."

Source: *New York Times* (National Edition), 2 September 1988, B1.

If you desire to have the kind of vocal communication that conveys an aura of rhetorical competence, pay attention to three specific factors of speech sound: (1) vocal quality, (2) pronunciation, and (3) dialect.

Vocal quality

It is sometimes said that, of all the factors of voice, "voice quality is the most difficult to define and the most difficult to classify objectively."[20] Broadly stated, voice quality has to do with whether or not our voice sounds pleasing to a listener.

One way to understand the specifics of good vocal quality is to consider some *dis*pleasing characteristics of a speaking voice. These include:

- *Nasality:* Have you ever heard a speaker who sounds as if he is talking through his nose?
- *Denasality:* Here the speaker sounds as if her nose is stopped up because of a cold.

- *Breathiness:* The speaker's voice sounds too husky—there is too much breath used while vocalizing. This is the kind of sound you make when you speak after a long run or great exertion.
- *Harshness:* The speaker's voice sounds rough, as if her throat needs to be cleared.
- *Thinness:* The speaker's voice sounds child-like, as if his pitch were too high.
- *Throatiness:* The speaker's voice sounds hollow, as if she were speaking through a tube.
- *Stridency:* The speaker's voice shows a combination of harshness and high pitch—as you would sound if you were upset.

Do not become preoccupied with voice quality problems described in such clinical terms as listed previously. Discussions of this kind sometimes convince us that we suffer from imaginary afflictions. In fact, studies suggest that voice quality is a problem for probably less than one percent of college students.[21] If you think you may be among this one percent, talk with your instructor. Probably your problems are minor, and your teacher may refer you to a book that emphasizes voice, diction, and articulation. Books of this kind not only give a fuller description of voice quality problems, but also usually offer many useful suggestions for improvement.

Still, attention to the essentials of voice quality is quite appropriate for a general class in public speaking. Qualities of voice often call to mind unfavorable personality stereotypes. Have you noticed how comedians modify their voices to suggest humorous characters? To create the character of an obnoxious telephone operator, Lily Tomlin makes her voice sound excessively nasal: "Tat's wun ringi-dingi." Denasality is the way Hollywood often portrays an oaf: "Duh, dhad's rhide, bozz." Movies also give us the vocal thinness of the stereotyped blond dingbat or the throaty harshness of the gangster. Research shows that a moderately poor quality of voice does not reduce comprehension of the speech.[22] Progressively greater credibility losses occur, however, as a voice exhibits thinness, nasality, tenseness, denasality, and throatiness.[23]

Pronunciation

How we pronounce words has to do with how we make the sounds of vowels and consonants. Do you sound the word "aunt" as ANt or ONt? Do you pronounce "fire" as fiUR or fiAH?

Attitudes on pronunciation have varied through the centuries. Before the twentieth century, teachers commonly prescribed rigid standards of correct pronunciation. Later, a more descriptive approach was taken in which the common usage of the educated public became the standard of pronunciation. In the 1960s, *Webster's Third New International Dictionary* took an even more liberal attitude toward pronunciation. The designation of "preferred" pronunciation was dropped.

Today's tendency, then, is not to label any widely-used pronunciation as "incorrect." Research findings further suggest that even unusual pronunciations of key words in a speech do not reduce the ability of listeners to understand the speech.[24] Ours would seem to be an age of official tolerance in pronunciation. However, remember that good pronunciation is a traditional mark of an educated person—and many people still hold to the one-correct-way theory of sounding words. Individuals and audiences continue to determine *for themselves* what is desirable, bothersome, or even offensive in pronunciation. Probably, listeners will not rate your speech as less effective simply because of unaccepted pronunciation, but your listeners are quite able to identify words that are sounded in a disagreeable fashion.[25]

Dialect

Speech scholars traditionally distinguish among three major dialects in the continental United States. These include: (1) the General American dialect, spoken by those living in the midwestern, northern, and western portions of our country, (2) the Northeastern dialect, and (3) the Southern. Recent practice is to divide the "General American" dialect into separate groups to reflect, for example, the influence of Southern speech patterns on lower portions of the Midwestern states. Further sub-regional variations abound, with distinct speech patterns associated with such areas as Brooklyn, New York. As compared to speech in Great Britain, however, American English shows far fewer variations in dialect.[26] The differences among American dialects chiefly is one of word pronunciation, although vocabulary, grammatical and other differences become involved when such ethnic dialects as Black English or "Tex-Mex" are considered.

As a rule, we may say that the best dialect is that which calls the least attention to itself. This proviso means that all dialects are acceptable—pleasing to the ear—to some audiences. When overall national preferences are considered, however, the General American dialect is the most preferred. After all, this speech pattern is the one least associated with regional, ethnic, social, or racial differences. Although people sometimes prefer their local dialect, a classic study showed that "speech preferences of college students in all sections of the United States are similar, and show a tendency to accept General American speech as the preferred dialect."[27]

Dialect is an important factor in the impressions that we form of a speaker.[28] When we perceive that a speaker "sounds like me," we also assume that the person holds attitudes and values similar to our own.[29] He or she is OK. In contrast, when we hear a person speaking in a different dialect, we may stereotype the person as a typical member of that particular outside group. Research done in Canada shows that dialect seems particularly powerful in triggering an either/or kind of perception in listeners. When a speaker using a French Canadian accent talked to English-speaking Canadians, the speaker was perceived stereotypically. But when the speaker was introduced as being a French Canadian, and yet *sounded like an English Canadian,* stereotypes were less applied.[30] Seemingly, dialect causes listeners to view the speaker either as "just like *me*" or "just like *one of them.*"

Public speakers must pay attention to matters of dialect because speech patterns are not just part of general interpersonal perception—*they are also relevant to building credibility.* When compared to speakers using regional or ethnic dialects, persons having the General American speech pattern are frequently taken as having a higher level of intellectual competence.[31] This result held true even for listeners who themselves spoke in the regional or ethnic dialect.[32] These findings do *not* mean that rhetorical competence requires using only the General American speech patterns. All nonstandard dialects are legitimate means of communication that reflect the culture of a region or social group. Regional and ethnic speech is always pleasing to members of that group. In 1976, for example, Southerners liked to comment that Jimmy Carter was the first president in a long time who did not speak with an accent! Differences in dialect can be generally pleasing, as when Americans listened with fascination to John F. Kennedy's Bostonese.

The best advice for public speakers on matters of dialect is that we avoid extreme aspects of our dialect that inhibit communication with general audiences. As a college educated individual, you are likely to interact with a wider range of persons than is the average. Being able to tone down extreme aspects of a regional or ethnic dialect may be helpful, generally, in speaking before groups in the larger society. Our society, as a whole, traditionally aspires to middle class status; and reliance on dialect as a tool of human perception seems to be greater for middle class individuals than for upper or lower economic groups.[33] Furthermore, modifying extremes of dialect may prove effective in speeches given in the work context. Attitudes of employers toward the dialect of job applicants can influence who gets hired.[34]

Matters of dialect and foreign accent are particularly troublesome for nonnative speakers of English. Nonnative speakers sometimes pause between each word in a way that sounds choppy to Americans. On the other hand, they may speak too fast for Americans to pick out the words. The solution for this latter problem is to hold the vowel sounds longer, since vowels are keys to distinguishing one word from another (e.g., p*a*t versus p*o*t). American English also tends to require somewhat greater mouth opening and lip movement than foreign tongues. Furthermore, for speakers whose native language is an oriental one, it is important not to swallow the final consonant of English words. "The final consonants of American English are exploded out of the mouth with a puff of air (unvoiced consonants such as t, p, k) or with an 'uh' sound (voiced consonants such as b, g, d)."[35]

If you suspect that a foreign accent may be reducing your comprehensibility, tape record a brief segment (say, thirty seconds) of speech you hear from a TV newscaster. Transcribe this segment into written English. Now, tape record yourself reading over the passage. Identify words and phrases where your speech seems to deviate most from the mainstream. Then work with individual words and sounds. Tape record yourself pronouncing the problem words. Pronounce them slowly, isolating the syllable and sound that give you trouble. Keep comparing your pronunciation to what you hear from the accomplished speaker. Ask a friend whose pronunciation seems standard to listen to your practicing and to help you work on individual sounds and words. Check with your instructor to see if your university has a speech lab with a program for practicing accent reduction.

Your voice makes a difference in your progress as a public speaker. True, perceptions based on dialect and other vocal factors tend to be first impressions, which may be later revised.[36] But this finding gives us no excuse to remain unconcerned about our voice. Characteristics of voice—clarity, quality, pronunciation, and dialect—are linked to social stereotypes. Be sure your voice conjures up a good image of you. After you have practiced making your speech articulate and fluent, be sure that your quality of voice is one that audiences consider pleasing. The same holds true for pronunciation. Listen to how people around you pronounce their words—people to whom you will be speaking. Avoid the needless risk that someone will believe you are pronouncing a word incorrectly. Finally, for Americans who aim to be taken as credible, reducing extremes of dialect can be a further useful skill when we face both community and business audiences.[37]

Vocal Variety

The rhetorically competent speaker has a voice that is both easy to follow and interesting. This effective speaking voice is usually marked by what we may call *vocal variety.* Nothing is harder for listeners to understand and enjoy than a speech delivered in a dull, expressionless monotone. For instance, complaints that Senator John Glenn, the former astronaut, is a dull speaker usually focus on his tendency to talk in an unchanging tone of voice. Glenn's lack of vocal variation is all too typical in our age of silent reading and written examinations. Gone are the days when college students presented their lessons orally in every class period and when debating societies were central to college life.

However, lively oral dialogue is not completely forgotten in our era. Television, especially live events, reminds us of the old culture of oral expression that our great-grandparents took for granted. Your public speaking class provides opportunities for overcoming today's dull speech. As an aspirant to rhetorical competence, you need both education and practice in appropriately varying your rate, volume, and pitch. Furthermore, you should consider changing how you emphasize words and how you combine them into phrases. Rhetorical competence in oral expression begins when we understand and appreciate these five key elements of vocal control. Skillful vocal communication means mastering the five elements.

Box 11.2

Bringing Back Oral Communication

Fathers and mothers, teachers, Boy Scout leaders, babysitters, uncles and aunts, *we must read out loud to children.* But first we must learn again to perform the text, out-ham our ancestors, take pleasure in word and story and hand this pleasure on. We must encourage our children to memorize and recite. As children speak poems and stories aloud, by the pitch and muscle of their voices they will discover drama, humor, passion and intelligence in print. In order to become a nation of readers, we need again to become a nation of reciters.

Source: "Bring Back the Out-Loud Culture," by Donald Hall, *Newsweek,* 15 April 1985, 12.

Elements of Variety

Vincent Price, the actor, expresses well the connection of vocal variety to public speaking. Price observes that there is something about listening to another person talk that "puts people off." Listeners often are lulled and bored when listening; in contrast, the person speaking feels stimulated. Price advises the public speaking student to pay attention to interesting speakers—to note how they use their voices to get and sustain attention.[38] Heed this advice. Listen carefully to speakers who impress you. What can you observe about their vocal rate, volume, pitch, phrasing, and emphasis?

Rate

Rate of speech is a measure of the number of words (or syllables) a communicator speaks in a given period of time. Experimental research bears out what most of us realize intuitively: people like the flow of speech to be neither too hurried nor too slow. Research suggests that listeners favor a rate of speaking that falls between 150 and 225 words per minute. A rate of 175 W.P.M. seems most popular.[39]

You will find that your rate of speaking affects both your ability to get across information and your credibility. When you speak as fast as 275–325 words per minute, comprehension of your speech by listeners declines significantly.[40] If you want to speak at breakneck pace, your only hope is that you can motivate your audience to listen carefully. When receivers are highly motivated to retain the information, they can master the higher rates of speech.[41] However, when *credibility* is the criterion—rather than comprehension—the lower rate of speech may sometimes be preferable. In one study, researchers found that speakers using a 145 W.P.M. rate were perceived as significantly more authoritative than speakers whose vocal rate was 296 W.P.M.[42] The only advantage of vocal speed seems to be in possibly creating the perception that a speaker is dynamic.[43]

Keep your vocal rate between 150 and 225 words per minute. This rate of speech probably will produce the best comprehension and credibility ratings for you. Fortunately, checking your rate of speech is a relatively straightforward task. Use a tape recorder during one of your practice sessions. Select a minute of talk from the center of the speech. Count the number of words to determine whether your speaking rate is within the bounds of normal listener preference.

Volume

The issue of vocal volume gets right to the heart of why people take a course in public speaking—a speech often differs from regular conversation. Compared to chatting with one or two persons, a public speech is often delivered to a greater number of people over a larger area. For this reason, speechmaking typically requires increased volume and volume control. David Stern, a voice coach, points out that "loudness without tension" is one of the "basic skills of vocal expression."[44] These are standards you should use to judge whether your speaking volume is appropriate. As you practice, first consider your overall volume. Are you audible, that is, loud enough to be heard by your audience? Is your volume consistently audible throughout the speech? You might find it helpful to have a friend listen and take notes about how well you make yourself heard across a distance.

Effective volume, however, should not make your voice harsh. Try to increase the stream of breath rather than tightening the pressure of the vocal cords.[45] Loudness without tension will increase the understandability of your voice without making it less pleasing for listeners. This advice to attain loudness without tension corresponds to the two elements of the scientific measurement of understandable speech: loudness (measured in decibels) plus the vocal frequency (measured in cycles per second).[46]

Loudness without tension is the key to a clear and pleasing voice.

Pitch

The human vocal cords open and close to produce high-pitched and low-pitched sounds in a manner similar to a musical instrument. When speaking, we can vary pitch in several ways. First, we can change our pitch as we move from one word to another. For instance: "Go *now,*" with a shift to a higher pitch on the word "now." Second, we can vary pitch from one syllable to another, as we shift pitch upward to ask a question. "Going fish*ing*?" (with an upward shift of pitch on "ing"). Third, we can vary pitch within a syllable as in saying "goo-*ood.*" Here we register an upward shift in pitch, perhaps to signify sarcasm.

Changes in pitch boost both the interest and conceptual clarity of our speech. Pitch adjustments provide complementary advantages for listener and speaker. For listeners, they "jog the attention," as well as help receivers "see the progression of ideas." For the speaker, pitch variations help the speaker "call attention to various parts of statements" as well as "give special emphasis to important points."[47] Furthermore, changes in pitch are a good device to show the transition from one idea to the next. Generally, we pick up the pitch when we begin a new train of thought.

Finally, pitch plays a role in how we are perceived. Speech critics and experimental researchers agree that you should avoid a monotone voice, seeking to employ variety in pitch. A monotonous voice will reduce your perceived competence, dynamism, and trustworthiness.[48] A monopitch voice sometimes even reduces the amount of information that listeners comprehend.[49]

Box 11.3

How Mrs. Thatcher Trained Her Speaking Voice

Pitch can pose problems for all public speakers, whatever their sex, because it tends to rise when a speaker is nervous or speaks louder than usual, both of which are likely to happen in oratory. For women, however, the problem is more acute because the natural pitch of their voices has a higher starting-point. . . . lower-pitched female voices tend to be regarded as more attractive than high-pitched voices. . . .

Viewed in these terms, the fact that Mrs. Thatcher [British Prime Minister] has taken positive steps to lower the pitch of her voice can be seen as a perfectly rational response to a very real problem. Under the guidance of a tutor from the National Theatre, she underwent a training programme which included special humming exercises aimed at lowering the pitch level at which she formerly spoke.

Source: Max Atkinson, *Our Masters' Voices,* (London: Methuen, 1984), 112–113.

Your pitch influences how you come across partly because changes in pitch indicate your emotional involvement with the words you speak. Researchers have long established that the different emotions seem to be characterized by different patterns of pitch.[50] The connection between pitch and emotion makes your vocal expression into a statement about what you are thinking and feeling at the moment you speak. Pretend that you are defending yourself against an undeserved attack and read the following sentence: "Well, what did you expect?" Unless you made an effort to speak in a monopitch, you probably heard the pitch of your voice rise and fall. Listeners are good at picking out what your pitch reveals about your attitudes.

Phrasing

The phrasing of speech is how we group words and use pauses while we speak. Printed words can be strung together without end. But we must group spoken words, since speechmaking calls for us simultaneously to think, breathe, and talk. How we phrase our words contributes to making our talk both comprehensible and interesting.

To get a feel for the role of phrasing in delivery, read the following excerpt from the Declaration of Independence, pausing where indicated:

> When in the Course of human events/it becomes necessary for one people to dissolve the political bands which have connected them with another/and to assume among the Powers of the earth the separate and equal station to which the Laws of Nature and Nature's God entitle them/a decent respect for the opinions of mankind requires that they should declare the causes that impel them to the separation.

Go back over this first sentence of the Declaration again, and read it without pauses or breaths. Then, to get a feel for another extreme of vocal phrasing, mark the Declaration with additional slashes, dividing each of the sections marked above. With the extra marks, your reading may seem choppy. Make a few completely random marks; does this make the reading seem less logical?

The above exercise is one that illustrates the importance of phrasing. Grouping words and pausing both can increase or decrease the listenability and meaningfulness of your speaking. With too few pauses, the reading is one rushing mass of material that is hard to comprehend. When read in a choppy manner, Jefferson's masterpiece sentence is understandable, but less interesting to hear—and more frustrating. A good exercise to develop your ear for phrasing is to read aloud. Pick a story out of a newspaper or magazine. Read the passage several times. Practice different ways to phrase the words to make them as interesting and meaningful as possible.

Emphasis

Vocal emphasis is the use of vocal control to highlight important syllables and words. The vocal control necessary for rhetorical emphasis is a product of the four factors of variety mentioned thus far—rate, volume, phrasing, and pitch—as well as two further factors, *duration* and *inflection.* Duration is the time taken to produce each sound. For instance, if you were using the word "annual," you could draw out the first syllable and, thus, increase its duration: "aaaan-nu-al." Inflection is a change of pitch within a single sound. We use inflection when we ask a question, for instance, "Is it free?" Here our pitch slides upward on the "ee."

When we speak, we create different meanings through the emphasis we give to words. This is why no printed text of a speech gives the full flavor of the speaker's intent. Take a moment to practice with the elements of emphasis. Use the sentence, "Your idea is the best so far," experimenting to change the meaning of the words by sounding them differently. First, speak the sentence in a straightforward way—as if you intended to communicate the literal meaning of the words. Then sound the word "best" in a way that is sarcastic, reversing the meaning. Now turn the sentence into a question. Here you would use an inflection with a shift to a higher pitch on vowel "a" in "far."

In ordinary speech, few of us are fully conscious of the ways we emphasize words. However, if you are like most speakers, you will find that you rely most on changes in volume, duration, and pitch to modify your meanings.[51]

Achieving Variety

Attaining vocal variety is one of the surest ways to give your delivery the aura of rhetorical competence. Greater variety actually increases the ability of listeners to understand what you say.[52] But the major effect of using variety is to make your speaking more interesting.

Much of President Franklin Roosevelt's rhetorical success can be attributed to his exceptionally effective voice. Not only did FDR use a crisp and distinct pronunciation, but he also showed exceptional vocal variety. FDR made his speaking more interesting by varying how he grouped words and used pauses. Sometimes he would divide sentences into short packages of four to six words. As a contrast to these short phrases, the President would speak long sections or entire sentences without any pause. FDR modified his volume to mark important words. In fact, when speaking from manuscript, he underlined those words he wanted to speak more loudly. Two speech critics noted how Roosevelt delivered important passages "more slowly and with more pauses than less important passages." A typical Roosevelt sentence: "Our acts must be guided by one / single / hard-headed / thought / —keeping America / out / of this war." Furthermore, the president emphasized important sentences by stressing the syllables of key words and by giving greater duration to the vowel sounds of important words. Making his voice match the verbal style of the speech, Roosevelt "was particularly effective in pointing up parallel structure by repeating patterns of intonation and inflection."[53]

In contrast to the exceptional vocal communication of Franklin Roosevelt, we may turn to President Jimmy Carter. While Carter's delivery usually showed an appealing friendliness, his vocal communication often worked against him. Carter tended to pause at the wrong places, to run words together, and to emphasize inappropriate words and syllables. With effort and practice, however, Carter was able to rise to the occasion. In his July 1979 television message on the energy crisis, Carter's phrasing and emphasis both showed notable improvement. The reason? Carter had practiced his speech several times, even using audio- and videotapes.[54] Carter's more forceful delivery won wide attention and praise, showing that all of us can improve vocal communication through effort.

Practicing your vocal delivery is worth the time because good vocal delivery makes speech easier to understand.[55] Skilled vocal communication also can make you more credible and persuasive.[56] Profit from the example of Jimmy Carter. If your voice lacks force, practice vocal variety using a tape recorder. Later, when you prepare your speeches, do not practice them silently—work *out loud.* Another way to lessen the monotony of your voice is to read out loud. Take paragraphs from a magazine or book and read them several times. As you work on the paragraphs, you should notice that your vocal presentation becomes more animated, more interesting, and more meaningful.

Movement and Action

What *they see* can be what *you get.* The visual dimension of public speaking—your movement and action—is directly linked to rhetorical success. In two studies, researchers found that actually seeing a speaker—rather than just hearing him—can boost what listeners remember about the talk.[57] Head and general body movement probably has less bearing on speech effectiveness than does voice. However, experimental research shows that visual cues are directly related to speech effectiveness.[58] We have ample reason to consider standards for good posture, gestures, facial expression, eye contact, and clothing.

Posture and Body Action

Posture refers to how we carry our body, whether we are standing in an erect or in a slouched manner. Straighter posture usually indicates alertness, interest, and readiness. Slouching communicates disinterest. These generalizations about posture apply fully to speechmaking. The ***basic body stance*** in speechmaking is often described by speech teachers as one of "comfortable erectness." Here our back is straight, arms are at our sides, and our weight is distributed relatively equally on both feet. We stand straight, but unlike a soldier at dress inspection, we feel comfortable. We bear our bodies alertly without slouching, leaning, or slumping.

When we speak, we may feel a certain amount of psychological resistance to good posture. Watch others give speeches, noticing how their bodies often seek outside support. A speaker bends over, leaning on an available podium; hands disappear into the safe haven of pockets; arms clutch a lectern; weight shifts aimlessly from one leg to another. To be sure, no one expects a speaker to stand rigidly. Rather, the straight posture of good speakers marks a base line or starting point from which movement and gestures most easily and smoothly spring. Standing straight, weight apportioned relatively equally on legs, arms at your sides—from this position, you may easily move or gesture. For practice, as you speak, make a point to return to the basic stance from time to time.

A major difference between people and plants is that people move. Human life is one of action—but how to move during a speech? The key consideration in departing from the basic speaking stance is *purpose.* Body action in public speaking should serve a useful purpose. For instance, movement can help maintain attention. When you step to the side of a podium, you will attract notice. Second, you may use movement to signal a transition from one point to another. You might take a small step to the side while stating "next we should consider. . . ." Finally, movement can helpfully complement the words you speak. A step forward can be a nonverbal statement that "this is important."

Sometimes the situation—time and place—of speech helps decide what sort of movement will be appropriate to your purpose. There is no use trying to deliver an address to three people from behind a podium. Move out in front. If you are speaking to a group seated around a long table, your range of movement—even if you are standing—may be quite limited. In a classroom setting, attempts to appear informal, such as sitting on a table, may help or hinder depending on the topic or your relationship with listeners.

Gestures

Gestures are movements of the hands, the arms, the trunk of the body, the shoulders, or the head, often in combination. Needless to say, gestures are closely linked to body movement; although in a gesture only part of our body is put into motion. Gestures are also linked to facial expression, since a movement of the head often accompanies a change in what our faces register. For instance, we are likely to move our heads slightly upward when we smile.

Combined movements of the hand and arm probably are the most consciously used gesture for the public speaker. Paul Ekman and Wallace Friesen classify three types of hand-arm gestures. First is the *emblem.* This is a conventional gesture that has an agreed-upon meaning for members of a group or culture. An example would be the hitchhiker's "thumb." Second is the *adaptor,* which represents an effort to meet a personal need, for instance, when we scratch our head or adjust clothing. Finally, there is the *illustrator,* a gesture that accompanies and complements something we say.[59]

The Ekman-Friesen classification scheme is useful for analyzing gestures in speechmaking. Very likely, you will have little occasion to use conventional emblem-type gestures. American society recognizes only a relatively small number of such gestures (and many are obscene). Adaptor-type gestures in the main are irrelevant to your message, and may be distracting. Adaptors often are nervous mannerisms such as jingling keys in a pocket. Furthermore, adaptors often leave an unfavorable impression. An increase in adaptor behavior normally signals others that we are nervous, uncomfortable, or are bottling up aggression.

Emblems and adaptors are largely irrelevant or counterproductive in public speaking; in contrast, when we use illustrator gestures to accompany and reinforce our words, we tap a useful reservoir of rhetorical power. Gestures can reinforce our words when we:

- Time a gesture to emphasize a word or phrase.
- Point to an object, place, or event.
- Show a spatial relationship—closeness or apartness.
- Gesture rhythmically in tempo with a sequence or pattern of words.
- Depict some physical action, e.g., throwing a ball.
- Draw a kind of picture in the air of what we are talking about.

Illustrator gestures have a proven benefit for both audience and speaker. Speeches with gestures help listeners, since audiences better comprehended such speeches.[60] For the speaker, gestures create an image of dynamism. In small group settings, speakers who use more gestures of the shoulders and arms tend to emerge as leaders.[61] Comments in 1988 that Michael Dukakis, Democratic presidential candidate, was a wooden speaker seemed to stem from his limited range of gestures. A writer for *The New Republic* described Dukakis's gestures as consisting of elbows "stapled" to his sides, arm movements as if holding a beach ball, awkwardly cupped hands, and shrugs of the shoulders.[62]

Not only do gestures affect the perceived image of a speaker, but they also are relevant to the speaker's fluency. Ekman and Friesen found that illustrators serve what they term a self-priming function. Gestures of the hand and arm typically help the speaker "past an awkwardness in his speech or thought, accelerating the flow of his ideas."[63] You should use illustrator gestures because these actions, in fact, will help you mentally organize as well as verbally present ideas.[64]

As you practice speaking, incorporate gestures into your delivery. Look for places in the verbal content that seem to call for a gesture. Probably you will feel your arms tugging toward a gesture. Using gestures may seem awkward at first, but effort and practice make your gesturing natural.

Facial Expression

The face is an inlet to our feelings and thoughts. Visual cues often give a more accurate picture of our emotions than do vocal ones.[65] People readily recognize the different feelings signaled by the face.[66] Surprise is signified chiefly in the brow and forehead and happiness in the eyes and mouth. Sadness and fear are seen mainly in the eyes and disgust in the cheeks and mouth. Anger seems to be the most ambiguous of emotions and is not clearly detected unless "registered in at least two and usually three areas of the face."[67]

The face gives listeners a view of our attitudes as well as our emotions. Research in television broadcasting shows that TV-watchers consistently pick out a raised eyebrow as indicating an unfavorable bias by a news reporter.[68] Furthermore, when a newscaster reads the name of a political candidate, television viewers can tell whether the reporter's face registers approval or disapproval.[69]

What should you do about facial expression? Your aim should be to have a facial expression that is consistent with the thesis, topic, and occasion of your speech. It is possible to control facial expression to an extent. Also, it helps to put yourself into a frame of mind that leads inevitably to appropriate expression. However, the face remains a natural sign of our internal thoughts and feelings. John C. Calhoun, pre-Civil War spokesman for the South, was known as a speaker whose expressive face contributed to his effectiveness. Tall, gaunt, forceful, Calhoun's eyes seemed to flash, and one observer commented that "his brow seemed charged with thunder."[70] You may find attaining the facial intensity of a Calhoun hard. However, it is relatively easy for you to incorporate smiles and head nods into your speaking. Assuming that the purpose of your speech allows positive facial indicators, appropriate smiles and nods may cause listeners to perceive you as more personable and credible.[71]

Eye Contact

To say that a person "couldn't look me in the eye" is to express doubt about the individual's honesty, sincerity, or competence. General American culture places importance on direct eye contact in contrast to other cultures in which this may be seen as aggressive. When we are talking to people, we expect them to look at us. This is why most of us find talking to someone wearing reflecting sunglasses so annoying.

When we speak in public, we generally are more separated from our listeners than in ordinary conversation. This greater distance should not make us overlook the importance of eye contact in speechmaking. Experimental research confirms what we know intuitively about speakers. When they maintain direct eye contact with us, we are more impressed with their

Direct eye contact is a sign of real communication.

delivery.[72] We should learn from skillful speakers who know the importance of giving roughly equal eye contact to all listeners. As your speech progresses, be sure that your gaze sweeps the room. Furthermore, be sure that you really look at your listeners. Pause a bit to create a real meeting of eyes with individuals. In the Communispond executive speech program, students go through an exercise where everyone in the audience holds up a hand. Listeners drop their hands only when the speaker has looked at them for at least five seconds. This kind of real eye contact is possible unless, of course, your audience numbers hundreds of persons. Even with a giant audience, you can have true eye contact with people in all parts of the room.

Get accustomed to making real eye contact with listeners. You will be surprised at the feeling of enjoyment—and power—you experience. When you look at listeners *as people* you acquire a handle on their attention. Your audience becomes more involved; listeners sense that authentic communication is taking place. To the extent that you maintain a direct eye-to-eye relationship with listeners, they are likely to view you as more honest and more qualified.[73] Furthermore, the more eye contact, the more the audience is likely to rate you as a very good speaker.[74] Eye contact even seems to contribute noticeably to how much information listeners comprehend from a speech.[75]

Personal Appearance

The clothing we wear plays a role in our speech delivery. Generally, clothing should be in accord with the setting of the speech. John Molloy, clothing consultant to executives, notes that clothes must stand out from the background. In class, if you will be speaking in front of a green colored chalkboard, be sure to leave the emerald outfit at home. Outside class, how you dress depends largely on the expectations of the audience. Your clothing and grooming should reflect the standards of listeners. For instance, Molloy recommends suits for both men and women who want to be taken seriously in business. The same may apply to politics. When Jesse Jackson decided to campaign for the presidency in 1984 and 1988, he left his casual, open-collared outfits at home.

Molloy also recommends dressing in a way that positively accents your physical characteristics and personality. Dark colors help a person be taken more seriously as a professional. Persons of smaller stature are helped most by dark, solid colors. In contrast, Molloy recommends that a person of large physical stature avoid dark, solid colors and select sportier items. Women who want to be credible in the business context should avoid high fashion, boots, or pants suits.[76]

The Conversational Manner

Teachers of speech use the term *conversational manner* to describe the ideal delivery. Conversational delivery is one in which you combine natural movement and gestures with vocal variety. The essence of the conversational mode of delivery is *balance.* Today's speaker must strike a good compromise between the twentieth century's tendency to dull, monotonous, and "facts only" delivery and yesterday's frequent oratorical theatrics. To get a feel for conversational delivery, imagine a speaker who looks directly at people, whose face is expressive, whose gestures keep tempo with his words, whose voice commands attention with interest. Imagine a speaker whose voice is neither monotonous nor dramatic, but animated, with variations in her rate, volume, pitch, and emphasis. Such a speaker differs noticeably from the dull, downward-gazing podium clutcher. Such a speaker differs equally from many a young speaker of yesteryear who strove to emulate the great orators. An early teacher of speech, James Winans, recalled the students of his youth who "spoke before us, not to us, and certainly not *with* us."[77]

Box 11.4

The Conversational Manner

When a person gets up in front of an audience to talk, you can't expect that person to sound as though he or she was in a casual conversation with a friend, but political speeches have got to go in the conversational direction. I think potential voters are often turned off by bombast and the cliches of politics.

Source: Andy Rooney, *Times Tribune* (Palo Alto edition), 27 August 1988, A10.

To attain the kind of delivery appropriate for the 1990s, follow the guidelines in the chapter to accentuate the natural way you speak to friends. The effort will prove worthwhile. A conversational type of delivery—rather than an artificially dynamic one—produces the best responses from listeners. The only exception is that a speaker with an initially high level of credibility may succeed with more extreme levels of vocal variety and movement. For ordinary situations, maintaining a conversational relationship with listeners will bring you higher ratings of sincerity, personability, and competence.[78] Take stock of your habits of delivery. Assess the clarity, quality, and variety of your voice. Pay attention to your movement and gestures. Begin a program of practice based on the suggestions given in this chapter. Remember that unless you make a commitment to improve your delivery, it will remain unchanged, so take action. Practice. Use a tape recorder. Consult the mirror. Follow through—and persist.

Concepts for Review

Can you summarize the meaning of these terms or expressions? How does each relate to speechmaking?

articulation
lip laziness
fluency
voice shows emotions
voice shows personality
voice quality
pronunciation
dialect
General American speech
dialect and stereotypes
vocal variety
rate
volume
pitch
phrasing
emphasis
duration
inflection
posture
"comfortable erectness"
gestures
adaptors
illustrators
facial expression
eye contact
dress appropriately
conversational manner

Things to Try

1. Identify a speaker who impressed you favorably or unfavorably. Now think about that speaker in action. Mentally picture the speaker as you heard him or her. Identify three characteristics about this speaker that you remember most. Are these verbal or nonverbal factors? Compare your list with other classmates.
2. In a bookstore, leaf through one or two self-improvement books. Do the books have a section on public speaking? If not, what advice do they give that would be appropriate for public speakers?
3. Make a commitment to improve your voice by reading aloud. Pick out a passage of one hundred or so words in a book or magazine. Read the passage several times—aloud. Make an effort to try variations. Consult the advice on vocal variety given in this chapter and listen to yourself critically. Now, tape record yourself as you read. Listen carefully to the clarity and interestingness of your voice. Mark places in the text where you need to improve. Reread and recheck.
4. Have a friend help you with your delivery. Review the advice on how to improve aspects of voice and body communication. For instance, a way to practice clear articulation is to whisper to another person over a distance. Here you cannot use volume to project sound (and be sure not to strain your voice). Brief your friend on what factors of delivery you are trying to improve, and ask for his or her reaction as you practice.

Endnotes

1. Cicero, *De Oratore,* III. 56.
2. Plutarch, *Demosthenes,* 7.
3. James T. Wooten, *Courier-Journal* (Louisville), 2 February 1978, A11.
4. Paul Heinberg, "Relationships of Content and Delivery to General Effectiveness," *Speech Monographs 30* (1963): 105–107 and D. F. Gunderson and Robert Hopper, "Relationships Between Speech Delivery and Speech Effectiveness," *Communication Monographs 43* (1976): 158–165.
5. *San Francisco Chronicle,* 19 August 1988, A1.
6. *Newsweek,* 10 October 1983, 40.
7. David W. Addington, "The Effect of Mispronunciations on General Speaking Effectiveness," *Speech Monographs 32* (1965): 159–163.

8. Milton W. Horowitz, "Fluency: An Appraisal and a Research Approach," *Journal of Communication 15* (1965): 4–13.
9. *San Francisco Chronicle,* 10 May 1988, A9.
10. Jess Yoder and Howard Mims, "The Significance of Written Texts," *The Great Debates: Carter vs. Ford, 1976,* ed. S. Kraus (Bloomington: Indiana University Press, 1979), 452.
11. William G. Powers, "The Rhetorical Interrogative: Anxiety or Control? *Human Communication Research 4* (1977): 44–47.
12. See Gerald R. Miller and Murray A. Hewgill, "The Effect of Variations in Nonfluency on Audience Ratings of Source Credibility," *Quarterly Journal of Speech 50* (1964): 36–44; Kenneth K. Sereno and Gary J. Hawkins, "The Effects of Variations in Speakers' Nonfluency upon Audience Ratings of Attitude toward the Speech Topic and Speaker's Credibility," *Speech Monographs 34* (1967): 58–64; James C. McCroskey and R. Samuel Mehrley, "The Effects of Disorganization and Nonfluency on Attitude Change and Source Credibility," *Speech Monographs 36* (1969): 13–21.
13. *San Francisco Chronicle,* 17 May 1988, B4.
14. Delwin Dusenbury and Franklin H. Knower, "Experimental Studies of the Symbolism of Action and Voice—II," *Quarterly Journal of Speech 25* (1939): 67–75; Grant Fairbanks and LeMar W. Hoaglin, "An Experimental Study of the Durational Characteristics of the Voice during the Expression of Emotion," *Speech Monographs 8* (1941): 85–90; Joel R. Davitz and Lois J. Davitz, "The Communication of Feeling by Content-Free Speech," *Journal of Communication 9* (1959): 6–13; John A. Starkweather, "Vocal Communication of Personality and Human Feelings," *Journal of Communication 11* (1961): 63–72; William F. Soskin and Paul E. Kauffman, "Judgment of Emotion in Word-Free Voice Samples," *Journal of Communication 11* (1961): 73–80.
15. Davitz & Davitz, "Communication of Feeling," and Soskin & Kauffman, "Judgment of Emotion."
16. Starkweather, "Personality and Feeling," 64.
17. L. S. Harms, "Listener Judgments of Status Cues in Speech," *Quarterly Journal of Speech 47* (1961): 164–168 and James D. Moe, "Listener Judgments of Status Cues in Speech: A Replication and Extension," *Speech Monographs 39* (1972): 144–147.
18. Roland J. Hart and Bruce L. Brown, "Interpersonal Information Conveyed by the Content and Vocal Aspects of Speech," *Speech Monographs 41* (1974): 371–380.
19. Hart & Brown, "Interpersonal Information," compare their work to that of psychologist Albert Mehrabian.
20. Jesse J. Villarreal, "Consistency of Judgments of Voice Quality," *Southern Speech Journal 15* (1949): 10.
21. J. Buckminster Ranney, "Incidence of Speech Disorders in the Student Population of a Southern University," *Southern Speech Journal 32* (1966): 113–116 and Samuel R. Faircloth, "A Descriptive Study of 133 Speech Deficient College Students," *Southern Speech Journal 32* (1966): 117–123.

22. Charles R. Petrie, Jr., "Informative Speaking: A Summary and Bibliography of Related Research," *Speech Monographs 30* (1963): 79–91 and Herbert F. Schliesser, "Information Transmission and Ethos of a Speaker Using Normal and Defective Speech," *Central States Speech Journal 19* (1968): 169–174.
23. David W. Addington, "The Effect of Vocal Variations on Ratings of Source Credibility," *Speech Monographs 38* (1971): 242–247.
24. Robert J. Kibler and Larry L. Barker, "An Experimental Study to Assess the Effects of Three Levels of Mispronunciation on Comprehension for Three Different Populations," *Speech Monographs 35* (1968): 26–38 and Kibler & Barker, "Effects of Selected Levels of Misspelling and Mispronunciation on Comprehension and Retention," *Southern Speech Communication Journal 37* (1972): 387–401.
25. Addington, "Effect of Mispronunciations."
26. Robert McCrum, William Cran, and Robert MacNeil, *The Story of English* (New York: Viking, 1986), 236–244.
27. Walter H. Wilke and Joseph F. Snyder, "American Speech Preferences," *Speech Monographs 9* (1942): 109. This finding also appears in Anthony Mulac and Mary J. Rudd, "Effects of Selected American Regional Dialects upon Regional Audience Members," *Communication Monographs 44* (1977): 185–195.
28. H. Thomas Hurt and Carl H. Weaver, "Negro Dialect, Ethnocentricism, and the Distortion of Information in the Communication Process," *Central States Speech Journal 23* (1972): 118–125.
29. Jesse G. Delia, "Dialects and the Effects of Stereotypes on Interpersonal Attraction and Cognitive Processes in Impression Formation," *Quarterly Journal of Speech 58* (1972): 285–297.
30. Dale T. Miller, "The Effect of Dialect and Ethnicity on Communication Effectiveness," *Speech Monographs 42* (1975): 69–74.
31. Mulac & Rudd, "Regional Dialects"; Joyce F. Buck, "The Effects of Negro and White Dialectical Variations upon Attitudes of College Students," *Speech Monographs 35* (1968): 181–186; Nancy Z. Flores and Robert Hopper, "Mexican American's Evaluations of Spoken Spanish and English," *Speech Monographs 42* (1975): 91–98.
32. Also, in Canada, French Canadians sometimes rate a speaker as more credible when the individual uses the standard English-Canadian accent. See Wallace E. Lambert, Hannah Frankel, and G. Richard Tucker, "Judging Personality through Speech: A French-Canadian Example," *Journal of Communication 16* (1966): 305–321. However, in England, Howard Giles, "Communicative Effectiveness as a Function of Accented Speech," *Speech Monographs 40* (1973): 330–331, found that while standard British pronunciation conferred *more prestige* on speakers, the speakers of standard dialect were *less persuasive* when speaking to listeners who used a regional accent.
33. Brenda Bochner and Arthur Bochner, "The Effects of Social Status and Social Dialect on Listener Responses," *Central States Speech Journal 24* (1973): 75–82.

34. Robert Hopper, "Language Attitudes in the Employment Interview," *Communication Monographs 44* (1977): 350. See also, Robert Hopper and Frederick Williams, "Speech Characteristics and Employability," *Speech Monographs 40* (1973): 296–302 and Nancy De La Zerda and Robert Hopper, "Employment Interviewers' Reactions to Mexican American Speech," *Communication Monographs 46* (1979): 126–134.
35. Beth Von Till, "Instructions for Assisting Nonnative Speakers of American English," San Jose State University Communication Lab, Spring 1987, 3.
36. Delia, "Dialects and Stereotypes."
37. This advice holds particularly true for members of racial minorities. See Walt Wolfram, "Sociolinguistic Premises and the Nature of Nonstandard Dialects," *Speech Teacher 19* (1970): 177–184; Richard R. Lee, "Linguistics, Communication and Behavioral Objectives: A Remedial Curriculum," *Speech Teacher 20* (1971): 1–9; Dennis R. Preston, "Social Dialects and College English," *Speech Teacher 20* (1971): 237–246; Delorese Tomlinson, "Bi-Dialectism: Solution for American Minority Members," *Speech Teacher 24* (1975): 233–236; Beatrice G. Popper, "Remediation of Selected Speech Patterns of Disadvantaged Black College Students," *Texas Speech Communication Journal 2* (1977): 17–26.
38. Lecture to students in communication, Indiana University Southeast, New Albany, Indiana, 28 September 1981.
39. Norman J. Lass and C. Elaine Prater, "A Comparative Study of Listening Rate Preferences for Oral Reading and Impromptu Speaking Tasks," *Journal of Communication 23* (1973): 95–102.
40. Ralph R. Behnke and Michael J. Beatty, "Effects of Time-Compressed Speech on Confidence-Weighted Comprehension Scores," *Southern Speech Communication Journal 44* (1977): 309–317 and Gerald Goldhaber and Carl H. Weaver, "Listener Comprehension of Compressed Speech when the Difficulty, Rate of Presentation and Sex of the Listener Are Varied," *Speech Monographs 35* (1968): 20–25.
41. Michael J. Beatty, Ralph R. Behnke and Deidre L. Froelich, "Effects of Achievement Incentive and Presentation Rate on Listening Comprehension," *Quarterly Journal of Speech 66* (1980): 193–200.
42. Lawrence R. Wheeless, "The Effects of Comprehension Loss on Persuasion," *Speech Monographs 38* (1971): 327–330. Note that Addington, "Vocal Variations and Credibility," found little connection between speaking rate and credibility.
43. Mulac & Rudd, "Regional Dialects."
44. David A. Stern, "Teaching and Acting: A Vocal Analogy," *Communication Education 29* (1980): 260–261.
45. Stern, "Teaching and Acting."
46. John W. Black, "Speech Intelligibility: A Summary of Recent Research," *Journal of Communication 11* (1961): 87–94.
47. Stern, "Teaching and Acting," 261.
48. Addington, "Vocal Variation and Credibility."

49. See George M. Glasgow, "A Semantic Index of Vocal Pitch," *Speech Monographs 19* (1952): 64–68 and Charles F. Diehl, Richard C. White, and Paul H. Satz, "Pitch Change and Comprehension," *Speech Monographs 28* (1961): 65–68.
50. Grant Fairbanks and Wilbert Pronovost, "An Experimental Study of the Pitch Characteristics of the Voice during the Expression of Emotion," *Speech Monographs 6* (1939): 87–104.
51. Joseph Tiffin and Max D. Steer, "An Experimental Analysis of Emphasis," *Speech Monographs 4* (1937): 69–74.
52. Stafford H. Thomas, "Effects of Monotonous Delivery on Intelligibility," *Speech Monographs 36* (1969): 110–113.
53. Earnest Brandenburg and Waldo W. Braden, "Franklin D. Roosevelt's Voice and Pronunciation," *Quarterly Journal of Speech 38* (1952): 25–26.
54. *Newsweek,* 3 July 1979, 19.
55. These studies show either slight or statistically significant increases in comprehension accompanying good vocal delivery: Kenneth C. Beighley, "An Experimental Study of the Effect of Four Speech Variables on Listener Comprehension," *Speech Monograph 19* (1952): 249–258; Beighley, "An Experimental Study of the Effect of Three Speech Variables on Listener Comprehension," *Speech Monographs 21* (1954): 248–253; Petrie, "Informative Speaking"; John L. Vohs, "An Empirical Approach to the Concept of Attention," *Speech Monographs 31* (1964): 355–360.
56. These studies show either slight or statistically significant increases in credibility and persuasion resulting from good vocal delivery: Erwin P. Bettinghaus, "The Operation of Congruity in an Oral Communication Situation," *Speech Monographs 28* (1961): 131–142 and John W. Bowers, "The Influence of Delivery on Attitudes toward Concepts and Speakers," *Speech Monographs 32* (1965): 154–158.
57. Edward J. J. Kramar and Thomas R. Lewis, "Comparison of Visual and Nonvisual Listening," *Journal of Communication 1,* No. 2 (1951): 16–20 and William T. Rogers, "The Contribution of Kinesic Illustrators toward the Comprehension of Verbal Behavior within Utterances," *Human Communication Research 5* (1978): 58.
58. Howard Gilkinson, "Indexes of Change in Attitudes and Behavior among Students Enrolled in General Speech Courses," *Speech Monographs 8* (1941): 23–33 and Frederick Williams, Sally A. Webb, and Ruth A. Clark, "Dimensions of Evaluation in High School Debate," *Central States Speech Journal 17* (1966): 15–21.
59. Paul Ekman and Wallace V. Friesen, "Hand Movements," *Journal of Communication 22* (1972): 353–374.
60. Ray Ehrensberger, "An Experimental Study of the Relative Effectiveness of Certain Forms of Emphasis in Public Speaking," *Speech Monographs 12* (1945): 94–111 and Petrie, "Informative Speaking."
61. John E. Baird, Jr., "Some Nonverbal Elements of Leadership Emergence," *Central States Speech Journal 42* (1977): 352–361.
62. *San Francisco Chronicle,* 10 May 1988, A9.
63. Ekman & Friesen, "Hand Movements."

64. Peter Wolff and Joyce Gutstein, "Effects of Induced Motor Gestures on Vocal Output," *Journal of Communication 22* (1972): 277–288 and Akiba A. Cohen, "The Communicative Functions of Hand Illustrators," *Journal of Communication 27,* No. 4 (1977): 54–63.
65. Dusenbury & Knower, "Action and Voice" and Kenton L. Burns and Ernst G. Beier, "Significance of Vocal and Visual Channels in the Decoding of Emotional Meaning," *Journal of Communication 23* (1973): 118–130.
66. Delwin Dusenbury and Franklin H. Knower, "Experimental Studies of the Symbolism of Action and Voice—I: A Study of the Specificity of Meaning in Facial Expression," *Quarterly Journal of Speech 24* (1938): 424–435.
67. Jerry D. Boucher and Paul Ekman, "Facial Areas and Emotional Information," *Journal of Communication 25,* No. 2 (1975): 27.
68. James W. Tankard, Jr., J. Sean McCleneghan, Vijay Ganju, Eui B. Lee, Cheryl Olkes, and Diane DuBose, "Nonverbal Cues and Television News," *Journal of Communication 27,* No. 4 (1977): 106–111.
69. Howard S. Friedman, Timothy I. Mertz, and M. Robin DiMatteo, "Perceived Bias in the Facial Expressions of Television News Broadcasters," *Journal of Communication 30,* No. 4 (1980): 103–111.
70. Herbert L. Curry, "John C. Calhoun," *A History and Criticism of American Public Address,* ed. W. N. Brigance, 2 vols., (New York: Russell & Russell, 1943), 2:647.
71. W. Gill Woodall, Judee K. Burgoon, and Norman N. Markel, "The Effects of Facial-Head Cue Combinations on Interpersonal Evaluations," *Communication Quarterly 28,* No. 3 (1980): 47–55.
72. Martin Corbin, "Response to Eye-Contact," *Quarterly Journal of Speech 48* (1962): 415–418.
73. Steven A. Beebe, "Eye Contact: A Nonverbal Determinant of Speaker Credibility," *Speech Teacher 23* (1974): 21–25.
74. Edward L. Black and Garry L. Martin, "A Component Analysis of Public-Speaking Behaviors across Individuals and Behavioral Categories," *Communication Education 29* (1980): 273–282.
75. Petrie, "Informative Speaking."
76. Molloy, *Dress for Success* (New York: Warner, 1975) and Molloy, *The Women's Dress for Success Book* (Chicago: Follett, 1978).
77. James A. Winans, "The Sense of Communication," *Southern Speech Journal 9* (1943): 4.
78. W. Barnett Pearce and Forrest Conklin, "Nonverbal Vocalic Communication and Perceptions of a Speaker," *Speech Monographs 38* (1971): 235–241 and Pearce and Bernard J. Brommel, "Vocalic Communication in Persuasion," *Quarterly Journal of Speech 58* (1972): 298–306.

Chapter

12

Presenting the Speech

Outline

Speaking to an American Legion Convention in Louisville, Kentucky, on September 7, 1988, George Bush wanted to make a point about military preparedness. Departing from his speech text, Bush asked: "I wonder how many Americans remember today is Pearl Harbor Day. Forty-seven years ago to this very day we were hit and hit hard at Pearl Harbor and we were not ready."[1] Did he say *September seventh?* The words were hardly out of candidate Bush's mouth when members of his audience began to whisper to one another. One Legionnaire leaned over to a friend and commented: "I thought nobody would forget that date." Noticing the surprised expressions of veterans, and their confused murmuring, Bush suddenly stopped. "Did I say September seventh? Sorry about that." He corrected the date of the attack, and the audience applauded as Bush continued his speech.

George Bush's error, and his recovery from it, remind us that a speech is not simply a plan or a text. A speech is nothing less than a message spoken in a particular situation before real people. Bush's experience at the American Legion Convention could happen to anyone. We forget a date; we see puzzled looks on the faces of listeners; we skip over a point and find we must return to it later. What should we do? Are there any tips for presenting the speech *on the spot?* What are some ideas for responding to feedback or for answering questions that come spontaneously from listeners? In sum, what can we say about the speaking situation itself?

Preparing a speech that is good *on paper,* or in front of a mirror, is one thing. But rhetorical competence means successfully taking a speech before living listeners. We need to review four important aspects of bringing ideas into a live speaking situation. We turn first to our need to choose from among the general forms of speech presentation. Second, we focus on extemporaneous speaking, the most widely applicable form of presentation. Third, we consider how to recognize, use, and even anticipate audience responses—feedback. Finally, we take a look at how to handle the tricky impromptu question-and-answer period that often follows a prepared message.

Forms of Speech Presentation

Adlai Stevenson once commented that "I think a speaker really makes four speeches: the speech he thinks about ahead of time; the speech he writes; the speech he gives; and the speech he gives on the way home."[2] Stevenson, reflecting on his experience as Illinois governor and two-time Democratic candidate for president, puts well the basic problem of rhetorical competence. Every instance of communication takes place in a unique situation. How do we prepare and deliver a speech that simultaneously meets our own purposes, the expectations of listeners, and the unique circumstances of time and place?

Basic to the question of success in a particular situation is choosing the right vehicle of presentation. Here we select from among the four general ways to present speeches: extemporaneous speaking, delivery from manuscript, impromptu speaking, or memorized presentation. These four methods, however, do not offer equally effective pathways to rhetorical success. If your aim is general rhetorical competence, you will be biased in favor of extemporaneous speaking and against memorization of words. What you need is to understand the essentials of extemporaneous speaking and, more important, to appreciate the value of this method.

The Extemporaneous Method

To speak extemporaneously means that you have prepared an outline, and that you have practiced your speech for delivery using a minimum of notes. Because you have rehearsed your extemporaneous speech, you have begun to commit certain phrases almost to memory. However, your speech is no word-for-word recitation of a written text. You have prepared in advance, but you construct your ideas spontaneously, at the moment of delivery, just as in ordinary conversation.

Speech communication teachers strongly endorse the extemporaneous mode of speech. Extemporaneous speaking offers you two major advantages. First, because you rely on only a few notes, your remarks fit easily into the conversational pattern. A good extemporaneous speech possesses that prepared-but-spontaneous look that is associated with great speakers. Not only does extemporaneous speaking allow for a personal style of language, but it also encourages you to use a direct-to-people mode of delivery. When you take the person-to-person approach, you are less tempted to launch into literary flights of fancy or to lapse into a dull recitation. For instance, Harry Truman was a wooden speaker when using a manuscript. But during the 1948 presidential campaign, he came alive as a communicator who could speak directly to ordinary citizens who came to his campaign stops. Capitalizing on Truman's desire to speak off-the-cuff in a direct and easy manner, his staff coached him on extemporaneous speaking.[3]

A second advantage of extemporaneous speaking is the flexibility it offers. You can adapt to whatever is happening at the moment, unlike the speaker who feels tied to a memorized script or to a briefcase full of notes. When speaking extemporaneously, you may easily include extra examples if your audience does not seem to be getting the point. If your listeners grow restless, you may easily shorten your remarks. In fact, the extemporaneous method often allows for an ideal mixture of polish and spontaneity. Henry Ward Beecher, the great nineteenth century preacher, prepared speeches by working out his aim and gathering information in the days before his speech. Several hours before the service, Beecher developed an outline.

Then as he faced his Sunday audience, Beecher drew upon his research and filled out the content of the outline while speaking. Beecher believed that once he put down all his ideas on paper he precluded any fresh and spontaneous variations on his prepared theme.[4] No wonder Beecher was viewed as the leading churchman of his era.

Even if we cannot all become modern day Beechers, extemporaneous speaking clearly represents the best method to *learn* speechmaking. This method gives you an attitude of confidence as well as specific skills to liberate you from notes, props, tripping over single words, dread of surprises, and resistance to spontaneous adaptation. You are ready, come whatever! The method also encourages you to use a conversational type of vocal delivery that is highly prized in today's world of personal and often informal relationships.

Because extemporaneous speaking is the preferred method of practice and study, we will take a detailed look at its specific characteristics after briefly reviewing other methods of presentation.

The Manuscript Method

When speaking from a manuscript you prepare and deliver the text of your speech word-for-word. The manuscript method offers some advantages for busy public figures who must use ghost writers. Since the time of Woodrow Wilson, demands of time have kept U.S. presidents dependent on the help of their speechwriting staffs. Second, the manuscript method of speaking gives advantages where words must be carefully measured and refined in advance. Just such a case occurred when William Agee, Chairman of the Board of Bendix Corporation, gave a speech to stem rumors that rapid promotions given to Mary Cunningham, his prized manager, resulted from an alleged romance between the two. Unfortunately, Agee's description of the situation was careless, only making matters worse. Cunningham, who resigned soon thereafter, commented: "His wording might have been a little better. That's one speech I would like to have written."[5]

The manuscript approach also has a place in public speaking for the mass media. Speakers on radio and television usually face absolute time limits. For instance, during a televised debate with Ronald Reagan on the issue of the Panama Canal, William F. Buckley, Jr. apparently was so carried away by the clever style of his speech that he exceeded his allotted time. As Buckley prepared to launch into his final point, Senator Sam Ervin, moderator of the debate, broke in: "I'm now going to perform one of the most painful things I've ever done. As one who loves to filibuster, I hate to stop a speech, but I am going to remind you that your time is gone."

Clearly the advantages of the manuscript method apply to a few rather restricted occasions. Most people will never play the role of a spokesperson for a major governmental or private organization. Few people give speeches that are supposed to live for the ages, and few will be speaking live on national television. If the benefits of manuscript speaking usually are restricted, the penalties often are not. By using a word-for-word text, you are tempted to skip practicing the speech. Furthermore, manuscript speaking creates a psychological barrier against responding to audience feedback. I once observed a keynote speaker forget this simple lesson while giving an address to an audience of college debaters. The students knew that they could not get the contest results until after the speech was done. For the first fifteen minutes they listened politely, but gradually their anxiousness to leave became obvious. Disregarding signs of the audience's growing impatience, the speaker—himself a teacher of speech—doggedly read every word of his forty-five minute masterpiece.

A final problem with a speech manuscript is that, while delivering your text, you are in less of a position to keep close eye contact with listeners. Audiences notice the stilted delivery that results. During a United States-Soviet summit meeting in Geneva, Switzerland, the First Ladies of the two countries both gave speeches at various public meetings around the city. The speaking of Raisa Gorbachev was more impressive to Swiss audiences because she spoke without notes. In contrast, Nancy Reagan hardly ever looked up from her notes.[6]

Practice, and a willingness to adapt, are keys for making sure that your manuscript speeches do not bring severe rhetorical penalties. When you have practiced delivering the manuscript several times, and when you have marked the text, you will be able to keep frequent eye contact with listeners. If you must give a manuscript address, remember that effective speakers modify their text when the occasion demands it. President Franklin D. Roosevelt was particularly good at speaking from a prepared text. If we compare the original texts of FDR's speeches to the addresses he actually presented, we find that Roosevelt changed his speeches to create a closer relationship with listeners. He added words of stronger motivational power; he included shorter and more vigorous words; and he interjected forceful phrases.

More evidence on how to present a manuscript speech comes from Adlai Stevenson's speaking during his second campaign for the presidency in 1956. A speech critic compared certain effective and ineffective addresses by Stevenson. In the effective presentations, Stevenson "made copious alterations in his manuscript, while speaking, mainly in an effort to gain more directness and identification" with listeners.[7]

Box 12.1

Please Don't Bore the Justices

For lawyers speaking before the United States Supreme Court comes this advice:

"Don't read. Reading from prepared materials is forbidden by Court rules, and it bores the Justices."

Source: "Tips for Taking on the Justices" *National Law Journal,* cited in *Chronicle of Higher Education,* 26 January 1983, 13.

Below are some suggestions for using a manuscript and, at the same time, keeping eye contact and a conversational orientation.

1. Prepare a text that is easy to use. This means that the manuscript should be neatly typed and triple-spaced.
2. Practice using the text. Do not be afraid to "mess up" the draft of the manuscript with marks as you practice, but if you make a great number of changes in wording, retype the text.
3. Mark the text. Highlight the manuscript to aid your delivery, for instance, underlining key words and phrases.
4. Practice delivering the text. Work on vocal variety as you practice, finding just the right places to change volume, to speed up or slow down, to raise or lower pitch, to emphasize particular words.
5. Concentrate on keeping eye contact. In your practice sessions, check to see if you are looking up from the text. If not, keep practicing the speech until you know important portions *almost* from memory. When you have this level of familiarity with your text, then you will be able to look up after you begin a section of the speech, or make eye contact when you are about to conclude a passage.
6. Practice movement and gestures. Probably you will be speaking from a lectern. This places some limitations on you, but still allows for upper body movement, for gestures, and for animated facial expressions.
7. Use a podium while practicing the speech. Most manuscript speeches are given from a lectern or podium, so get familiar with using one. Become accustomed to laying your notes flat on the podium and looking down occasionally at them.

Impromptu Speech

As you enter the world of business and society, you will occasionally find yourself called upon to give a speech without advance notice. During a business meeting, your boss may suddenly volunteer you to give a summary

Use a lectern when practicing the delivery of a manuscript speech.

of your work on a project. The chair of a club meeting may surprise you by asking for an impromptu report. What should you do?

If you have mastered rhetorical competence, such requests for impromptu remarks will not represent a major hurdle. Impromptu speakers are well served by Aristotle's observation that a speech consists of essentially two parts: (1) a statement of the major points and (2) proof of the points.[8] Aristotle's observation suggests that organization can become a key to effective impromptu speaking.

You are most likely to be asked for an impromptu speech when you are presumed to be knowledgeable about content. The hard part is to decide quickly upon an organizational pattern to handle the content. Consider using a sequence that includes (1) enumeration, (2) elaboration, and (3) summary. In other words, begin by saying that you would like to make a number of points on the subject. For instance, "I have found several reasons why we should delay introducing our new product." Then you *enumerate* each point, beginning with a capsule phrase such as "First, the engineering department has not yet worked out all the bugs." Next, you *elaborate* on each point, giving details. Finally, you *summarize* however many points you made: "So, I see four reasons why we should delay introducing the new product."

In general, the training you get from your speech class in extemporaneous speaking will carry across to impromptu situations. However, if you are one of those persons who frequently give impromptu remarks, pay particular attention to several additional aspects of rhetorical technique. Study the *topoi* method of inquiry (chapter 6), the ways to begin and end speeches (chapter 9), the message-centered organizational patterns (chapter 13), and the listener-centered organizational patterns (chapter 14). Mastering these principles of analysis and organization will make you ready for all on-the-spot opportunities to speak.

Memorized Speech

Why do some speakers cling to the idea that memorizing solves the problems of speechmaking? Memorization, in itself, is no evil. In fact, memory work is a great way for preschool children to prepare for literacy. Furthermore, to learn interesting passages by heart is to tutor the ear in good style, voice, and variation. But as a technique for the ordinary presentation of speeches, memorization contradicts several of the attitudes and skills of rhetorical competence.

First, when you write out a text and learn it word-for-word, you are apt to forget that public speaking is an art of direct communication with listeners. Memorization focuses your attention on frozen words instead of a living audience. Once the speech is down on paper, and you begin to recite it, the words become unchangeable. The content of your address can never become better, and your delivery of the speech may become worse. You cannot respond to surprises of the moment. By memorizing, you also make yourself vulnerable to disaster because you are focusing on individual words instead of ideas. One omitted word can bring your whole enterprise to a screeching halt.

Box 12.2

Don't Memorize, Conceptualize

Clinton C. Johnson, Vice-President of Chemical Bank and Trust Company, reported how he learned not to memorize his speeches:

> At that time I was president of a young people's organization which annually gave a concert in the Brooklyn Academy of Music. During the intermission in the program the president was called upon to give a little address of welcome, expressing appreciation for patronage, and informing the audience that the proceeds from the concert were being devoted to an excellent charity—namely, summer camp for underprivileged children.
>
> I appeared on the platform bedecked in white tie and started to give my talk, which I had written out and memorized. I thought it was going along perfectly until I forgot one word—and then I came to an abrupt stop to try to recall it, but couldn't. The only thing to do was to proceed extemporaneously, which I did; and according to my good wife the second part was better than the first.

Source: "My Toughest Speech Problem—And How I Licked It," *Today's Speech 2,* No. 4 (1954): 3.

In addition to taking you into harm's way, memorized speaking fails as a method for building rhetorical competence in delivering speeches to real audiences. Early in the twentieth century, many speech teachers still used the declamation method, in which their students delivered classic orations from memory. Speech researchers then discovered that declamation did not help students learn how to give their own speeches. In fact, declamation actually discouraged students from using extemporaneous methods.[9] Declamation remains a fine contest event for student clubs, and it helps cultivate an appreciation for verbal style. But as a method of speech presentation, memorized declamations are inferior to the extemporaneous method.

Delivering Your Extemporaneous Speech

Now it is time to look at the fine points of extemporaneous speaking. Extemporaneous delivery embodies the essential knowledge, attitudes, and skills of rhetorically competent speechmaking. This method stresses *personal research and composition* in contrast to the assumption of manuscript delivery that you have access to a speech writing staff. Extemporaneous speaking stresses *improvement through practice* in contrast to the stultifying effects of memorization. Extemporaneous speaking allows you *really to communicate with people* in contrast to the focus on mere words that can result from frozen manuscripts and memorized texts.

Another way to look at the vitality of extemporaneous delivery is to consider its prevalence. Most speaking situations are of the routine, practical sort—in business or in social groups. Occasions of this kind require the spontaneous give-and-take that only extemporaneous delivery can convey. For instance, members of the United States Senate report that they use all four methods of speech preparation in committee work and on the Senate floor. However, most legislative speeches are extemporaneous. In the executive branch of government, Harry Truman acknowledged that his presidential role sometimes required manuscript speaking. But he added that "If I had my choice, I would always speak extemporaneously. . . . Like almost everyone else, I talk more effectively than I read."[10]

To become effective in making extemporaneous presentations, you should pay particular attention to techniques for remembering phrases and for working from speech notes.

Memory in Speechmaking

One of the Roman world's greatest teachers of speech, Quintilian, concluded that "extempore eloquence, in my opinion, depends on no mental activity so much as memory."[11] As an extemporaneous speaker, you will not learn an address word for word. But you still must remember the main ideas, the arrangement of points, and relevant remarks of previous speakers. Also, good memory is required to use effectively your speaking notes, since each notation must bring to mind a longer train of thought. In fact, if you could memorize your speech notes you could give your speech entirely without them.

Several elements of memory pertain to giving extemporaneous speeches. First, you are concerned with *long-term* as opposed to short-term memory. Our short-time memory contains information retained only briefly, such as a telephone number recalled while dialing but forgotten a minute later. In contrast, long-term memory is a repository of things we retain because we have reflected on them several times. Second, you are concerned with the aided memory as opposed to the natural, unaided memory. You will be taking specific steps to increase your ability to recall information when you need it.

There are several ways that your aided memory can help in speechmaking. Each marks a natural human tendency that can be enhanced for use in recalling speeches.

Mental pictures

Effective memory involves visualization. Memory expert Harry Lorayne contends that a person's trained memory "will be based almost entirely on *mental pictures* or images."[12] This observation suggests that the way to remember a speech is to picture the sequence of events. Visualize real people, real places, real action. Lorayne suggests that your pictures be exaggerated, since vivid images are more easily brought to mind than conventional ones. If your speech is organized around the social and political effects of censorship, visualize someone snooping in a window or a speaker with a handkerchief stuffed in his mouth.

A variation of the picturing method is the technique of creating relevant pictograph symbols. *Pictograph* means, literally, a written picture—a thumbnail-size sketch such as in Egyptian hieroglyphics. Applied to speechmaking, the pictograph method would have us create a vivid pictograph to represent each point or some particular points in the speech. Quintilian gives the example of a speaker using a spear to represent the idea of a battle.

The pictograph method was one favored by Mark Twain in his many humorous lectures across America. Twain first tried to remember his lectures by memorizing key sentences and the first letters of each key sentence. The approach didn't work; he got mixed up and needed to shuffle through his papers. Twain finally arrived at the pictograph approach, finding that six or so pictures gave him an unforgettable summary of the content of his talk. For instance, he might use a haystack with a wiggly line underneath (representing a rattlesnake) to remind him to talk about ranch life in the West.

Twain initially inked his pictographs onto his thumbnails; but he found that someone would always come up after the lecture to ask what was wrong with his hands! Then Twain began to draw out his line of symbols on paper, fix the image of the pictures in his mind's eye, and then discard the paper. Though the pictograph method was taught by Quintilian and used by Mark Twain, we should not assume the method is too antique for the contemporary world. Pictographic notes are the recommended approach in today's Communispond program of speech workshops for business executives.[13]

The peg system

Effective memory can be stimulated by remembering sequences of sound and sight. Speechmaking is served by location, a natural peg system. Quintilian taught Roman students to remember the organization of their speeches by mentally placing ideas into familiar locales. Beginning with vivid symbols that conveyed the ideas of a speech—such as a spear to represent a battle—Quintilian suggested that students place these symbols mentally in a familiar geographic pattern. In your case, why not use your house? Suppose your speech consists of five points, and that you have created vivid mental symbols for each point. Now, visualize each symbol in a room of your house; by picturing each symbol in a room, you could remember the order of points by mentally taking a tour of home. The Roman world's greatest orator, Cicero, recommended this method for extemporaneous speaking.[14]

Association

George Miller's classic study of memory shows that people can improve their recall of information by "chunking" together miscellaneous data around a central core of thought. The association principle of memory has great value for your speeches. Generally, you will use the association method to keep details of the speech tightly organized around each point. Lorayne, the memory expert, advises that you use what he calls the "link method." This system would find you capsulizing each main point of the speech with a key word—a single term that brings to mind a whole thought. You would link each successive key word to the next, so that when you finished one point, you would be led to the next.[15] For example, say the first point in your speech dealt with the automobile industry (key word, "car"), and the second point treated the telephone industry (key word, "phone"). You would find some mental picture that linked the two key words, for instance, visualizing sitting in a car eating a telephone (remember, the unusual stimulates recall).

Sounds

Vivid sounds stimulate the memory. One application of this principle to speechmaking includes Quintilian's advice that the speaker practice out loud "so that the memory may derive assistance from the double effort of speaking and listening." This advice is underscored by research showing that people remember more about a passage when they read it out loud rather than silently.[16]

Style is a second way to stimulate thought by means of sound. We observed this earlier in the case of the ancient Greeks who used rhyme, rhythm, and personification to recall information. The stylistic figures discussed in chapter 10 would help you recall ideas. For instance, Douglas MacArthur, then 82 years of age, delivered his address on "Duty, Honor, Country" (text at end of chapter 10) without notes. Can anyone doubt that his detailed descriptions, repetition, and stylistic figures all aided his memory?

Gradualism and repetition

In memory work, learning one section of the speech at a time helps. Try recalling one unit or one link at a time; only then, try to recall the whole structure of the speech.

Repetition is a crucial element of learning the speech. By definition, long-term memory, the basis of learning a speech, involves repetition. In physiological terms, long-term memory is a "relatively permanent alteration [that] occurs among neurons" as a result of repetition of an experience.[17] When you picture and practice the speech frequently, you will better impress upon your mind its structure and style.

Visual aids

Do not overlook visual aids as a help to your memory. Just about any type of visual will help you picture and link the main concepts of the speech. A typical exercise for students is a speech to demonstrate the operation of something. Even beginners find themselves able to give such a speech with few or no notes. Why? The visual elements of the speech lead you through the key points.

Pay attention to memory and memorization in public speaking. Rhetorically competent speakers recognize that memory is the vehicle by which content and style reach the audience. Why not experiment with the Roman method for speaking entirely without notes? B. F. Skinner, the famous behavioral scientist, says that a presentation without notes is particularly impressive.[18] However, even if you are not ready to abandon the safety net of written notes, remember that memory techniques still can work for you. Memory methods will make the ideas and phrases of the speech more familiar, increasing your chances for success.

Speech Notes

If you are like most speakers, you will want to use notes while speaking extemporaneously. Notes become crucial when you begin to practice your speech, and most speakers begin by using the outline as their first speaking notes. A caution, however: one sure sign that you have not sufficiently practiced your speech is when you carry your original outline to the podium to use as notes. In the normal course of events, active practice on the speech will cause you to change your notes. Most changes will be in the direction of deleting and slimming down written notes as you become more and more familiar with the speech. What began in your original speech outline as whole sentences could, through practice, be reduced to phrases, key words, or even pictographs.

Sometimes practice will lead you to add material to your notes. For instance, you might discover an especially appropriate short quotation. This idea brings us also to the question of how to handle evidence in speech notes. Probably the best idea is to keep evidence cards separate from the basic notes. Mark your notes to indicate when you should read your quotation cards.

Following are some essential guidelines for using notes in speechmaking:

1. Less is better. Most students err on the side of having too many notes. Avoid the temptation to substitute bulky notes for extensive practice. If you start out with notes consisting of six sheets of paper, or a dozen 3 × 5 cards, boil this mass down to one page or a couple of cards.
2. Simple is better. Try to use key words and phrases rather than sentences. And why not experiment with a pictograph or two?
3. If notes are solely in words, use an outline form. Keep the outline symbols from your full preparation outline.
4. Make the notes orderly. Type or print your notes neatly, with letters as large as possible.
5. Be sure your notes do not flip, flap, shuffle, or creak. If you use a sheet of paper, find something to use as a backing; otherwise the paper will flutter and flap. Do not shuffle through a half-inch stack of cards. Avoid creaky notebooks that will squeak every time you turn a page.
6. Keep your notes out of your hands as much as possible; they inhibit gestures. Try laying them on the podium or table. If you must hold them, just use one hand.
7. Glance at your notes occasionally, *but do not read them.* Your notes should be a familiar friend by now. Try glancing inconspicuously at your notes when you shift positions or when you make a transition. The audience—and you—will hardly realize you have notes.

Box 12.3

The Only Time Bulky Notes Saved a Speaker

On October 14, 1912, Theodore Roosevelt's life was saved by a scripted speech when the folded text in his coat pocket slowed the bullet of a would-be assassin. Had the former president been more concise or had the advent of TelePrompTers eliminated the need for his typed version, he might not have lived to declare to the stunned audience, "I will make this speech or die!"

Source: Kathleen H. Jamieson, *Eloquence in an Electronic Age* (New York: Oxford University Press, 1988), vii.

Extemporaneous speaking requires attention to memory and speech notes. Both of these presentation factors presuppose that you will be practicing the speech. Do not think you can attain rhetorical competence without practice. A speech is not something you contemplate—it comes off only when you get up to speak. If you are tempted merely to review your original outline silently before class, think again. Do not lull yourself into the mistaken view that extemporaneous delivery is the easiest mode of preparation because of freedom to use notes. True, you don't have to type out a whole speech or memorize 1000 words of text. But you should use the time you would spend typing or memorizing to practice. A lack of practice will show. Do not volunteer for a handicap; instead, set aside some special practice time. Mentally review your speech during moments when you are doing something with your hands—driving, washing dishes. Live with the speech a bit.

Feedback

Feedback is a modern term that refers to the responses that listeners make to a speech. The audience's immediate reaction to the speech is, at once, your privilege and your cross to bear. On the one hand, responding to feedback allows you to create a spirit of unity with listeners. Like George Bush, who corrected his gaff about Pearl Harbor Day, you can win approval by immediately responding to feedback—by correcting, adding, deleting, or elaborating. Yet, feedback can represent a burden. Knowing that you have the power to adapt, listeners expect that you will heed their feedback. Attitude is important. The rhetorically competent speaker is always alert for and responsive to feedback.

Looking for Feedback

Market researchers help persuaders and advertisers to pretest their messages and refine their appeals. Already by the early 1940s, researchers had developed the Program Analyzer, a machine that allowed receivers to press buttons indicating whether they liked or disliked a segment of film. You might envy market researchers in view of their ability to get and use precise data about audience response. However, even without a Program Analyzer, you already *can* and *do* correctly read feedback from listeners.

You and your audience are fellow human beings, people experienced in interpreting nonverbal behavior. Therefore, when you give a speech, you are already in a position to understand whether or not the audience is favorable. For instance, you do not need a Program Analyzer to know that restless movement in the audience signals a lack of interest. True, some audiences are easier to read than others. For instance, persons highly involved with a subject tend to exhibit their views more clearly.[19] Although experience as a speaker will give you an edge in interpreting feedback, even inexperienced speakers can accurately read their audiences.[20]

Specifically, what should you expect to see when you look out at the audience?[21] Sometimes listeners will signal that they like what you are doing in the speech. *Favorable feedback* includes:

- smiling.
- heads nodding in agreement.
- direct eye contact with you.
- comfortably straight posture.
- absence of extra nervous movement.
- taking notes.

On other occasions, you may find your audience signaling disapproval. Signs of *unfavorable feedback* include:

- frowning.
- heads shaking in disagreement.
- listeners looking down and around—but not at you.
- slouched posture and/or randomly shifting posture.
- restless movement—listeners touching themselves or playing with objects.
- doodling with pencil and paper.

In judging the posture and facial responses of your audience, remember two things. First, look for the general reaction. Do not base your assessment of the audience on one or two listeners. Second, recognize that your speech may not be the sole cause of the audience's behavior. Reactions could stem in part from the layout of the room or the time of day. Whatever its cause, however, feedback reports the impact of *your* presentation. A hallmark of your becoming rhetorically competent is a constant interest in finding and using feedback.

Responding to Feedback

Most speakers believe they will perform better and experience less nervousness when looking directly at listeners.[22] Clearly, reactions of listeners do directly affect the performance of speakers. Unfavorable responses are unsettling and tend to reduce a speaker's fluency and satisfaction.[23] Therefore, knowing your options for responding to feedback will be crucial for you.

What should you do about feedback? Where the feedback is favorable or *positive,* the answer is easy; *keep doing what you are doing and what you plan to do.* Favorable responses indicate the audience approves of your approach. Keep on with it!

Negative feedback is a more complicated issue. First, we should note that negative feedback is not a disaster. For one thing, *experienced* speakers do *not* lose fluency when faced with unfavorable feedback.[24] Over your career as a speaker, you may expect to become better in handling negative reactions. Furthermore, speech students who receive training in using feedback exhibit fewer nonfluencies in the face of negative responses.[25] Expect to increase your composure in crisis when you use your speech class as an opportunity to practice responding to feedback.

Now we turn to some specific suggestions for handling negative feedback. To respond to negative feedback you must accept the idea that unfavorable responses mean *the audience wants you to do things differently.* The rhetorically competent speaker has the attitude of being willing to adapt to cues from listeners. Of course, there are features of your speech that you cannot change, for instance, the topic. And presumably you will not throw away your entire thesis at the first hint of difficulty. Nevertheless, there remain a number of changes that you can make to reconcile better your intention with the reactions of the audience. Below are four general skills of preparing for and responding to negative feedback.

Expect the unexpected

Speakers may be bothered less by unfavorable feedback than by feedback that is different from what they expected. For instance, a speaker is likely to exhibit more nonfluencies when receiving feedback that differs *in any way* from that given to a previous speaker.[26] This finding suggests that you should prepare for feedback by not fixing your mind on how the audience "should" respond to your speech. As you practice the speech, visualize the audience responding in different ways. Practice handling these responses.

Anticipate responses

As you prepare your speech, you can anticipate ways the audience may react—and build your response into the structure of the speech. This advice takes us back to the subject of audience analysis (chapter 5). Audience analysis gives you clues about likely responses of listeners to various ideas and arguments. Once you have identified these possibilities, you can respond *in advance* to feedback. How? Look at the points you will be making, in each case considering how listeners might react. When you anticipate possible obstacles to successful informative and persuasive speaking, you will be motivated to try harder. You will work to find stronger arguments and you will develop habits for effectively adapting your points to the views of listeners.[27] Booker T. Washington, the early civil rights leader, followed this advice. Washington believed that the most effective way to win support for a disagreeable point was to tell a story. Washington developed a repertoire of tales to illustrate his points, complete with dialogue between characters.[28]

Act on feedback

While you deliver your speech, pay particular attention to changes in the nonverbal responses of listeners. When listeners signal disapproval, don't just stand there—respond! You have three general options in using feedback to adjust your speech plans: (1) deleting material, (2) adding material, (3) rearranging material. In addition, you need to decide whether or not explicitly to indicate that you are changing your speech plans to respond to the immediate situation.

The most straightforward response to unfavorable cues from the audience is to delete material. William T. Foster, a great teacher of speech, advised speakers to have a conclusion firmly in mind and to end the speech quickly when necessary. Wrote Foster, "no speech is wholly bad which has terminal facilities."[29] Sometimes you will find shortening your speech necessary because of environmental conditions over which you have no control—for instance, noisy machinery outside the room. In such a case, you might want to acknowledge what you are doing so that listeners will not misinterpret your rushed ending.

Sometimes responses by listeners suggest that you should add material. Puzzled looks call for more explanation, description, or examples. When listeners show disinterest, you need to make the speech more personal, for example, by using an anecdote or a story in place of statistical evidence. If you believe the audience is disagreeing with a key point, you might try to bolster the idea with more evidence. Or you might make the point strike closer to home by showing its direct connection to the situation of listeners.

Finally, it is possible to respond to feedback by rearranging your material. Perhaps you originally chose to organize your speech by making a series of related arguments. If the audience seems unpersuaded, you might decide quickly to shift to a need-solution pattern of organization. You would try to arouse concern in a problem and then show how your ideas led to a desirable solution.

A classic instance of diagnosing feedback and changing the speech occurred when John F. Kennedy addressed the 1959 Alfred E. Smith Memorial Dinner in New York City. This event was immediately prior to JFK's formally beginning his campaign for the presidency, and Kennedy shared the platform with a political rival, Nelson Rockefeller. Kennedy had brought a prepared manuscript address, which he ultimately discarded in favor of brief impromptu remarks. Why? Kennedy noticed that the audience had become lulled into a comfortable indifference. The result? Kennedy made a stronger impression with his extemporaneous remarks than his rival Nelson Rockefeller did by plodding along with a prepared manuscript.

Box 12.4

How JFK Abandoned His Text and Saved the Day

The Alfred E. Smith Foundation banquet at the Waldorf Astoria in October, 1959, reveals [John F. Kennedy's] practice of making sudden and significant changes in his speaking plans so that he could adapt his remarks to the prevailing mood of the audience and to the lateness of the hour. For two reasons Kennedy viewed this setting as crucial to the success of his future political goals. First, he recognized the possibility that he might become a candidate for the Democratic nomination in 1960. Second, he regarded Governor Nelson Rockefeller, who also was scheduled to speak, as a potential Republican nominee. During the dinner hour, therefore, Kennedy nervously played with his manuscript while noting his opponent's animated conversation and carefree manner. Later, at the close of the governor's manuscript speech, Kennedy decided to put aside his own text to change the atmosphere of comfortable indifference which, according to the *New York Times,* had settled over the 2,500 people in the audience. After making humorous references both to himself and to Rockefeller, he alluded to General Winfield Scott, Alf Landon, and Richard Nixon who, he suggested, was perhaps standing on the steps of the Nation's Capitol with the spyglass turned toward Albany. His witty and spontaneous presentation evoked laughter and applause ten times in nine minutes. More important, in his first encounter with Rockefeller, Kennedy had made a stronger impact on the audience.

Source: James L. Golden, "John F. Kennedy and the 'Ghosts,' " *Quarterly Journal of Speech* 52 (1966): 355.

John F. Kennedy's switch from a manuscript address to impromptu remarks amounts to a drastic response to feedback. While all your responses need not be that extensive, Kennedy's choice is consistent with the attitude and skill that a rhetorically competent speaker brings to a speaking situation. If the mood of listeners casts doubt on your advance plans, then let your plans give way to your purpose of attaining success with the audience.

Respond to noise and interruptions

Circumstances other than your speech can determine the mood of an audience. Time and place often play perverse tricks. You are about to speak and jackhammers set up a distraction. As you begin your most important point, a waiter drops a trayful of glasses. You begin to suffer from a persistent cough. You are covering a tough point and someone shouts a sarcastic remark. Unexpected events, yes, but things such as these happen often enough that you should anticipate something of the kind—and be ready to deal with it.

In this day of machines and ventilation systems, noise is a frequent obstacle. If the distracting noise seems likely to be temporary, as with a jet airplane passing over the building, calmly stop and wait. If the noise is persistent, request appropriate help, for instance, to close a window or door. Cut the speech short if nothing else works. If your audience generates background noise in the form of shuffling, whispering, or creaking chairs, you might speak louder or ask for quiet. Or you might bring your speech rapidly to a close, since these are signs of disinterest.

Interruptions come in many forms, and they call for varying responses. Sometimes the distraction will be coincidental or accidental, as when a baby says something cute or a waiter drops a tray. In these cases, wait until the group settles down, then smile and begin again as if nothing had happened. If the interruption seems to weaken your hold on the group, another option would be to regain psychological control by briefly, pleasantly, or humorously acknowledging what happened. Daniel Webster took the humorous tack in a campaign appearance in 1840. During Webster's address, the hastily constructed speaker's platform suddenly collapsed, tumbling Webster and other dignitaries onto the ground. Wanting to regain some degree of dignity, Webster quickly took to his feet, saying "the great Whig platform [is] more solid than the frail structure on which [I have been] standing."[30]

Interruptions sometimes come in the form of questions or comments from the audience. If the interruption is a question, treat it as friendly until proven otherwise. Answer the question briefly, and move on; or open the floor for more questions if this suits the purpose. A particularly difficult kind of obstacle is *heckling* from the audience—derogatory comments, repeated hostile questions, or insulting suggestions. Geraldine Ferraro, campaigning for vice president in 1984, found herself frequently in competition with hecklers. At a campaign stop at the University of Texas, Arlington, Ferraro sometimes ignored the chanting protesters; at other times she confronted them. Once, unable to complete a sentence, Ferraro chided the hecklers: "I want to tell you—if I had a record like Ronald Reagan's, I wouldn't want anybody to talk about it either."[31]

Heckling is not something you would expect in the normal run of speech situations. However, the experience of heckling is dramatic enough that you will want to understand how to deal with it. If you are like most speakers, you would prefer to avoid heckling. Disruptive heckling can reduce your credibility, especially when the hecklers are of the same social background as the rest of the audience.[32] Your range of options for dealing with heckling basically are these:

1. Ignore the remark, especially if it is isolated.
2. Postpone by telling the heckler that his or her point will be covered soon.
3. Answer the objection briefly, if this does not detract from your speech plan.
4. Answer the objection at length, letting the audience know that this approach is a departure from your planned remarks.
5. Use a reprimand, pointing out the unfairness or rudeness of the interruption.
6. Ask for help—ask members of the audience to persuade one or two individuals to listen.
7. Squelch the heckler with sarcasm or insult, especially if the audience is sympathetic with you, the speaker.[33]

The best general advice on handling heckling is to keep your cool and, if possible, your sense of humor. Remember that it is better to show good character in a shortened speech than to reveal bad character while fighting to be heard over hecklers.

Sometimes distractions result from your personal situation. Typical problems include losing your place, becoming excessively nervous, or lapsing into a troublesome cough. If the problem is at all persistent, briefly acknowledge it; then take corrective measures. Organize your notes, pause to reflect, or take a drink of water. Bring the speech rapidly to a close if temporary measures do not work.

At some point in your speaking career you will probably have to deal with the problem of someone's introducing your speech in an inept, inaccurate, or too-long-winded fashion. If this is the case, you might ignore

The question and answer period can enhance or undermine your prepared speech.

the introduction. Or you might find it necessary to correct significant errors tactfully and briefly, resisting the temptation to make a joke at the expense of the person who introduced you.

You will find that feedback represents both a key question and a key answer for your career as a public speaker. As a question, feedback is an attitude toward the audience that makes you want to (1) predict how listeners might respond and (2) keep tabs on how you are coming across. As an answer, feedback is a plan that invites you to adapt to the immediate speech situation, making your ideas stronger and your credibility more appealing.

The Question and Answer Period

For many speakers, especially for those giving business presentations, the speech is not over until the post-speech question and answer period is adjourned. The question period is a time when the effects of your prepared speech can be undermined or underscored. Not surprisingly, training in how to respond to questions is a major part of the public speaking workshops for executives.[34] What are your objectives and options in answering questions after the speech?

Reinforcement of the Speech

The purpose of the question and answer period is to enhance the original purpose of the speech itself—to inform, persuade, inspire, or entertain. So that your answers may best support your speech, keep in mind that a question period deserves advance practice—just like the speech itself. In rehearsing the question period, first predict those questions that either are likely or that are the toughest to answer. Questions tough to answer would include those that require complex answers, that are hostile, that are personally sensitive, that point to personal weak points, or that pertain to your reputation. After identifying the toughest questions, use research and practice to prepare your answers. Do necessary background research—be able to handle all the troublesome points. Practice your answers—write out some responses. Have a friend listen to you and give you advice.

Beyond strengthening your speech, the question and answer period should enhance your credibility. First, be sure to allow a brief break between your prepared speech and the question session. This will give persons who need to leave a convenient opportunity to do so. Second, when you begin your answers, avoid showing excessive hostility toward the questioner—no matter what the question. Avoid an *ad hominem* attack, one that dodges the issue by impugning the questioner or group he represents. Also, do not "tell off" your interrogator. Remember that people do not like mudslinging, and that you can often win greater credibility by praising rather than denigrating an opponent.[35] To keep your answer from becoming an attack, focus on what the question actually says, rather than your interpretation of the questioner's motives in asking it. Of course, you sometimes will feel it necessary to criticize the question, the questioner, or the implied tone of the question. In such a case, be sure to use good humor. This is how John F. Kennedy handled a hostile question asked during a news conference:

> *Question*: The Republican National Committee recently adopted a resolution saying you were pretty much of a failure. How do you feel about that?
> *President Kennedy*: I assume it passed unanimously.[36]

Finally, do not believe that your credibility inevitably suffers when you must beg off from a question. If you are not able to give a definite answer, admit your ignorance. No additional loss in credibility will result from acknowledging what will become obvious anyway. Perhaps you can explain why the information is unobtainable or difficult to obtain. Refer the audience to sources where the information may be found. Try to conclude by focusing on some part of your original speech that pertains to the question.

Options for Answering Questions

OK, you have prepared in advance for your question and answer session; now what are your options for handling a trial by inquiry? In general, be wary of hypothetical questions that can draw you into an endless trail of speculation. Answering with a declarative statement can help you avoid getting into a sticky "what if" situation. For instance:

Q: "If your plan fails, what then?"
A: "Once we adopt this plan, we're going to make it work."

In addition to hypothetical questions, you may also face requests to speculate on another person's motives. President Ronald Reagan once used this apt answer, refusing to speculate on why the Russians wanted arms talks. Responded Reagan, "You'll have to ask them what their reasons are for accepting."[37]

Be responsive in answering questions; but remember that you are free to structure your answer to help your cause. Here are some specific tips:

1. Repeat the question for the audience. Normally, you must repeat a question so that the entire audience will hear it clearly. It is OK to take fair advantage of this duty. Paraphrase the question in a way that facilitates your own purpose. If the "question" really is a statement or a series of questions, be sure to explain what approach you are taking in answering it. For instance, you might decide to answer only the first question in a series or to refute what is not a question but an opposing argument.
2. Use the following basic organization for your responses: (a) repeat the question, (b) give your response, and (c) state a conclusion that refers to a theme or important argument you made in your speech.
3. Do not allow yourself to be drawn into the questioner's slant on the subject. Questioners may try to put you into a dilemma by requesting a "yes" or "no" answer, asking if the answer is X or Y, or trying to force you to rank one idea as more important than another. Your main concern here should be to stay on your own ground. Make a statement that reflects the point you want to make:

   Q: "Do you support X or Y?"
   A: "I think our objective should be to [your summary of your position]."

4. Look at the questioner while he or she makes the inquiry. Direct eye contact not only helps you listen, it also aids you in understanding the questioner's motive. Direct attention also makes clear to the questioner that you *are* listening.

5. Look at the audience—not the questioner—when you are giving your response. Looking at the whole audience while responding helps to remind you that your interest is more to satisfy the whole group than the single questioner. By not looking at the questioner, it becomes more difficult for him or her to interrupt your answer.
6. Ask the questioner a question if this works to your advantage. You may need more clarification before responding, or responding with your own question might help you reveal the questioner's ignorance or bias. Be careful not to give the questioner an opportunity to deliver a speech.
7. Organize your answer to highlight the important ideas of your original speech. Some useful patterns are:

- Need-Solution: restate the objection raised by the question, then give your solution; or identify an important value and show how your position helps attain it.
- Agreement-Disagreement-Agreement: identify the aims or motives you hold in common with the questioner; then focus on disagreement (the objection stated in the question); then show that your answer meets the common aims.
- Refutation: answer by explicitly refuting the reasoning, evidence, or assumptions of the questioner.
- Elimination of Alternatives: answer by sketching out a small number of alternatives and show why only one (your position) is acceptable.

Your objective for the question and answer session is to advance your thesis and credibility. However, keep in mind that the audience expects you to be *responsive.* Audiences will notice if you skirt the substance of a question. A clear answer to a tough question can positively enhance your credibility.[38] The objective of clarity does not mean to emphasize views that the audience may find disagreeable. Naturally, you will want to phrase your answer strategically, emphasizing what listeners will find positive in your ideas.[39] In general, responsiveness is a matter of perception. Sometimes hearers will accept a vague message because they read an agreeable answer into it.[40] However, if you are speaking during an extended debate, the protection offered by vague answers may be short-lived, since opponents can point out the evasions. For example, one economist complained that Ronald Reagan answered between zero and three of the six questions asked by reporters during a political debate with Representative John Anderson.[41]

Good skills in answering questions can be important if you are seeking rhetorical competence on a career-long basis. Keep in mind the advice on how to answer questions. You may expect to lose credibility when you refuse to answer questions, ridicule and dismiss questions, or respond evasively.[42]

When you present a speech to a real audience, you bring together all your knowledge, attitudes, and skills of speechmaking. Your goal is to transform the speech from a plan drawn on paper to a living moment of real communication. Once you have prepared your outline, you must choose one of the four modes of presentation. Usually you will settle on the extemporaneous method, sometimes the impromptu or manuscript modes, but usually not the method of memorization. Although verbatim memorization of words is not the route to rhetorical success, memory work is an asset to your extemporaneous delivery. Use picturing, association, sounds, repetition, and visual aids to remember your key ideas and phrases. If you are like most speakers, you will combine memory work with brief written notes. This approach allows you maximum flexibility to respond to audience feedback or to unexpected events. Your skill in adapting to the unpredictable also will serve you well during the question and answer period that follows many speeches. You want to answer responsively, but your replies also should be strategic, simultaneously boosting your credibility and reinforcing points developed in your speech.

Concepts for Review

Can you summarize the meaning of these terms or expressions? How does each relate to speechmaking?

extemporaneous speech
manuscript speech
impromptu speech
enumerate-elaborate-summarize
memorized speech
long-term memory
mental pictures
pictograph
peg system
association
sound and memory
repetition
visual aids and memory
brief and simple notes
feedback
favorable feedback
unfavorable feedback
anticipate feedback
delete, add, rearrange
heckling
answer to build credibility
answer to reinforce speech

Things to Try

1. Trade the notes for your most recent in-class speech with a classmate. Review your partner's notes. Circle words that could be eliminated while still keeping the notes useful as an aid to the memory.

2. Work to boil down your notes for the next speech. Start with a sentence outline of your speech. Practice delivering the speech, each time crossing out words in your notes that you no longer need. Try to reduce your notes to a few key words or phrases.
3. Try using the no-notes method once or twice as you practice your next speech. Construct a vivid pictograph symbol for your introduction, for each main idea in the speech body, and for your conclusion. Use the Roman method of mentally placing each pictograph in a familiar location, such as the order of rooms in a familiar building. Practice giving the speech with only your mental notes. Do you think you would be confident enough to try this method in class?
4. During the next session of speeches, sit in a seat that allows you to observe the class. Review the various signs of favorable and unfavorable feedback. During one speech, carefully watch for the flow of feedback from audience members. Use the first twenty seconds of the speech as a benchmark. Note when feedback becomes less favorable and more favorable. Try to connect the feedback to what the speaker is saying and doing.

Endnotes

1. *Times Tribune* (Palo Alto Edition), 8 September 1988, A11.
2. Russel Windes Jr. and James A. Robinson, "Public Address in the Career of Adlai E. Stevenson," *Quarterly Journal of Speech 42* (1956): 230.
3. Cole S. Brembeck, "Harry Truman at the Whistle Stops," *Quarterly Journal of Speech 38* (1952): 42–50.
4. Lionel Crocker, "Henry Ward Beecher," *A History and Criticism of American Public Address,* ed. W. N. Brigance, 2 vols. (New York: Russell & Russell, 1943), 1:279.
5. *Newsweek,* 15 December 1980, 84. Herbert Hildebrant and Walter W. Stevens, "Manuscript and Extemporaneous Delivery in Communicating Information," *Speech Monographs 30* (1963): 369–372, found that some speakers are better able to convey information with the manuscript method while others are better served with extemporaneous delivery.
6. *Courier-Journal* (Louisville), 21 November 1985, A4.
7. Laura Crowell, "Word Changes Introduced *Ad Libitum* in Five Speeches by Franklin Delano Roosevelt," *Speech Monographs 25* (1958): 229–242 and Russel Windes, Jr., "A Study of Effective and Ineffective Presidential Campaign Speaking," *Speech Monographs 28* (1961): 48.
8. *Rhetoric,* III. 13. 1414a.

9. See R. A. Tallcott, "Speech Training through Acting, Reading, and Declamation," *Quarterly Journal of Speech Education 11* (1925): 8–17 and J. Garber Drushal, "An Objective Analysis of Two Techniques of Teaching Delivery in Public Speaking," *Quarterly Journal of Speech 25* (1939): 561–569.
10. See Phillip K. Tompkins and Wilmer A. Linkugel, "Speech in the Senate," *Today's Speech 7,* No. 1 (1959): 30–32; Tompkins and Edward J. Pappas, "Speech in the Senate '65," *Today's Speech 15,* No. 2 (1967): 3–4, 6; Eugene E. White and Clair R. Henderlider, "What Harry S. Truman Told Us about His Speaking," *Quarterly Journal of Speech 40* (1954): 41.
11. *Institutio Oratoria,* XI. 2. 3.
12. Harry Lorayne, *How to Develop a Super-Power Memory* (New York: Frederick Fell, 1957), 39.
13. Lydel Sims, "How Mark Twain Solved the Speechmaker's Dilemma," *TWA Ambassador,* August 1976, 16, 32 and Herbert E. Meyer, "A $900 Lesson in Podium Power," *Fortune,* August 1977, 196–204.
14. See Quintilian, *Institutio Oratoria,* XI. 2. 19–22 and Cicero, *De Oratore,* II. 88.
15. George A. Miller, "The Magical Number Seven, Plus or Minus Two," *Psychological Review 63* (1956): 81–97 and Lorayne, *Memory,* 72–80.
16. Quintilian, *Institutio Oratoria,* XI. 2. 33 and Ray E. Collins, "A Study of Oral and Silent Reading Comprehension," *Western Speech 28* (1964): 217–221.
17. Lloyd R. Peterson, "Short Term Memory," *Scientific American 215* (July 1966): 90–95.
18. B. F. Skinner, *Beyond Freedom and Dignity* (New York: Bantam/Vintage, 1971), 46.
19. Joe Ayres, "Observers' Judgments of Audience Members' Attitudes," *Western Speech 39* (1975): 40–50.
20. See Milton Dickens and David H. Krueger, "Speakers' Accuracy in Identifying Immediate Audience Responses during a Speech," *Speech Teacher 18* (1969): 303–307; C. Franklin Karns, "Speaker Behavior to Nonverbal Aversive Stimuli from the Audience," *Speech Monographs 36* (1969): 126–137; David A. Williams and Dennis C. Alexander, "Effects of Audience Responses on the Performances of Oral Interpreters," *Western Speech 37* (1973): 273–280; James E. Sayer, "Debaters' Perception of Nonverbal Stimuli," *Western Speech 38* (1974): 2–6.
21. See Elwood A. Kretsinger, "An Experimental Study of Gross Bodily Movement as an Index to Audience Interest," *Speech Monographs 19* (1952): 244–248; Jon A. Blubaugh, "Effects of Positive and Negative Audience Feedback on Selected Variables of Speech Behavior," *Speech Monographs 36* (1969): 131–137; James C. Gardiner, "The Effects of Expected and Perceived Receiver Response on Source Attitudes," *Journal of Communication 22* (1972): 289–299; Ronald Bassett, *et al.,* "The Effects of Positive and Negative Audience Responses on the Autonomic Arousal of Student Speakers," *Southern Speech Communication Journal 38* (1973):

255–261; Williams & Alexander, "Audience Responses"; Steven C. Rhodes and Kenneth D. Frandsen, "Some Effects of Instruction in Feedback Utilization on the Fluency of College Students' Speech," *Speech Monographs 42* (1975): 83–89.

22. James W. Welke, "The Effects of Intensional and Extensional Audiences on Communicator Anxiety," *Central States Speech Journal 19* (1968): 14–17.

23. Bassett, *et al.,* "Positive and Negative Audience Responses"; Williams & Alexander, "Audience Responses"; John W. Vlandis, "Variation in the Verbal Behavior of a Speaker as a Function of Varied Reinforcing Conditions," *Speech Monographs 31* (1964): 116–119; Gardiner, "Expected and Perceived Response"; Gerald R. Miller, "Variations in the Verbal Behavior of a Second Speaker as a Function of Varying Audience Responses," *Speech Monographs 31* (1964): 109–115; Blubaugh, "Audience Feedback."

24. Karns, "Nonverbal Aversive Stimuli."

25. Rhodes & Frandsen, "Feedback Utilization."

26. Miller, "Verbal Behavior of Speaker."

27. Michael D. Hazen and Sara B. Kiesler, "Communication Strategies Affected by Audience Opposition, Feedback and Persuasibility," *Speech Monographs 42* (1975): 56–68.

28. Karl R. Wallace, "Booker T. Washington," *A History and Criticism of American Public Address,* 1:418–419.

29. William T. Foster, "Random Notes on Public Speaking," *Quarterly Journal of Speech 33* (1947): 140.

30. Robert G. Gunderson, "Webster in Linsey-Woolsey," *Quarterly Journal of Speech 37* (1951): 29.

31. *Courier-Journal* (Louisville), 21 September 1984, A7.

32. P. Dale Ware and Raymond K. Tucker, "Heckling as Distraction: An Experimental Study of Its Effect on Source Credibility," *Speech Monographs 41* (1974): 185–188 and Michael J. Beatty and Michael W. Kruger, "The Effects of Heckling on Speaker Credibility and Attitude Change," *Communication Quarterly 26,* No. 2 (1978): 46–50.

33. See Arthur A. Eisenstadt, "Speech Blocks—How to Deal with Them," *Today's Speech 6,* No. 3 (1958): 13–15.

34. See Robert Haakenson, "Training for an Industrial Speakers Bureau," *Today's Speech 13,* No. 1 (1965): 20–22; Mark Knapp, "Public Speaking Training Programs in American Business and Industrial Organizations," *Speech Teacher 18* (1969): 129–134; Meyer, "Podium Power," 196–204.

35. Judee K. Burgoon, Miriam Wilkinson, and Ralph Partridge, "The Relative Effectiveness of Praise and Derogation as Persuasion Strategies," *Journal of the American Forensic Association 16* (1979): 10–20.

36. Bill Adler (ed.), *The Kennedy Wit* (New York: Citadel, 1964), 81.

37. *San Francisco Chronicle,* 10 November 1986, 25.

38. M. Lee Williams and Blaine Goss, "Equivocation: Character Insurance," *Human Communication Research 1* (1975): 265–270 and C. Jack Orr and Karen E. Burkins, "The Endorsement of Evasive Leaders: An Exploratory Study," *Central States Speech Journal 27* (1976): 230–239.

39. Blaine Goss and Lee Williams, "The Effects of Equivocation on Perceived Source Credibility," *Central States Speech Journal 24* (1973), 162–167 and Williams & Goss, "Character Insurance."
40. M. Lee Williams, "The Effect of Deliberate Vagueness on Receiver Recall and Agreement," *Central States Speech Journal 31* (1980): 30–41 and Orr & Burkins, "Evasive Leaders."
41. *Newsweek,* 6 October 1980, 42.
42. J. Donald Ragsdale and Alan Mikels, "Effects of Question Periods on a Speaker's Credibility with a Television Audience," *Southern Speech Communication Journal 40* (1975): 302–312.

Part

V

Kinds of Speeches

Chapter

13

The Informative Speech

Outline

- "MORTE ALLA FRANCIA ITALIA ANELO. It's not a greeting, it's a battle cry."
- "On November 10 we learned that Ohio State University is to be subjected to another state budget cut, effective December 15. This cut of three percent amounts to $5.4 million."

Two speakers begin their informative talks. In the first excerpt, a student speaker uses a striking sentence to begin an explanation of the Mafia. The second excerpt, by a university president, opens in the manner of a news story with the journalists' *topoi* of who, when, and what. From the beginning, each speaker not only conveys information, but also makes sure that the data are vital, important, even striking to the audience.

In chapter 13 we are concerned with the special features of informative speaking. We begin by reviewing what it means to enter a speech situation with the aim of presenting information. Our interest then shifts from informative speaking in general to several specific how-to's. To implement your informative purpose, you have available various basic approaches, organizational patterns, and useful tips.

Speaking to Inform

Can you summarize all your rights under your dorm or apartment contract? Do you know exactly what your auto insurance covers—and does not cover? Can you explain all the deductions on your paycheck? Are these unfair questions? Perhaps; but these probes show how we can always learn more details about otherwise familiar ground. Informative speaking is socially important because people rarely understand everything they need to know about daily life.

Before you research and organize your informative speech, be sure that you understand the basic ingredients of giving new data to listeners. Begin your work by considering (1) your own material, (2) what listeners already know, (3) how you can motivate listening, and (4) your relationship with the audience.

Knowledge of Your Material

If you cannot explain something in clear terms, then you probably do not fully understand the topic yourself. To be effective as an informative speaker, you need to have such a command of the material that you can make things clear even to the complete novice. Full understanding of the speech subject comes only through careful personal attention to the material. We live in an era when high officials often hire ghostwriters, and books by celebrities frequently carry the notice "as told to." Wealthy celebrities may have resources to escape the ordinary chores of writing and speaking, but most students are not members of the rhetorical leisure class. Furthermore, many who today use ghostwriters once advanced themselves through personal attention to details. Lee Iacocca, for instance, spent one of his first days at Ford hunched over a drafting board preparing a picture of a clutch spring. We should not let today's era of ghostwritten books and speeches blind us to the connection between personal effort and successful informative speaking.

Adlai Stevenson, Illinois governor and twice Democratic nominee for president, advised people to prepare their own speeches. Stevenson's own experience taught him that only by personally researching and organizing ideas could he master them. Stevenson believed in speechmaking as a personal "learning and synthesizing process."[1]

Can audiences tell when a speaker doesn't know the material? You bet, especially when listeners doubt what they are hearing. Bruce Carnes, Deputy Under Secretary of Education, discovered this fact in March 1988 when speaking to a group of officials from black colleges. Carnes's purpose was to explain the Education Department's statistics on student loan defaults. The college audience was already suspicious of Carnes because they believed Federal policies to reduce defaults would weigh most heavily on black colleges. When Carnes had trouble presenting the Education Department's data, listeners interrupted him. Sarcastic remarks followed Carnes' admission that he had gotten some of the figures wrong.[2]

Anyone can have trouble explaining material in a clear fashion. Why not reduce this problem by pre-testing your knowledge of the material? Knowledge always is a matter of degree. On one level, you may understand a subject to the extent that you feel comfortable talking about it. A more demanding level of knowledge is the ability to explain something to people who already have a basic understanding of the topic. Edgar Dale, well-known professor of education, once coined the expression "clear only if already known" to designate this second plateau of informative speaking. Unfortunately, neither of these first two levels of knowledge guarantees that you can explain things to a group of complete beginners. You need to understand your subject so well that you *cannot be misunderstood* even by novices.

Listeners' Knowledge

The more you know your material, the better are your chances for giving clear explanations. Still, your informative speaking will be influenced by the capacity of listeners to understand. This principle may be seen in one version of a story about St. Thomas Aquinas, the medieval theologian. The story has Aquinas meeting a little child on the beach and watching the child try to shovel all the beach's sand into his pail. When Aquinas remarks that so much sand could never fit into such a small pail, the child replies that neither would Thomas understand all the mysteries of God.

Knowing the capacity of your audience is important. Before putting together your informative speech, identify and/or predict what listeners initially know about the topic. Use what the audience already knows as a foundation for bridging gaps in their understanding.

One student speaker who planned a talk about post-college careers followed this advice and made predictions about what his listeners already knew. The speaker predicted that "the majority of people in the class are aware of the abundance of people out of work—and some of those being degree holders." The speaker believed that he could build his informative speech around what listeners already knew. The speaker organized his talk around the main idea that "degree holding people will have a better chance of employment if they are willing to, at times, take jobs not directly in line with their degree."

Box 13.1

Use a Mini-Poll to Find What Listeners Know

In preparing for my speech, I gave the class a brief two-question survey. The questions were: (1) What does ozone do in the upper atmosphere that is helpful to humans and most other living creatures? and (2) What is the ozone hole over the Antarctic? Two of the people responding (out of a total of 15) did not know the answer to the second question, but did correctly answer the first question. For these people I will have to give a brief, concise overview of what the problem is.

From a preparation report by a public speaking student, fall 1988.

Another student speaker similarly considered her audience in preparing to explain biorhythms. The speaker believed that "the audience will have little knowledge about the topic." This observation gave her clues to organizing her explanation. "To solve this problem. . .I am going to start with the discovery of biorhythms and then lead into how the theory is used and practiced in our world today."

Motivation of Listening

The more your audience is interested in what you say, the more they will hear and understand. As an informative speaker, you always run the risk of sounding *pedantic.* The pedantic speaker assumes that everyone else in the room shares his or her interest in the topic. An almost sure sign of pedantic thinking is listing a host of reasons why listeners "should be" interested in your topic. *Should be* and *are* represent two different kinds of reality. All of us have things pending that we should do right now, but that we will do only later—if ever. If you have taken on the attitude of rhetorical competence, you will avoid wishfully assuming that listeners are interested in your topic. You will base your speechmaking on predictions about what actually is or realistically might be. You will look for realistic ways to adjust ideas to the people receiving them.

One student speaker, who planned an informative talk on smoking, was realistic in recognizing that "most people have heard these facts and have become bored with them." To maximize the interest value of her presentation, she planned to focus exclusively on the less understood subject of passive smoking. The speaker believed that since everyone is affected by second-hand cigarette smoke, the subject would have greater interest value. This speaker was on solid ground in believing that *personal relevance* is an important factor in what people remember. In one research study, for instance, receivers better remembered a message on civil defense if this particular topic was important to them.[3]

Box 13.2

Make Facts Come Alive

Deliver your data with vitality. Robert M. La Follette, the Wisconsin governor, senator, and Progressive Party candidate for president, was known for his ability to make figures come alive. Campaigning for railroad legislation in 1903, La Follette did not merely present net statistics on the burden of railroad rates. The governor related the figures to the farmers who stood in front of him. La Follette told them that unregulated freight rates cost each of them 38 cents per acre. When preparing your informative speeches, try to think like La Follette.

Source: Carroll P. Lahman, "Robert M. La Follette, *A History and Criticism of American Public Address,* ed. W. N. Brigance, 2 vols., (New York: Russell & Russell, 1943), 2:954.

Further research supports the idea that motivation is a key to informative speaking. Listeners remember more about a speech when they believe that the content will be *personally useful.* If you are like most people, you pay greater attention when you expect an immediate quiz on course material. Research shows that when people know they are going to be tested for effective listening, they apply their full mental potential to the task of remembering.[4] Similarly, when students are promised extra class credit for correct answers, they recall more information from a speech. In one study, the lure of extra credit boosted listening even when the rate of speaking was doubled from 140 to 280 words per minute.[5]

Your Relationship With Listeners

We observed that a hallmark of the rhetorically competent speaker was the effort to act as adviser to the audience. Sometimes informative speakers believe they can escape the ethical demand to be a good adviser since they are "only giving information." Remember, however, that when you inform people, you are also changing their outlook on life. For instance, research shows that people become more favorable to new terms merely by repeatedly seeing them. Researchers prepared a list of meaningless terms that included "The Zabulon Proposal," the "Dilikli Theory," and "The Representative from Lokanta." Groups of students saw these terms on slides projected for two seconds. The students saw the terms from 1 to 25 times, and, as a control, some did not see the terms in advance of rating them as good or bad. Results showed that the greater the exposure to the terms, the more that students expressed a favorable rating of the terms. The researchers called this phenomenon, "persuasion via mere exposure."[6]

Furthermore, we have direct evidence that an informative speech can change attitudes. Researchers prepared a speech on medical care for the elderly that was consistently rated as informative by experts in public speaking. The researchers found that this informative talk had the effect of making listeners significantly more favorable to the idea that the elderly required a special program of medical care. At the same time, the speech caused listeners to take positions on how medical care should be provided to the elderly.[7] The point is that you should remember your responsibilities as an adviser when you prepare your informative speeches.

In addition to remembering your role as adviser, work to identify every possible connection you share with your listeners. The more you are able to place yourself in the audience's world, the greater you will succeed in getting across information. Experimental research shows that when two persons have similar backgrounds, the two are more successful in giving clues and guessing answers in a password game. In another study, members of the same social group (in this case, clergymen) were better able to communicate information with fellow ministers than with laypersons. The same may be observed in negotiations between plains Indians and United States government officials during the nineteenth century. Indian speakers focused on establishing trade with whites, while the United States Army's representatives emphasized an end to shooting. The different viewpoints of the two groups precluded achieving either clear communication or successful treaties.[8] Both experimental research and historical examples show the need for you to keep in mind your connections with the audience while you prepare your informative speeches.

Do not overlook your need to master the basics of informative speaking. To prepare and deliver an informative talk effectively, you should know your material and understand what receivers already know. You should also start with the three attitudes of wanting to motivate listening, wanting to establish an advisory relationship, and wanting to enter the mental world of listeners.

Approaches to Presenting Information

What are your general strategic options for informative speaking? Robert Jeffrey and Owen Peterson summarize the work of the informative speaker as defining, narrating, explaining, demonstrating, and analyzing.[9] This roster represents a good starting point.

Defining

To define is to lay out the meaning or essential nature of a thing or idea. One student speaker began her talk with this definition: "Now, *Webster's New World Dictionary** defines dust as any finely powdered matter. Scientists who study dust define it more specifically as any particulate matter over one micron in size."[10] You can even use a definition to make a point humorously, as when former Senator Sam Ervin introduced Ronald Reagan: "I will introduce him as a politician rather than a statesman because they tell me the statesman is a dead politician and I want Governor Reagan to be around a long, long time" (full text in chapter 15).

You have available several options for using definitions. You may classify according to characteristics, give examples, make comparisons, give historical background, and state an operational principle.

Box 13.3

Use a Definition to Clarify

When I was preparing for my speech on animation, I was assuming that the audience didn't know much on my topic. I decided to give a definition of animation and how animation differs from live-action films. . . .I tried not to use extremely technical terms so I wouldn't bore the audience.

From a preparation report by a public speaking student, fall 1988.

Classification

Logicians and dictionaries use the method of classification when they give us a definition that places something in a class and then specifies particular characteristics of the thing being defined. For instance:

> A horse is an animal that stands on four legs, is about six feet tall at the shoulders, has a flowing mane and tail, and has been domesticated for use in carrying loads and for racing.

The first part of this definition places the horse in the category of animals. The remainder of the definition provides characteristics that distinguish the horse from other animals.

Examples

When you use the method of examples, you identify instances or representative cases of something. In one of the speeches reprinted in this chapter, Harold L. Enarson takes up definition by example, identifying specific items that contribute to quality in a university. Enarson begins his point by asking "what things do make a difference in the quality of this University?" He then lists five examples of quality, including top-notch faculty, recreation facilities, keeping the library and labs up-to-date, and making cultural events available to students.

Comparison

You may use similarities and differences as a basis for definition. Jacquelyn Flanigan uses this method when she notes the irony that the Mafia share many values generally held by Americans. "In summary, I have emphasized values that encompass the life of a Mafioso. We can see that these values are those of the traditional American value system, are based on needs we *all* share as human beings."

Harold L. Enarson defines by stressing dissimilarities when he makes the point that "a university is not a factory." Enarson says that the factory analogy is a bogus analogy that misleads state officials into thinking that university "production" can easily be scaled back.

Historical background

In using the historical approach to defining key concepts, you may look at the origins of a word. For instance, the term "propaganda" came into use as an expression for the missionary work of the Roman Catholic Church. The term was first used in connection with the *Congregatio de propaganda fide,* or College for the propagation of the faith, founded in 1622 to oversee the spread of the Catholic denomination.[11]

A second way to define things historically is to review general background. In this way, Jacquelyn Flanigan defines Mafia by tracing the group's origins to historical experiences of Italians and Italian immigrants in the United States. Definitions grounded in history can be useful, not only in amplifying ideas, but in giving legitimacy to them. Winston Churchill was most effective in defining contemporary events through the lens of history. Churchill likened the threat of Hitler to Napoleon's earlier attempts at invasion. He defined the heroic dimensions of the evacuation of British troops from France in 1940 by comparing the conduct of the soldiers to the Charge of the Light Brigade.[12]

Operational definition

An operational definition specifies the set of actions, or operations, necessary to produce something. If you were to say that happiness is sitting in front of a warm fire on a cold winter's night, you would be giving an operational view of the word. Douglas MacArthur gives operational definitions of duty, honor, and country by describing specific attitudes and actions that these words imply. "They build your basic character, they mold you for your future roles as the custodians of the nation's defense. . . ."

Social science research represents probably the most prominent context for operational definitions. Operational definitions are basic to statistical-experimental studies of speech comprehension. For instance, a researcher might set a specific score on a listening test as an operational definition of good listening.

Narrating

Informative speaking often requires us to relate events, describe what has happened, or tell stories. These actions are part of the narrative element of speaking. Harold Enarson's speech on the Ohio State University budget illustrates narration as a chronicling of events. Following the method of a

Table 13.1 Defining

Method	How to use it
Classifying	Put something into a general category and then give particular characteristics.
Examples	Identify representative instances or essential components.
Comparison	List similarities and differences.
Historical Background	Review the origins of a word or put a concept into a general historical situation.
Operational Definition	Specify the actions (operations) necessary to produce something.

news story, Enarson begins his speech by describing four years' worth of cuts in appropriations. The focus is on factual information presented in a plain, chronological order.

Narration need not always be factual description. Speakers often use anecdotes as narrative material. Edward Everett, the nineteenth century's favorite ceremonial speaker, was frequently praised for his ability to portray historical events vividly. Everett often spoke on themes dealing with the American Revolution. He was particularly known for his effective narrations of the incidents leading up to the Declaration of Independence. In addition, Everett developed a habit of sprinkling into his addresses various episodes of local history that would be especially familiar and flattering to particular audiences.[13]

Narrative story-telling allows you both to clarify and to reduce hostility. Story-telling *clarifies* by allowing you to portray an unfamiliar situation in terms of something familiar. For instance, in the 1949 spy trial of Alger Hiss (former State Department official), the prosecuting attorney used an anecdote to argue Hiss' guilt. According to the prosecutor, Hiss passed secret State Department data to a Soviet agent as evidenced by document summaries written in Hiss' hand or typed on his machine. The prosecutor's narration likened Hiss and his document summaries to a boy accused of sneaking sweets: "Admitted you did not see him . . . [but] normal, everyday intelligence . . . tells you that the boy is lying. Why? Why, there is the jam on his face."[14]

Story-telling not only clarifies, but also helps you *reduce hostility* to ideas. Booker T. Washington, the black educator, made a habit of searching the audience for unfriendly faces. He found that the best method to thaw out the hostile listener was to tell a story. For instance, Washington liked to make the point that blacks had a special mission in American life, since they were the only group that came over to America by "special invitation." In contrast, Washington observed, whites took their place in America over the active protests of the original inhabitants.[15]

Narration is particularly useful for your informative speeches because it allows you to make a point without stressing a persuasive purpose. Narration is different from hard-and-fast proof because narration soft peddles arguments. The difference between proof and narration may be seen in a change in the format of American sermons. Before the Civil War, American preachers tended to use an argumentative approach that found them working to prove the truth of doctrines. Toward the latter part of the nineteenth century, a new style of preaching- through-illustration took hold in which preachers narrated instances of appropriate belief and conduct. Rather than make a case for new modes of thought and action, preachers could present the point in a more pleasing fashion by illustrations that connected accepted ideas to new ways of living.[16]

Explaining

Informative speaking is a natural by-product of an age of science and engineering. With the emergence of mass industrial economies has come an increase in the amount of available information. Today's specialization creates a place for the expert who enlightens nonspecialists in matters of finance, health, consumer purchases, and even movie choices.

The ability to explain well is *not* a natural talent akin to the automatic ability of many mammals to swim. Even when an expert *is* an expert, clarity of explanation does not follow inevitably. After a career of teaching public speaking to engineering students, Thomas Sawyer concluded that expert knowledge sometimes works against clear explanation. Sawyer liked to challenge senior engineering students to explain a twin-turbine transmission. After several speeches on the subject—complete with diagrams—Sawyer confessed that "I still don't understand it, and neither do the engineers, even faculty members."[17] Special knowledge does not necessarily bring special articulateness.

To gain greater skill in informative speaking, take advantage of three useful ways to present explanation: topical, historical, and process-oriented. Harold Enarson takes the *topical* approach when he relates steps he has taken to cut the Ohio State University budget. He cites the new hiring freeze, curtailment of purchases, and spending limits. He then lists several steps that might be necessary if financial deterioration continued, including selling university facilities and curtailing student activities.

An instance of explanation by means of *history* may be observed in Jacquelyn Flanigan's treatment of the origins of the Mafia. She explains the traditional role of the Don in Italy. Continuing, she shows how this tradition shifted to the United States when the close-knit Italian immigrant community relied on powerful kinsmen to smooth the harsh realities of urban America.

The *process-oriented* approach to explaining will serve on occasions when you must clarify how something functions. In such a case, one teacher recommended that a technical explanation should "start with a simplified statement of the principles or functions of the device." Thus, to explain the refracting telescope, you might begin with the idea that the device works by means of lenses that bend rays of light. Secondly, a technical explanation works best when given in a logical sequence supplemented with simple analogies. To explain a torque converter, you might set up the situation of "two electric fans facing each other: turn on one, and the air it pushes out will spin the other fan; the torque converter simply uses oil, rather than air."[18]

Demonstrating

To inform by demonstrating is to combine verbal explanation with a visual presentation. Visual demonstration, described earlier in chapter 7, works well as a supplement to your explanations in words.

Look for places in your informative speeches where visual support might help. For instance, in a talk on cameras or nuclear power plants, a diagram would help you get listeners to visualize a whole process. Demonstration may also work for topics having no apparent need of visual support. Planning a talk on career opportunities for college graduates, a student speaker found several possible uses of visual demonstration:

- Diagram: "maybe a flowchart of entry into the job market."
- Graph: "to show the population growth, number in the work force, change in blue and white collar workers, inflation, and the labor force."
- Map: "one of the United States showing movement of population during the next ten years."
- Overhead projector: "to use different colors to illustrate differences in year groups (ten years each, 70s, 80s, 90s)."
- Slides: "slides of labor statistics, or pictures of working people, maybe one of future cities."
- An object: "a black box, or a maze; a cap and gown; or a picture of a computer or space craft to depict the future; or a crystal ball."
- Printed handout: "possibly a pamphlet on career decision-making or careers that are available, or data on the economy in this area."

Naturally, this student used only one or two of these resources in his speech. However, the student's survey shows an essential attitude of rhetorical competence. He looked for every possible way of making his subject comprehensible, important, and interesting to his audience.

Visual demonstration supplements oral explanation.

Do visuals really help explanation? Common sense and the experience of speakers suggest that they do. Furthermore, research (cited in chapter 7) shows that visual aids generally boost comprehension of information and the credibility of speakers. Also, the research on "persuasion via mere exposure," mentioned earlier, suggests that you might profitably use slides or charts to show unfamiliar technical terms or jargon.

Analyzing

When we analyze, we apply a standard of judgment. A familiar instance of informing by analyzing occurs whenever you observe and rate speeches given in your public speaking class. You better understand a speech by assessing it according to the criteria of validity, ethics, quality, truth, and effectiveness.

Many features of society, such as morals, business, politics, and religion, are too complex simply to be described. Analysis of these topics—breaking them up and examining smaller elements—is necessary. To discuss religion, for instance, you might need to consider different religious organizations and doctrines as well as the ever-present issue of separation of church and state. The basic problem here is to keep an informative tone while taking apart complicated social institutions and issues. Analysis of religion or business without treading on deeply-felt values is difficult. The informative speaker necessarily intrudes on sensitive feelings.

A second problem of analytic speaking relates to your goals as a speaker. Analyzing ordinarily requires applying a framework to a complex topic, as when Jacquelyn Flanigan compares the values of Mafia members to those held by other Americans. You must decide whether you want listeners to retain the framework or the topic—or both. In the case of Jacquelyn's speech, to what extent should listeners take away a memory of the Mafia (the topic) or remember the idea of human values (the framework of analysis)?

If your goal is to impart understanding solely about a topic, such as the Mafia, then you must be sure that your analytic framework does not distract from the subject. On the other hand, you might apply a framework to a topic chiefly to illustrate the framework. The difficulty in explaining an analytic framework is shown in a study of techniques for teaching propaganda analysis. Researchers wondered if a sixty-minute lecture on detecting propaganda would immunize students against later messages that contained fallacious arguments. Results showed that an audience of students could learn details of a propaganda analysis framework. However, despite learning about the framework, students still could be tricked by weak arguments in later propagandistic messages.[19]

When seeking to inform, your basic options are to define, narrate, explain, demonstrate, and analyze. Probably you will follow the example of the speakers cited in this text and combine several methods to get across your information.

Organizing the Informative Speech

As with all speeches, the informative speech is built around an outline consisting of major points and subpoints. Beyond these two provisos, we may identify two specific helps to organizing the informative talk. First are five organizational patterns especially suited to conveying information. Second are several tips that flow from research on how to make ideas memorable.

Message-Centered Organizational Patterns

Experienced speakers sometimes organize speech materials seemingly without step-by-step planning. United States Senator Wayne Morse once reported that he was not "conscious of following any pattern or sequence of events in the body of my speeches."[20] The *intuitive approach* to organization may work for veteran speakers who have internalized the various patterns of arrangement. However, as a student of public speaking, you will want to review systematically those organizational patterns that are specially suited for giving information.

To organize the body of your informative speeches, turn to each of these five specialized patterns: topical, chronological, spatial, causal, and systemic patterns of organization. These five patterns allow you to arrange material according to *what needs to be said about the subject.* For this reason, these patterns may be called the *message-centered* ways of organizing a speech.

Topical pattern

The topical pattern is *the* standard way of organizing a speech. When you use the topical pattern, you discover what naturally seems to demand attention; you then pattern the speech around these points. This approach is the heart of the classical method, and Harry S. Truman relied on this advice. Truman believed that "an audience approves of Cicero's method, which was to state his case and then prove it." Truman read Cicero's speeches in the original Latin to study this Roman orator's methods.[21]

In using the topical method, begin by surveying your subject. Out of your research will fall three, four, or five key topics. These key points become the major ideas of the body of your speech, and you find appropriate subpoints for each. This approach has you divide the content of your topic into its natural constituent parts. For instance, Jacquelyn Flanigan begins the body of her informative speech by enumerating values traditionally held by Americans. She then shows the ironic connection between Mafia and customary American values. The body of her speech is organized into three major points.

I. Americans traditionally hold several important values— family, freedom, liberty, and church.
II. The Mafia value system was developed in Italy and was refined with Italian immigration to the United States.
   A. The Mafia originated in Italy.
   B. The Don functioned as a guardian in Italian immigrant communities in America.
III. The Mafia value system focuses on security, family, and religion.
   A. The vow of silence is the root of security and freedom.
   B. Mafia members have strong family bonds.
   C. Mafia members are devout Roman Catholics.

The topical method often unfolds through a process of trial and error. You first identify key points that must be communicated. Then you tinker with an outline to find how these points may best be coordinated.

Chronological pattern

Frequently you will find that information can best be presented according to time. A student speaking on the topic of smoking decided that her best option for getting across data was to give a chronology of research on smoking. The body of her speech presented five major ideas (subpoints omitted):

I. In 1972 it was established that smoking by expectant mothers is harmful to their unborn children.
II. In 1974 it was established that children passively exposed to smoke are less healthy than children who are not exposed.
III. In 1980 it was determined that smoke is harmful to a smoker's co-workers if they are exposed on a regular basis and are nonsmokers.
IV. In 1981 it was determined that regular exposure to smoke is harmful to a nonsmoking spouse.
V. Just recently passive smoking was found to aggravate symptoms in patients who already have some diseases.

You may use time as an organizing principle not only for your major ideas but also for your subpoints. In major point II of Jack Dodds's speech on Agent Orange (chapter 2), we find him describing successive developments in the controversy over its health effects. First, veterans filed claims with the Veterans Administration. Later, the VA tests showed the presence of dioxin in veterans. Then, Agent Orange International filed suit against the manufacturers, and the VA called for more tests.

Spatial pattern

Along with time, space is one of the major ways that people organize their thinking. Matters of geography will serve you as a natural method for arranging ideas.

Travelogues and vacation slide shows often rely on the ability of listeners to visualize geographic space. A report of a student's study tour might present main ideas in the order of travel:

I. We started in Chicago with orientation and classes.
II. Our flight took us to London where we spent four days.
III. We took a side trip to Norwich, England.
IV. We traveled to Paris via ship-train.

Causal pattern

Connections of cause are basic to human perception. Even animals are sensitive to causal relationships. According to the old saying, if a cat touches a hot stove with its paw, it won't touch a cold one either.

It is easy to see how you might use causal relationships to arrange your material. For instance, you might start a speech on national economic policies by treating the policies as causes. Then you would explain present economic conditions as effects of the policies. Turning things around, it would also be possible for you to treat economic conditions as causes that required particular economic policies (effects).

A student speaker used the causal approach in an informative talk on the temporomandibular joint (TMJ) in the human jaw. She began with symptoms (effects) and then moved to causes.

I. Several symptoms indicate the Ernest Syndrome, that is, imbalance in the TMJ.
II. There are three common causes of the imbalance.
III. Treatments for the imbalance include several options and steps.

This particular outline also shows how organizational patterns sometimes overlap. We could consider points I and II to be a statement of the problem, with point III giving the solution.

Box 13.4

Organizing According to Cause

The first and most important of these lines of argument [used by Clarence Darrow, the famous attorney] is causal. Either Darrow attempts to justify his clients by an inquiry into the motives behind their acts, or he delves into the historical, causitive factors of the act itself. In the Loeb-Leopold case, much of Darrow's plea dealt with the psychological factors behind his clients' crime; his argument ran that Loeb and Leopold had murdered Robert Franks because of certain physical and psychological defects for which they could not be held responsible. . . . In most of his labor cases, Darrow dealt with the historical causes of the acts in question. . . . When Darrow defended [Bill] Haywood, he used his client as a symbol for the whole labor cause, and so related the trial to all the struggles of the poor.

Source: Martin Maloney, "Clarence Darrow," *A History and Criticism of American Public Address,* ed. M. K. Hochmuth [Nichols] (New York: Russell & Russell, 1955), 298–299.

Systemic pattern

Frequently, you will want to organize a speech around the steps, elements, or parts of a system. The systemic pattern will serve you well on such varied topics as nuclear power, running for public office, or the process of photography.

Experimental evidence validates the usefulness of systematic organization in informative speaking. Researchers constructed two speeches that explained how to play the game, *Risk*. They organized one speech according to a progression of twenty-eight steps needed to learn the game. The other version of the speech presented the rules in no particular order. Listeners heard the different versions and then took a test to measure their knowledge of the game. Those who heard the explanation based on specific steps recalled a significantly greater amount of information about *Risk*.[22]

A student speaker discussing illegal drugs used the systemic pattern when she arranged her speech according to the structure of society. These were the three major ideas in the body of her speech:

I. Cocaine has always been used by the upper class.
II. Cocaine is spreading into the middle class.
III. Cocaine is used by the lower class in America.

The message-centered organizational patterns are important in your progress toward rhetorical competence. Understanding when and how to use the topical, chronological, spatial, causal, and systemic patterns will help you convey your information in the best way possible. Social science research overwhelmingly shows that comprehension of your ideas depends on how well you arrange major points and subpoints.[23]

James Benson, a veteran speech coach, emphasizes the importance of considering all the message-centered patterns before preparing your speech. Benson observed that many students participating in extemporaneous speaking contests habitually use one favorite organizational pattern (usually the topical or chronological)—whether or not the pattern exhibits the subject to best advantage.[24] Instead, you should look for the organizational pattern that has a hand-in-glove fit with your particular subject. Look at all the message-centered patterns to see which one seems most promising for your needs.

Tips for Organizing Informative Speeches

The five message-centered patterns provide you with a basic organizational strategy for informative speaking. Seven tips, below, will help you maximize whatever plan of arrangement you choose.

1. Use previews. Be sure to give a preview of major points at the beginning of your informative speech. Research shows that, by listing major points at the outset of a speech, you can increase comprehension by listeners.[25]
2. Use transitions. Be sure to connect major points of your speech with specific internal transitions. Research shows that transitions, especially of the preview and summary type, boost comprehension of a message by receivers.[26]

Table 13.2 Message-centered organizational patterns

Topical	Find the natural key points of a topic.
Chronological	Identify what happened first, second, etc.
Spatial	Divide the subject according to locations.
Causal	Look at effects and causes.
Systemic	Organize according to the parts of a system.

3. Use repetition. Restate your major points at different times during the speech. Research of the last forty years consistently demonstrates that repeating central points significantly increases comprehension of them.[27]
4. Use emphatic phrases. To highlight one or two major points of your speech, make statements that call special attention to the points. For instance, if you use such phrases as "now get this," you will help listeners retain your crucial points.[28]
5. Concentrate on key points. Be sure to develop all major points extensively—with specific arguments and evidence. Research shows that the audience will better remember those points in the speech that you develop fully.[29]
6. Present important points first or last. Material presented in the middle of your speech is less likely to be remembered, so you should cover the essential material at the beginning or end.[30]
7. Conclude by reviewing. Your informative speeches will be particularly well served by conclusions that review major points. Reiterating major points at the end of the speech significantly increases comprehension of them.[31]

When speaking to inform, your goal is to *help listeners actually to understand and remember your important points.* Generally, the five message-centered patterns represent strategies of arrangement particularly suited to informative speeches, but also take particular note of seven tactical tips for making what you say memorable. Significant gains in comprehension are likely to follow when you use previews, transitions, repetition, and emphatic phrases as well as when you focus on major points, put key points at the beginning or end, and review essentials in the conclusion.

Ours is an era of information explosion. Gone are the days when scholars such as Aristotle (384–322 B.C.) or Roger Bacon (1214–1294) could have a personal command of everything written in all branches of knowledge. Today, even the brightest thinker and fastest reader cannot hope to keep up with advances in the many fields of knowledge. For instance, just one bibliographic service, *Language Abstracts,* lists 2464 items published on

Informative talks help us cope with the flood of data and discoveries.

the subject of pronunciation between 1973 and July 1989. Modern life, with its flood of discoveries and details, will find us constantly giving and receiving informative presentations.

As you prepare your informative speeches, take advantage of your many options. Begin your preparation by gaining a confident familiarity with your subject. At the same time, think about your listeners—their knowledge and level of interest. When you put together your speech material, consider what each of the five general informative approaches has to offer. Which of your ideas are best served by defining? Which are best served by narration, explanation, demonstration, or analyzing? Next consider what your best options are for arranging the information. Review each of the five important message-centered organizational patterns, not only the topical pattern, but also the chronological, spatial, causal, and systemic patterns. When putting the final touches on your speech, and when practicing it, review the seven tips on presenting a clearly organized speech. Look for opportunities to include previews, transitions, repetition, and emphatic phrases. Be sure to concentrate on your major points, to present your key ideas either first or last, and to include a review of points in your conclusion.

Sample Speech

Criminal Scruples: A Rhetorical Look at a Non-Traditional Value System

By Jacquelyn Flanigan

Morte Alla Francia Italia Anelo. It's not a greeting, it's a battle cry. But listen and look closer at the first letter of each of the five words: M-A-F-I-A. In Italian, this phrase symbolizes what is now the most structured and most highly organized crime group in America. Later in my speech, I will explain the meaning of this phrase.

We've all heard the names and the stories about "Lucky" Luciana, Al Capone, and the St. Valentine's Day Massacre. Because we have heard too much from Eliot Ness and "The Untouchables," I will not be covering that in my speech. What we haven't heard, and what I will be covering, is the structure, that is, the value system of the Mafia.

My topic is "Criminal Scruples: A Rhetorical Look at a Non-Traditional Value System." In my speech, I am going to show that even members of the Mafia have a certain code, a system of values that govern their lives.

My speech will be broken down into two main points: (1) the origin and development of the Mafia value system and (2) examples of these values as they exist today.

But first, I will take a brief look at some values Americans traditionally hold. In his book, *The Art of Persuasion,* W. C. Minnick categorizes a summary of these values into six headings. These headings are (1) scientific, (2) economic, (3) aesthetic, (4) social, (5) political, and (6) religious. Under these headings are specific values. Americans traditionally believe in the sanctity of the family. They value the freedoms and liberties protected by the Constitution. Americans believe a person should belong to and support a church. These values are part of a system that I as an American believe in.

Morte Alla Francia Italia Anelo! Now, for the meaning of the phrase with which I began my speech and promised to define. It translates simply, "Death to the French is Italy's Cry!": M-A-F-I-A.

During the Napoleonic campaign, Italy was invaded by the French. All over the Italian countryside, peasant farmers became French subjects. The takeover was short-lived, however. The Italians revolted and gained control of their land once more. The battle cry for this revolt was "Death to the French is Italy's cry!"

Upon regaining control of their country, the Italians established a system of city-states. A nobleman assumed the leadership role in order to act as protector and social arbitrator for his particular city-state. This nobleman was called "the Don," a title of honor given to priests and noblemen.

Centuries later came the days of mass immigration of Europeans to America. Immigrants, who came to this "land of milk and honey" seeking a better way of life, included thousands of Italians. But for many, there was no "milk and honey," only poverty and degradation. With very little money and a pronounced language barrier, many of the Italians were forced to seek help. Help was often a wealthier, more established "paesano," a fellow countryman. The "paesano" would see to it that his own people were cared for. He arranged employment. He dealt with relentless landlords. He guaranteed passports for family members still in Italy. These are but a few of his many tasks that earned the "paesano" the honored title of "Don." He thus provided a sense of security for those who sought it.

As you can see, the Mafia began quite honorably. We as Americans established our own freedom by overthrowing the British oppressors. And in America, where the family is the basic social unit, we are all concerned with protecting our own by guaranteeing them freedom and security.

Admission to the Mafia requires something Americans are learning to value: silence. Each new member must pledge to maintain the vow of silence and his allegiance to "La Fratellanza," another name for the Mafia, which means "The Brotherhood." This vow is known as "Omerta." The Mafioso who breaks this sacred code invites a gruesome death. Two much publicized men who have broken the code and lived are Joe Valachi and Vincent Teresa. Valachi died of natural causes protected in solitary confinement in a federal penitentiary. Mr. Teresa has undergone a complete identity change at the hands of the CIA. If his true identity is ever discovered, he awaits the same fate of others who have desecrated the "Omerta" and not lived.

The vow of silence extends to Mafia family life. According to *Newsweek* magazine, May 16, 1977, "Marriages reflect the old country values of silence and obedience." *Newsweek* continues, saying, "neither the generation gap nor suburban diaspora" has dissolved these strong family bonds. The wives lead an isolated but secure life. The children attend the best of schools—for they can afford the best of everything. Social life revolves almost solely around the family.

Another important American value within the Mafia is religion. With very few exceptions, Mafia members are devout Roman Catholics. Most attend Mass daily and contribute large sums of money to the church and charities. Social functions are a cycle of baptisms, weddings, and funerals.

Religion—family—security—freedom—these are all values listed under Minnick's six categories of American values. As stated earlier, I, being an American, believe in and respect these values. However, being an Italian-American, I know that many of the values I believe in are strongly supported within the Mafia.

I do wish to interject at this point that in no way have I ever condoned nor do I now condone the criminal aspects of their lifestyle. These same men murder for money. They steal and arrange for illegal narcotic trafficking. They are heavily involved in gambling, loansharking, and prostitution.

In summary, I have emphasized values that encompass the life of a Mafioso. We can see that these values are those of the traditional American value system, are based on needs we *all* share as human beings. These needs can be seen in Maslow's hierarchy of human needs, discussed by William J. Reddin in his book *Managerial Effectiveness.* These needs are (1) physiological or life-sustaining needs, (2) safety or security needs, (3) social, belonging and love needs, (4) esteem needs, and (5) the need for self-actualization.

The most conclusive illustration of the truly ironic relationship between the American value system and that of the Mafia can be seen in the name of a man who is at present a prominent Mafia leader. This man was once an assassin for Albert Anastasia's Murder, Inc., a group of hired hit-men who murdered on contract. He is the graying and grandfatherly, the gruesome and gory Aniello Dellacroce—"Little Lamb of the Cross." His contradictory characteristics remind us of the admonition to "Judge not, lest you be judged."

Sample Speech

Price, Quality and the Bottom Line

By Harold L. Enarson

On November 10 we learned that Ohio State University is to be subjected to another state budget cut, effective December 15. This cut of three percent amounts to $5.4 million. It comes on the heels of another three percent state cut imposed last July. This means that in less than six months, Ohio State has been directed to cut $10.8 million from its budget.

The three percent cut announced then is but the latest in a series of budget cuts made by the state since 1976. Except for the worst days of the Depression, this series of cuts is unprecedented in higher education in our state. Unprecedented, too, is the growing erosion of Ohio State's programs as a direct result.

It is absolutely imperative that all of us—students, faculty, administrators, and particularly our many alumni and friends across Ohio—understand clearly what these cuts mean. There must be no illusions about the damaging impact of these cuts on Ohio State.

From Harold L. Enarson, "Price, Quality and the Bottom Line" in *The Ohio State University Monthly,* December 1980.

To understand the full force of this most recent state cut, we need to go back and track what has been happening since 1976.

During 1976–77, the state imposed a two percent cut in its funding of the university. In 1977–78, this cut in state funding was increased to three percent. These cuts to the university's base funding level have not been restored.

Federal funding for the general support of university programs also has declined. A prime example is in capitation grants for the health sciences where the university will receive approximately $1 million in 1980–81. In 1973–74 we received $4.8 million, and in today's dollars it would take $8.8 million to meet those same commitments.

State subsidy for 1980–81, projected in June to increase only by 7.8 percent over 1979–80 levels, has now been reduced to 1.8 percent, as a result of the two state cuts since July. When corrected for inflation, our state subsidy has been reduced in one year alone by more than 10 percent in dollars of constant value. . . .

Now, less than six months later, we are requested to do it all over again. As a result, we have taken the following emergency steps, effective immediately:

- Frozen all hiring, except where absolutely necessary, for example to protect the health and safety of the campus or to meet contractual obligations.
- Stopped the purchase from the General Fund of all scientific, instructional, office, or other equipment costing more than $500.
- Imposed new limits on spending on each administrative unit of the University.

In addition, there is absolutely no way we can sustain cuts of $10.8 million in this year alone without considering the possibility of a further increase in student fees. . . . We are also acutely aware of the anxiety which the prospect of mid-year increases of unknown magnitude can create. We pledge, therefore, that any increase proposed to the Trustees will not exceed $15 per quarter.

You have heard the bad news. Now let's talk a moment about exactly what is at stake, as the State of Ohio continues its budget-cutting course of recent years.

In my opinion, this most recent budget cut—against a backdrop of earlier cuts, high inflation, loss of federal support, and general instability throughout the economy—threatens the very quality of Ohio State's programs and has placed in real jeopardy the ability of this university to hold its position of national rank. . . .

As faculty and administrators, we have failed to communicate to the people of Ohio and their elected representatives the connection between price and quality. We have failed to make them understand that when the funds the state provides for higher education are cut back the quality goes down. And this lack of understanding has been one of higher education's central problems.

There exists in this beautiful land of ours the utterly quaint notion that price and quality in higher education are somehow wholly unrelated. Nowhere else in American life is this proposition advanced. For example, as consumers we buy cars and television sets and clothes and houses and many other things. And, generally, we believe that price and quality are reasonably well correlated. Simply put, we believe that we get what we pay for.

When it comes to the services provided by a university, however, the public apparently thinks that different rules apply. Why should this be so? Perhaps it is because educational quality seems less tangible, something the public can't get its hands on and measure. . . . There seems to be an underlying assumption that a university can readily decide which courses or services to cut or drop, if it will only run the numbers through the computer enough times.

But a university is not a factory. In hard budget times, such as we now face, a university is not able to shut down a "product line" and furlough the workers in courses where enrollment is low. And no amount of cost-benefit analysis can ever help decide whether to phase out a foreign language, cut back the counseling service, or close a wing of the library. These are decisions that relate to the very quality of a university. There are some things that simply cannot be decided "by the numbers. . . ."

Having said that, it also needs to be said that educational quality is very real. It is not a matter of mystique. In education, as in all things in life, some things are better than others. And often the better things are a direct function of the budget available.

Let's see if we can't identify some of the elements of quality. What things do make a difference in the quality of this University?

It makes a difference whether we win or lose the intense competition with other universities for top-flight faculty. . . .

It makes a difference whether the marvelous recreation facilities in Larkins Hall are available to our students 18 hours a day or eight hours a day. . . .

It makes a difference whether the library is able to keep up-to-date in its acquisition of books and periodicals. If it can't, the single most important resource for students and scholars has been compromised.

It makes a difference whether laboratory equipment is up-to-date. To students, the difference may have a direct bearing on their job opportunities. To faculty, the difference will have a direct bearing on their teaching and research.

It makes a difference whether students are exposed to the arts—through free or low-cost concerts, plays, and events of all kinds—or whether tight budgets eliminate for many students the cultural dimension of their education.

I need not continue my list. The point has been made. In higher education as in everything else, you get what you pay for. . . .

Now the state once again has asked us to do with less. Can we do with less at Ohio State? Let me say it loud and clear to our elected officials and to the people of Ohio—something our students and faculty and administrative staff know well: Ohio State *has* been doing with less. We have also pursued aggressively every opportunity to save money and to increase our income. Let me cite but two examples:

Since 1973–74, we have assessed retrenchments equivalent to $29.4 million on the budgets of the University's Colleges and Offices. These reductions, which have reduced our base budget by 15 percent, have resulted in reduced staffing levels for many units and serious curtailments of equipment and operating expenditures.

We have aggressively sought out other sources of income to augment the state's support and student fees. Since 1976–77, income from these sources—for example, from our cash management program, from indirect cost recovery and from gifts and endowments—has more than doubled from $11.6 million to $25.0 million. . . .

Perhaps the time has come for some dramatic action that would capture public attention. What would you do to sound the alarm? Here are some of the possibilities that have been suggested to me—*all bad*:

Sell one or both of the OSU golf courses, or the airport property, or some of our agricultural lands.

Shut down our University radio or television stations that serve virtually all of Ohio. . . .

Disband the marching band for a year or two, the orchestra, choir, theater and dance groups—all those organizations that give students invaluable experience.

I trust that we will not be driven to take such drastic and self-defeating action. But somehow we have got to break through the confused notion that has gripped Ohio that it can have quality universities at bargain-basement prices. . . .

We have talked about price. We have talked about quality. Now it is time to talk about the bottom line. And the bottom line is this: Unless the people of Ohio, through their elected representatives in the General Assembly, quickly come to grips with the tax and money issues facing our state, they will witness—indeed, they will be accessories to—the unraveling of the basic quality of our state university programs. . . .

> I know the strengths of this University today as perhaps no one else in our state. I see the full sweep of its almost unimaginable array of programs. I understand the many ways it is serving the people of Ohio. I cannot believe that they or their elected officials, will stand by, in silence and inaction, and allow their University to slip into the ranks of the second-rate and the mediocre. This must not be allowed to happen in Ohio.

Concepts for Review

Can you summarize the meaning of these terms or expressions? How does each relate to speechmaking?

"clear only if already known"
what listeners know
motivate listening
"persuasion via mere exposure"
define by classifying
define by examples
define by comparison
define by historical background
operational definition
narrating
topical explanation
historical explanation
process explanation
demonstrating
analyzing
message-centered patterns
topical pattern
chronological pattern
spatial pattern
causal pattern
systemic pattern
previews
transitions
repetition
emphatic phrases
important points first/last
"conclude by reviewing"

Things to Try

1. Identify the two most important points you want to make in an informative speech you are preparing. Considering your specific audience, how can you make these two points motivating for your listeners? That is, how can you present each point to make it appear important, vital, and directly relevant to the audience?
2. Consult an issue of *Vital Speeches* in your library, and identify an informative speech. Read the speech to find places where the author is defining, narrating, explaining, demonstrating, or analyzing.

3. As you listen to one set of informative speeches given in class, take a census of the organizational patterns used. Outline the body of each speech. Which of the message-centered patterns do you find: topical, chronological, spatial, causal, systemic?
4. Find five texts of informative speeches in *Vital Speeches* or in other collections. Looking at the body of each speech, what organizational patterns do you find? Did the speakers select the best pattern given their purposes and information?

Endnotes

1. Russel Windes, Jr., and James A. Robinson, "Public Address in the Career of Adlai E. Stevenson," *Quarterly Journal of Speech 42* (1956): 229.
2. *Chronicle of Higher Education,* 30 March 1988, A23.
3. Judee K. Burgoon, "Conflicting Information, Attitude, and Message Variables as Predictors of Learning and Persuasion," *Human Communication Research 1* (1975): 133–144.
4. Charles M. Kelly, "Mental Ability and Personality Factors in Listening," *Quarterly Journal of Speech 49* (1963): 152–156.
5. Michael J. Beatty, Ralph R. Behnke, and Deidre L. Froelich, "Effects of Achievement Incentive and Presentation Rate on Listening Comprehension," *Quarterly Journal of Speech 66* (1980): 193–200.
6. Raymond K. Tucker and Paul D. Ware, "Persuasion Via Mere Exposure," *Quarterly Journal of Speech 57* (1971): 437–443.
7. Phillip K. Tompkins and Larry A. Samovar, "An Experimental Study of the Effects of Credibility on the Comprehension of Content," *Speech Monographs 31* (1964): 120–123.
8. Charles F. Vick and Roy V. Wood, "Similarity of Past Experience and the Communication of Meaning," *Speech Monographs 36* (1969): 159–162; Patrick R. Connolly and William E. Knabe, "Assessing Inter-Group Differences in the Use of Language: A Method and a Case Study," *Central States Speech Journal 24* (1973): 43–47; Theodore Balgooyen, "A Study of Conflicting Values: American Plains Indian Orators vs. the U.S. Commissioners of Indian Affairs," *Western Speech 26* (1962): 76–83.
9. Robert C. Jeffrey and Owen Peterson, *Speech: A Text with Adapted Readings,* 2nd ed., (New York: Harper and Row, 1975), 67.
10. Theresa Buescher, *1987 Championship Debates and Speeches,* ed. J. K. Boaz and J. R. Brey (Annandale, VA: Speech Communication Association, 1987), 142.
11. *The Compact Edition of the Oxford English Dictionary,* 2 vols., (New York: Oxford University Press, 1971), 2:1466.
12. See Charles W. Lomas, "Winston Churchill: Orator-Historian," *Quarterly Journal of Speech 44* (1958): 155–156.
13. Ronald F. Reid, "Edward Everett: Rhetorician of Nationalism, 1824–1855," *Quarterly Journal of Speech 42* (1956): 279–280.

14. Allen Weinstein, *Perjury: The Hiss-Chambers Case* (New York: Vintage Books, 1978), 463. Hiss was tried for perjury because the statute of limitations precluded prosecution on charges of espionage.

15. Karl. R. Wallace, "Booker T. Washington," *A History and Criticism of American Public Address,* ed. W. N. Brigance, 2 vols. (New York: Russell and Russell, 1943), 2:418.

16. Lionel Crocker, "Henry Ward Beecher," *History and Criticism,* ed. W. N. Brigance, 1:272.

17. Thomas M. Sawyer, Jr., "In Defense of Explanatory Speeches," *Speech Teacher 6* (1957): 196–199.

18. Sawyer, "Explanatory Speeches," 199.

19. Roy V. Wood, James J. Bradac, Sara A. Barnhart, and Edward Kraft, "The Effect of Learning About Techniques of Propaganda on Subsequent Reaction to Propagandistic Communication," *Speech Teacher 19* (1970): 49–53.

20. Emery V. Hildebrandt, "Senator Wayne Morse on Speech Preparation," *Today's Speech 6,* No. 2 (1958): 8.

21. Eugene E. White and Clair R. Henderlider, "What Harry S. Truman Told Us About His Speaking," *Quarterly Journal of Speech 40* (1954): 39.

22. Christopher Spicer and Ronald E. Bassett, "The Effect of Organization on Learning from an Informative Message," *Southern Speech Communication Journal 41* (1976): 290–299.

23. Ernest Thompson, "An Experimental Investigation of the Relative Effectiveness of Organizational Structure in Oral Communication," *Southern Speech Journal 26* (1960): 59–69; Charles R. Petrie, Jr., "Informative Speaking: A Summary and Bibliography of Related Research," *Speech Monographs 30* (1963): 79–91; Donald K. Darnell, "The Relation Between Sentence Order and Comprehension," *Speech Monographs 30* (1963): 97–100; Ernest Thompson, "Some Effects of Message Structure on Listeners' Comprehension," *Speech Monographs 34* (1967): 51–57; Arlee Johnson, "A Preliminary Investigation of the Relationship Between Message Organization and Listener Comprehension," *Central States Speech Journal 21* (1970): 104–107; John E. Baird, Jr., "The Effects of Speech Summaries Upon Audience Comprehension of Expository Speeches of Varying Quality and Complexity," *Central States Speech Journal 25* (1974): 119–127; Richard F. Whitman and John H. Timmis, "The Influence of Verbal Organizational Structure and Verbal Organizing Skills on Select Measures of Learning," *Human Communication Research 1* (1975): 293–301; Tom D. Daniels and Richard F. Whitman, "The Effects of Message Introduction, Message Structure, and Verbal Organizing Ability Upon Learning of Message Information," *Human Communication Research 7* (1981): 147–160.

24. James A. Benson, "Extemporaneous Speaking: Organization Which Inheres," *Journal of the American Forensic Association 14* (1978): 150–155.

25. John P. Parker, "Some Organizational Variables and Their Effect Upon Comprehension," *Journal of Communication 12* (1962): 27–32 and Baird, "Speech Summaries."

26. Petrie, "Informative Speaking" and Thompson, "Effects of Message Structure."

27. Ray Ehrensberger, "An Experimental Study of the Relative Effectiveness of Certain Forms of Emphasis in Public Speaking," *Speech Monographs 12* (1945): 94–111; Petrie, "Informative Speaking"; Warner Wilson and Howard Miller, "Repetition, Order of Presentation, and Timing of Arguments and Measures as Determinants of Opinon Change," *Journal of Personality and Social Psychology 9* (1968): 184–188; Idolene Mazza, William Jordan, and Ronald Carpenter, "The Comparative Effectiveness of Stylistic Sources of Redundancy," *Central States Speech Journal 23* (1972): 241–245.

28. Ehrensberger, "Emphasis in Public Speaking" and Petrie, "Informative Speaking."

29. Petrie, "Informative Speaking" and Burgoon, "Learning and Persuasion."

30. Petrie, "Informative Speaking"; Burgoon, "Learning and Persuasion"; Daniels & Whitman, "Verbal Organizing Ability"; and Norman Miller and Donald T. Campbell, "Recency and Primacy in Persuasion as a Function of the Timing of Speeches and Measurements," *Journal of Abnormal and Social Psychology 59* (1959): 1–9.

31. Parker, "Organizational Variables and Comprehension" and Baird, "Speech Summaries."

Chapter

14

The Persuasive Speech

Outline

One speech *can* make a difference. In the case of Corazon Aquino's speech to a Joint Session of the United States Congress, the difference was 200 million dollars. Aquino, President of the Philippines, inspired members of Congress by describing the effort of Filipinos to restore democracy, prosperity, and stability to their country. Thomas (Tip) O'Neill, Speaker of the House of Representatives, called Aquino's speech "the finest speech I've ever heard to move Congress in my 34 years here." Members of the House responded by approving an emergency aid package of $200 million for the Philippines. Representative David Obey observed that "this could never have passed before the speech."[1]

Are you confident that *your* persuasive speeches will make a difference? To succeed as a persuasive speaker, you need specific advice about the proven doorways into the hearts and minds of listeners. Aristotle described the art of persuasive speech as "observing in any given case the available means of persuasion."[2] What are the pathways to persuasion? We begin this chapter with the essentials of persuasive speaking. To be a successful persuader, you must influence sentiments and modify behavior—ideally, for the long term. Next comes a survey of how you can win over listeners by strong arguments, by "inoculating" the audience against opposing ideas, by building personal credibility, and by avoiding needlessly offending the audience. Finally, we focus on strategies and tactics for organizing speech materials persuasively.

The Persuasive Purpose

Richard Weaver, Chicago professor of English, coined the expression "language is sermonic." Weaver meant that when you speak, you reveal how you look at the world. Whenever you state your preferences, you invite others to adopt and share your views. Every persuasive speech necessarily becomes a kind of sermon on how you view life and think it ought to be lived.[3]

Persuasive speaking requires the fullest application of rhetorical competence. To influence others requires more than stating arguments. Instead, your effort is to convey points that make listeners rearrange their minds on your topic. You need to search for all possible ways to connect your ideas and reasons to the thoughts and feelings of listeners. To understand this kind of speaking, we must consider four interrelated goals of the persuasive speaker: (1) to influence beliefs, (2) to influence attitudes, (3) to influence values, and (4) to influence behavior.

Box 14.1

The Great Presidential Speakers

Where does President Bush stand as a public speaker among this century's seventeen presidents? Tough call. But a study by New York's Burson Marsteller, which trains executives how to speak publicly, puts the current chief executive about in the middle of the pack—seventh. And, no the "great communicator" was not No. 1. Ronald Reagan was No. 3 behind runner-up Theodore Roosevelt and top finisher John F. Kennedy, who was called "an electrifying presence behind the podium," by Marsteller trainer Gail Quattlebaum.

Also finishing ahead of Bush were Harry Truman, Franklin D. Roosevelt, and Woodrow Wilson. Finishing dead last in a tie were Dwight Eisenhower and Calvin Coolidge.

Source: *San Jose Mercury News*, 21 February 1989.

Influencing Beliefs

To succeed as a persuasive speaker, you will need to influence what listeners believe. We may apply this point to William F. Buckley's speech on the Panama Canal (reprinted at the end of this chapter). Clearly, Buckley gives considerable attention to presenting facts about the Canal. He points out that 75 percent of the Canal's work force is Panamanian. He discusses finances of the Canal. He points to certain realities of human nature, noting that Panama's national pride is tied up with control of the Canal.

The belief dimension of Buckley's speech is directly related to his persuasive purpose. Buckley's educational review of the Canal is calculated, for he cites data that lead listeners to a particular conclusion. To understand and remember Buckley's data is to move closer to his thesis that the United States should allow Panama to operate the Canal.

Getting receivers to comprehend basic data takes your audience along the road to persuasion. To illustrate this principle, we may turn to an experiment in which an audience of high school students heard a speech advising them to seek a college education. Results showed that the more the audience remembered about the speech, the more they changed attitudes. In a related study, researchers analyzed the persuasive power of a booklet promoting fallout shelters. They found a direct connection between what people learned and how much they changed their attitudes. To be sure, the link between education and persuasion is neither automatic nor uniform for all listeners. However, do not overlook the power of information to boost your chances for successful persuasion.[4]

One reason that information contributes to persuasion is that it allows you to create *new beliefs* favorable to your ideas. Thomas Hart Benton, Senator from Missouri, practiced a brand of persuasion heavily based on the power of education. Benton's typical method was to reduce questions of policy to questions of fact. Benton used this method in his speech to the United States Senate on American claims to the Oregon Territory in 1846. Benton described control of Oregon as simply a matter of which power, the United States or Britain, had superior claims to the basins of the Columbia and Frazer rivers and to the coastal islands. Benton then presented a factual review of who first discovered the territories, who actually settled them, and who had continuously occupied them. These historical facts served as the basis for Benton's proposed division of the disputed Oregon Territory.[5]

In addition to getting across new information, beliefs boost persuasion when you *make old knowledge more important.* William Jennings Bryan relied on this method in his "Cross of Gold" address to the 1896 Democratic Party national convention. Bryan knew that most delegates favored a policy of free coinage of silver instead of the restrictive policy of backing currency only with gold. Rather than state new facts about this question, Bryan relied on the existing beliefs of listeners. In the words of one biographer, Bryan worked to "articulate their resentment." Bryan attacked the gold standard for keeping prosperity limited to the rich. Ending the gold standard, he argued, would spread wealth to the masses of small businessmen—the nation's farmers, shopkeepers, and workers. Bryan reminded listeners of how they had petitioned for relief against economic policies that benefitted the wealthy. Bryan railed against foreign influences on the American economy, something he described as an outrage for a nation born through a war of independence.[6]

Bryan's address shows that existing beliefs can serve as a touchstone for persuasive speaking. Research confirms that Bryan's success in 1896 was not a historical accident. Whenever you remind listeners of beliefs relevant to your topic, you are helping them renew their commitment to the beliefs.[7] When listeners are committed to an idea, their beliefs about the idea represent firm foundations for persuasion.

Influencing Attitudes

An attitude is a tendency to favor or oppose some concept or thing. When receivers hold positive attitudes toward an idea, they listen to it gladly—they try to hear more.

Persuasive speakers want to make their ideas appear consistent with the attitudes of listeners. For instance, in advocating that the United States turn over operation of the Panama Canal to Panama, William F. Buckley emphasizes that this policy would be *good for the U.S.A.* Buckley's whole speech is pitched against the natural desire of Americans to retain an important symbol of American ingenuity. Buckley also refutes the idea that relinquishing administration of the Canal would be costly for the United States. By presenting the Panama Canal treaties as good *for the U.S.A.* Buckley works on the basis of shared attitudes—common ground—with his audience.

Samuel Gompers' career as a labor movement speaker further illustrates how persuasion flows from shared attitudes. A founder of the American Federation of Labor, Gompers was shrewdly able to connect his persuasive aims to the attitudes of American workingmen. Gompers recognized the strength in America of the values of individualism and personal freedom. Gompers recognized that these general American values led to specific American working class attitudes. For instance, Gompers understood that American workers wanted good jobs more than a labor-based political party. Gompers' labor speeches show his effort to make the union movement consistent with traditional American attitudes about work.[8]

Effective persuaders have a knack for demonstrating the importance of overlooked ideas. In his classic speech on "The New South," Henry Grady, Atlanta newspaper editor, appealed to the common aims of North and South in winning over his audience of northern businessmen. Northerners (in 1886) still were suspicious about the former states of the Confederacy. Nevertheless, Grady was able to build attitudes favorable to the South by emphasizing the common heritage and common business interests of North and South.[9]

The example of Grady's success is especially interesting because his speech effectively worked against attitudes aroused by preceding speakers. Before Grady gave his address, a number of speakers had emphasized the old anti-South themes of the post Civil War period. Grady took the podium only after the Northerners had finished a rousing rendition of "Marching Through Georgia." In sharp contrast to Grady's success against adversity is the failure of the 1930s Union Party to capitalize on anti-establishment attitudes during the Great Depression. Organized as a right-wing third party alternative in 1936, the persuasive appeals of the Union Party became bogged down in complicated monetary doctrines. The party's candidate for president, William Lemke, typically gave abstract speeches on the bond market or the national debt, but his audiences didn't care much about such generalities; they wanted to learn how Lemke's program would help individuals.[10] Lemke failed to show why listeners should become committed to the Union Party's economic attitudes.

As you plan your persuasive speeches, be sure to highlight the importance of your ideas for listeners. If you make your points strike home, your listeners will adopt the attitudes you want to get across.[11]

Influencing Values

You may build persuasion through value appeals as well as through arguments directed to beliefs and attitudes. John F. Kennedy's Houston speech (reprinted at the end of this chapter) relied on traditional values of religious freedom and separation of church and state. Appeals grounded on these values helped Kennedy make his audience of Protestant ministers better accept the idea of a Catholic as president. William F. Buckley similarly showed how acceptance of the Panama Canal treaties was consistent with the American idea that even weak nations deserve fair treatment. Buckley encouraged listeners to adopt the value of generosity, forsaking pride. Kennedy and Buckley both used value appeals as a way of getting through to listeners who might hold anti-Catholic or anti-Panama attitudes.

American history shows many examples of how values set limits for speakers. Changes in American values had a significant impact on the career of Edward Everett, educator, politician, and one of the nineteenth century's most popular public speakers. No important occasion was complete without an address by Everett, and his specialty was the patriotic oration focused on the American Revolution. During the period 1820–1850, a shift in public attitudes away from nationalism and toward sectionalism made reliance on the value of national unity as a foundation for public speaking more difficult for speakers. In the introduction to his first Bunker Hill monument oration in 1825, Daniel Webster remarked at the "uncounted multitude" of shining faces that inspired him to reflect on the theme of nationhood. By 1850, as Everett prepared his own Bunker Hill address, he recalled spending an entire day "in vain attempts to say something interesting about Bunker Hill." Everett despaired of preparing a patriotic address in a time when national unity was collapsing as a result of issues dividing North and South.[12]

Everett's career shows the importance of shared values in rhetorical success. Value appeals are important in persuasive speaking because values serve as *sources of motivation* (as we saw in chapter 5). Experimental research indicates that you must do two things to achieve persuasion through value appeals.[13] First, you must select ***values that are important*** for the listener. You must express goals that people really want to attain or avoid. For instance, candidates for president typically stress values of economic progress and national security. Candidates for mayor usually stress social services. Candidates for sheriff normally emphasize curtailing crime.

A second requirement for value-centered persuasion is making listeners believe that a value truly *is* connected to your arguments. For instance, in political speaking, voters must believe that a candidate for president can provide greater economic progress or that a candidate for sheriff can bring greater community safety. Value appeals worked for William Jennings Bryan, in his "Cross of Gold" address, because he convinced listeners that abandoning the gold standard really would boost their well-being. In contrast,

William Lemke failed to win much support for his monetary policies during the era of the Depression. Lemke failed because he did not make a connection between his economic policies and what voters wanted—jobs.

The failure of value appeals can be seen as a contributing cause to the defeat of Walter Mondale in his quest to unseat President Reagan in 1984. Mondale proposed a tax increase (a policy) that he said was necessary to attain a balanced federal budget (an American political value). Mondale further contended that the tax increase would help promote economic stability and growth by ending the record budget deficits of the Reagan era. Mondale's value appeal failed because the Republicans were able to focus the attention of voters on the obvious sacrifice required by more taxes. By contrast, Mondale's promises of balanced budgets and future prosperity seemed abstract and distant.

Influencing Behavior

Beliefs, attitudes, and values often function as steps to the final goal of changing behavior. For instance, John F. Kennedy did not strive simply to improve the image of the Catholic faith in the eyes of Houston's protestant ministers. Kennedy gave his Houston speech to get votes. Similarly, when William Jennings Bryan spoke against the gold standard, he aimed to change national policy by getting the Democratic Party to take up this cause.

What is the connection between winning support for a belief or attitude and getting people to act? In one sense, changing beliefs, attitudes, and values always modifies behavior. Kenneth Boulding, American social scientist, notes that "behavior depends on the image."[14] People have no alternative but to act according to how they see the world. People know they can't leap tall buildings in a single bound, so they don't try. Beliefs, attitudes, and values set the boundaries of normal behavior.

However, the link between opinion and behavior is murky. For instance, all of us occasionally act in ways that we know are harmful to our health. Some of us smoke, do drugs, drive too fast, avoid exercise, eat poorly. Why do we act contrary to expressed beliefs, attitudes, or values? For one thing, our actions may be driven along by biological urges or by the crowd. We also frequently minimize the dangers of what we do. After all, we don't have an accident or get a ticket every time we run a red light. To reassure ourselves about bad habits, we rationalize that we will quit—"later."

Social scientists have long been interested in the connection between attitude and behavior. In one classic study, researchers examined the effect of health pamphlets in causing students to get immunizations. Researchers gave students booklets explaining the benefits of receiving a tetanus inoculation and recommending that students get the free shot at a campus clinic. Researchers used a questionnaire to measure attitudes toward a tetanus immunization and also checked records at the clinic to see how many

Clarence Darrow always focused on his audience.

of the students actually went for the shot. Only nine of fifty-nine students got the shot. Not everyone whose attitude was changed actually went for the shot, showing that attitudes were not absolutely connected to behavior.[15]

How can you make sure that your persuasive speeches will influence behavior as well as attitudes?[16] Four principles seem to apply. The first factor making for greater consistency in attitude and action is that the attitude itself is consistent. If beliefs, feelings, and intentions are in harmony, then behavior likely will conform to mental attitude. To apply this finding, be sure to build your persuasive speeches around all aspects of the audience's mental world: beliefs, attitudes, values, feelings, and motives. Take the path of Clarence Darrow, the great attorney, who believed that a defense counsel needed to do more than give information and reasons to the jury. In Darrow's view, a defense attorney should make the defendant likeable to jurors. Darrow believed that when jurors liked the accused, they would look for ways to free him.[17]

The social situation represents a second condition affecting your ability to connect attitude and behavior. People behave consistently with their attitudes when the social situation points in one clear direction. When personal beliefs, the beliefs of society, and the demands of the situation all lead to the same point—only then may you be confident that listeners will act consistently with their attitudes. This finding suggests that you should emphasize how action flows logically from beliefs, attitudes, and values. For instance, William F. Buckley argued that relinquishing control of the Panama Canal was consistent with treating other nations according to American values.

A third way to increase the link between attitude and behavior is to make sure that listeners have a highly developed understanding of a speech topic.

Your audience will be more likely to take action when you supply sufficient information for them to picture clearly what is going on. The earlier example of Thomas Hart Benton's factually-oriented persuasion applies here. Benton had a passion for evidence. He studied every possible document on a question so that he was the master of the material. His speeches were crammed with facts that presented an overwhelming case for action.

A fourth factor making for a link between attitude and action relates to how much behavior change you are demanding. When you advocate an action requiring minor effort, you are more likely to succeed, so do not appeal for more action than you absolutely need. Also, you should look for ways to minimize the difficulty involved in your recommendations. The importance of *making action easy* may be seen in experimental findings. For instance, students were more likely to obtain a tetanus shot when they received explicit directions on where and when to get the shot.

As a persuasive speaker, you work with beliefs, attitudes, values, and behavior. Your success will depend on how well you solidify beliefs and build attitudes that favor your case. Furthermore, you will be more likely to influence listeners when you use values as sources of motivation. Your persuasive speeches will meet the highest test of effectiveness when you link beliefs, attitudes, and values to necessary actions.

Box 14.2

He'll Get Them Back

No, thank God, it wasn't a case of mind-altering drugs in the dormitory water supply. That really *was* Ted Kennedy speaking to 5,000 students and townsfolk at Jerry Falwell's Liberty Baptist College in Lynchburg, Va. And he *was* getting applause—for one of the best speeches he has ever given.

Kennedy's appearance resulted from the mass-mailing equivalent of crossed wires: the senator received a membership card in Falwell's Moral Majority. . . . When [Cal] Thomas [a Moral Majority vice-president] invited him to visit the campus, Kennedy offered to speak. . . .

Kennedy did not trim his rhetoric for the religious right. In a pluralist state, he said, "the real transgression occurs when religion wants government to tell citizens how to live uniquely personal parts of their lives. . . . In such cases—cases like prohibition and abortion—the proper role of religion is to appeal to the conscience of the individual, not the coercive power of the state." But if it was wrong to call ERA-supporters "blasphemers," he suggested, it was equally wrong for liberals to call Falwell a "warmonger." Kennedy drew applause by calling the shoot-down of Korean Air Lines Flight 007 "outrageous and barbarous," and by criticizing Reagan for not cutting economic aid to Poland.

"You might have gotten to a few of them tonight," Falwell said later, "but I'll get them back."

Sources of Persuasion

Getting results from your speeches begins when you recognize that people balance their perceptions of a speech situation. In other words, your listeners seek a consistent view of you (the speaker), the topic, and your specific arguments.[18] As a result, you may turn to several entry-points for persuasion that exist in every speech situation. These include: (1) establishing claims as strong, (2) inoculating receivers against opposing arguments, (3) building credibility, and (4) avoiding giving offense to the audience.

Establishing Strong Claims

"Show me," says the proverbial Missourian. "Prove it," says the skeptical scientist. Experience suggests that proof is a vital source of persuasion. Follow these tips for using argument and evidence to maximize your influence on listeners.

First, *remind listeners of beliefs they hold that favor your conclusions.* To illustrate this principle, we may turn to an experiment in which students wrote out ideas they associated with the concept "politician." Students later undertook the task of explaining to a foreign student the basic meaning of "politician." This educational task caused students to recall chiefly neutral or positive meanings of "politician." When students focused on their positive beliefs about politicians, they shifted to a more positive attitude toward the concept.[19] The lesson is that you may collect dividends in persuasion when you remind listeners of beliefs that favor your ideas.

A second way to strengthen claims is to *show that good results will come from what you advocate.* Research indicates that a good predictor of people's attitude toward a change in policy is their belief that good or bad effects *are likely* to result from the change.[20] This finding helps explain Walter Mondale's problem in his 1984 campaign for president. Mondale simply could not convince voters of the likelihood that a tax increase would bring good results. You may expect to be more persuasive when you give strong reasons that good effects will come from what you recommend.

Citing outside evidence will also increase your chances for persuasion. Evidence works best when you find sources that your listeners are likely to view as credible.[21] The speech by Jack Dodds (chapter 2) illustrates how to pursue persuasion through credible evidence. Jack cites such sources as the *Congressional Quarterly,* a Harvard biochemist, a University of Illinois professor of medicine, and an article taken from the *New York Times.* Don't waste your time with sources of evidence that receivers doubt—poor evidence can actually reduce persuasion![22] Also remember that evidence works best when listeners view it as directly relevant to the issues being discussed.[23] Finally, do not overlook *visual aids* as a form of evidence. Graphs, pictures, and other visual support sometimes lead to greater persuasiveness.[24]

Finally, *arguments based on comparison* are particularly useful in attaining persuasion. *Metaphors* are a form of comparison in which you describe one thing or situation in language taken from an unrelated area of activity. For instance, in chapter 10, we observed how Martin Luther King made an argument about civil rights through the language of banking. King said that the demand of blacks for equal treatment under law was an effort to cash a check promised them in the United States Constitution. Experimental studies suggest that including metaphors in a speech can boost its persuasiveness, particularly if the metaphor appears in the conclusion of the speech.[25]

A *simile* is a type of comparison that amounts to a simplified, briefly-stated metaphor. For instance, a speaker might state that "suspicion is like quicksand," or "the telephone is like a confession box." Using similes can increase your persuasiveness, though to a somewhat lesser extent than metaphors.[26]

An *analogy* is a comparison that explains one thing or situation by examining an apparently related object or situation. For instance, suppose you wanted to argue that the United States should stop sending weapons to right-wing guerilla forces in Central America. You could develop an analogy between this policy and the United States entry into the Vietnam War. In other words, arming one side in a civil war might lead to the eventual commitment of United States troops as in the case of Vietnam. Research suggests that messages containing analogies may be more persuasive than messages not containing them.[27]

Box 14.3

Lincoln Kept Practicing

The countryside was Abe's auditorium. Wherever he could find one or two eager listeners he practiced his art. He found them at home, the country store, the neighborhood sociables, the blacksmith's shop. "He kept his audiences at the country store until midnight, listening to his shrewd wisdom, native wit and vivid recitals." "He was so odd, original and humorous and witty that all the people in town would gather around him," said Dennis Hanks [Lincoln's boyhood friend] to Herndon. "I would get tired, want to go home, and cuss Abe most heartily."

Source: Mildred F. Berry, "Abraham Lincoln: His Development in the Skills of the Platform," *A History and Criticism of American Public Address,* 2 vols. (New York: Russell & Russell, 1943), 2:841.

Inoculating Receivers

Achieving image and behavior change is the first task of persuasion. The second is to *make the changes stick,* to make them persist. The problem of persistence in persuasion harkens back to the World War I-era song, "How 'Ya Gonna Keep 'Em Down on the Farm? (After They've Seen Paree)." Like farm boys turned loose in the big city, your listeners are going to experience many temptations that beckon them to forget or abandon your ideas.

Rhetorically competent speakers realize that a speech is only one part of a continuing stream of information and opinion beamed at people. The persuasive effects of a single speech tend to diminish with time. This result creates an important objective for persuasive speaking. You need to speak not only to persuade, but also to secure lasting changes in attitude and behavior. The basic idea is to prepare a talk that *inoculates receivers against later contrary information and opinion.* How? Following are some ideas.

First, don't just support your points well; to gain lasting persuasion, *be sure to refute opposing arguments.* In many cases, listeners already have in mind some ideas that work against your purposes. It is also inevitable that your audience will later hear arguments that contradict some of your ideas. Take the extra step of refuting major counter-arguments whenever you believe listeners will weigh your points against these opposing claims. Refutation will protect your success as a persuader.[28]

William F. Buckley's entire persuasive speech is strongly oriented to persuasion through refutation. To strengthen his case for giving up United States control of the Panama Canal, Buckley considers whether his opponents are right to believe that Panamanians would never sabotage the Canal. Buckley offers the example of the Egyptians, who closed off their Suez Canal to protest Israeli occupation of the Sinai Peninsula. Buckley argues by analogy that Panamanian national pride makes United States insistence on continued control of the Canal risky.

Sometimes you may refute opposing arguments by using a technique called *forewarning.* Here you warn listeners that a later speech will present contrary ideas. This technique is useful when you are sure that listeners are on your side. Research shows that forewarning listeners significantly reduces the effect of a later speech that opposes your thesis. For instance, researchers told a group of high school seniors that they were about to hear a talk on "Why Teen-Agers Should Not Drive." Another group got advance word only that they would be hearing a talk. Those students who knew in advance that the speech would present a disagreeable thesis were significantly less persuaded by the speech.[29]

Another way to help persuasive effects persist is to *use arguments shown to stand up well against later refutation.* Certain kinds of argument seem particularly resistant to refutation. Example-based arguments appear most immune to counter-claims. Listed in the order of their power to resist refutation are a number of other types of arguments: dilemma argument, the method of residues (*i.e.,* refuting all alternatives to your plan), analogy, and causal argument.[30]

Using evidence is another way to make persuasion persist. Evidence reduces the impact of a later speech that opposes the thesis of the earlier speech.[31] As a rhetorically competent speaker, you will want to do more than present plausible arguments. You will be most likely to succeed as a persuader when you clinch each crucial point with outside evidence.

Building Credibility

Speech is a personal process of influence. As a writer, you never know who will read your work; but as a speaker, you stand directly before your audience. It follows that *who you are* influences *what you say.* There is little doubt that when listeners find you believable—credible—they will be more open to persuasion.[32]

Sometimes we hear the argument that a message should be judged only on the "issues." For instance, media critics decry modern practices that encourage voters to "reach out and elect someone"—someone attractive and personable.[33] Critics have a point in worrying about political spots that "package" candidates to hide their defects. However, a live speech is not an artificially-staged event—it is a real performance under the spotlight. Oral performance is the essence of rhetorical competence. Speakers sometimes lie or harbor self-serving motives, so audiences are quite rational to evaluate speakers *as people.* Furthermore, practical affairs always concern the future as well as the present. We need to estimate whether a leader is the kind of person who can handle issues of tomorrow in addition to those of today.

What produces a credible speaker? Such a question admits to no certain answer. Every speaker, every era, every public dispute produces unique possibilities for credibility. In the 1988 election, Michael Dukakis's command of the Spanish language gave him credibility among Hispanic voters. George Bush enjoyed the endorsement of the sitting president, Ronald Reagan. Nevertheless, we may turn to a number of generalizations on how to build credibility through speechmaking.

First, to build credibility, *use factual arguments.* Unless you already have high credibility with an audience, factual arguments will work better than value-oriented ones. A factual argument focuses on specific beliefs and information. A factual treatment of the nuclear arms race would have you identifying specific weapons and particular military policies. A value-centered treatment would find you talking about the "extinction of human life" or "the need to deter the evil enemy." Generally, belief-oriented arguments confer greater credibility than do value-oriented ones. Value arguments are more controversial. They work best when you are seen as either being an expert or holding opinions similar to those of listeners.[34]

Further, in building credibility, *making specific references to your personal experience with the topic helps.* If you have first-hand experience with the topic, be sure to mention it. Speaking on the use of Agent Orange in Vietnam, Jack Dodds noted that "I am a Vietnam-era veteran: I served six years in the Navy." Speaking on the Panama Canal treaties, William F. Buckley similarly used personal references to help establish his credentials on foreign policy. "I have sat in Hawaii with Admiral McCain when he was commanding officer of CINCPAC." References to personal experience boost credibility.[35]

Third, to retain the aura of credibility, *be sure that none of your major points is logically contradictory.* Researchers tested this principle by having a speaker present contradictory statements about wire tapping. First, the speaker argued that wire tapping is ineffective because people can easily detect the tap. Later in the same speech, the advocate contended that wiretapping forces people to make incriminating statements because people are unaware that their conversations are being recorded. Results showed that when listeners notice a contradiction between two major points in a speech, the speaker's credibility suffers—and persuasion declines.[36]

Finally, be sure that your speech *marks you as well-informed.* An informed speaker talks in specifics. Make statements about real persons, particular events, actual situations. For instance, Jack Dodds asked his audience of fellow public speaking students to support specific legislation that would help veterans get help for illnesses caused by Agent Orange. Jack encouraged speakers to "let them know that we care and that we support legislation such as S1872, S1480, HR6050 and HR5291, which will create a superfund, financed largely by industry, and would pay benefits to their families." Citing outside evidence also helps build positive credibility because it conveys your expertise.[37]

"Persuasion is achieved by the speaker's personal character when the speech is so spoken as to make us think him credible."[38] Aristotle's observations of the Athenian assemblies and law courts also apply to our own era of live and televised speeches. How you present your ideas builds an impression of you. When you are viewed as credible, you will be more likely to attain persuasion.

Avoiding Offending the Audience

Many a speaker has assumed he was on the road to success, only to discover that he had offended the listeners. Usually such failures have come from misusing or misapplying persuasive techniques. Avoiding errors of persuasive practice is crucial for rhetorical competence.

When predicting the future, be sure to *use fear appeals carefully.* A fear appeal is an argument in which you warn listeners about a horrible danger that threatens them. Appeals to fear are the basis of grade school anti-smoking assemblies as well as the "Scared Straight" program that gives juvenile delinquents a look at life in real prisons. Fear appeals find their place in politics as well. In 1987, Colonel Oliver North argued in Congressional hearings that without American aid to the Contra rebels in Nicaragua, the United States itself would soon be under attack.

Fear appeals are a controversial style of persuasion whose effectiveness often is challenged. Strong fear appeals may sometimes cause listeners to become defensive and believe that they are exempt from the danger.[39] In other words, to adjust psychologically to the warning, listeners may tend to discount the threat as unreal or exaggerated. Research on the "Scared Straight" program found that allowing convicts to intimidate troubled youngsters actually increased the chances that the juveniles would turn to crime.[40]

How to use fear appeals successfully is no simple matter. Research on the topic is complicated, but we may identify two conditions that make fear appeals workable for your persuasive speeches. First, show that the fearful consequence threatens something personal and close-at-hand, such as your audience's own families. Citing an immediate, personal threat can be more persuasive than emphasizing one that is impersonal or far off.[41] Also, when describing fearful results, explain specifically how listeners can avoid the bad consequence.[42] This allows you to show that what you propose is rewarding.

Second, to avoid offending your audience, remember that *humor may backfire.* Speakers are attracted to humor in the belief that jokes help win over an audience. One of President Gerald Ford's speech writers, Robert Orben, argued that humor "enables the President or anybody else to establish a link with an audience so that the audience will listen and listen with a favorable view of the speaker."[43] Humor does allow you to soften the hard edges of your attacks on opponents. And Adlai Stevenson often used a mildly self-critical humor that gave him an aura of confidence. A typical Stevensonism: "My job is to speak. Your job is to listen. Let us hope that we both complete our jobs at about the same time."[44]

Though humor may lighten an audience's mood, experimental studies are inconsistent on whether humor significantly boosts credibility.[45] Furthermore, satirical humor may be misinterpreted. A classic example of satire occurred when Jonathan Swift criticized harsh British policy in Ireland by recommending that Irish children be used as food. When you use satire, listeners sometimes find identifying your actual opinion difficult.[46] Satire may actually decrease persuasion by "turning off" listeners who resent a light treatment of ideas. Audiences may not like humorous material if they view the topic as too serious for joking.[47]

Third, remember that you may offend listeners by making *intensely opinionated statements.* Speechmaking is an assertive activity that seemingly requires us to show certainty and aggressiveness. Intense language allows us to express vividly our attitudes. So we say "he is a liar" rather than "he is loose with the facts." While intense language seems natural in a persuasive speech, it sometimes hinders persuasion. For one thing, opinionated language can reduce credibility.[48] Furthermore, listeners do not like speakers to eliminate freedom of choice. Listeners may find you less credible if you make demands of this kind: "As a decent American, you absolutely cannot do other than totally agree with me."[49] In general, you should be wary of stating your views in extremely opinionated language unless you have initially high prestige or unless listeners already agree with you.[50]

If there were any automatic or fool-proof method of achieving persuasion, then politicians, advertisers, and public relations counsels would have discovered it long ago. No single, sure route to persuasion exists; social influence is an elusive goal. Some speakers, such as Thomas Hart Benton, find research and evidence a congenial path to social influence. Other speakers make an effort to inoculate receivers against the opposing arguments. Research shows that refutation, forewarning, and example-based arguments seem best in making your listeners resistant to later counterpersuasion by opposing speakers. In addition, you will find that citing facts and specifics, emphasizing your experience and avoiding contradiction helps you build the kind of credibility that supports persuasion. Finally, persuasion is all the more likely when you realize that success and failure often mean walking a thin line between appropriate and inappropriate fear appeals, humor, and intense language.

Organizing the Persuasive Speech

No aspect of speechmaking is more straightforward to control than organization. How we arrange our major ideas and our subpoints is a strategic decision that we can make days before delivering the speech. This is not to say that organization comes easily or automatically. President Theodore Roosevelt, although an energetic and inspiring speaker, had a tendency to skip from one idea to another. Even when he prepared addresses carefully, Roosevelt digressed by talking about miscellaneous experiences and memories irrelevant to his main theme. Once giving an address on "Productive Scientific Scholarship," Roosevelt's speech became an excursion into his Rough Rider days, the Iroquois Indians, and the once flourishing populations of elephants and moose in New York State.[51]

Teddy Roosevelt's career as a speaker shows that even an experienced speaker may have trouble keeping to a planned speech structure, so take heed when your public speaking course offers theory and practice in arranging materials. Pay particular attention to the following listener-centered patterns that are especially suited for persuasion.

Listener-Centered Organizational Patterns

Listener-centered patterns of organization are proven ways to keep arguments, evidence, and delivery consistently focused on the target of persuasion. What does it mean to call a pattern listener-centered? This question may best be answered by comparison. In chapter 13 we looked at various message-centered patterns that arranged materials according to the features of the subject. For instance, a chronological pattern seemed naturally suited for a talk on travel. In contrast, listener-centered patterns *focus on the characteristics and background of the audience rather than the demands of the topic.* The rhetorical process is one of adjusting ideas to people—and people to ideas.[52] Six listener-centered patterns of organization give you specific strategies to make your ideas relevant and important to other people.

Familiar-unfamiliar pattern

Frequently you will stand before people who know nothing about your topic. To meet this rhetorical problem, why not begin the speech with concepts already familiar to listeners and then give the new information?

A student's speech on the subject of biorhythms illustrates how major ideas in a speech may be sequenced according to degree of familiarity. The student predicted that "most of my audience will be unfamiliar with my topic"; nevertheless, she believed that everyone "will have come in general contact with the subject." Given her audience, the speaker arranged the body of her speech around two major points:

I. Rhythms are a natural part of life.
  A. The Moon's gravity produces tides.
  B. Cell reproduction is cyclic.
  C. Cycles are present in work and rest.
II. The theory of biorhythms is useful in daily life.
  A. There are three important cycles.
  B. Behavior is a composite of these three cycles.
  C. Biorhythms are used by business and industry.

In arranging your ideas according to the familiar-unfamiliar pattern, look for everything about your topic that has high explanatory power. Think of examples. Look for ways to translate abstract ideas into everyday experi-

Listener-centered organizational patterns help you keep direct contact with the audience.

ence and language. Use comparisons and analogies that link something well-known, such as a 24-hour day, to something less known, such as biorhythms.

Agreement-disagreement pattern

On some occasions, most or all of your listeners may be unfavorable to your thesis or to a major point. When your task is to adjust people to disagreeable ideas, begin with arguments your listeners already accept and, only later, present the less agreeable points. Your general goal here is to establish *common ground* with listeners. Theodore Roosevelt mastered the art of looking for ideas and experiences that linked diverse people. Roosevelt, a Republican, showed this talent in a speech to the Democrat-controlled Texas State Legislature. To minimize party differences, Roosevelt observed that 95 percent of the time, public officials were doing work of a nonpartisan character.[53]

Establishing common ground early in a speech is useful because it helps the audience see the speaker as "one of us." This sets up a nice psychological frame for presenting less popular ideas. People accept criticism better from one of their own as compared to outsiders. For instance, scientists enjoy their own satirical publications, such as the *Journal of Irreproducible Results.* It's OK when a scientist makes fun of the pompous language of research studies. Yet, scientists resent Senator William Proxmire's "Golden Fleece" awards because Proxmire, the nonscientist, "satirizes a piece of work, knowing nothing about it other than the title of the paper."[54]

One public speaking student saw an opportunity to use the agreement-disagreement pattern when preparing a speech on capital punishment. The speaker believed that her audience viewed capital punishment as immoral, since everyone has a right to life, and useless, since execution would not bring back someone already dead. She decided to focus on the situation of victims of crime rather than accused criminals. She argued:

I. We are born with basic rights.
   A. We have rights to freedom and life.
   B. Our rights are often violated by others.
   C. The worst violation of our rights is murder.
II. Violators must be held responsible for their actions.
   A. Anyone who takes the life of another should forsake his own.
   B. The death penalty would deter murder.

In this speech, the student worked up to the controversial point about the death penalty only after presenting points with which few would disagree.

The *progressive agreement* pattern is one common variation of working from agreeable to disagreeable points. If you have ever listened to a telephone sales pitch, you probably will be aware of the progressive agreement approach. The pitch might begin with a harmless point such as "the weather certainly is getting colder, isn't it Mrs. Burns." Next the caller might mention that "we're all concerned about our heating bills, aren't we?" Next the sales person might make the point that "most heating loss is the result of poor insulation." Finally, the sales pitch would try to commit the home owner to the conclusion that buying storm windows is a good idea. And, of course, "our representatives will be visiting your neighborhood this week."

Two-sided pattern

Often, your listeners will already have in mind ideas and arguments that oppose a point you want to make. Probably, listeners will later be exposed to information that contradicts your thesis. What should you do? You can respond to opposing ideas by using the two-sided pattern. In organizing your speech in a two-sided manner, you would balance the pros and cons. For every opposing argument, you would give an argument that supported your case.

Research supports the idea that the two-sided pattern minimizes resistance to persuasion when (1) your audience initially disagrees with your thesis or (2) you want to immunize receivers against opposing arguments.[55] Research suggests that the best way to present a two-sided speech is first to give arguments that support your thesis, then cite opposing points. When giving arguments that support your case, organize your points in reverse order of strength, that is, the strongest last. On the other hand, when you present opposing arguments, end with the weakest point.[56]

Speeches by John F. Kennedy and William F. Buckley illustrate the two-sided arrangement. In his Houston address, Kennedy begins with his strongest points about religious freedom and political equality. Then Kennedy identifies and immediately disassociates himself with out-of-context statements by past Catholics on church-state relations. Kennedy also refutes the claim that he would promote public aid to Catholic schools. In a like manner, Buckley organizes his speech in a two-sided fashion, mentioning and then refuting arguments by opponents of the Panama Canal treaties.

Theodore Parker's persuasive sermon on Daniel Webster shows how an entire speech may be organized around alternating pro-con subpoints. Parker, a well-known Unitarian minister, wanted to criticize Webster, the Massachusetts Senator and giant of the pre-Civil War United States Congress. This approach carried risks because attacks on Webster's political career and philosophy might provoke disagreement from Bostonians. Given Webster's recent death, the criticism might seem inappropriate and create resentment. To meet this rhetorical situation, Parker used the two-sided approach. Throughout the speech, Parker treated the two themes of (1) Webster as a great man and (2) Webster as a politician who ignored fundamental principles of justice. For every positive aspect of Webster's life and career, Parker included a point of blame.[57]

In using the two-sided approach, sometimes you will merely mention the opposing point. More often, you will cite and then *explicitly refute* a contrary argument. Experimental studies show that refutation is an effective way to inoculate receivers against being swayed by opposing arguments they later hear.[58] Also it is wise for you specifically to *object to the reasoning* that supports a contrary claim.[59] Finally, you may want to include in your two-sided speech a *forewarning statement.* You would let the audience know that they should be wary of a certain argument they may later encounter. Warning the audience about an argument and then refuting it significantly weakens an opposing argument that follows your speech.[60]

Elimination of alternatives pattern

When you want to advocate adoption of a new plan, it is effective to consider—and then eliminate—alternatives to your proposal. Persuasion often deals with matters of policy, that is, questions about what should be done to solve a problem. Policy situations are usually complex. If a problem is one currently in the news, members of your audience are likely already to have in mind their own pet solutions. Why not organize the speech around this tendency of the audience? By arranging the speech to eliminate solutions, one by one, you are in a position to lead listeners gradually to your own plan.

Eliminating alternatives sometimes is termed the *method of residues.* That is, you conclude your speech by proposing adoption of the final remaining choice—the residue. Research shows that the method of residues is a particularly strong way of refuting opposing ideas.[61] This pattern will help when you want to support one policy and simultaneously attack another.

As an example of the method of residues approach, consider how a speaker might use the method in a campaign speech. The persuader might support one candidate by first examining and rejecting each competitor. Applied to Republicans running for president in 1988, the body of the speech might be organized around the merits of the several candidates:

1. Alexander Haig: Too little political experience.
2. Pierre DuPont: No national visibility.
3. Jack Kemp: Not yet ready.
4. Pat Robertson: Runs well only among fundamentalists.
5. Robert Dole: Better suited to the United States Senate.
6. George Bush: The inevitable choice.

In this hypothetical campaign speech, the method of residues permits the speaker actually to compare politicians. By keeping focus on actual candidates, instead of beginning with an abstract discussion of the ideal political leader, the advocate keeps the speech fixed on the goal of promoting one particular candidate.

Reflective thought pattern

Sometimes it is wise not to tip your hand at the beginning of a speech. If some members of your audience disagree with your conclusion, you might better succeed by inviting listeners to join with you in thinking through the problem. John Dewey, the philosopher, originated the reflective thought pattern. Dewey was interested in a modern, scientific approach to reasoning, and he developed a five-step format.[62] Dewey's theory of thinking offers a useful plan for persuasive speakers.

1. Identify a difficulty needing attention.
2. Define, locate, and describe the difficulty.
3. Identify several possible solutions.
4. Evaluate the different solutions.
5. Choose and analyze the best solution.

The persuasive impact of Dewey's steps lies in their apparent objectivity. While acting as a persuader, you look reasonable by fully dissecting a situation. Furthermore, the pattern tends to get listeners involved. They follow along. The reflective thought approach also contains elements of the two-sided and elimination of alternatives patterns. You have a chance to identify and refute competing solutions.

Need-solution pattern

Persuasion is based on an audience-centered psychology. Human nature suggests that your chances for success are greater when you create a need and then satisfy it. The need-solution approach is more psychologically satisfying than the more academic approach of presenting a proposal and working back to explain its benefits.[63]

Here is how one public speaking student used the need-solution pattern.

I. The American people are not eating properly.
   A. Americans are not eating a balanced diet.
   B. Our methods of cooking strip away nutrients.
II. Everyone should eat a balanced diet.
   A. This includes representatives of all four food groups.
   B. Eat three meals per day.
   C. Cook food to retain its nutritional value.

The first major point in the speech sets up a problem that lends both importance and credibility to the solution given in point II. Harry Emerson Fosdick, the Baptist preacher, built a career around the need-solution pattern. In sermons before packed houses at New York City's Park Avenue Baptist Church, Fosdick focused on human problems—modern tensions and anxieties. Fosdick then showed how listeners could relieve stress through a life based on religion.[64]

The *motivated sequence* is a variation of the need-solution pattern. This mode of organization has you begin by winning the *attention* of listeners, perhaps by a visual aid or startling statement. Next you describe some *need* or difficulty that exists. Third, you show how the need may be *satisfied* by some action. Next, you invite listeners to *visualize* how much better things will be once your solution is put into practice. Finally, you conclude by asking listeners to take some specific *action* to improve conditions.[65]

Martin Luther King's "I Have a Dream" address offers us an example of how the motivated sequence looks in practice. King's attention step begins with references to Lincoln, "in whose symbolic shadow we stand." King then describes the present situation of blacks who are "sadly crippled by the manacles of segregation and the chains of discrimination." Next comes King's specific description of what blacks want to overcome—police brutality, lack of public accommodations, lack of the vote. The visualization step comes in the form of King's dream. Several times, King holds out a vision of a future America—"I have a dream!" Finally, King calls for continued action to change America when the civil rights marchers returned home.

Box 14.4

The Motivated Sequence

I think my speech could best fit the motivated sequence pattern:

Attention: There is money to be made in real estate—a lot of it.

Need: Housing prices in Silicon Valley are now higher than what most can pay.

Satisfaction: Buying in Central California is one way of attaining the great American dream.

Visualization: Imagine you could make a lot of money and buy your dream house.

Action: The time is now.

From a speech preparation report by a public speaking student, fall 1988.

Tips for persuasive organization

The six listener-centered patterns represent general strategies for adjusting ideas to people and people to ideas. However, it is one thing to prepare an outline that looks good on paper; getting your points across clearly is another matter. Generally, well-organized speeches produce more persuasion than poorly-organized ones.[66] Furthermore, researchers supply us with three useful tips for making organization into a resource for persuasion.

1. Usually, you should *specifically state your thesis.* Do not let listeners guess what conclusion you draw from your arguments and evidence; instead, cite a specific thesis. Speeches with explicit conclusions typically produce more attitude change than those that leave the conclusion to be inferred by listeners.[67] Of course, we have already noted the exceptions to this rule. When your

audience initially disagrees with your thesis, or you have initially low credibility, you are better advised not to state the thesis at the beginning of the speech. Present your arguments first, and state the thesis later.

2. To make sure your listeners focus on what is important, *present your strongest points at the beginning or end of the speech.* We saw in chapter 13 that this tip also applies to informative speaking: arguments presented first or last are better remembered. In addition, presenting arguments at the beginning or end makes them more persuasive.[68] Don't bury vital ideas in the middle of your talk.
3. When preparing your conclusion, consider *using a metaphor to leave a vivid impression of what you are advocating.* Metaphorical conclusions can be more persuasive than literal ones—as we observed earlier in this chapter. Such a finding comes from research in which one speaker used metaphors of death to attack federal grants to students. The speaker contended that federal aid would "strangle individuality," leading to the "murder" of American values and the "death-rattle" of liberty. Literal conclusions, which were less persuasive, made the same point minus the terms of death.[69]

Good organization keeps you on target as a persuasive speaker. Arrange your arguments and evidence in ways that are shown to produce results. Remember that each one of the listener-centered patterns caters to a particular condition of your listeners: lack of knowledge, unfavorable attitudes, or ignorance of the personal benefits resulting from what you advocate. After deciding what pattern best adjusts your ideas to the audience, you must decide how to make your major points stick in the minds of listeners. Be sure to state your thesis explicitly, present your best points first or last, and use metaphors in your conclusions.

Your range of choices in successful persuasive speaking is laid out in chapter 14. Your career as a persuader begins when you set as your goal to change beliefs, attitudes, values, and behavior. Your chief working tools are your ability to make strong claims, to inoculate receivers, to build credibility, and to avoid offending your audience. How do you implement all this advice? Organization is the key to putting your speech materials on target. Listener-centered patterns are the ways for you to adjust your ideas to the thoughts and personalities of receivers.

Sample Speech

Speech to the Greater Houston Ministerial Association
By John F. Kennedy

I am grateful for your generous invitation to state my views.

While the so-called religious issue is necessarily and properly the chief topic here tonight, I want to emphasize from the outset that I believe that we have far more critical issues in the 1960 election: the spread of Communist influence, until it now festers only ninety miles off the coast of Florida—the humiliating treatment of our President and Vice President by those who no longer respect our power—the hungry children I saw in West Virginia, the old people who cannot pay their doctor's bills, the families forced to give up their farms—an America with too many slums, with too few schools, and too late to the moon and outer space.

These are the real issues which should decide this campaign. And they are not religious issues—for war and hunger and ignorance and despair know no religious barrier.

But because I am a Catholic, and no Catholic has ever been elected President, the real issues in this campaign have been obscured—perhaps deliberately, in some quarters less responsible than this. So it is apparently necessary for me to state once again—not what kind of church I believe in, for that should be important only to me, but what kind of America I believe in.

I believe in an America where the separation of church and state is absolute—where no Catholic prelate would tell the President (should he be a Catholic) how to act and no Protestant minister would tell his parishioners for whom to vote—where no church or church school is granted any public funds or political preference—and where no man is denied public office merely because his religion differs from the President who might appoint him or the people who might elect him.

I believe in an America that is officially neither Catholic, Protestant nor Jewish—where no public official either requests or accepts instructions on public policy from the Pope, the National Council of Churches or any other ecclesiastical source—where no religious body seeks to impose its will directly or indirectly upon the general populace or the public acts of its officials—and where religious liberty is so indivisible that an act against one church is treated as an act against all.

For while this year it may be a Catholic against whom the finger of suspicion is pointed, in other years it has been and may someday be again, a Jew—or a Quaker—or a Unitarian—or a Baptist. It was Virginia's harassment of Baptist preachers, for example, that led to Jefferson's statute of religious freedom. Today, I may be the victim—but tomorrow it may be you—until the whole fabric of our harmonious society is ripped apart at a time of great national peril.

Finally, I believe in an America where religious intolerance will someday end—where all men and all churches are treated as equal—where every man has the same right to attend or not to attend the church of his choice—where there is no Catholic vote, no anti-Catholic vote, no bloc voting of any kind—and where Catholics, Protestants and Jews, both the lay and the pastoral level, will refrain from those attitudes of disdain and division which have so often marred their works in the past, and promote instead the American ideal of brotherhood.

That is the kind of America in which I believe. And it represents the kind of Presidency in which I believe—a great office that must be neither humbled by making it the instrument of any religious group, nor tarnished by arbitrarily withholding it, its occupancy, from the members of any religious group. I believe in a President whose views on religion are his own private affair, neither imposed upon him by the nation or imposed by the nation upon him as a condition to holding that office.

I would not look with favor on a President working to subvert the First Amendment's guarantees of religious liberty (nor would our system of checks and balances permit him to do so). And neither do I look with favor upon those who would work to subvert Article VI of the Constitution by requiring a religious test—even by indirection—for if they disagree with that safeguard, they should be openly working to repeal it.

I want a chief executive whose public acts are responsible to all and obligated to none—who can attend any ceremony, service or dinner his office may appropriately require him to fulfill—and whose fulfillment of his Presidential office is not limited or conditioned by any religious oath, ritual or obligation.

This is the kind of America I believe in—and this is the kind of America I fought for in the South Pacific and the kind my brother died for in Europe. No one suggested then that we might have a "divided loyalty," that we did "not believe in liberty" or that we belonged to a disloyal group that threatened "the freedoms for which our forefathers died."

And in fact this is the kind of America for which our forefathers did die when they fled here to escape religious test oaths, that denied office to members of less favored churches, when they fought for the Constitution, the Bill of Rights, the Virginia Statute of Religious Freedom—and when they fought at the shrine I visited today—the Alamo. For side by side with Bowie and Crockett died Fuentes and McCafferty and Bailey and Bedillio and Carey—but no one knows whether they were Catholics or not. For there was no religious test there.

I ask you tonight to follow in that tradition, to judge me on the basis of fourteen years in the Congress—on my declared stands against an ambassador to the Vatican, against unconstitutional aid to parochial schools, and against any boycott of the public schools (which I attended myself)—and instead of doing this do not judge me on the basis of these pamphlets and publications we have all seen that carefully select quotations out of context from the statements of Catholic Church leaders, usually in other countries, frequently in other centuries, and rarely relevant to any situation here—and always omitting, of course, that statement of the American bishops in 1948 which strongly endorsed church-state separation.

I do not consider these other quotations binding upon my public acts—why should you? But let me say, with respect to other countries, that I am wholly opposed to the state being used by any religious group, Catholic or Protestant, to compel, prohibit or prosecute the free exercise of any other religion. And that goes for any persecution at any time, by anyone, in any country.

And I hope that you and I condemn with equal fervor those nations which deny their Presidency to Protestants and those which deny it to Catholics. And rather than cite the misdeeds of those who differ, I would also cite the record of the Catholic Church in such nations as France and Ireland—and the independence of such statesmen as de Gaulle and Adenauer.

But let me stress again that these are my views—for, contrary to common newspaper usage, I am not the Catholic candidate for President. I am the Democratic party's candidate for President who happens also to be a Catholic.

I do not speak for my church on public matters—and the church does not speak for me.

Whatever issue may come before me as President, if I should be elected—on birth control, divorce, censorship, gambling, or any other subject—I will make my decision in accordance with these views, in accordance with what my conscience tells me to be in the national interest, and without regard to outside religious pressure or dictate.

And no power or threat of punishment could cause me to decide otherwise.

But if the time should ever come—and I do not concede any conflict to be remotely possible—when my office would require me to either violate my conscience, or violate the national interest, then I would resign the office, and I hope any other conscientious public servant would do likewise.

But I do not intend to apologize for these views to my critics of either Catholic or Protestant faith, nor do I intend to disavow either my views or my church in order to win this election. If I should lose on the real issues, I shall return to my seat in the Senate satisfied that I tried my best and was fairly judged.

But if this election is decided on the basis that 40,000,000 Americans lost their chance of being President on the day they were baptized, then it is the whole nation that will be the loser in the eyes of Catholics and non-Catholics around the world, in the eyes of history, and in the eyes of our own people.

But if, on the other hand, I should win this election, I shall devote every effort of mind and spirit to fulfilling the oath of the Presidency—practically identical, I might add, with the oath I have taken for fourteen years in the Congress. For without reservation, I can, and I quote, "solemnly swear that I will faithfully execute the office of President of the United States and will to the best of my ability preserve, protect and defend the Constitution, so help me God."

Sample Speech

Speech in Favor of the Panama Canal Treaties

By William F. Buckley, Jr.

Thank you, Mr. Chairman. Ladies and gentlemen. If Lloyds of London had been asked to give odds that I would be disagreeing with Ronald Reagan on a matter of public policy, I doubt they could have flogged a quotation out of their swingingest betting man because, judging from Governor Reagan's impeccable record, the statisticians would have reasoned that it was inconceivable that he should make a mistake. But, of course, it happens to everyone. I fully expect that someday I'll be wrong about something.

Ronald Reagan told me over the telephone last Sunday that he would treat me very kindly tonight as he would any friend of his suffering temporarily from a minor aberration. He does not, in other words, plan to send the Marines after me. Perhaps he is saving them to dispatch to Panama.

I find myself, Mr. Chairman, in your company, and in the present company, disarmingly comfortable. I have sat in Saigon with Ellsworth Bunker and heard him confide to me that in his opinion we should militarily cut off the Ho Chi Minh Trail. I have sat in Hawaii with Admiral McCain, when he was commanding officer of CINCPAC, fretting privately over the failure vigorously to work our will on the Vietnamese. Admiral "Bud" Zumwalt, on my program, *Firing Line*, deplored three years ago the progressive deterioration in American military strength. Patrick Buchanan is probably the author of every truculent anti-Communist statement uttered by Richard Nixon—the old Nixon—over a period of ten years. Roger Fontaine is that anomaly in the academic world—a scholar wholeheartedly devoted to the anti-Communist enterprise. George Will is probably the most consistent journalistic critic of the SALT treaties, insisting that they play into the hands of the Soviet Union. And my colleague James Burnham is, after all, author of *The Struggle for the World* and has been the leading anti-Communist strategic prophet in the United States, whose books and articles have illuminated the international understanding of the global threat of the Communist world beyond those of any other scholar.

And yet, here we are, disagreed on a matter of public policy impinging on our common concerns. We should, I think, make this dispute as easy on ourselves as possible. We are here to ask the question—should the treaties submitted by the president to the Senate be signed? If I were in the Senate of the United States, I would sign that treaty—so would Will, so would Burnham, so would Zumwalt, so would Bunker.

Now, this does not commit us to saying anything more about that treaty, or more popularly, these treaties, . . . than that we should vote for them rather than against them. To vote for them is not to renounce the foreign policy of Theodore Roosevelt. To vote for them is not to endorse the foreign policy of President Carter. To vote for them is not to say that we are frightened by any threat directed at us by Omar Torrijos [former dictator of Panama]. Or to vote for them is not to say that we are in the least influenced by the desires of the Security Council of the United Nations, which is dedicated to the decolonization of any part of the world not under Communist control.

I think I speak for my associates when I concede that the means by which we achieved our present position in Panama were a part of what one might call pre-Watergate international morality. But then if we look around us at the activity during that period of our sister states, we do not—those of us who do not suffer from the sin of scrupulosity—think ourselves historically unique. Indeed. . .I happen to believe that there is a great deal to be said, historically, for the achievements of colonialism. . . .

Nor does our belief that it is wise to sign these treaties suggest that we harbor any illusions about the character of the head of government of Panama or the stability of his regime, or that we find that the 32 governments that have ruled over Panama since it became an independent state are an indication of creeping stability because the current government has lasted almost ten years. And finally, we are not unaware of the friendship struck up by General Torrijos with Fidel Castro, the premier barbarian of this hemisphere.

What we are maintaining is that the United States, by signing these treaties, is better off militarily, is better off economically, and is better off spiritually.

Why militarily? The question needs to be examined in two parts. If there is a full-scale atomic war, the Panama Canal will revert to a land mass. . . . In a situation of hostility short of the exchange of missiles, we would desire mobility through the canal. That mobility is more easily effected if we have the cooperation of the local population. As matters now stand, 75 percent of the work force in the canal is Panamanian.

It is frequently asserted that the natural economic interest of Panama is sufficient to keep the Panama Canal open and operating. Those who come too readily to that kind of economic reductionism fail to take into account great passions that stir not only in the breasts of members of the Third World, but also in our own. The same man who built the Panama Canal once spoke of millions for defense but not one cent for tribute. Theodore Roosevelt would not have been surprised by the closing of the Suez Canal in 1967 even though the loss of revenues to Egyptians was roughly comparable over such a loss to Panamanians.

The Panama Canal is responsible for 12 percent of the gross national product of the Republic of Panama. Subtract 12 percent, and you have 88 percent left over, plus national pride. I hope that Governor Reagan will not tell us tonight that Panamanian pride is not involved in the matter of the treaties. He may tell us that Panamanian pride must, in this case, be subordinated to the national interest, and if he convinces me that the national interest requires the subordination of Panamanian pride, I shall side with him. But he must not tell me that pride does not count. He must not tell us that the Panamanians should not be expected to share those passions which moved Egyptians only a decade ago to undertake huge sacrifices, closing their canal, and he ought not to suggest that American pride is one thing, Panamanian pride quite something else.

I take it then that the cooperation of the two million people in whose territory the canal lies, whose personnel already do three-quarters of the work required to keep the canal open, is—to put the matter unobtrusively—desirable. At the same time, I deem it essential—along with Admiral McCain—that the United States should continue to exercise responsibility for maintaining access to the canal. And I note, therefore, with satisfaction, that the first treaty reaffirms the absolute right of the United States to defend access to the canal and to continue to garrison our troops in Panama until the year 2000. And I note with satisfaction that the second treaty reaffirms the right of the United States to defend the canal and to guarantee access to it, even after the canal itself shall have become the physical property of the Republic of Panama.

It is appropriate to reflect at this moment on the words of William Howard Taft, reiterated by Theodore Roosevelt in another context. Taft said, "We do not want to own anything in Panama. What we want is a canal that goes through Panama." I should add before leaving the military point that if we cannot secure access to the canal after the year 2000 from bases outside Panama—i.e., if our power is so reduced that we cannot control the waters at either end of the little Isthmus of Panama—it is altogether unlikely that the situation would change in view of our having the technical right to bivouac a few thousand Marines within the territory of Panama.

Why would we be better off economically—because, under the first treaty, the revenues from the use of the canal flow to the United States. The royalty retained by Panama is—at 30 cents per ton—approximately twenty-five percent of the tolls, plus a share in the profits, not to exceed $10 million. Ancillary economic commitments do not spring directly from the treaty, by which I mean our extra-treaty commitment to help Panama achieve credits from the Export-Import Bank, from AID, and OPIC, and our commitment to give it—over the terms of the treaty—$50 million of military equipment for the purpose of relieving us of expenses we currently shoulder.

Those who have made a huge production over the financial price of these treaties—which figure approaches $60 million per year, the whole of it derived from canal revenues—are perhaps most readily sedated by comparisons that come readily to mind: $1,290,000,000 to Spain during the last 20 years. I know, I know, we are paying Spain for the privilege of protecting Spain. Such are the burdens of great nations. Or there is Turkey. For the privilege of protecting Turkey from the Soviet Union we have spent $2,828,000,000 and are now committed to spend an extra one billion over the next four years. Dear Turkey. Lovely people. And unlike the canal, we have no offsetting revenues from Turkey. Perhaps we should send Mr. Bunker to Ankara and argue that we should receive a royalty on every pound of heroin sent out from Turkey for sale in the streets of the United States. Or there is Greece: $1,800,000,000 with $700,000,000 committed over the next four years. Or the Philippines which is asking for a cool billion. I do hope and pray that Mr. Reagan, whose propensity to frugality with the public purse is one of his most endearing characteristics, will not devote an extravagant amount of our time tonight to telling us how ignominious it is—under the circumstances—to cede 40 or 50 million dollars a year out of revenues to the Republic of Panama.

I said finally we'd be better off spiritually. Perhaps—I fear it is so—this is the most provocative point I have made, particularly in this company. And that is so, Mr. Chairman, because we are—most of us—agreed that the people who have been responsible for United States foreign policy during the postwar years—Republicans and Democrats—have tended to suffer from grievous misconceptions . . . concerning what it is that makes a country popular or prestigious. . . . The conventional wisdom is that we earn the respect of the world by prostrating ourselves before the nearest Cherokee Indian and promising to elect Marlon Brando as president. The factual situation suggests the world works very differently. General Torrijos has criticized the United States far more than he has criticized Fidel Castro. American liberals accept solemnly plebiscites conducted in Panama when they validate something they want validated, while scorning plebiscites conducted in Chile when they see validated what they don't want to see validated.

I happen to believe that the surest road to international prestige is to pay absolutely no need whatever to foreign opinion. However, in order to do this successfully, it helps, though it is not required, that you be a gentleman. Nikita Khrushchev had no problems whatever in getting admired by Pandit Nehru—the greatest ethical heart throb of the century—not even when Khrushchev took to expressing his crochets by sending Russian tanks to run over Hungarian students who wanted a little liberty. In the corridors of the United Nations the representatives of the anti-colonialist world don't rise and walk out in indignation when the Soviet overlords walk into the room—or the Chinese. They don't pass resolutions calling for the freedom of Tibet or of Lithuania—let alone Poland which, last week, we were advised by our pleasantly befuddled president, shares American principles and ideals. No.

Finally, we do not believe—those of us who favor this treaty—that it is to be favored because it will cause the president of Libya to smile upon us as he lubricates his megaphones with expropriated American oil, happily joining a consortium of extortionists whose respect for the United States paradoxically enough, diminishes as we agree to pay the price that they exact from us as a reward for our defective diplomacy. No, it is another kind of satisfaction, Mr. Chairman. I mean the approval, given by reflective men and women, to nations that disdain a false pride.

Nothing should stand in the way of our resolution to maintain United States' sovereignty and freedom, and nothing should distract us from the irrelevance of prideful exercises—suitable, rather, to the peacock than to the lion—to assert our national masculinity. We have great tests ahead of us. Are we going to disarm unilaterally? Is our word to our allies a reliable covenant? Do we really believe in human rights? Do we believe in sovereignty—even for little countries . . . whose natural resources, where and when necessary, we are entitled to use but not to abuse? The kind of satisfaction a nation truly consistent in the practice of its ideals seeks for itself is the kind of satisfaction, at this moment in history, we can have by ratifying treaties that at once enhance our security and our self-esteem. Thank you.

Concepts for Review

Can you summarize the meaning of these terms or expressions? How does each relate to speechmaking?

"language is sermonic"
create new beliefs
reinforce beliefs
use shared attitudes
value appeals
values as sources of motivation
attitudes and behavior
establishing strong claims
inoculating receivers
forewarning
building credibility
avoid contradiction
use fear appeals carefully
humor may backfire
opinionated language
listener-centered patterns
familiar-unfamiliar
agreement-disagreement
two-sided pattern
elimination of alternatives
reflective thought pattern
need-solution
motivated sequence
state your thesis
strongest points first/last
metaphors as conclusions

Things to Try

1. Select the text of a persuasive speech in *Vital Speeches* or in another source. Read through the speech to find examples of where the speaker is working with beliefs, attitudes, and values. Where does the speaker build upon existing beliefs, and what appeals to new beliefs do you find? Where does the speaker build upon existing shared attitudes? What value-oriented (motivational) appeals do you find?
2. In preparing your persuasive speech, make an effort to inoculate receivers against counter-persuasion. Pick at least one of your important claims and identify the strongest opposing arguments that listeners may later (or have already) encountered. Practice using the technique of forewarning to inoculate listeners against this counter-argument. Practice refuting the opposing argument.
3. In planning your next persuasive speech, assess your level of credibility with your audience. (Review the sources of credibility mentioned in chapter 5.) Now, to what extent does your existing credibility with the audience allow you to use value appeals? Or to what extent should you stick to factual arguments? Consult the advice on using factual and value-based arguments given in this chapter.
4. Using a collection of speeches, or *Vital Speeches,* consult the texts of two or three persuasive addresses. How are the speeches organized? Do the speakers use any of the listener-centered patterns?

Endnotes

1. *San Francisco Chronicle,* 19 September 1986, A1, A22.
2. Aristotle, *Rhetoric,* I. 2. 1355b.
3. Richard M. Weaver, *Language Is Sermonic,* ed. R. L. Johannesen, R. Strickland, and R. T. Eubanks (Baton Rouge: Louisiana State University Press, 1970), 201–225.
4. Dennis S. Gouran, "Attitude Change and Listeners' Understanding of a Persuasive Communication," *Speech Teacher 15* (1966): 289–294; Bradley S. Greenberg, "On Relating Attitude Change and Information Gain," *Journal of Communication 14* (1964): 157–171; Lawrence R. Wheeless, "The Effects of Comprehension Loss on Persuasion," *Speech Monographs 38* (1971): 327–330.

5. Norman W. Mattis, "Thomas Hart Benton," *A History and Criticism of American Public Address,* ed. M. K. Hochmuth [Nichols] (New York: Russell and Russell, 1955), 76.
6. "Speech Concluding Debate on the Chicago Platform," in William J. Bryan, *The First Battle: A Story of the Campaign of 1896* (Chicago: W. B. Conkey, 1896), 199–206 and Myron G. Phillips, "William Jennings Bryan," *A History and Criticism of American Public Address,* ed. W. N. Brigance, 2 vols. (New York: Russell & Russell), 2:903.
7. Vernon E. Cronen and Richard L. Conville, "Belief Salience, Summation Theory, and the Attitude Construct," *Speech Monographs 40* (1973): 17–26.
8. Walter B. Emery, "Samuel Gompers," *History and Criticism,* ed. W. N. Brigance, 2: 566–567.
9. Marvin G. Bauer, "Henry W. Grady," *History and Criticism,* ed. W. N. Brigance, 1:388–391.
10. Harry P. Kerr, "The Rhetoric of Political Protest," *Quarterly Journal of Speech 45* (1959): 146–152.
11. Donald J. Cegala and Robert J. Kibler, "Object Importance and Commitment to Position: Predictors of Attitude Position," *Central States Speech Journal 24* (1973): 108–116.
12. Ronald F. Reid, "Edward Everett: Rhetorician of Nationalism, 1824–1855," *Quarterly Journal of Speech 42* (1956): 278–279.
13. Gary Cronkhite, *Persuasion: Speech and Behavioral Change* (Indianapolis: Bobbs-Merrill, 1969), 90–91; Dominic A. Infante, "Predicting Attitude from Desirability and Likelihood Ratings of Rhetorical Propositions," *Speech Monographs 38* (1971): 321–326; Infante, "Cognitive Structure as a Predictor of Post Speech Attitude and Attitude Change," *Speech Monographs 39* (1972a): 55–61.
14. Kenneth E. Boulding, *The Image* (Ann Arbor: University of Michigan Press, 1956), 6.
15. Howard Leventhal, Robert Singer, and Susan Jones, "Effects of Fear and Specificity of Recommendation Upon Attitudes and Behavior," *Journal of Personality and Social Psychology 2* (1965): 20–29.
16. David R. Seibold, "Communication Research and the Attitude-Verbal Report-Overt Behavior Relationship: A Critique and Theoretic Reformulation," *Human Communication Research 2* (1975): 3–32.
17. Martin Maloney, "Clarence Darrow," *History and Criticism,* ed. M. K. Hochmuth [Nichols], 296.
18. Erwin P. Bettinghaus, "The Operation of Congruity in an Oral Communication Situation," *Speech Monographs 28* (1961): 142.
19. Vernon E. Cronen, "Task Requirements, Belief Salience and Attitude: Beyond the Hullian Model," *Today's Speech 22,* No. 2 (1974): 11–17.
20. Infante, "Predicting Attitudes"; Infante, "Cognitive Structure as a Predictor"; Infante, "The Function of Perceptions of Consequences in Attitude Formation and Communicator Image Formation," *Central States Speech Journal 23* (1972b): 174–180; Infante, "Differential Functions of Desirable and Undesirable Consequences in Predicting Attitude and Attitude Change Toward Proposals," *Speech Monographs 42* (1975): 115–134.

21. Irving D. Warren, "The Effect of Credibility in Sources of Testimony on Audience Attitudes Toward Speaker and Message," *Speech Monographs 36* (1969): 456–458.
22. Bradley S. Greenberg and Gerald R. Miller, "The Effects of Low-Credible Sources on Message Acceptance," *Speech Monographs 33* (1966): 127–136 and Joseph A. Luchok and James C. McCroskey, "The Effect of Quality of Evidence on Attitude Change and Source Credibility," *Southern Speech Communication Journal 43* (1978): 371–383.
23. Luchok & McCroskey, "Quality of Evidence."
24. Cf. William J. Seiler, "The Conjunctive Influence of Source Credibility and the Use of Visual Materials on Communicative Effectiveness," *Southern Speech Communication Journal 37* (1971): 174–185 and Seiler, "The Effects of Visual Materials on Attitudes, Credibility, and Retention," *Speech Monographs 38* (1971): 331–334.
25. John W. Bowers and Michael M. Osborn, "Attitudinal Effects of Selected Types of Concluding Metaphors in Persuasive Speeches," *Speech Monographs 33* (1966): 147–155 and N. Lamar Reinsch, Jr., "An Investigation of the Effects of the Metaphor and Simile in Persuasive Discourse," *Speech Monographs 38* (1971): 142–145.
26. Reinsch, "Effects of Metaphor and Simile."
27. James C. McCroskey and Walter H. Combs, "The Effects of the Use of Analogy on Attitude Change and Source Credibility," *Journal of Communication 19* (1969): 333–339.
28. William J. McGuire, "Persistance of the Resistance to Persuasion Induced by Various Types of Prior Belief Defenses," *Journal of Abnormal and Social Psychology 64* (1962): 241–248; Michael Burgoon and Lawrence J. Chase, "The Effects of Differential Linguistic Patterns in Messages Attempting to Induce Resistance to Persuasion," *Speech Monographs 40* (1973): 1–7; W. Clifton Adams and Michael J. Beatty, "Dogmatism, Need for Social Approval and the Resistance to Persuasion," *Communication Monographs 44* (1977): 321–325; Bert Pryor and Thomas M. Steinfatt, "The Effects of Initial Belief Level on Inocuation Theory and Its Proposed Mechanisms," *Human Communication Research 4* (1978): 217–230.
29. Jonathan L. Freedman and David O. Sears, "Warning, Distraction, and Resistance to Influence," *Journal of Personality and Social Psychology 1* (1965): 262–266.
30. Dick A. Bridges and John C. Reinard, Jr., "The Effects of Refutational Techniques on Attitude Change," *Journal of the American Forensic Association 10* (1974): 203–212.
31. James C. McCroskey, "The Effects of Evidence as an Inhibitor of Counter-Persuasion," *Speech Monographs 37* (1970): 188–194.
32. Carl I. Hovland, Irving L. Janis, and Harold H. Kelley, *Communication and Persuasion* (New Haven, CT: Yale University Press, 1953); Kenneth Andersen and Theodore Clevenger, Jr., "A Summary of Experimental Research in Ethos," *Speech Monographs 30* (1963): 59–78; Henry E. McGuckin, Jr., "The Persuasive Force of Similarity in Cognitive Style between Advocate and Audience," *Speech Monographs 34* (1967): 145–151; Gerald R. Miller and John Baseheart, "Source Trustworthiness, Opinionated

Statements, and Response to Persuasive Communication," *Speech Monographs 36* (1969): 1–7; R. Samuel Mehrley and James C. McCroskey, "Opinionated Statements and Attitude Intensity as Predictors of Attitude Change and Source Credibility," *Speech Monographs 37* (1970): 47–52; Loren Anderson, "An Experimental Study of Reluctant and Biased Authority-Based Assertions," *Journal of the American Forensic Association* 7 (1970): 79–84; M. Lee Williams and Blaine Goss, "Equivocation: Character Insurance," *Human Communication Research 1* (1975): 265–270.

33. Neil Postman, *Amusing Ourselves to Death: Public Discourse in the Age of Show Business* (New York: Viking, 1985), 125–141.

34. Stephen W. King and Kenneth K. Sereno, "Attitude Change as a Function of Degree and Type of Interpersonal Similarity and Message Type," *Western Speech 37* (1973), 218–232 and Michael D. Scott and H. Thomas Hurt, "Social Influence as a Function of Communicator and Message Type," *Southern Speech Communication Journal 43* (1978): 146–161.

35. Terry H. Ostermeier, "Effects of Type and Frequency of Reference Upon Perceived Source Credibility and Attitude Change," *Speech Monographs 34* (1967): 137–144 and Lawrence R. Wheeless, "Effects of Explicit Credibility Statements by More Credible and Less Credible Sources," *Southern Speech Communication Journal 39* (1973): 33–39. Less gain in credibility comes when the speaker mentions that he or she is acquainted with someone else having first-hand experience.

36. John F. Schunk, "Attitudinal Effects of Self-Contradiction in a Persuasive Communication," *Central States Speech Journal 29* (1969): 20–29.

37. James C. McCroskey, "A Summary of Experimental Research on the Effects of Evidence in Persuasive Communication," *Quarterly Journal of Speech 55* (1969): 172, 174.

38. Aristotle, *Rhetoric,* I. 2. 1356a.

39. Cronkhite, *Persuasion,* 180.

40. "Does 'Scaring' Work?" *Newsweek,* 14 May 1979, 131.

41. Frederic A. Powell, "The Effect of Anxiety-arousing Messages When Related to Personal, Familial, and Impersonal Referents," *Speech Monographs 32* (1965): 102–106.

42. Frances Cope and Don Richardson, "The Effects of Reassuring Recommendations in a Fear-Arousing Speech," *Speech Monographs 39* (1972): 148–150.

43. Gage W. Chapel, "Humor in the White House: An Interview with Presidential Speechwriter Robert Orben," *Communication Quarterly 26,* No. 1 (1978): 47–48.

44. William L. Miller, Stevenson speechwriter, quoted in Lois J. Einhorn, "The Ghosts Talk: Personal Interviews with Three Former Speechwriters," *Communication Quarterly 36* (1988): 100.

45. Two studies of informative speeches give different answers to the question of whether humor significantly increases credibility. Cf. Charles R. Gruner, "The Effect of Humor in Dull and Interesting Informative Speeches," *Central States Speech Journal 21* (1970): 160–166 and Pat M. Taylor, "An Experimental Study of Humor and Ethos," *Southern Speech Communication Journal 39* (1974): 359–366. In a study by Charles R. Gruner and William E. Lampton, "Effects of Including Humorous Material in a Persuasive Sermon," *Southern Speech Communication Journal 38* (1972): 188–196, the researchers found that humor added nothing to the persuasive power of a sermon.
46. Larry Powell, "Topic Salience and Responses to the Source of Satirical Messages," *Southern Speech Communication Journal 44* (1978): 60–72.
47. Larry Powell, "Satirical Persuasion and Topic Salience," *Southern Speech Communication Journal 42* (1977): 151–162.
48. Mehrley & McCroskey, "Opinionated Statements and Attitude Intensity" and Dominic A. Infante, "Effects of Opinionated Language on Communicator Image and in Conferring Resistance to Persuasion," *Western Speech Communication 39* (1975): 112–119.
49. Mary J. Smith, "The Effects of Threats to Attitudinal Freedom as a Function of Message Quality and Initial Receiver Attitude," *Communication Monographs 44* (1977): 199.
50. Michael Burgoon, Stephen B. Jones, and Diane Stewart, "Toward a Message-Centered Theory of Persuasion: Three Empirical Investigations of Language Intensity," *Human Communication Research 1* (1975): 240–256; William J. McEwen and Bradley S. Greenberg, "The Effects of Message Intensity on Receiver Evaluations of Source, Message and Topic," *Journal of Communication 20* (1970): 340–350; James J. Bradac, John W. Bowers, and John A. Courtright, "Three Language Variables in Communication Research: Intensity, Immediacy, and Diversity," *Human Communication Research 5* (1979), 257–269.
51. Richard Murphy, "Theodore Roosevelt," *History and Criticism,* ed. M. K. Hochmuth [Nichols], 343–345.
52. Donald C. Bryant, "Rhetoric: Its Functions and Its Scope," *Quarterly Journal of Speech 39* (1953): 413.
53. Murphy, "Theodore Roosevelt," 339.
54. *Chronicle of Higher Education,* 25 November 1981, 23.
55. Arthur A. Lumsdaine and Irving L. Janis, "Resistance to 'Counterpropaganda' Produced by One-Sided and Two-Sided 'Propaganda' Presentations," *Public Opinion Quarterly 17* (1953): 311–318.
56. Anthony J. Clark, "An Exploratory Study of Order Effect in Persuasive Communication," *Southern Speech Communication Journal 39* (1974): 322–332.
57. Valerie Schneider, "Parker's Assessment of Webster: Argumentative Synthesis Through the Tragic Metaphor," *Quarterly Journal of Speech 59* (1973): 330–336.

58. McGuire, "Resistance to Persuasion"; Burgoon & Chase, "Messages Attempting to Induce Resistance"; Adams & Beatty, "Dogmatism, Approval, Resistance"; Pryor & Steinfatt, "Inoculation Theory."
59. Bridges & Reinard, "Refutational Techniques."
60. Dominic A. Infante, "Forewarnings in Persuasion: Effects of Opinionated Language and Forewarner on Speaker Authoritativeness," *Western Speech 37* (1973): 185–195.
61. Bridges & Reinard, "Refutational Techniques."
62. John Dewey, *How We Think* (Boston: D. C. Heath, 1910), 72.
63. Cronkhite, *Persuasion,* 196–197.
64. Robert D. Clark, "Harry Emerson Fosdick," *History and Criticism,* ed. M. K. Hochmuth [Nichols], 434.
65. Douglas Ehninger, Bruce E. Gronbeck, Ray E. McKerrow, and Alan H. Monroe, *Principles and Types of Speech Communication* 10th ed. (Glenview, IL: Scott, Foresman, 1986), 153–155.
66. Raymond G. Smith, "An Experimental Study of the Effects of Speech Organization Upon Attitudes of College Students," *Speech Monographs 18* (1951): 292–301 and James C. McCroskey and R. Samuel Mehrley, "The Effects of Disorganization and Nonfluency on Attitude Change and Source Credibility," *Speech Monographs 36* (1969): 13–21.
67. Stewart L. Tubbs, "Explicit Versus Implicit Conclusions and Audience Commitment," *Speech Monographs 35* (1968): 17.
68. Norman Miller and Donald T. Campbell, "Recency and Primacy in Persuasion as a Function of the Timing of Speeches and Measurements," *Journal of Abnormal and Social Psychology 59* (1959): 1–9; Ralph L. Rosnow, "Whatever Happened to the 'Law of Primacy?'" *Journal of Communication 16* (1966): 10–31; Warner Wilson and Howard Miller, "Repetition, Order of Presentation, and Timing of Arguments and Measures as Determinants of Opinion Change," *Journal of Personality and Social Psychology 9* (1968): 184–188; Clark, "Order Effect."
69. Bowers & Osborn, "Concluding Metaphors."

Chapter

15

Special Occasion Speeches

Outline

The most memorable speeches often are tied to a particular time and place. Special occasion speeches are uniquely able to connect us powerfully and vividly to real experiences in life. Inaugural addresses, dedications, and tributes predominate in rosters of the greatest American speechmaking.[1] For generations, Lincoln's eulogy at Gettysburg has been considered the greatest American speech. Significant discourses of our own time include Kennedy's Inaugural Address, Reagan's Welcome Home to the Iran hostages, and Reagan's memorial address on the Challenger disaster. Some of the greatest persuasive speeches also are closely connected with dramatic events. Winston Churchill's "Blood, Sweat and Tears" speech powerfully stimulated Britons to the defense of their land against Hitler. Martin Luther King's "I Have a Dream" address served as the rhetorical capstone of the 1963 March on Washington.

Because of their unparalleled ability to capture human interest and imagination, special occasion speeches offer particular opportunities for demonstrating your rhetorical competence. One of Jimmy Carter's most effective speeches was his formal address to the Parliament of India. Carter forged a close inspirational link with his listeners by showing that fellow Georgian, Martin Luther King, was "a spiritual son of Mahatma Gandhi," founder of modern India.[2]

Although occasion-centered remarks create a context for impressive speaking, audiences often adjust their expectations upward, creating the maximum challenge for a speaker. If we ignore their expectations, if we flout the demands of the situation, if we present an *un*fitting address, chances for rhetorical failure are great. At the Democratic National Convention of 1988, Governor Bill Clinton's overly-long, unmemorable nominating speech for Michael Dukakis drew significant applause only for his phrase, "in conclusion." Adverse reaction to the address led some commentators to believe that the poor speech might destroy Clinton's career. Later, Clinton was able to turn the event into good publicity, with TV appearances that included Johnny Carson's "Tonight" show. As a gag, Carson used a sand glass timer after asking his first question of Clinton.

In the special occasion speech our task is closely focused on a person, event, or object. The facts of the immediate occasion dictate (or should) how we select our purposes to inform, persuade, entertain, or inspire. In this chapter, we will look at seven kinds of special purpose speeches. These are speeches of (1) welcoming, (2) introducing, (3) nominating, (4) presenting a gift or award, (5) accepting a gift or award, (6) giving an after dinner (entertainment) address, and (7) offering words of tribute (eulogy). Read over this list again. Can you see yourself in one or more of these situations? Unless you plan to live as a hermit, you surely will be called upon to give one or more special occasion speeches to fulfill work or community commitments.

Special occasion speeches share a number of common elements that we should examine before we treat each kind separately. As the name "special occasion" suggests, the most fundamental feature of occasional speeches is their association with a particular context of people, location, ideas, and physical facilities. For a special occasion speech to succeed, you must not forget that the occasion gives rise to the message. In one of his first important addresses as president of the United States, Lyndon Johnson overlooked the way in which specific circumstances shape an address. During his first presidential swing through the West, Johnson spoke to an audience of 35,000 on the campus of the University of California at Los Angeles. The occasion was the University's Charter Day celebration; however, Johnson's speech contained no reference to the founding of the university. In fact, Johnson only once acknowledged the school's existence. Many listeners were particularly conscious of LBJ's omission because Mexico's President Lopez Mateos, who shared the platform with Johnson, organized his entire speech around the purpose of a university. Understandably, President Johnson received only polite applause. Later, the campus newspaper likened Johnson's address to an ordinary "news conference" when compared to the eloquent remarks of Lopez Mateos and the often inspirational university addresses of Johnson's predecessor, John F. Kennedy.[3]

A second aspect of occasional addresses is that their connection with events may be so strong that the speaking becomes a direct part of a ritual ceremony. Ronald Reagan's tribute to the crew of the space shuttle Challenger helped the nation accept and relieve grief. Reagan's memorial talk was a ceremonial centerpiece in the process by which Americans came to understand not only the loss of the crew, but also the abrupt fall from grace of America's manned space program. Reagan's words served to bind together listeners as a grieving community. The speech stressed what listeners held in common, including feelings of sorrow as well as a hope for the future of space exploration.[4]

When connected to a ritual event, special occasion speeches sometimes create a situation in which the *words themselves perform a function*. For instance, Reagan's Challenger speech helped restore a sense of community through appropriate eloquence. In contrast, LBJ's address at UCLA was a journey through various topics that ignored the feelings of hurt that lingered in the months after the Kennedy assassination. Some special occasion speeches are marked by particular phrases that implement the purpose of the speech. Just as the words "I do" mark a performative point in the marriage ceremony, so too is the phrase "I welcome you" the essence of the welcoming speech. The substance of a nominating speech is the phrase, "I nominate"; the rest of the words serve chiefly to make the basic performative statements clear, important, vital, and vivid.

A third characteristic feature of special occasion speeches is that the logical content of the words often counts for less than their emotional force. Words not only persuade but also satisfy and heal. The therapeutic aspect of words is particularly important when a speech is part of a ritual event. Rituals such as nominations, awards, dedications, and memorials help people understand and cope with important changes taking place in their lives. When a speech is a direct part of a ritual ceremony, the words help in emotional adjustment. Alma Sarett, a veteran speech teacher, puts the point nicely: "Often the final significance lies not so much in the 'intellectual content' of the words as in their appropriateness to the occasion, in the sincerity of their utterance, and in the very fact that they are uttered."[5]

Because special occasion speeches are fixed on particular situations, they allow you relatively greater freedom to select from among the general purposes of public speaking—informing, persuading, inspiring, and entertaining. To illustrate this fourth general feature of occasional speeches, consider how Robert Ingersoll mixed inspiration and persuasion in his nomination of James G. Blaine. At the same time that Ingersoll persuades Republican Party delegates of James G. Blaine's fitness to lead the party, Ingersoll invokes warm memories of the glories of the Republican Party. Similarly, Senator Sam Ervin's speech of introduction not only informs us about Ronald Reagan and William F. Buckley. Ervin makes us appreciate the significance of the public debate in which Reagan and Buckley participated.

To give the best special occasion speeches, you keep a close focus on the specific situation. Your remarks thereby become a natural part of a public ritual. In addition, you add the open hand of therapeutic words to a closed-fisted logic of ideas. Finally, memorable eloquence most often follows when you combine informing, persuading, entertaining, and inspiring into a blend uniquely tailored to the needs and expectations of a particular time and place.

With four general characteristics of occasional speeches in mind, we now turn to specifics of welcoming, introducing, nominating, presenting an award, accepting an award, entertaining, and eulogizing.

The Speech of Welcome

At some time in the future, you may find yourself welcoming an individual or group. In preparing and delivering a speech of welcome, pay attention to the following general guidelines.

First, be sure that your speech clearly expresses the greeting on behalf of the organization you represent. The specific statement of welcome—which is the performative part of the speech—is crucial, usually coming at either the beginning or end of the speech. Second, you should gather and mention complimentary facts about the person or group you are welcoming. As a rule, the more complimentary the tone, the greater number of specific facts you should cite. If you praise a visitor as "America's greatest athlete," listeners expect more illustration and proof than when you welcome "one of today's finest tennis professionals." To be specific in your praise of the visitor(s), you may need to do some specific research. Read about the person or group; talk to him, her, or them.

In giving a speech of welcome, identify the purpose behind the visit. Describe for listeners the general circumstances or events that surround the visit—or mention relevant past history. You may want to impress upon the audience the significance of the visit or the importance of the ideas (values) that are symbolized by the presence of the guests. Connect the purpose of the visit to the needs or beliefs of the audience. Be specific as to how the visit relates to the interests or attitudes of listeners. If you are unsympathetic to the visitors or their purposes, decline the opportunity to serve as speaker. Otherwise you will be giving a speech that you don't believe in, or you will become enmeshed in an embarrassing scene. J. Patrick Liteky, a Santa Cruz County (California) supervisor, took the latter course when asked to say a few appropriate words at a ribbon-cutting ceremony for a new Safeway grocery store. Liteky stunned his hosts by refusing to welcome the new store "in honor of Cesar Chavez and the just cause of the farm workers" who were then boycotting this supermarket chain.[6]

Finally, the speech of welcome links the interests and aims of the welcoming group with those of the guest. If you are highly favorable to the visitor, you may predict that the visit will benefit those present at the ceremony. Show how the visit will benefit either the material or spiritual well-being of audience members. In addition to showing that a visit will directly *cause* benefits, perhaps you can treat the visit as a general *symbol* of good things to come.

President Ronald Reagan's address on the occasion of the return of the Americans held hostage by Iran serves as a useful model of the speech of welcome. Reagan's remarks were given at the White House on January 27, 1981.

Sample Speech

Cardinal Cooke, thank you, I think, for delivering this weather. We had been promised showers. We're most grateful.

Welcome to the Ambassadors of our friends in neighboring countries who are here today. And I can think of no better way to let you know how Nancy and I feel about your presence here today than to say on behalf of us, of the Vice President and Barbara, the Senators, the members of Congress, the members of the Cabinet, and all of our fellow citizens, these simple words: Welcome home.

You are home, and believe me, you're welcome. If my remarks were a sermon, my text would be lines from the 126th Psalm: "We were like those who dreamed. Now our mouth is filled with laughter and our tongue with shouts of joy. The Lord has done great things for us. We are glad." You've come home to a people who for 444 days suffered the pain of your imprisonment, prayed for your safety, and most importantly, shared your determination that the spirit of free men and women is not a fit subject for barter.

You've represented under great stress the highest traditions of public service. Your conduct is symbolic of the millions of professional diplomats, military personnel, and others who have rendered service to their country.

We're now aware of the conditions under which you were imprisoned. Though now is not the time to review every abhorrent detail of your cruel confinement, believe me, we know what happened. Truth may be a rare commodity today in Iran; it's alive and well in America.

By no choice of your own, you've entered the ranks of those who throughout our history have undergone the ordeal of imprisonment: the crew of the *Pueblo,* the prisoners in two World Wars and in Korea and Vietnam. And like those others, you are special to us. You fulfilled your duty as you saw it, and now like the others, thank God you're home, and our hearts are full of gratitude.

I'm told that Sergeant Lopez here put up a sign in his cell, a sign that normally would have been torn down by those guards. But this one was written in Spanish, and his guards didn't know that "*Viva la roja, blanco, y azul*" means "Long live the red, white, and blue." They may not understand what that means in Iran, but we do, Sergeant Lopez, and you've filled our hearts with pride. *Muchas gracias.*

Two days ago, Nancy and I met with your families here at the White House. We know that you were lonely during that dreadful period of captivity, but you were never alone. Your wives and children, your mothers and dads, your brothers and sisters were so full of prayers and love for you that whether you were conscious of it or not, it must have sustained you during some of the worst times. No power on Earth could prevent them from doing that. Their courage, endurance, and strength were of heroic measure, and they're admired by all of us.

But to get down now to more mundane things, in case you have a question about your personal futures, you'll probably have less time to rest than you'd like. While you were on your way to Germany, I signed a hiring freeze in the Federal Government. In other words, we need you, our country needs you, and your bosses are panting to have you back on the job.

Now I'll not be so foolish as to say forget what you've been through; you never will. But turn the page and look ahead, and do so knowing that for all who served their country, whether in the Foreign Service, the military, or as private citizens, freedom is indivisible. Your freedom and your individual dignity are much cherished. Those henceforth in the representation of this Nation will be accorded every means of protection that America can offer.

Let terrorists be aware that when the rules of international behavior are violated, our policy will be one of swift and effective retribution. We hear it said that we live in an era of limit to our powers. Well, let it also be understood, there are limits to our patience.

Now, I'm sure that you'll want to know that with us here today are families of the eight heroic men who gave their lives in the attempt to effect your rescue. "Greater glory hath no man than that he lay down his life for another." And with us also are Colonel Beckwith and some of the men who did return from that mission. We ask God's special healing for those who suffered wounds and His comfort to those who lost loved ones. To them, to you, and to your families, again, welcome from all America and thank you for making us proud to be Americans.

And now, ladies and gentlemen, I call on, to speak for this wonderful group of returnees, Bruce Laingen, Deputy Chief of Mission [Charge d'Affaires] in Tehran. Mr. Laingen.

The Speech of Introduction

Perhaps the most familiar special occasion speech is the speech of introduction. While introductions often are quite brief, these speeches are usually built around three principles. First, your fundamental purpose is to acquaint the audience with the upcoming speaker. You name the person who will speak next, and you say some appropriate things about him or her. How you introduce a speaker will directly affect that speaker's level of credibility. You can help the speaker you are introducing by emphasizing his or her qualifications, such as education and experience. As a result of your care, listeners will view the speaker as more informed and intelligent.[7]

Do research to be sure you can implement the informative dimension of the introduction speech. Talk to the speaker, read about him or her, interview others about the speaker. In selecting details to include in your introduction, remember that a speaker is most credible when an audience believes him or her to possess an ideal mixture of personal similarity and objective expertise. Audiences like to think of a speaker as someone who is "one of us" and at the same time "knows more than we do."[8] So include details that both humanize the speaker and that testify to his or her objective competence.

A second principle of introducing another speaker is to try to promote the purposes of the speaker. The person you are introducing wants to inform, persuade, entertain, or inspire the audience. Help him along; give her a boost in attaining the purpose. Direct the audience's attention to the subject or theme of the upcoming speech—but don't actually deliver the speech for the next speaker! Instead, mention the general significance of the upcoming speech for the audience. If you are introducing an alumnus who made good in the outside world, mention that the speaker will be able to give career tips. If the upcoming speech will be inspirational in nature, try to focus on the idea behind the speech.

Introducing a speaker is a way to help him or her attain the purpose.

In helping the speaker attain his or her purpose, be alert for ways to help the speaker overcome problems. For instance, Benjamin Hooks, executive director of the National Association for the Advancement of Colored People, helped Texas Senator Lloyd Bentsen through a rocky start to his 1988 NAACP address. Shortly before the speech, Michael Dukakis, winner of the Democratic party's race for delegates, had chosen Bentsen as his running mate, spurning Jesse Jackson. Some in the crowd booed as Bentsen moved toward the podium. Hooks stepped to the microphone and told Bentsen, "You've got a hard act today, so do your best." Hooks then noted that "many of our delegates wanted to see Jesse in this position," giving listeners a chance to let off steam. Then Hooks told Bentsen, "I empathize with you," and gave a brief anecdote. "I've been preaching when they wanted somebody else to preach. I went to one church and they said, 'We ain't going to say amen one time.' They didn't." By this time, the NAACP audience was laughing rather than jeering. Hooks continued: "I lived. But I didn't go back. So we want to give Mr. Bentsen the kind of welcome that he will come back."[9]

Finally, avoid several temptations to talk too long or to undermine the speaker you are introducing. Do not make yourself the focus of the introduction, for instance, by stressing details of your connections to the speaker. Also, do not tell the audience how it will react or should react to the next speech. Consider the burden you place on a speaker if you tell listeners that they will experience the greatest inspiration of their lives or that they will laugh until their sides hurt. Do not raise expectations that even a good speech may not fulfill. Another way to keep from placing unrealistic demands on the speaker is to avoid praising the speaker lavishly or excessively. Furthermore, do not emphasize your own views on the topic, since your ideas may conflict with those of the speaker. Do not use the occasion of your introduction to apologize to the audience for unrelated problems. Do not apologize to the speaker for poor attendance. Such apologies may insult the speaker or make the people who did show up think they made a mistake. Do not include in your introduction irrelevant material such as criticism of a previous speaker. The key is to be brief. Do not speak for more than three minutes.

The following speech by former United States Senator Sam J. Ervin, Jr., is our model for the speech of introduction. Ervin introduced Ronald Reagan and William F. Buckley, Jr. on the occasion of their nationally-televised debate on the subject, "Resolved: The Senate Should Ratify the Proposed Panama Canal Treaties." This debate was held at the University of South Carolina on January 13, 1978.

Sample Speech

John Milton, who knew much about the power of words and the ideas they express, said, "Give me the liberty to know, to utter, and to argue freely according to conscience about all liberties."

The men who gave us the First Amendment to make and keep America politically, intellectually, and spiritually free shared in full measure John Milton's idea on this subject. So they gave to all Americans the right of freedom of speech, the right of a free press, the right to debate freely, the right to agree with government programs and the right to dissent from government programs.

And tonight we will witness an exercise of this invaluable right which must exist and will exist if America is to endure. Tonight we're going to have a debate on the subject "Resolved: The Senate should ratify the Panama Canal Treaties." This is a question on which American people are divided. It's a highly controversial question, and we are very fortunate in having two truly great Americans to debate the subject. One is William Buckley, the founder of the *National Review,* an author of many books, a courageous columnist, and an internationally famous debater. The other is a man who served with great distinction as governor of the State of California. I will introduce him as a politician rather than a statesman because they tell me the statesman is a dead politician, and I want Governor Reagan to be around a long, long time. He is a unique person in politics.

Now it's easy enough for a columnist to be courageous like William Buckley is, but it takes a lot of courage for a politician to stand up. And the great thing about Governor Reagan is that he has the courage to stand up for what he actually believes, and I would say that that is a quality which is in shortest supply among politicians.

At this time William F. Buckley will open the debate, speaking in favor of the affirmative; that is, in favor of ratification.

The Speech of Nomination

Every large organization that elects officers has need for speeches of nomination. Familiar to all of us are the nomination speeches for candidates at national political party conventions. "I give you a man [woman] who. . . ." When your turn comes to offer a nomination, here are some pointers to follow. First, remember that actually placing the name in nomination is the key element to the speech. The statement in which you say "I nominate" represents the performative aspect of the speech, the act around which your address is built. You may give the statement of nomination at the beginning of the speech, especially if you believe that listeners will react enthusiastically. Sometimes, for reasons of suspense, the name of the person being nominated is not spoken until the end of the speech. Saving the act of nomination for last is OK as long as the suspense does not seem contrived. The shorter the speech, the better the suspense approach works.

Next, give information about the position for which you are nominating the individual. Your options here include describing the present state of affairs or citing issues facing the group. Another approach is to explain what type of person is needed, focusing on requirements of the office or needs of the group.

After describing the position, show how your nominee is especially fit for the position. Here you establish the speaker's credibility. You may center your remarks on any of the many aspects of credibility, including character, competence, and sincerity. As with the speech of welcome, the more lavish your praise of the nominee, the more of the person's achievements you should cite. If the nominee's attainments are well-known, you can use inspirational language to impress the audience with their significance. In the sample speech following, Robert Ingersoll takes just this approach. If the achievements are largely unknown, you must give a more detailed description of them, possibly including proof in the form of testimony or statistics.

Fourth, it is often useful to include an element of prediction in giving a nominating speech. Help listeners visualize the successes that your candidate will bring to the group when elected. To flesh out your predictions, consider again the advice given for the visualization step in the motivated sequence pattern of organization (pp. 415–416). Help the audience picture how things will be after your candidate has acted on current problems or difficulties. It is worth mentioning, in this connection, that the motivated sequence provides a nice structure for the speech of nomination. You get *attention* by nominating the candidate. Then you show a *need* by describing the present state of affairs. Then you *satisfy* the need by describing your candidate's fitness for office. Then you help listeners *visualize* success under the nominee's leadership. Finally, you encourage the group to *act* to elect your candidate.

Robert G. Ingersoll's nominating speech for James G. Blaine is a classic of political speechmaking. The speech was given at the 1876 Republican National Convention, at a time when Blaine was the leading national figure of the G.O.P. A few of the specific political issues and controversies cited by Ingersoll are unfamiliar today. His references to the notorious Confederate prison at Andersonville were vivid for listeners of 1876 but now are a matter for history books. However, most of the points Ingersoll makes are surprisingly current. How little the basics of American politics have changed in 100 years. Ingersoll's speech was delivered in Cincinnati on June 15, 1876.

Sample Speech

. . . The Republicans of the United States demand as their leader in the great contest of 1876 a man of intelligence, a man of integrity, a man of well-known and approved political opinions. They demand a statesman; they demand a reformer after as well as before the election. They demand a politician in the highest, broadest and best sense—a man of superb moral courage. They demand a man acquainted with public affairs—with the wants of the people; with not only the requirements of the hour, but with the demands of the future. They demand a man broad enough to comprehend the relations of this government to the other nations of the earth. They demand a man well-versed in the powers, duties and prerogatives of each and every department of this government. They demand a man who will sacredly preserve the financial honor of the United States; one who knows enough to know that the national debt must be paid through the prosperity of this people; one who knows enough to know that all the financial theories in the world cannot redeem a single dollar; one who knows enough to know that all the money must be made, not by law, but by labor; one who knows enough to know that the people of the United States have the industry to make the money, and the honor to pay it over just as fast as they make it.

The Republicans of the United States demand a man who knows that prosperity and resumption, when they come, must come together; that when they come, they will come hand in hand through the golden harvest fields; hand in hand by the whirling spindles and the turning wheels; hand in hand past the open furnace doors; hand in hand by the flaming forges; hand in hand by the chimneys filled with eager fire, greeted and grasped by the countless sons of toil.

This money has to be dug out of the earth. You cannot make it by passing resolutions in a political convention.

The Republicans of the United States want a man who knows that this government should protect every citizen, at home and abroad; who knows that any government that will not defend its defenders, and protect its protectors, is a disgrace to the map of the world. They demand a man who believes in the eternal separation and divorcement of church and school. They demand a man whose political reputation is spotless as a star; but they do not demand that their candidate shall have a certificate of moral character signed by Confederate Congress. The man who has, in full, heaped and rounded measure, all these splendid qualifications, is the present grand and gallant leader of the Republican party—James G. Blaine.

Our country, crowned with the vast and marvelous achievements of its first century, asks for a man worthy of the past, and prophetic of her future; asks for a man who has the audacity of genius; asks for a man who is the grandest combination of heart, conscience and brain beneath her flag—such a man is James G. Blaine.

For the Republican host, led by this intrepid man, there can be no defeat.

This is a grand year—a year filled with recollections of the Revolution; filled with proud and tender memories of the past; with the sacred legends of liberty—a year in which the sons of freedom will drink from the fountains of enthusiasm; a year in which the people call for the man who has preserved in Congress what our soldiers won upon the field; a year in which they call for the man who has torn from the throat of treason the tongue of slander—for the man who has snatched the mask of democracy from the hideous face of rebellion; for the man who, like an intellectual athlete, has stood in the arena of debate and challenged all comers, and who is still a total stranger to defeat.

Like an armed warrior, like a plumed knight, James G. Blaine marched down the halls of the American Congress and threw his shining lance full and fair against the brazen foreheads of the defamers of his country and the maligners of his honor. For the Republican party to desert this gallant leader now, is as though an army should desert their general upon the field of battle.

James G. Blaine is now and has been for years the bearer of the sacred standard of the Republican party. I call it sacred, because no human being can stand beneath its folds without becoming and without remaining free.

Gentlemen of the convention, in the name of the great Republic, the only republic that ever existed upon this earth; in the name of all her defenders and of all her supporters; in the name of all her soldiers living; in the name of all her soldiers dead upon the field of battle; and in the name of those who perished in the skeleton clutch of famine at Andersonville and Libby, whose sufferings he so vividly remembers, Illinois nominates for the next President of this country, that prince of parliamentarians—that leader of leaders—James G. Blaine.

Speech to Present Gift or Award

Most of us will be in the position of presenting a gift or award in connection with an office we hold, a group we belong to, or a task we are assigned. Generally, you will be brief; but, if you have acquired rhetorical competence, you will make your remarks memorable through resources of thought and style. Overall, your goal is to give fair but not excessive tribute to the recipient of the gift or award. True, you are focusing the rhetorical spotlight on a deserving individual or group; but remember to keep the person's or the group's accomplishments in perspective against the attainments of others.

A good speech of presentation is informative. You explain the nature of the gift or award, and you also describe why the chosen recipient is deserving. To inform listeners of the impressive features of the gift, you may mention that an award carries a major cash prize. You may also emphasize the history of the gift or award, particularly if these details are interesting, unusual, or particularly relevant to the audience. You may cite further data about the gift or award, such as the criteria used to determine the winner, or the persons who granted the gift. Finally, you may explain the nature of the gift or award by focusing on the ideas or values that stand behind it. For instance, you might describe a scholarship as symbolizing excellence of personal determination by the scholar. Or you might treat a scholarship as evidence of society's appreciation for the value of academic study.

Along with your explanation of the gift or award comes your description of why the recipient deserves this recognition. Your purpose here is to satisfy both the donor(s) and the recipient(s), a fact that suggests two possible methods. On the one hand, you may focus on the achievements of the recipient, such as what it took to win the honor of "top employee." On the other hand, you may emphasize how wonderful it is that your group has decided to grant the gift or bestow the award. On some occasions, you will judge that the merits of donor and recipient are equally important, and you will structure the speech accordingly.

The last feature of the speech of presentation—the performative one—may seem too simple for comment. But this simplest of tasks is the most crucial. You should explicitly transmit the gift or award. In a short phrase or sentence, call the recipient, and in a friendly and dignified manner, give the actual gift or award, or a symbol of it.

The following sample speech of presentation is an address given to members of the Speech Association of America, the national professional organization for teachers in speech communication (now called the Speech Communication Association). The address is by Karl Wallace, a leading figure in the association whose writings we have encountered earlier in relation to the theory of rhetorical competence. In simple language, Wallace's speech satisfied the donors—a group of scholars who completed an important study for the association. Wallace's remarks also met the needs of the listeners, members of the association gathered in annual convention. The speech was given in Chicago on December 29, 1954.

Sample Speech

Professor Braden, at this time I have the special privilege of presenting to the Speech Association of America a volume of studies which I trust is not only symbolic of the long and honorable history of our subject in centuries past, but signalizes the maturity of our subject today, and prophesies our scholarship in the decades to come.

The volume bears the title *History of Speech Education in America.* It is the immediate product of thirty-six scholars in the fields of speech and the educational theatre who have labored for six years to present some of the fundamental facts of the development of their subjects in the public school and college. It is the ultimate fruit of the energy and wisdom of those mentors whose faith in our work and its history led the Association to undertake the project officially. Hence these studies represent more than the time and labors of the editorial board and of the contributors. They are a monument to the original Committee on the History of Speech Education, whose members were John Dolman, Jr., Alexander M. Drummond, Bert Emsley, Wilbur Gilman, Ota Thomas Reynolds, Mary Margaret Robb, Lester Thonssen, Russell Wagner, and Giles Gray.

In presenting this volume to the Association on behalf of the editorial board, I wish to acknowledge particularly the fine cooperation of our contributors and of our publishers. Many of the contributors are recognized as authorities in their lines of study; they were asked to take a fresh look at their materials, to extend their research, and to prepare new studies. This they gladly did. A few of the authors were asked to undertake what to them were new lines of investigation. They, too, responded superbly.

Although it is too early to know how others will judge their work, we believe that their contributions are worth the close observation and critical analysis which both mature scholars and graduate students in speech can exercise. We are, of course, particularly grateful to our publishers, Appleton-Century-Crofts, and their editorial assistants, because their faith in this venture has been as great as ours.

Mr. Secretary, if this volume should stimulate in the next ten years new and better studies in the history of our subject, our work will have been well rewarded. The seed may be essential, but it's the harvest which not only multiplies but tests the stock.

From Karl R. Wallace, presenting volume of *History of Speech Education in America* to SAA, in *Quarterly Journal of Speech, 41*(1): 62–63, February 1955.

Speech to Accept Gift or Award

For every presentation of a gift, there comes an acceptance. The acceptance speech is no simple matter. If you are like most people, you may find it easier to give praise than to receive it. We are conditioned by society not to appear boastful, so we modestly minimize our worthiness for any recognition we are given. But if we downplay our fitness for the gift or award, we are also insulting the judgment of the donors. Following is a recommended approach to handle the dilemma of the acceptance speech.

First, accept the award and express thanks to the donors. Your statement, "I accept," is the performative part of the speech. Therefore, the words themselves are less important than the fact that you pronounce your acceptance with appropriate thanks. Still, you would be wise to avoid such trite expressions as "I have no words to express."

In accepting a gift or an award you may minimize your own attainments, but do not deny them. To insist your unworthiness for the award is to suggest that the donors acted stupidly or with ulterior motive. Instead, give appropriate thanks and recognition to other persons who may have contributed to your success. If you know ahead of time that you will receive the award, you should review everyone who needs recognition.

Acceptance speeches may include a word or two about the award you have received. (This kind of statement also was a feature of the speech to present an award.) But be sure not to deprecate the gift or award, for instance by saying "Well, I guess it was a woman's turn to get the award this year—but thanks anyway." In accepting your gift or award, you may recognize the past or present relationship between you and the donors, or look to future connections.

Finally, be brief. Unless your acceptance is the featured address, remember that the audience does not expect more than a simple statement. Convey your acceptance, give thanks, recognize those who helped, and finally, mention what the award means to you.

The following speech by a student, Betty Ann Whelchel, illustrates how a speaker can simply and appreciatively accept an award. The speech was given at the national convention of the Chi Omega sorority, June 23, 1978.

Sample Speech

First, I would like to say thank you to all of you. Without the support of Chi Omegas, the Mary Love Collins Memorial Scholarship and its tribute to the ideals Mary Love represented, would not exist.

I feel very honored to be a recipient of the Mary Love Collins Memorial—particularly when I read of her extraordinary accomplishments. I am especially awed when I think of the time in which she

From Betty Ann Whelchel, "Mary Love Collins Scholarship Winner Accepts Award at Chi Omega Convention" in *The Eleusis of Chi Omega, 80*(3): 68–69, fall 1978.

achieved so much. Mary Love predated our era of relative acceptance of professional women in fields such as law. Yet, she not only became a lawyer, but became a lawyer widely respected among her contemporaries.

When I think of the opportunities women now have—opportunities made possible by the achievements of women such as Mary Love—I feel very fortunate. Women are in the position as never before in our history to choose what we wish to do with our lives. Law, medicine, business, and homemaking are equally viable options. Although it is still not as easy for women to pursue some fields as others, the obstacles are not insurmountable. The *only real limits* on what we can accomplish rest in our own imagination, ability, and initiative.

The ideals of Chi Omega also predated our era. From its inception, Chi Omega embodied the affirmation of the potential of women. The spirit of our Fraternity stresses a belief in our highest qualities and our personal capabilities. It lives through the lives of Chi Omegas—not only the exceptional, such as Mary Love, but in all Chi Omegas. It was evident in many of the older girls I admired as a pledge, the friends I had as sisters, my chapter advisers, and other alumnae. These relationships meant much to me in my college years. Chi Omegas, by example or active encouragement, have often brought me to attempt that which I would not have considered on my own. Chi Omegas have often shown me the way to enrich my own life and accomplish my goals. Most of all, Chi Omegas have often believed in me when I am not sure I believed in myself.

The ideals of Chi Omega illuminate the path to excellence. The sisterhood of Chi Omega provides the support for us to achieve that goal.

In this, our Fraternity could well serve as a model for all women. I believe we need today to focus on achieving a life with meaning in whatever vocation we follow. We need to retain respect for others and support them in their pursuits. We must encourage each other to achieve our maximum potential in whatever we do.

We are at the brink of new opportunity, new individualism. I urge you to make the most of it, as did Mary Love Collins. Take the unconventional path that is your way to fulfillment. Contribute all you can to your chosen field. We each have something we can give to our society—something that is as individual as each of us, but which is equally important to the enrichment of our world.

I think of one of the quotations used at Mary Love Collins' memorial service:

> "The enduring purposes of Chi Omega challenge creative abilities and give meaning to life."

I believe there could be no greater tribute to Mary Love Collins than for those purposes to be fulfilled—and for the ideals of Chi Omega, to which she dedicated her life, to live on through future Chi Omegas.

I challenge you, as well as myself, to undertake this task—to ensure the survival of the spirit of our Fraternity—not only for the sake of Chi Omega, but for the enrichment of our own lives and the greater happiness of those around us.

I wish I could have known Mary Love Collins. I thank you again for the opportunity to be here with you tonight. I thank you for making the scholarship possible, and I pledge to live up to her ideals in my own life.

Entertainment (after Dinner) Speech

Entertainment is frequently the aim of addresses given at banquets, recognition dinners, or "roasts." The basic elements of entertainment speaking were surveyed in chapter 4. Review these principles; then read the following excerpts from John F. Kennedy's speech given at the Alfred E. Smith Memorial Dinner in New York City, October 19, 1960.

Because the Al Smith Dinner is a traditionally Catholic event, Kennedy initially planned not to attend, believing that to speak there would only highlight his controversial position as a Catholic running for president. In the end, Kennedy decided to speak with a light touch. In the days before the speech, Kennedy's aides scurried to find every possible new joke about the 1960 presidential campaign.[10]

The following paragraphs are the opening one-third of Kennedy's original address. Kennedy's friendly and humorous intent is clear, although some of the specific names and events are now less familiar. Here is some background to help you follow Kennedy's remarks: Alfred E. Smith, former Governor of New York, was the first Catholic nominated for president by a major party. (John F. Kennedy was the second.) Also, both President Herbert Hoover and Vice President Richard Nixon had Quaker ancestry. Nelson Rockefeller, Governor of New York, had been a major rival of Mr. Nixon for the Republican presidential nomination of 1960. Casey Stengel was the longtime manager of the New York Yankees baseball team and had been recently fired. JFK's father, Joseph Kennedy, served as Ambassador to Great Britain under Franklin D. Roosevelt.

Sample Speech

I am glad to be here at this notable dinner once again and I am glad that Mr. Nixon is here also. [applause]

Now that Cardinal Spellman has demonstrated the proper spirit, I assume that shortly I will be invited to a Quaker dinner honoring Herbert Hoover. [laughter] Cardinal Spellman is the only man so widely respected in American politics that he could bring together amicably, at the same banquet table, for the first time in this campaign, two political leaders who are increasingly apprehensive about the November election—who have long eyed each other suspiciously and who have disagreed so strongly, both publicly and privately—Vice President Nixon and Governor Rockefeller. [laughter]

Mr. Nixon, like the rest of us, has had his troubles in this campaign. At one point even the *Wall Street Journal* was criticizing his tactics. That's like the *Osservatore Romano* criticizing the Pope.

But I think the worst news for the Republicans this week was that Casey Stengel had been fired. [laughter] It just shows that perhaps experience doesn't count. [laughter and applause]

On this matter of experience, I had announced earlier this year that if successful, I would not consider campaign contributions as a substitute for experience in appointing ambassadors. Ever since I made that statement, I haven't received one single cent from my father.

One of the inspiring notes that was struck in the last debate was struck by the Vice President in his very moving warning to the children of the nation and the candidates against the use of profanity by presidents and ex-presidents when they're on the stump. And I know after fourteen years in the Congress with the Vice President that he was very sincere in his views about the use of profanity.

But I am told that a prominent Republican said to him yesterday in Jacksonville, Florida, "Mr. Vice President, that was a damned fine speech." [laughter] And the Vice President said, "I appreciate the compliment, but not the language." And the Republican went on, "Yes, sir, I liked it so much that I contributed a thousand dollars to your campaign." And Mr. Nixon replied, "The hell you say." [laughter and applause]

However, I would not want to give the impression that I am taking former President Truman's use of language lightly. I have sent him the following wire: "Dear Mr. President: I have noted with interest your suggestion as to where those who vote for my opponent should go. While I understand and sympathize with your deep motivation, I think it is important that our side try to refrain from raising the religious issue." [laughter and applause]

A eulogy is an expression of tribute and sorrow.

Speech of Tribute (Eulogy)

Speeches of tribute—eulogies—allow us to pay special honor to significant persons, living or deceased. Speeches of tribute call for true eloquence of spirit and fluency of expression. If you ever have to deliver a eulogy, you will want to review the following traditional advice given by speech experts.

First, since your subject is a person (or persons), be sure to structure your speech around the character—the essential nature—of this person. Cite specific facts and events to show the character or theme of your subject's life. Next, tell how your subject affected others. You may mention particular people influenced by your subject, or you may describe the person's influence on society at large. Remember that the eulogy is a ceremonial speech, part of a ritual event. It is designed to help listeners understand the significance of a larger-than-life individual or the loss occasioned by a death.

In giving a eulogy, you may connect the person to a value; then you may focus the speech on that value. In the sample speech following, Ronald Reagan associates the crew of the Challenger space shuttle with the values of discovery and exploration. In like manner, you might want to connect your subject with such values as courage, wisdom, justice, or determination. Focusing the speech of tribute on a transcending value is especially appropriate when the particular value connects the audience to the person(s) being honored. In Reagan's eulogy for the Challenger Seven, he emphasized the crew as representatives of the nation.

In a eulogy, you should humanize the person receiving tribute. Making your subject seem human balances your praise of the individual. Mention events that show the person acting as a real human being. Another way to humanize a person is to include a quotation from his or her own speaking or writing—or cite someone else's testimony. Look for words that epitomize the person being honored or remembered.

Literally, the word eulogy means praise, but be sure to avoid extravagant or excessive praise. Do not think you are doing the honoree, or the deceased, any favors by treating him or her as more saintly than commonly believed. Excessive praise may be taken as sarcasm—or may cause listeners to focus on the person's shortcomings.

Finally, you may express your own personal feelings of praise—or grief, in the case of eulogizing someone deceased. Remember, however, that a eulogy is not a personal testimony. It is an expression of tribute or sorrow felt by a community of people. You serve only as spokesperson, so do not center the speech on your own reactions or feelings. You will find, in fact, that the speech is easier to deliver the less you personalize the speech and the more you take an objective approach.

The following text is Ronald Reagan's eulogy for the Challenger astronauts. His remarks were given in a nationally-televised address, January 28, 1986.

Sample Speech

Ladies and gentlemen, I planned to speak to you tonight to report on the State of the Union, but the events of earlier today have led me to change those plans. Today is a day for mourning and remembering. Nancy and I are pained to the core by the tragedy of the shuttle Challenger. We know we share this pain with all of the people of our country. This is truly a national loss.

Nineteen years ago, almost to the day, we lost three astronauts in a terrible accident on the ground. But we've never lost an astronaut in flight. We've never had a tragedy like this. And perhaps we've forgotten the courage it took for the crew of the shuttle. But they, the Challenger Seven, were aware of the dangers, and overcame them, and did their jobs brilliantly.

We mourn seven heros: Michael Smith, Dick Scobee, Judith Resnik, Ronald McNair, Ellison Onizuka, Gregory Jarvis, and Christa McAuliffe. We mourn their loss as a nation, together.

The families of the seven—we cannot bear, as you do, the full impact of this tragedy; but we feel the loss, and we're thinking about you so very much. Your loved ones were daring and brave, and they had that special grace, that special spirit that says, "Give me a challenge and I'll meet it with joy." They had a hunger to explore the universe and discover its truths. They wished to serve and they did—they served all of us.

We've grown used to wonders in this century; it's hard to dazzle us. For twenty-five years the United States space program has been doing just that. We've grown used to the idea of space, and perhaps we forget that we've only just begun. We're still pioneers. They, the members of the Challenger crew, were pioneers.

And I want to say something to the school children of America who were watching the live coverage of the shuttle's take-off. I know it's hard to understand that sometimes painful things like this happen. It's all part of the process of exploration and discovery. It's all part of taking a chance and expanding man's horizons. The future doesn't belong to the fainthearted. It belongs to the brave. The Challenger crew was pulling us into the future, and we'll continue to follow them.

I've always had great faith in and respect for our space program, and what happened today does nothing to diminish it. We don't hide our space program; we don't keep secrets and cover things up. We do it all up front and in public. That's the way freedom is, and we wouldn't change it for a minute. We'll continue our quest in space. There will be more shuttle flights and more shuttle crews and, yes, more volunteers, more civilians, more teachers in space. Nothing ends here. Our hopes and our journeys continue.

> I want to add that I wish I could talk to every man and woman who works for NASA, or who worked on this mission, and tell them, "Your dedication and professionalism have moved and impressed us for decades, and we know of your anguish. We share it."
>
> There's a coincidence today. On this day 390 years ago, the great explorer, Sir Francis Drake, died aboard ship off the coast of Panama. In his lifetime, the great frontiers were the oceans, and a historian later said, "He lived by the sea, died on it, and was buried in it." Well, today we can say of the Challenger crew, their dedication was, like Drake's, complete. The crew of the space shuttle Challenger honored us by the manner in which they lived their lives. We will never forget them nor the last time we saw them this morning as they prepared for their journey and waved goodbye and "slipped the surly bonds of earth to touch the face of God."
>
> Thank you.

Welcoming, introducing, nominating, presenting, accepting, entertaining, eulogizing—special occasion speeches mark transitions in our lives and in society. The seven speeches given in this chapter provide models for how a speech must respond to the occasion for which you prepare it. When circumstances place you in the position of giving one of the special occasion speeches, keep in mind the basic flavor of the masterpieces cited above. Tuck away some impressions for later use.

Concepts for Review

Can you summarize the meaning of these terms or expressions? How does each relate to speechmaking?

"the occasion gives rise to the message"
words perform a ritual function
logical content may count for less than appropriateness
make compliments proportional to facts
connect events to values
promote the purposes of a speaker you introduce
visualization step in the nomination speech
satisfy both donor and recipient when presenting an award
don't downplay your fitness for an award
have your eulogy connect a person to a value

Things to Try

1. List all the special occasions speeches that you remember hearing. Select one of these speeches and indicate whether or not the speech was satisfying. How did you react at the time? How did others react? What made the speech successful or unsuccessful? Did the success or failure of the speech have anything to do with the advice given in this chapter?
2. Collect two samples of a particular kind of special occasion speech. To find them, look in your library's card or computer catalogue for collections of speeches (usually listed under the subject headings of "speeches" or "public speaking"). Do the two speeches follow all the points of advice given in this chapter for the particular kind of speech? Compare the two speeches, listing similarities and differences.
3. Take one of the special occasion speeches you identified in item 2 above. Compare it to a contemporary informative speech in *Vital Speeches.* Rhetorical theory suggests that the language of a special occasion speech is more eloquent in style than that of an informative speech. Does this generalization hold true for your comparison? Consult chapter 10 on style to support your judgment.
4. Which one of the special occasion speeches are you most likely to give? Describe the situation in which you might give the speech—at work, in a community organization, etc. Prepare an outline for the speech.

Endnotes

1. See Hugo E. Hellman, "The Greatest American Oratory," *Quarterly Journal of Speech 24* (1938): 36–39 and survey by the International Platform Association, cited in *Spectra,* June 1982, 4.
2. *Courier-Journal* (Louisville), 3 January 1978, A4.
3. Waldo Phelps and Andrea Beck, "Lyndon Johnson's Address at the U.C.L.A. Charter Day Ceremony," *Western Speech 29* (1965): 162–171.
4. Steven M. Mister, "Reagan's Challenger Tribute: Combining Generic Constraints and Situational Demands," *Central States Speech Journal 37* (1986): 158–165.
5. Alma J. Sarett, *Basic Principles of Speech,* 4th ed. (Boston: Houghton Mifflin, 1966), 491.
6. *Courier-Journal* (Louisville), 8 April 1985, B9.

7. Helen Fleshler, Joseph Ilardo, and Joan Demoretcky, "The Influence of Field Dependence, Speaker Credibility Set, and Message Documentation on Evaluations of Speaker and Message Credibility," *Southern Speech Communication Journal 39* (1974): 389–402.
8. Mark I. Alpert and W. Thomas Anderson, Jr., "Optimal Hetrophily and Communication Effectiveness: Some Empirical Findings," *Journal of Communication 23* (1973): 328–343.
9. *San Francisco Chronicle,* 14 July 1988, A12.
10. Theodore H. White, *The Making of the President 1960* (New York: Atheneum, 1961), 298.

Appendixes

Outline

Appendix

Speaking in Group Discussion

"You are here to *solve* problems, not to create them." This bit of advice for managers makes a good motto when you speak in the group setting. You and your fellow discussants want to resolve issues rather than create loose ends and hard feelings. Task group speaking is a crucial context for decision-making in today's work and social organizations. In a survey of Fortune 500 executives, 97.6 percent expressed the view that managers needed instruction in group discussion; the same percentage recommended specific training in how to manage meetings.[1]

If your experiences are typical of college-educated persons, much of your speaking will come in the context of a task group. A *task group* is a small number of persons (usually between three and ten) meeting together to solve a common problem or achieve a common goal. When you speak in a task-oriented group, your audience of fellow discussants is not merely a collection of listeners. The listeners are equal participants with you. Therefore, group discussion requires more than knowing how to give impromptu speeches. You pitch into a wide-ranging conversation about problems and decisions.

In group discussion, rhetorical competence means helping to move a group toward its objectives. To speak effectively in the group setting, you need to (1) understand the problem solving process, (2) appreciate the special situation of cooperating with others, and (3) execute skills of decision making, leadership, and meeting management. Appendix A takes you through the key elements of problem solving and decision making.

Problem Solving

Group problem solving requires systematic thinking. You and the other participants proceed through several steps that take you from a perceived problem to implementation of a solution. These include: (1) identifying the problem, (2) analyzing crucial issues, (3) gathering information, (4) specifying and evaluating solutions, and (5) choosing and implementing the best solution.

"What's wrong? What's your problem?" Group problem solving begins with these typical questions that we hear every day. For your group to make progress on a problem, you and the others first must cooperatively identify what *is* the problem. Problem solving begins with the perception by group members that a difficulty exists. We find problems when we encounter obstacles, detrimental conditions, and deviations from the ideal. What are some potential problems that a student task group might encounter on your campus? Parking? Bookstore policies? Closed classes?

If members of your group share a *mutual concern* about a problem, then your group has completed the first stage of problem solving: discovery of a problem. Remember, however, that a group problem must be of general interest to all members of the group. If only one or two group members are concerned about the problem, then the group may fail to make progress later on. For instance, if only two of the five members of your group are commuter students, then the "parking problem" at your campus may be a topic that your group cannot effectively pursue with mutual interest. On the other hand, if everyone has trouble in scheduling classes needed for graduation, then your group has found a truly common problem. Members will probably be sufficiently motivated to pursue the whole process of problem solving.

A second step in problem solving is analysis. You carefully assess present conditions. What are the issues needing investigation? Here your group puts feelings of dissatisfaction into a form suitable for discussion. Group members make observations that throw light on the problem. For instance, on the problem of bookstore policies, each member might report personal experiences with availability of books, textbook costs, or buy-back procedures. As discussion proceeded, group members would discover certain issues emerging. *Issues* are vital questions that must be confronted to solve a problem or make a decision. Once your group begins to identify issues, the group is well on the way to developing goals and an agenda of questions to pursue. The group's *agenda* lists the items of business that must be pursued for the group to complete its task. With discussion organized around an agenda of business, group speaking increasingly focuses on specific issues, allowing members to measure their progress systematically against their developing goals.

To be effective as problem solvers, you and your fellow group members must analyze the problem from every angle. Don't be one-sided. For instance, if your group feels dissatisfied with the bookstore's buy-back policies, try to look at the situation from the bookstore's point of view. Consider what might be the risks of buying back used books. Also, be sure to compare and contrast. If the bookstore pays only a small percentage of the original textbook price, how does this compare with selling other used items—such as cars, furniture? Finally, work not only to locate the fixed points that cannot be changed, but also to see if there is room to maneuver. For instance, on the parking problem, is there vacant land near the campus or does parking require the building of garages?

Issue-oriented analysis finds members offering observations, providing analysis, and looking for explanations. Issue-oriented speaking helps move your group toward goals that lay the foundation for solutions. However, analysis itself is not the ideal way to resolve matters of fact. When your task group will be meeting over a period of time, data gathering becomes a third step that is separate from analysis. For instance, on the topic of closed classes, group members might begin to perceive that the problem is worse for some academic majors than for others. But such a factual question cannot be completely resolved by the personal anecdotes of five students on a campus of 10,000. Similarly, if you and the others began to wonder whether parking was harder to find at certain times of the day, this factual issue could only be resolved effectively through systematic observation. As your group pursues the problem, members will began to identify items for outside research and data gathering.

The research step in group discussion is similar to that in general public speaking. You may do library work to find relevant printed material. When problems are local, however, you and your fellow discussants most often make progress though interviews, questionnaires, and personal observation. On the topic of bookstore policies, your group would profit by interviewing the bookstore manager. To find facts on the topic of closed classes, group members might prepare a questionnaire and distribute it to students. To get facts about parking, group members might walk through parking lots and garages at different times of the day to count the available spaces.

After analysis and data gathering comes the fourth step of problem solving—identifying solutions. Of course, you and your fellow discussants began to have solutions in mind even before you had clearly formulated the problem. If your group has done a good job of identifying the problem, issues, and data, then you are now in a position to specifically state and evaluate solutions. Still, to make sure your group does not overlook any solution, it helps to brainstorm for responses to the problem. *Brainstorming* is a process in which group members call out ideas without pursuing any one of them. The idea is to hold off analysis and criticism of the ideas until group members have filled up a blackboard or piece of paper with thoughts. Let's say that your group has identified a lack of parking spaces between 9:00 and 11:00 A.M. and also between 6:00 and 7:00 P.M. What are all the possible solutions to this problem? If your group's brainstorming has been comprehensive, you might consider not only building more parking spaces, but also changes in the scheduling of classes, ride sharing, and incentives to use public transportation.

Now that your group has identified solutions, the job is to evaluate them. Which are the more practical, the most desirable? Here you must decide how your solutions respond to the issues and goals your group identified earlier. For instance, if the main issue in the parking problem was convenience, then ride sharing might not work. If the main assumption of the group was the need for a quick solution, then building more parking spaces might not be the best approach. In other words, group members work to decide which solutions best respond to the real difficulties. Clearly each solution brings its pros and cons. Ride sharing is cheap but less convenient. Building a parking garage is efficient but costly and time-consuming. Now the group is in a position to look at which solutions would create the most support and the most opposition. Ride sharing and public transportation would require changing habits of commuter students. Building more parking would require getting support of the administration and possibly higher parking fees.

In evaluating solutions, you and your group must decide which solution, in the final analysis, is the most desirable. Here you must be sure to consider which solution seems least likely to generate negative side effects. For instance, suppose your group decided that the quickest, cheapest, and most convenient solution to campus parking was scheduling fewer classes during times when parking lots were overflowing. Here you have solved the parking problem; but perhaps your group has now created new problems. Presumably the college's class schedule reflects the times when most students want to go to school. If the college offers fewer classes during the most popular times, then the class schedule becomes less convenient, although parking may be easier. Now students have the new problem of going to school more days per week or not having afternoons free for paying jobs.

Finally, when your group has identified the best solution, you choose and implement it. If your group session was part of a panel discussion, then implementing the solution would be to announce it at the end of the meeting. For a task group that meets over a period of days or weeks, implementing the solution usually requires writing a report and winning support for it. As long as group members share a mutual concern about the problem, and as long as members agree on the solution, then these steps are quite manageable. It helps to have the group as a whole decide on the overall organization of the report. If everyone is satisfied with the general structure of the emerging document, then assigning sections to individual writers is possible. When dividing the writing chores, the key principle is to make sure that whoever writes a section of the report has access to all the relevant information. In some cases, the group as a whole may cooperate in writing a section of the report. This will work as long as members are agreed on the content and do not try to vote on every sentence. If the final report consists of sections drafted by different members, the group must devise a way to harmonize the various sections.

After the group completes the written report, members are ready for the job of implementing it. Group members must present the report to appropriate officials or organizations and lobby for the solution. Sometimes a solution can be implemented through administrative action. In the case of bookstore policies, your group could start by taking findings to the bookstore manager. The manager might be able to accommodate several recommendations without much effort—for instance, changing the schedule of the book buy-back period. However, for the group's more ambitious suggestions, members might want to identify the higher administrators responsible for the bookstore. In addition to seeking administrative action for the group's solution, members will want to consider a political solution. For instance, your group might take the report on bookstore policies to the student government or to the university senate. Sympathetic student leaders or faculty delegates might introduce your group's report in one of these legislative bodies.

Group speaking calls for skills of informative and persuasive talk. Speaking to solve group problems means to make comments that move the group to identify problems, confront issues, gather data, discover solutions, and create institutional change.

Decision Making

Decision making is problem solving with people. Your task group works to identify problems and solutions that have objective validity. However, your group is not a machine. No task group ever makes decisions without cultivating and maintaining good interpersonal relations. Furthermore, your group will prosper when members actively contribute to a healthy leadership process.

Task groups operate not only in response to problems, but also in response to *interpersonal relations.* Important factors of group relations include the self-concepts, needs, and relationships of members. Group members bring unique *self-concepts*—generalized notions of who they are—to group work. Differences in self-concept help account for why some members are more talkative, agreeable, or friendly than others. Similarly, if a group member feels secure, then he or she may find compromise easier. On the other hand, a dogmatic person may find giving up even on small points difficult. *Human needs* also account for patterns of group participation and decision making. Individuals in your group want to be included in the group's activities, and they want to have a say in what happens. Group members speak not only in relation to issues, but also to satisfy needs for inclusion and control. For instance, one member's need to control may cause him to persist in proposing a solution that other members have decided to reject or ignore. The fact that group discussion meets human needs accounts for the relative slowness of group work. Giving everyone a say can take more time. On the other hand, when group members all have had a chance to participate in making a decision, they are more committed to it. Finally, *relationships* are an interpersonal factor that affects group decision making. In any group some people get along better; therefore, factions that are based on interpersonal attraction may emerge in your group.

Group discussion mixes issue-oriented speaking and interpersonal relations; therefore, a group always operates according to *issue agendas* and *hidden agendas.* When people get together to solve problems, much of the speaking is oriented to objective issues. What is the problem? What are possible solutions? How shall we determine which solution is best? Such questions point to official agendas in group work. In addition to a task-oriented agenda, hidden agendas influence what is said and how talk leads to decisions. Hidden agendas are below-the-surface objectives of individual members (resulting from self-concept, needs or relationships) that block cooperation and consensus in the group. "They won't listen to me, so I won't listen to them." "I'm going to win a point in this discussion no matter what." "I wish Joe wouldn't talk so much." When hidden agendas overcome issue-oriented agendas, then the group will find making satisfactory decisions difficult.

Group norms and group cohesiveness are measures of your group's progress in creating a climate of productive decision making. *Group norms* are rules, usually unspoken, concerning acceptable group behavior. Norms will emerge in your group concerning such routine matters as whether the meetings start on time and how long meetings last. More complicated norms emerge on how your group identifies and handles issues. For instance, your group may gradually adopt a working procedure in which members solve one issue before moving to another. Other groups may develop norms that allow handling two or three related issues simultaneously. Norms also usually develop concerning how group members handle and resolve conflict. One group may feel comfortable in allowing conflict to continue unresolved for a time, whereas another may work quickly to smooth all major disagreements.

When members of a task group conform to group norms, we may say that the group is a *cohesive* one. Cohesiveness is an overall measure of how much members enjoy participation in their group. Groups usually enforce their norms in a subtle fashion. For instance, if one member persists in raising a point that others have rejected, members may simply ignore the comments. On other occasions, members may enforce group norms more explicitly. For instance, assume that your group has developed a norm that social talk comes only after the job is done. If, in this context, one member persists in telling jokes, another may tell him to "knock it off." When a group is unable to enforce common norms, then the group's problem-solving competence may decline as the group splits into factions. For instance, to avoid one uncooperative individual, the other members may begin to meet when the offending member cannot be in attendance. Decision making patterns of this kind show that the group is becoming less cohesive. Members begin to like their group work less and less, and productivity declines.

Leadership is a crucial element in developing cohesive, productive groups. We may define leadership as actions that move the group toward goals or that help maintain a cohesive work climate. Decision making leadership typically takes two forms. In the most general sense, leadership is a role shared by all members of the group. A more formal kind of leadership comes when one individual is designated to take leadership responsibilities.

A *role* is a position that a group member plays in relation to other discussants or with respect to the social situation. For instance, one member may play the role of expert, while another more typically acts to harmonize conflict, and a third tends to play devil's advocate. Considered as a group role, leadership occurs when any member behaves to help in completing the task or in maintaining good interpersonal relations. *Task-facilitating* roles include the following:

- Initiating: Making comments that get the group started in some new phase of action. For instance: "I think we're ready to compare these two solutions."
- Giving information: Supplying data or reasons that help resolve questions being discussed. For instance: "Nobody I've talked to knows anything about how to get a car pool priority parking permit."
- Seeking information: Asking for factual or interpretive ideas relating to an issue. For instance: "Has anyone tried using the main street bus?"
- Coordinating: Clarifying or summarizing what the group has done. For instance: "It looks like we've identified three departments to check on this problem."
- Setting procedures: Suggesting ways that the group can make a decision. For instance: "Why don't we rank order the possible solutions and then discuss them in that order?"

In addition to task-facilitating roles, group leadership includes behaviors that help maintain good interpersonal relations. Important *group maintenance* roles include the following:

- Encouraging: Giving verbal or nonverbal support to other members to encourage their contributions. For instance: "Bob, I'd like to hear more about your conversation with Dr. Matthews."
- Harmonizing: Making comments, including use of humor, that help resolve disputes among members of the group. For instance: "Couldn't we include Andy's point under the section of our report dealing with 'future research?' "
- Compromising: Offering to yield on a point in the interest of reaching consensus. For instance: "I'm concerned with the parking problem; but only two of us use cars, so I guess it would be better to discuss closed classes."

Conflict over issues is inevitable in group discussion—and is productive in helping the group identify the full range of information and solutions. However, for a task group to succeed, conflict must eventually give way to consensus about decisions. For this reason, everyone in a group discussion can exert leadership by taking on a task-facilitating role. At the same time, when group members play maintenance roles, they keep the discussion from getting bogged down as a result of poor interpersonal relations. Group maintenance roles allow you and others to reduce tensions that result when members seek to get attention, to divert, to control, or to withdraw from participation.

Sometimes a group has a *designated leader.* Designated leadership is the norm in formal organizations and is typical of panel discussions and public forums. The designated leader will want to specialize in the task-facilitating and group maintenance roles treated above. In addition, he or she must understand the key principles of how to *manage meetings.*

The organization of a group discussion is never as tidy as that of a single-person speech. Therefore, a first principle of meeting management is to keep the meeting targeted on the task. Get the meeting started on time. Make sure that the meeting is organized around an agenda. The agenda is your group's road map for the discussion. The agenda specifies the major topics for discussion, making clear the purpose for the meeting. Other aspects of keeping the meeting on target are deciding how long the meeting will last, who needs to be in attendance, and what people should do in preparation for the meeting.

Important to managing a meeting is helping to define issues and thereby stabilize the group's progress. As a designated leader, you will want to summarize points and to keep discussion from becoming one-sided. At the same time, you will want to help create a climate conducive to solving the problem. Solicit opinions. Keep one or two aggressive members from dominating. Ask open-ended questions. Probe. Listen and restate. Remember that your goal is open discussion. You want a cooperative, task-oriented climate in which hidden agendas are minimized. You want a solid group in which people do not have to be aggressive to contribute.

The final stage of meeting management is effective follow-up. As a designated leader, you need to make sure that the group's objectives are, in fact, met. You need to be sure that the group understands what comes next: another meeting, work on a report, or a joint meeting with another group.

Good leadership helps avoid three pitfalls of problem solving and decision making: (1) a dictatorial meeting, (2) a one-sided "group think" atmosphere, and (3) social loafing. A *dictatorial meeting* is a session in which one or more aggressive individuals control discussion. Meetings of this kind see a stress on individual power and status that impedes not only the cooperative spirit but also progress on the task. Remember: discussion is a slow process leading to consensus. An important part of discussion is the feeling that everyone has had a say and thus all claim some ownership of the decision. As a result of joint ownership, members feel commitment to the decision. They are more likely to have the motivation to do the follow-up work and lobbying.

Sometimes a designated leader feels a need to dominate the meeting. True, if you have formal leadership responsibilities, you may need to restrict the group's agenda and latitude of discussion. However, if you can tolerate only one decision, it is better not to meet at all than to manipulate members to your preconceived position. Furthermore, if quick action is needed, there is no point in browbeating members to ratify quickly a decision already made.

Good leadership also avoids the problem of *group think.* Group think represents an excessive effort to maintain group solidarity and cohesiveness. In an atmosphere of group think, dissent is not tolerated because it interrupts the smooth progress of step-by-step consensus. In his study of various foreign policy fiascoes, psychologist Irving Janis has documented the group think phenomenon in government decisions about the Bay of Pigs invasion (of Cuba), the Vietnam War, and Watergate.[2] In each case, decision makers participated in cohesive groups that come to consensus too quickly without fully exploring the implications of or alternatives to a decision. A leadership climate helps prevent premature consensus because individuals ask probing questions and they fully explore issues.

A third benefit of good leadership is that it can help arrest *social loafing.* One problem of speaking in the group situation is that no one individual may feel responsible for the group's work. A single speech demands that the speaker take responsibility for preparing the message. But responsibility for preparation is diffused in a group setting. Especially where there exists no agenda, people may prepare poorly—or not at all. Each person may count on the other to provide information and analysis. As a result, discussion may falter or come completely unhinged. Social loafing may be minimized when members take task-facilitating roles and when a designated leader prepares an agenda and keeps members on target.

Group discussion is an important context for speaking. Applied to the task group, rhetorical competence means to keep focus on problem solving and to abide by principles of good decision making. You will contribute to your group's progress if you take on task-facilitating and group maintenance roles and if you abide by principles of effective meeting management.

Endnotes

1. James C. Bennett and Robert J. Olney, "Executive Priorities for Effective Communication in an Information Society," *Journal of Business Communication 23,* No. 2 (1986): 20.

2. Irving L. Janis, *Groupthink,* 2nd ed., (Boston: Houghton Mifflin, 1982).

Appendix

B

Parliamentary Speaking

Rules of parliamentary procedure make it possible for a large number of advocates to give speeches on a single subject. Parliamentary speaking is a fundamental situation of modern democracy. Formal meetings are often governed by parliamentary rules—you have probably participated in some. Furthermore, legislative bodies always proceed by parliamentary debate. Remember that parliamentary procedure is designed to help a group manage its business. A meeting of ten people may become bogged down when formal parliamentary techniques are applied.

Parliamentary speaking gives the opportunity for practice in skills of extemporaneous and impromptu speaking. The following rules will help you adapt your knowledge of speechmaking to the specific demands of parliamentary debate.

1. Your group must have a *presiding officer.* The presiding officer (chair or president) recognizes individuals to speak and enforces time limits. The chair does not give speeches and should remain impartial concerning the issues being debated. The chair makes sure that the rules of parliamentary procedure are followed. The chair makes decisions about how various motions are handled, such as main motions and amendments (see following chart). The chair restates the motions that have been made and supervises voting on motions.
2. Parliamentary speechmaking is organized around *motions* or *resolutions.* The standard form of a resolution is as follows:

   A RESOLUTION TO . . .

   Whereas, ____

   ______________ ; and whereas ___________________________

   ________ ; therefore,

   Be it resolved that, ____________________________________

   ____

   ____ .

3. When parliamentary debate is used as an academic speechmaking exercise, speaking proceeds according to general rules that specify such considerations as the *length of speeches* (e.g., three minutes) and a *list of subjects* on which debate will occur (possibly developed by the class as a whole).
4. Parliamentary debate begins when an individual is recognized to present a resolution or motion. This is a *main motion,* that is, a new item of business. If the resolution is *seconded* by another member, then the chair calls for a speech in favor of the motion

(usually by the person who introduced it). After a speech has been given in support of a new resolution, speeches then *alternate*—against and for the resolution. Speaking continues until the group decides to *close debate* by *unanimous consent* (informal consensus) or with passage of a specific motion to close debate. Debate on a motion also stops when the motion is *referred to a committee* or *postponed* (tabled), each of these actions requiring a specific motion.

Debate shifts somewhat if someone moves to *amend* the main motion. If a motion to amend is moved, seconded, and approved, then the group debates the amendment before returning to the main motion. To avoid complications, prohibiting third level amendments (i.e., amendments to amendments) is wise. One form of amendment is a *substitute motion* in which a whole new resolution on a given subject replaces one being debated.

While debate is in progress, some resolutions cannot be made (they are *out of order*). However, amendments and motions to postpone, etc. are in order. Members may also at any time ask questions in the form of *motions of request.* A motion of request (addressed to the chair) allows the speaker to: inquire about what is taking place; ask a question of a speaker (through the chair); or make a procedural point about the conduct of business (e.g., to observe that a third level amendment is out of order).

The chair is responsible for *keeping order* and making decisions regarding resolutions and other motions. The decisions by the chair may be overturned by the group as a whole if a member proposes a *motion to appeal a decision of the chair,* and if this motion is seconded and approved.

5. To make possible orderly parliamentary speaking, the group must follow the basic *rules for handling motions.* A chart of parliamentary motions that provides the essential rules for treating each motion follows. You can check the chart to learn the procedures for handling each kind of motion:

- May the motion interrupt business (a speech or another motion on the floor)?
- Does the motion require a second?
- Is the motion debatable? That is, are speeches given for or against the motion?

- Can the motion be amended?
- What are the rules for voting? Most motions require a *majority vote.* A majority vote is 50 percent, plus 1. However, the motion to close debate requires a two-thirds vote. A majority is determined by counting those persons actually voting, not counting *abstentions.* Motions of request are decided by the chair without a vote.

In using the chart, below, remember that the motions are listed in *order of precedence.* In other words, the motion to adjourn (terminate the meeting) must be acted on before anything else is decided. On the other hand, the main motion has the least precedence—every other parliamentary motion must be taken care of before the main motion is voted.

Roster of basic parliamentary motions

	Procedural rules				
Motions (in order of precedence)	**Interrupt business?**	**Second required?**	**Debatable?**	**Amendable?**	**Vote**
1. Adjourn meeting	No	Yes	No	Yes	Majority
2. Restrict or close debate	No	Yes	No	Yes	Two thirds
3. Appeal decision of chair	Yes	Yes	Yes	No	Majority
4. Request (of chair)	Yes	No	No	No	None
5. Amend	No	Yes	Yes	Yes	Majority
6. Postpone	No	Yes	Yes	Yes	Majority
7. Refer to committee	No	Yes	Yes	Yes	Majority
8. Main motion	No	Yes	Yes	Yes	Majority

Credits

Photos

All photographs, unless otherwise indicated are © William C. Brown Publishers/ Photography by Arnold and Brown.

Page 4: UPI/Bettmann Archive; **p. 23**: Historical Pictures Service, Inc., Chicago; **p. 69**: AP/Wide World Photos, Inc.; **p. 36**: © James L. Shaffer; **p. 92**: UPI/Bettmann Newsphotos; **p. 118**: © Karl Schumacher/The White House; **pp. 132, 137**: © James L. Shaffer; **p. 148**: Aristides X. Maravel/CBS News Information Service; **p. 176**: UPI/ Bettmann Archive; **p. 198 top**: © James L. Shaffer, **bottom**: © Bob Coyle; **p. 232**: © James L. Shaffer; **p. 242**: Historical Pictures Service, Inc., Chicago; **pp. 248, 252**: UPI/Bettmann Newsphotos; **p. 258**: Source unknown; **p. 262**: Historical Pictures Service, Inc., Chicago; **pp. 277, 285, 304**: UPI/Bettmann Newsphotos; **pp. 317, 334**: AP/Wide World Photos, Inc., Chicago; **p. 340**: © Nancy Dawe; **pp. 364, 376**: © James L. Shaffer; **p. 394**: AP/Wide World Photos, Inc.; **p. 401**: UPI/Bettmann Newsphotos; **p. 441**: © James L. Shaffer; **p. 453**: UPI/Bettmann Newsphotos.

Illustrations

Figures 2.1, 2.2, 5.1, 7.1f, 7.1g, 7.1h: Precision Graphics.

Name Index

E

F

G

H

T

U

V

W

Y

Z

Subject Index

D

E

S

W